Harry Pfund

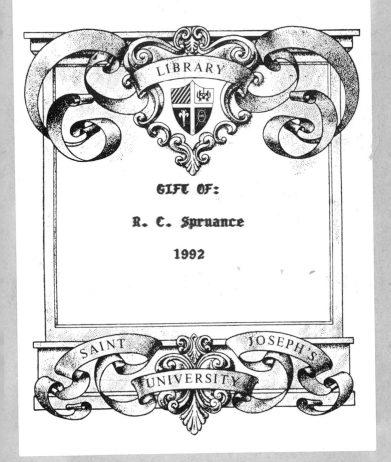

FRIEDRICH VON SCHILLER.

Maria Stuart

Ein Trauerspiel

von

Friedrich Schiller

EDITED WITH INTRODUCTION AND NOTES

BY

EDWARD S. JOYNES, M.A.

PROFESSOR IN SO. CAROLINA COLLEGE

AND

A VOCABULARY

BY

WM. ADDISON HERVEY, A.M.

INSTRUCTOR IN COLUMBIA UNIVERSITY

NEW YORK

HENRY HOLT AND COMPANY

PRINTED IN THE U. S. A.

PREFACE.

ABOUT fifteen years ago the present writer produced an edition of *Maria Stuart* with very brief notes, as one of the series of "Whitney's German Texts," begun and in part directed by that eminent and honored scholar, Professor W. D. Whitney. Now, as circumstances seemed to call for a new edition, it has been thought best to essay a fresh work, planned on new and larger lines, more suited, perhaps, to the demands of the present day in our schools and colleges. While, therefore, the present edition is the lineal descendant of the earlier one, it is in no sense the same, except, of course, in so far as the earlier materials have again been freely used.

In the present work the editor has especially endeavored to recognize and, so far as he could, to meet what he deems the most important needs of the student in reading a play like this, which, from its subject and style, is likely to be among the first to be read in the German classic drama. Besides such explanatory notes as might be necessary or duly helpful — and no more — it has been his chief aim to secure an intelligent and sympathetic interest in the play as a work of *literature*. This purpose, it is hoped, will be recognized both in the introductory matter and in the general character of the commentary; and the editor trusts also that it will be justified by thoughtful teachers. The student who begins a literary work like *Maria Stuart* should feel that he has now risen above the plane of mere language study, and should be helped, so far as may be, to read and enjoy Schiller or Goethe in the same spirit, if not yet to the same degree, as like masterpieces in his mother-tongue. The conviction that this spirit and this effort are the most important things in the study and teaching of German or French is here freely confessed as forming the key-note of this edition. Yet this chief object, while continually borne in mind, has been pursued, it is hoped, with such due reserve and simplicity as is essential to all good teaching — especially in literature, whose best lessons can be only suggested and aided, rather than directly taught.

This view has guided the editor both in what he has done and in what he has left undone. Much of purely critical comment, which lay ready to hand, has been purposely omitted. The edition is, therefore, specifically for the student; yet also it may prove, for that very reason, helpful to many teachers. The critical scholar it does not aim to instruct; enough if for such it may prove to be simply an acceptable and trustworthy instrument.

The execution in detail it is hoped will be found to correspond fairly to this indication. The introductions to the several scenes aim to trace clearly the connections of plot and of character; and the notes, to give all needful help for the full understanding of the language and of the thought. Detailed grammatical explanations are not given. Occasionally such points are briefly noted, or a reference is suggested to whatever grammar may be in hand. The student who needs more than this is not yet prepared for such reading.

The text is that of the standard *Cotta* edition, in the now current orthography. An occasional emendation has been borrowed, however, from the text of Oesterley (in Goedecke's *Historisch-kritische Ausgabe*), or of Boxberger (in Kuerschner's *Deutsche National-Litteratur*) — sometimes with brief mention in the notes. The more important changes in Act V. are added in an appendix, as is also a genealogical table for convenient reference.

It would be impossible, as it would be useless, for the editor to record the many sources from which he has derived help. Outside, however, of such as may be regarded as common property, he owes special acknowledgments only to the excellent edition of *Maria Stuart* by Dr. Karl Breul, from the Cambridge University Press.

SOUTH CAROLINA COLLEGE,
June, 1894.

SKETCH OF SCHILLER.

"AMONG the writers of the concluding part of the last century there is none more deserving of our notice than FRIEDRICH SCHILLER. Distinguished alike for the splendor of his intellectual faculties and the elevation of his tastes and feelings... the reputation which he enjoys and has merited excites our attention the more on considering the circumstances under which it was acquired. Schiller had peculiar difficulties to strive with, and his success has likewise been peculiar. Much of his life was deformed by inquietude and disease, and it terminated at middle age... yet his writings are remarkable for their extent and variety as well as their intrinsic excellence, and his own countrymen are not his only or perhaps his principal admirers. It is difficult to collect and interpret the general voice; but the World, no less than Germany, seems to have dignified him with the reputation of a classic; to have enrolled him among that select number whose works belong not wholly to any age or nation, but who . . . . are claimed as instructors by the great family of mankind."

With these words, Carlyle opens the first English biography of Schiller (1825). The lapse of time since then, while it has greatly increased our knowledge of Schiller's writings and of his life, has only confirmed and extended his fame. Sources of information, however, concerning his life and works are now so numerous and so accessible that only a brief sketch is here deemed necessary.

JOHANN CHRISTOPH FRIEDRICH SCHILLER was born at Marbach in Würtemberg, November 10, 1759. His father, Johann Casper Schiller, the son of a baker, was first a barber's apprentice, then surgeon, adjutant, captain in the army of the Duke of Würtemberg, and later was appointed to the superintendence of the public grounds of the Duke's country palace "Solitude," in which service he continued, with the confidence and approbation of his prince, till his death in 1796. He was a man of strong native sense and great energy and integrity of character; somewhat austere in temper and with the rigid habits of the soldier, yet of deep piety and tenderly devoted to his family. To him his son owed strong and positive traits of character, together with a somewhat rigorous discipline, which, by reaction, showed its effects especially in his early career. His mother, Elizabeth Dorothea Kodweis, daughter of a prosperous innkeeper at Marbach, was by nature the opposite of her husband, cheerful and warm-hearted, with much native taste and sensibility. Married, 1749, at sixteen years of age, and early trained by the lessons of war to self-denial and self-reliance, she grew into strong yet gentle womanhood, full of simple charm and wisdom. She lived till 1802, the object of the poet's affectionate care. He was the only son and inherited her enthusiastic temper and poetic sensibility, as well as her blond hair and soft blue eyes. During the father's absence in the army the care of the family fell much upon her alone; and the mother's sweet yet controlling influence left deepest traces upon the mind and heart of her gifted son.

Schiller's earliest school was at the village of Lorch, under good Parson Moser (afterwards remembered in *The Robbers*) ; later he entered the public school at Ludwigsburg. Under the influence, doubtless, of Moser and of his pious parents, the boy had early chosen the clerical profession. But in 1773 his father was reluctantly induced by the Duke to enter his son in the military academy lately founded near Solitude, afterwards as the *Karlsschule* transferred to Stuttgart, and thus to devote him to the service of the State. Here, then, at fourteen years of age, sorrowfully surrendering his cherished plans, the young Schiller begins the study of law, which he does not like. In 1775, now at Stuttgart, he is permitted to substitute medicine, which he dislikes hardly less, but still continues, until finally, in 1780, he becomes regimental surgeon, and is stationed at Stuttgart on a meagre pittance of salary. The enforced studies of this school and its rigorous military discipline had proved wholly repugnant to Schiller's temperament. He seems to have rendered only a reluctant and forced compliance with its duties, and more and more, as the instincts of his own genius revealed themselves, he began, in secret but restless rebellion, to cherish other aspirations. Clandestinely, as he found opportunity, he indulged his passion for imaginative and dramatic reading. He dreams of authorship, writes passionate poems, and essays themes of epic or dramatic composition; above all he conceives and begins *The Robbers*.

The duties of regimental surgeon proved to be hardly less uncongenial. This state of mind now found expression in the morbidly sentimental *Odes to Laura*, or in the wild despair of the *Infanticide*; yet some of the poems of this period (as *The Battle*) show a healthier power. But Schiller's chief thoughts were now given to *The Robbers*, which was printed, at the author's expense, in 1781. It fell upon Germany and upon Europe like a thunderbolt from

heaven.   Carlyle says : " The publication of *The Robbers*
forms an era in the literary history of the world.   It is the
production of a strong, untutored spirit grappling darkly
with the phantoms to which its own imprisoned energy gives
being."   He speaks of its " rude simplicity, combined with
a gloomy and overpowering force," and of its " tragic interest, so deep that it frequently borders upon horror " ; of its
style, " strong and astonishing, and sometimes wildly grand,"
yet often " coarse and grotesque " ; and he adds : " It is in
vain that we protest against its crudities ; its faults are re-
deemed by the living energy that pervades it." — Schiller
himself (as quoted by Carlyle) afterwards speaks of this
work as " an example of the offspring which genius, in its
unnatural union with thralldom, may give to the world."
The effect of *The Robbers* was deep and widespread.   In
spite of criticism the people at large, and especially the
young, were profoundly moved by its rugged eloquence and
wild spirit of revolt.   So it became a potent factor in the
moral upheaval of that age, and it still remains not only the
most remarkable work of its author, but the most extraordinary ever conceived by a school-boy and completed by
a youth of twenty-two.

The appearance of *The Robbers* was destined soon to produce important changes in the author's fortunes.   At the request of Dalberg, director of the theater at Mannheim, Schiller prepared a stage copy which was played there in January,
1782, with immense success, Schiller himself being present
incognito.   A second visit for a like purpose brought upon
him the severe rebuke of the Duke, with orders to write no
more (except with ducal approval), nor to hold correspondence abroad ; — still severer measures would follow future
transgression.   Thus driven to despair, Schiller determined

to free himself, at whatever cost, from his galling servitude. With a single faithful companion, the young musician Andreas Streicher, and with the knowledge only of his devoted mother, he escaped by night (Sept., 1782) in a close carriage, and made his way to Mannheim, where he hoped for employment from Dalberg.   Here he concealed himself under the assumed name of Dr. Ritter.   Such escapades are not without example : it is a narrow line that divides the ridiculous from the sublime — mere rebellion from glorious revolution ; but in this case the stake was at least boldly thrown, and Streicher's noble devotion to his friend was justified by the result.

But Dalberg was not yet ready to take the risk of offering employment to the young refugee.   He declined, moreover, Schiller's second play, *Fiesco*.   Schiller, now without means of support, retired from Mannheim and, with his faithful Streicher, spent some weeks of homeless and hopeless wandering, saved from actual want only by Streicher's slender means.   But now a noble lady, Frau von Wolzogen, whose sons he had known in the *Karlsschule*, invited him to her country house at Bauerbach near Meiningen.   Here, still under his assumed name, Schiller found most acceptable and fruitful refuge (Dec., 1782–July, 1783).   *Fiesco*, now completed and again rejected by Dalberg, was sold to the Mannheim bookseller Schwann, henceforth Schiller's constant friend, and was received with favor.   During the winter he completed his third play, *Kabale und Liebe* (Plot and Passion), and after meditating other themes (among these *Maria Stuart*), he began *Don Carlos*.   The sojourn at Bauerbach was destined also to be in other respects influential upon Schiller's life.

Fiesco and *Kabale und Liebe* belong still to the author's revolutionary (*Sturm und Drang*) period, yet they mark each a distinct advance. The latter especially, appealing to a more human sympathy, shows increasing simplicity of style and clearer dramatic insight. It is artistically the best, as on the stage it is the most popular, of Schiller's earlier works. Thus far all his plays had been in prose ; but meantime his reputation as a poet was increased by the publication of some pieces in an *Anthology* (1782).

But the retirement of Bauerbach — disturbed moreover by a hopeless love for the daughter of his hostess — could not long content Schiller's restless spirit. Renewed correspondence with Dalberg resulted in his return (July, 1783) to Mannheim as "theater-poet." Here he led a busy life. Early in 1784 *Fiesco* was brought on the stage and, soon after, *Kabale und Liebe*, the latter especially with great success. Theatrical criticism and essays also occupied his time. A little later, ambitious of a still wider field, he founded a literary journal, *Die Rheinische Thalia*, in which he published the first act of *Don Carlos*. Invited to read this at the court of Darmstadt in the presence of Duke Karl August of Weimar, the "German Mæcenas," he was honored by this prince with the title of *Rat* (Counsellor) of the Court of Weimar ; and in other respects, too, he was steadily growing in consideration and repute. But the engrossing and often disagreeable nature of his official duties, which, while not relieving his financial embarrassments, interrupted his literary work — added to some social and personal complications — had rendered the life at Mannheim irksome, and he gladly welcomed an opportunity of change. With his departure from Mannheim (1785) is usually dated the end of the first period of Schiller's life — the period of struggle and unrest. Severe indeed had been the experience and discipline of these early years.

Following the invitation of a group of enthusiastic admirers, among whom was Gottfried Körner, father of the heroic poet, Theodor Körner, Schiller removed (April, 1785) to Leipsic. Among these friends, and later especially with Körner in and near Dresden, he now spent some of the best and happiest years of his life. To Körner he owed not only immediate pecuniary aid, which was sorely needed, but, so long as he lived, an encouraging sympathy and a wise criticism and counsel which were of invaluable benefit. The first note of this brighter existence is sounded in the glorious "Hymn to Joy," full of the exultation of new-born hope and love for mankind. He was busy also with his *Thalia* in which, besides other lyrical pieces, he published his striking but unfinished prose story, *Der Geisterseher;* and at last he completed *Don Carlos*, of which, at long intervals, the first three acts had been already published in the *Thalia.* A more direct fruit of his intercourse with Körner were the *Philosophische Briefe*, in which (as *Julius* and *Raphael*) the two young friends discuss, without solving, the problems of human life and destiny. To Körner's influence is probably due the first direction of Schiller's mind towards philosophical study. His studies for *Don Carlos* also aroused his historic interest, and formed the starting point of his later history of the *Revolt of the Netherlands*. Altogether the short sojourn in Dresden was not only full of active work but rich in fruitful germs.

Don Carlos is the first of Schiller's plays in verse, and exhibits a wonderful growth beyond his earlier prose dramas. The long interval between its beginning and its completion impaired its dramatic unity, — indeed, the author was no longer the same man. This growth of his ideals is embodied in the figure of Posa, who becomes the true hero

of the latter part of the play, which had now outgrown its
original mould.   Yet with all its faults *Don Carlos* is still
read with delight.   It showed clearly the author's growing
power and gave pledge of better things to come.   In his
Briefe über Don Carlos Schiller offers a model of candid
and luminous criticism upon his own work.

But — besides another unfortunate love affair — his painful sense of dependence on Körner and his ever restless
ambition made Schiller soon long for a freer and wider
field.   In July, 1787, he visited his earlier Mannheim friend,
Frau von Kalb, in Weimar, the then " Athens " of Germany.
The kind reception here accorded him at court, and by such
magnates in literature as Herder, Wieland and others (Goethe
was absent in Italy), induced him to make his abode there.
Here, stimulated by his new connections and soon weary
of social distractions, he devoted himself eagerly to study
and work.   While continuing his *Thalia* and co-operating
with Wieland on the *Deutscher Merkur*, yet not neglecting
poetical composition, he renewed his study of Greek and
Latin by translations from Euripides and Vergil, and with
inexhaustible energy also pushed forward his history of
the *Revolt of the Netherlands*, which, though still incomplete, was published in 1788 and made a great impression.
In November, 1787, he made a visit to his old retreat
at Bauerbach, and at Rudolstadt was introduced by his
friend Wilhelm von Wolzogen to the Lengefeld family, con-
sisting of a mother and two charming daughters, the
younger of whom, Charlotte (" Lotte ") is destined to become his wife and begins already to shed new light and
hope in his heart.   At this house, in Sept., 1788, he meets
Goethe for the first time ; yet without other result, on Schiller's part, than the conviction that the two can never come

any nearer together ! To the same busy period belong some of his most thoughtful poems, as *Die Götter Griechenlands*, and a little later, *Die Künstler*, embodying his ideals of beauty and of art.

In December, 1788, through Goethe's official influence, Schiller was surprised by the offer of appointment as Professor of History in the University at Jena. With hesitation and reluctance, yet urged by the *angustæ res domi* and by the hope of a settled income which might justify his marriage, he accepted and entered upon his duties in May, 1789. His reception was enthusiastic ; yet his actual fees were small ; so that it was only by the help of an additional *pension* from the Duke that at last he was enabled to marry (Feb. 22, 1790). This is a red-letter date in the calendar of Schiller's life. His " Lotte," with her sound sense and bright temper, was just the wife he needed. His somewhat wayward heart had long felt the need of firm domestic ties, and henceforth ambition, labor, poverty, sickness were sustained and sweetened by the blessed influences of a virtuous and happy home. His labors were now unflagging. To his regular lectures on History he added others on the Philosophy of Art, some of which afterwards took the form of published essays, prepared historical *Memoirs* on special topics, and continued his *History of the Thirty Years' War*, devoted to the vindication of religious liberty, and connected also with his later drama of *Wallenstein*. On this work, with his *Revolt of the Netherlands*, rests Schiller's fame as an historian. While yet far removed from the more analytic and exhaustive methods of the present day, these volumes show a profound philosophical insight, and a power of description and portraiture, which have given them, with all their defects, a permanent place among the classics of historical literature.

In the midst of these active labors came severe sickness, followed by enfeebled health — the first symptom of that pulmonary disease to which he finally succumbed. Henceforth he was never well; but it only adds to our admiration to see what glorious works he was yet able to accomplish. For the present he was compelled to seek relief in rest and travel. Once more poverty, now more painful than ever, began to add its cares. But again unlooked-for succor came — this time from abroad. Two Danish admirers, the Prince of Holstein-Augustenburg and Count Schimmelmann, made offer of a gift of 1000 Thlr. for three years, in terms so delicate as to compel acceptance. By this generous gift Schiller was enabled to retire from academic service and realize (1793) the wish of revisiting his old home and friends in Würtemberg, where he spent nearly a year with great pleasure and benefit. To a visit to Tübingen at this time he owed also his connection with the great publisher COTTA, henceforth his generous and invaluable friend. During all this time he had bravely continued his labors in philosophy and æsthetics (as an earnest yet cautious disciple of Kant), and in literary study and criticism; and now with improving health he pushed forward his drama *Wallenstein*, the poetic fruit of his studies of the Thirty Years' War. The (so-called second) period of his life now concluding (1785–94) had been rich in study, reflection, self-culture, and helpful intercourse: — the restless apostle of revolt had grown into the mature and thoughtful historian, scholar, critic, philosopher and poet — ripe now for the great works yet to come.

In May, 1794, Schiller with improved health returned to Jena. Here he found stimulating and inspiring intercourse with Wilhelm von Humboldt and others. Above all he

was brought into friendly relations, and soon into close intimacy, with Goethe — mainly, at first, through their co-operation in a new journal, *Die Horen*, of which Schiller was editor.
This friendship, — which belongs to the glories of German
literature — marks a new era in the life of both. It is perhaps the most intimate and fruitful connection that ever
existed between two such men. Their very unlikeness only
made their intimacy more cordial and more helpful. It
would be impossible to measure what each owes to the other,
and what mankind therefore owes to their association ; but
henceforth hardly any work was conceived or done by either
of which the other was not confidant, adviser and critic.
Their correspondence is among the treasures of literature.
Schiller was doubtless the chief debtor ; and under this inspiration he enters upon the third and greatest period of his
life. For a time he is busy with his most important essay :
Ueber naïve und sentimentalische Dichtung; but soon the
poetic impulse resumes its sway. In 1795 he founds a poetical annual, the *Musenalmanach.* Now appear in rapid
succession the most thoughtful and finished of his minor
poems ; and a little later that splendid series of ballads —
partly classical, partly mediaeval, such as *Die Bürgschaft,
Die Kraniche des Ibykus, Der Taucher, Rudolf von Habsburg,* etc. — which are the most widely popular and, next
to his great dramas, the richest productions of his genius.
To these should be added, though not appearing till later
(1800) *Das Lied von der Glocke* (Song of the Bell), perhaps the most perfect of his minor works. In the *Musenalmanach* were also published, in co-operation with Goethe,
the famous *Xenien,* brief epigrams in classical metre, sometimes playful, sometimes profound, but usually ironical or
sarcastic, directed against the poetasters and superficial

critics — the "Philistines" of that day. They were a verit-
able literary *tour de force*, and their success was immense.

Meantime the great drama of *Wallenstein* was slowly ap-
proaching completion. Finding the vast material intract-
able for a single play, Schiller finally divided it into three
parts. *Wallensteins Lager*, a rollicking picture of camp life,
was put on the stage in 1788; *die Piccolomini*, showing the
progress of the war and of revolt, in 1799; followed soon
after by *Wallensteins Tod*, in which Schiller's genius reached
perhaps its highest point of grandeur and imaginative power.
This great success determined Schiller to devote himself
henceforth to dramatic composition. He now surrenders
other engagements, and in December, 1799, removes to
Weimar, where in conjunction with Goethe he undertakes
the direction of the Weimar theater. This was an excellent
school of practical *technique* — including criticism, stage
adaptations and translations, among which may be mentioned
Shakespeare's *Macbeth ;* from the French, *der Parasit* and
der *Neffe als Onkel*, and later Racine's *Phädra*. In the
midst of active official duty, and with feeble health yet still
inexhaustible energy, Schiller now began that rapid series
of great dramas which filled the last and most productive
years of his life. Fortunately they are so well known that
brief mention may here suffice.

In 1800, after many interruptions, appeared our own play,
Maria Stuart, begun in 1799. Here Schiller's desire for a
more romantic and independent theme found partial satisfaction in the freer treatment of the history. For us this
play is perhaps the most interesting in its subject, as it is
also among the strongest, of Schiller's dramas. A more romantic and freer theme he next found in *Die Jungfrau von
Orleans* (1801), in which the portraiture of the inspired

Maid — half history, half mystery — offered the most congenial field to his idealizing imagination. This was one of the most successful, as it is one of the most beautiful, of his plays. Still further in the direction of the ideal appeared, in 1803, *Die Braut von Messina,* an attempt to revive the spirit of the Greek drama, with its lyric chorus. Though, dramatically, the attempt was unsuccessful, this play is in Schiller's best style, full of force and beauty. But now, as if his longing for the ideal had been satisfied, he returned once more to a purely human — if only legendary — theme. In 1804 he produced his great drama of *Wilhelm Tell,* the most popular — perhaps the greatest — of his works, in which he again celebrates that love of liberty which had been his earliest inspiration. But what an interval between the mad iconoclasm of *The Robbers* and the rational liberty and sweet humanity of *Tell!* The success of *Tell* surpassed every other triumph.

Schiller had now reached the summit of his fame and of his powers. His person and manners had ripened with his mind and character. Early awkwardness and bashfulness had given way to a calm dignity and graciousness which bespoke a great and modest soul. Mme. de Stael gives a charming picture of him at Weimar : "His conscience was his muse . . . . no quality was lacking to that sweet and gentle character which genius alone inflamed . . . ." All contemporaneous accounts concur as to his personal charm. His figure was tall and slender, with a slight stoop from over-study ; his hair and eyes were light, his brow broad and clear ; his chin rather too massive ; his mouth and Roman nose exquisitely chiseled ; his countenance full of sweetness, dignity and light — "a face," says Carlyle, "at once meek, tender, unpretending, and heroic." Honored and beloved

abroad — endeared by his heroic struggles as well as by his
writings to the whole German people, — yet he was most
loved by those who knew him best. Public honors, too,
now rapidly followed the award of fame. In 1802 he received a patent of nobility and became *von Schiller* — an
honor which he modestly welcomes " for the sake of Lotte
and the children." In 1804 he was invited to Berlin, where
he witnessed the triumphant rendition of his own greatest
plays, and received, but declined, a flattering offer of official
appointment. It seemed now as if a life of assured fame
and prosperity was opened before him. But this was not
to be. The fell disease that had so long preyed upon his
strength now renewed its attacks. After his return from
Berlin he had a severe illness. He rallied slowly, but suf-
ficiently to produce in November his idyllic drama, *Die
Huldigung der Künste,* for a wedding at the Weimar court.
In the winter he was again busy with the grand outline of
Demetrius and with other labors, while looking forward
to his ardently desired visit to Switzerland in summer.
But at last his overtasked strength failed, and on the 9th
May, 1805 — after a life of struggle, of suffering and of
achievement almost unexampled — he expired, in the forty-
sixth year of his age. All Germany wept over the untimely
death of its best beloved, if not greatest, poet ; and the
common voice accorded to him a fame which has grown
from then till now, and will probably last forever. In the
words of his friend H. Grimm, written soon after his death :
" What might he not have become, if God had allowed him
a larger space of life, to develop all the germs that slum-
bered in his noble heart !" In conclusion, we quote again
from Carlyle : "Schiller is the poet of truth — he exalts
and inspires, but does not mislead. We not only admire,

we trust and love him. . . He was an apostle of the Sublime and Beautiful, whose inspirations constantly maintained the noblest temper in his soul. For him, Literature includes whatever speaks to our immortal part, and is the mirror of all that is spiritual and exalted. His influence has been deep and universal and bids fair to be abiding : for such nobleness of heart and soul, shadowed forth in beautiful emblems, is an everlasting treasure."*

---

* *Life of F. Schiller* (abridged). A new edition of Carlyle's Life of Schiller with Supplement (1845) is reprinted in cheap form in *Lovell's Literature Series* (N.Y.). A bright but somewhat cynical *Life of F. Schiller*, by H. W. Nevinson, is published in the " Great Writers " series. This is also inexpensive, and contains a valuable bibliography, to which the student may be referred for more elaborate works.

INTRODUCTION.

1. *MARIA STUART* follows next after *Wallenstein,* among Schiller's dramatic works. It was begun about May, 1799, and was completed, after many interruptions, in June, 1800. In the same month it was first played at Weimar, under the immediate direction of the author. On the stage — as, indeed, was foreseen and in part provided for by Schiller himself — it has undergone material modification ; but thus adapted, it still retains its place as a favorite acting play, and is often performed in our own country. As a literary performance it will always hold rank among the master-pieces of German literature. Its subject commends it especially to our reading ; and in style and treatment it is also well adapted to serve as an introduction to the German classic drama, in school or college. This object has been borne in mind, throughout this edition.

2. The basis of the play is of course historical, yet *Maria Stuart* is rather a romantic than an historical drama. On the completion of *Wallenstein*, in March, 1799, Schiller wrote to Goethe* : " Inclination and necessity draw me towards subjects of pure fancy, but not to historical ones, and towards such where the interest is of a purely sentimental and human character ; for of soldiers, heroes and commanders I am now heartily tired." It might seem strange

---

* Correspondence of Schiller and Goethe, No. 591. Bohn's translation, not always very good, is here quoted.

that he should find the satisfaction of this desire in an historical subject like Mary Stuart; yet the solution of the apparent contradiction is found in the mode of treatment. The historical canvas is used only as the background of the poet's picture : historical facts, dates, places and personages are handled with artistic freedom, and made to serve the ideal purpose of the drama. That Schiller was quite conscious of this appears in a later letter to Goethe (July 19), where he speaks of "the poetic struggle against the historical subject-matter," and of his effort "to obtain freedom for the fancy over the history," etc. That he was also conscious that this effort was consistent with the demands of dramatic art, and that in *Maria Stuart* he had attained it more successfully than heretofore, is equally clear from his letter to Körner (June 16, 1800), where he declares that he has at last begun "to master the dramatic *organ*." It has been questioned, indeed, whether such freedom might be fairly taken with an historical subject so recent and so notorious. But Schiller's object was art, not history ; and his work is entitled to be judged by its own purpose and point of view. To indicate these briefly is the design of this Introduction.

3. At a much earlier period, at Bauerbach in 1782, Schiller had thought of writing a drama on Mary Stuart, but had abandoned it in favor of *Don Carlos*. Now while seeking, as a relief from the "soldiers, heroes and commanders" of *Wallenstein*, a distinctly "sentimental and human" interest, he was disposed to turn again to the subject of *die feindlichen Brüder*, afterwards completed under the title of *die Braut von Messina*. But at this crisis he made a visit to Goethe, and to the influence of this good genius is due, probably, his return to the earlier theme.

April 26, he writes to Goethe that he has begun to study the history of the reign of Elizabeth and of the trial of Mary Stuart, and adds : " A few tragic motives presented themselves at once, and have given me great faith in the subject. . . It seems more especially adapted for the Euripidean style, which consists in giving the fullest representation of the state of affairs ; for I see a possibility of setting aside all the legal proceedings as well as political concerns, and of beginning the tragedy with the condemnation." *

4. By the " Euripidean Style " Schiller means the full presentation of a dramatic *situation*, rather than the development of a dramatic history ; and so, casting aside, or viewing only in retrospect, the complicated course of Mary's life and the political events of those troublous times, he assumes at once the tragic situation of her actual condemnation as the basis of his drama. This situation becomes, then, the point of view from which he treats all historical and political facts with romantic freedom, and with reference only to the crisis and the characters which it is his purpose to portray. These events, therefore, will be reviewed here only so far as necessary to describe the situation as conceived by the author, or to group together the more important events actually referred to in the play. More detailed explanations will be found in the Notes.

5. To most of the readers of this play the facts of Mary Stuart's career are already known ; for in the romance of English history, as well as in the galaxy of illustrious and unfortunate women, she holds a prominent place. Beauty, genius, misfortune and the never-ending question of her innocence or guilt have made her one of the most attract-

* Correspondence, No. 596.

ive figures as well as fascinating enigmas of history. Born
Dec. 7, 1542, she united the blood of both Scottish and
English royalty. Her father, James V., by his marriage
with Mary of Lorraine, of the brilliant Catholic house of
Guise in France, laid the foundation at once of his daughter's talents and of her misfortunes. By her father's death,
only a few days after her birth, she was, as Schiller says,
"in the cradle a queen." Henry VIII., the Blue Beard of
the English throne, yet an able and politic monarch, sought
to unite the thrones of England and Scotland by a marriage
between his son Edward (VI.) and the infant queen of
Scotland; but the influence of her French kindred prevailed,
and Mary was betrothed to the Dauphin, afterwards Francis II. of France. Thus her political and religious destiny
was determined by causes over which she had no control.
Taken to France at an early age, she was soon introduced
at court, "*den üppigen Hof der Medicäerin*," where in the
midst of adulation and gayety she grew into precocious
and brilliant womanhood. In 1558, she was married to
the Dauphin, who by the sudden death of his father, Henry
II., became king in 1559. Thus early Mary, born heir of
one throne, is called to another, while a fatal destiny has
made her already claimant to a third. In June, 1560, her
mother — till now Regent of Scotland — died, and, in
December of the same year, her young husband also. Her
mother-in-law, the famous and infamous Catherine de
Medici, now became Queen Regent; and the young
queen, moved both by Catherine's jealous dislike and by the
advice of her uncles (the Guises), determined to return to
her hereditary kingdom. With weeping eyes, August
1561, she bids adieu to France, and enters upon a new and
stormy history. In the meantime, after a dark and trou-

bled youth, in strong contrast with the brilliant opening of
Mary's career, her great rival Elizabeth had become Queen
of England.

6. Elizabeth Tudor, the " Virgin Queen," born 1533 and
thus nine years older than Mary, was daughter of Henry
VIII. and Anne Boleyn. To effect this marriage, Henry,
without papal sanction, had put away his first wife, Catherine of Aragon. Thus, in the view of the Catholic Church,
Elizabeth's birth bore the taint of illegitimacy ; and herein
was laid in advance one of the chief grounds of the struggle
between her and Mary. After a brief reign Edward VI.
was succeeded by Mary, daughter of Catherine of Aragon,
"*die spanische Maria*" — to us better known as " Bloody
Mary," from the religious persecutions in her reign.
Jealous of her sister Elizabeth, Mary, after the outbreak of
Wyatt's rebellion (1554), committed her first to the Tower
and afterwards had her removed to Woodstock, where she
was held for a time under strict surveillance. On the
death of Mary, 1558, Elizabeth was proclaimed queen.
The horror of the recent persecutions made her accession
welcome. Political conditions abroad concurred with ecclesiastical conflicts at home in her favor. The religious
propaganda of Rome, aided by Spain and the Catholic
party of France, in support of the claims of Mary Stuart,
identified the cause of the reformed religion in England
with that of national independence and national pride.
Thus Elizabeth became more and more the representative
of the new religion, on which depended her right to the
throne, while for the opposite reason Mary became identified with the cause of Catholicism and of foreign influence.
Those conditions intensified the contrast and antagonism
between these two women, which Schiller, with fine poetic

instinct, makes the central *motif* of the play. Outside of her strong personal qualities, all conditions, domestic and foreign, favored Elizabeth, and concurred to make her reign the golden age of England; yet, with personal gifts not less striking and far more attractive, Mary, dowered for the noblest destiny, becomes the victim of inexorable conditions, no less than of her own misguided passions, and dies upon the scaffold! It was, then, in the struggle between these two queenly women, standing for principles so momentous, with gifts so splendid yet so diverse, and under conditions so intense and so direful, that Schiller saw the elements of a great historic tragedy, in which all details of political history might be set aside, and a tragic theme be found in the portraiture, "in the Euripidean style," of the supreme event.

7. Already on the death of Queen Mary of England in 1558, the inevitable conflict had begun. Refusing to recognize Elizabeth's title to the succession, Mary Stuart and her husband assumed the title and arms of English royalty; and when in 1560, by the treaty of Edinburgh, framed by representatives of England, Scotland and France, Elizabeth secured the condition that no further claim should be made upon her throne during her life or that of her posterity, Mary refused to agree to this stipulation. It is not surprising, then, that when in the following year — now a widow — she determined to return to Scotland, her coming was regarded by Elizabeth as that of an enemy, and she was refused permission to pass through England; indeed, she narrowly escaped capture by English cruisers. Upon her arrival in Scotland the young queen was eagerly welcomed by a people long distracted by political and religious dissensions. At first her beauty, her grace and the

charm of her manners won all hearts, and for a time she seemed anxious to conciliate all interests. She sent an ambassador to Elizabeth, proposing that if the latter would recognize her succession in the event of her own death without issue, no further claim should be made during Elizabeth's life-time. But Elizabeth, well knowing that this concession would sow the seeds of dissension among her people and tempt her own destruction, refused, as she said, "to hang a winding-sheet before her eyes." Yet, though disallowing this claim, Elizabeth still made it the pretext for interfering in the question of Mary's marriage. She objected to Don Carlos of Spain, as a Catholic prince, and even proposed — though with doubtful sincerity — her own favorite, Dudley, Earl Leicester; but Mary was unwilling to share her throne with an English subject, a Protestant. Meantime, however, she was pushing her own plans, which she suddenly consummated by marrying, July 1565, Henry Lord Darnley, a kinsman of both herself and Elizabeth by common descent from Henry VII. (See Genealogical Table.) This marriage, however seemingly politic, was the beginning of Mary's downfall. Darnley was handsome but frivolous, and soon manifested a character of mingled arrogance and depravity which alienated Mary's affection, and brought the direst consequences upon himself and her.

8. This marriage, which seemed to strengthen at once the Catholic power in Scotland and Mary's claim upon the throne of England, was regarded as a menace both to the Scottish reformers and to Elizabeth. The Lords of the Congregation, under the lead of Mary's half-brother, James Stuart, afterwards Earl of Murray, rose in arms, but were easily defeated by Mary, who rode in person against them.

Never did the prospects of the Queen of Scots seem brighter. Soon, too, the news of her pregnancy still further strengthened the hopes of her supporters at home, in England, and in Catholic countries abroad. But these fair prospects were soon blighted by Darnley's arrogance and folly, and by the doom of her own misguided passions. Not content with the title of king, her husband claimed the legal rights of royalty, which being refused, he proceeded from insolence to violence. Mary's most trusted adviser at this time was an Italian, David Rizzio, who, entering her service as court musician, had been advanced to the post of private secretary. He it was who had secretly aided her marriage with Darnley; but now Darnley, jealous of his influence, resolved upon his destruction. At the head of a band of discontented nobles, he penetrated into the queen's presence, and Rizzio was stabbed to death, almost beneath her eyes. This outrage (March, 1566) was bitterly felt by Mary, who, however, veiled her resentment against Darnley in order to pursue her vengeance upon more dangerous foes. Fleeing to Dunbar, she quickly gathered her friends; the murderers fled; Murray and his adherents submitted, and the birth of her son (June, 1566) seemed once more to secure her power and her hopes. But she was destined soon to still darker disaster.

9. Mary, feeling herself secure, now treated Darnley with open contempt, while James Hepburn, Earl Bothwell, one of the boldest and most unscrupulous of the Scottish nobles, became her foremost favorite. What follows is wrapped in the mystery of crime and horror. Suddenly Mary's demeanor towards Darnley changes. He had fallen sick at Glasgow: she visits him and, with real or simulated sympathy, persuades him to come to Edinburgh. Here he is lodged in a suburban house, the Kirk o' Field, where she visits him on the evening of Feb. 9, 1567, and then rides gaily off to a wedding at her palace of Holyrood. In the depth of night a terrible explosion is heard; the Kirk o' Field is blown to pieces, and the body of Darnley, *strangled to death*, is found in the garden. This awful crime aroused universal horror. Bothwell was at once accused, while grave suspicions fell upon Mary. After a pretended trial, Bothwell was acquitted — the queen taking no part in the prosecution — and Parliament, overawed like the Court, confirmed the verdict. Bothwell now seized the Queen's person and carried her off to his castle at Dunbar, where he held her prisoner until, after a real or pretended reluctance, she consented to marry him, he divorcing his wife for this purpose (May, 1567). This fatal step sealed Mary's doom. Confirming the suspicions of her guilt in the murder of Darnley, it at once drove her friends to despair and strengthened her enemies at home and abroad. The fear of the murder by Bothwell of her infant son was added to the causes of revolt. The Scottish reformers, under Murray, again rose in arms. After a brief struggle Bothwell was driven into exile, and Mary, confined in a castle on Loch Leven, was compelled to abdicate her throne in favor of her son, for whom the Earl of Murray became regent. By the aid of young George Douglas, Mary made her escape and, revoking her forced abdication, essays a new struggle for her crown; but quickly defeated, she flees in a boat across the Frith of Solway and takes refuge at Carlisle in England. Here, in disaster and disgrace, begins her long captivity.

10. The question, how far Mary was actually guilty, how far only a weak, and reluctant or willing, victim, in the

murder of Darnley and in her marriage with Bothwell, can perhaps never be fully determined, though, as Green says, "taken simply by themselves, the facts have a significance which it is impossible to explain away." It is only one—one **of the gravest — of the enigmas presented by Mary's** enigmatical character. Schiller, however, assumes that she consented to Bothwell's crimes ; and this guilt, with its awful expiation, he makes the key-note of the tragedy. Coming now, a fugitive from rebellion, to seek help and restoration from a kindred queen, Mary — as she bitterly declares in our play — was held as a prisoner. Interview with Elizabeth and the privilege of passing into France were alike denied her. As exigency required, she was moved from place to place, for many years under the mild guardianship of Earl Shrewsbury, and finally to Fotheringhay Castle, where, under the strict oversight of the Puritan, Sir Amias Paulet, she is found at the opening of this play.

II. But what Mary might perhaps no longer have accomplished, if free, was effected by her imprisonment. Whatever may have been her crime in Scotland, neither Elizabeth nor English law was justly her judge. Her devotion to the Catholic religion, her beauty, her romantic career, and now her sufferings, wrought powerfully upon the minds of men. Her cause was strengthened by Catholic sympathy abroad, and especially by the Pope's excommunication of Elizabeth in 1570, which released the English Catholics from their allegiance. Yet the zeal of Mary's friends was met by equal zeal and bitterness. A Catholic rising in the north of England under Northumberland and Westmoreland was sharply suppressed. Stricter laws were passed against the Catholic religion, and Mary's right of succession was set aside by Act of Parliament. Yet Elizabeth's situation became not less difficult. Afraid either to prosecute or to release Mary, and threatened both at home and abroad, she again owed her triumph to the madness of Mary and her friends, and to the plots in her behalf.

12. The Duke of Norfolk, a powerful and hitherto loyal nobleman who aspired to a marriage with Mary, now entered into a conspiracy for her release, in which foreign aid was sought. But the plan was detected, and Norfolk was executed (1572). His confederate, the Bishop of Ross, was sent to the Tower and afterwards banished. Now followed a period of outward peace; yet still the religious troubles of Scotland, with Catholic influences abroad and, later especially, papal emissaries from the seminary at Rheims, kept alive the hopes of Mary's supporters, who now sought more secret and more desperate measures. In 1584 a conspiracy, headed by James Throckmorton, implicated the Spanish ambassador, Mendoza. In 1585, the plot of Dr. Parry aroused increased alarm. For these movements, which did not stop short of the purpose to murder Elizabeth, Mary was held to be responsible. She was now consigned to the care of Paulet, and a further Act was passed, which included not only all conspirators but, with manifest reference to Mary, all persons in whose behalf conspiracy should be made. These violent measures produced only renewed plots. Under the influence of emissaries from Rheims, Savage, a young officer who had served with Parma in the Netherlands, vows the death of the queen; a wealthy young enthusiast, Anthony Babington, with Tichburne and others, undertakes to secure Mary's release, and Mary herself takes part in the correspondence. But the plot is detected by Elizabeth's watchful ministers. The leaders are executed and Mary's own papers are

seized. She is now placed under strictest surveillance; and at last, with the conviction that there can be no safety for England while she lives, it is determined to bring her to trial, as a conspirator against the life of Elizabeth, under the Act of the preceding year.

13. For this solemn procedure a commission of forty-two judges was appointed, who sat at Fotheringhay. Mary at first refused to answer; but being persuaded that this would be construed as a confession of guilt, she at last consented to plead. With great dignity she maintained her innocence of all plots against the life of Elizabeth, while claiming her right, as a captive queen, to seek her own release. The alleged copies of her letters she declared to be falsified, and vainly demanded to be confronted with her secretaries, whose testimony, as well as Babington's dying confession, seemed to point to her guilt. The commission adjourned to Westminster palace, and there Mary was declared guilty of conspiracy against the life of the queen and condemned to death. She received the announcement with dignity, declaring herself an innocent yet willing martyr to the Catholic faith. Elizabeth still sought delay; but urged by Parliament, by her ministers and by public opinion, as well as by rumors of new perils (Schiller invents an overt act, and provides, besides, even more dramatic motives), she at last signed the fatal order and entrusted it to her secretary, Davison, to be provided with the Great Seal; yet still expressing the hope that other means might be found to relieve her from the dread necessity. Her ministers, knowing her hesitation, seized the opportunity and ordered the execution, which, under the direction of Shrewsbury and Kent (Schiller from dramatic motives substitutes Burleigh and Leicester), occurred at Fotheringhay, February 8, 1587.

On the scaffold Mary exhibited a courage, a dignity and a piety which aroused deepest sympathy and, more than anything in her life, have shed glory upon her name. Elizabeth showed surprise and horror, real or assumed, on the receipt of the news, and by public mourning and pro-testations, and the punishment of her faithful servants, she sought to turn from herself the odium of the deed. Davi-son was sent to the Tower, and even Burleigh was banished for a time from her presence. But her dissimulation was as vain as was the sacrifice. Upon her still rests the odium of the deed. On other fields she had still to fight for her "*angefochtenen Thron*"; and on this throne, at last, her successor was the son of Mary!

14. Such is a brief outline of the complex historical facts with which Schiller had to deal; which, however, he pro-posed to treat in retrospect or perspective only, assuming as the basis of his drama the *situation* presented at the time of Mary's condemnation. Thus the play opens at Fother-inghay, when Mary is about to receive the fatal announce-ment, which, by the poet's fiction, is communicated only two days before the execution. The final catastrophe is thus, from the first, fully in view, and in all its tragic significance becomes the *motif* as well as the end of the drama. In the first Act the exposition of the situation is impressively pre-sented, and the dramatic action already begun; which then moves forward with an unflagging interest worthy of high-est admiration, unequaled perhaps, in the skillful manage-ment of plot and of detail, by any other of Schiller's plays. Elaborate analysis would be out of place here; only a few suggestions will be added with regard to the general treat-ment of the plot and of the characters. More detailed re-marks will be found in connection with the several Scenes.

15. A few words, however, may here be inserted as to Schiller's historical authorities. His free treatment of the history does not, of course, imply neglect of such study, but rather the contrary, in view of his effort "to obtain freedom for the fancy over the history," and at the same time " to secure possession of all that the latter contained which could be used." * This, however, renders it unnecessary, except for purely critical purposes, to inquire into the authority for this or that view, or even to detail fully the list of the books used in preparation for this play. These, we may say briefly, included the chief authorities then known : The Latin " History " of Buchanan (Mary's bitter enemy) and " Annals" of Camden ; also Robertson, Hume, etc. It may suffice to say here, that Schiller used chiefly the German *Geschichte der Regierung der Königin Elizabeth,* by Archenholz, which gave a sympathetic view of Mary's life and sufferings; and the French Rapin Thoyras *Histoire d'Angleterre* (to which is due the French form of some proper names) ; and, for the fifth Act, the genial account of Mary's execution by Brantôme (author of *Les Dames Illustres,* etc.) ; and also, for the religious ceremonials of this Act, a volume of *Theological Miscellanies.* From what has been said already it follows that the historical details of the play should not be too closely questioned. In more important instances, however, an occasional comment is made in the Notes.

16. The purpose of the play is to exhibit the character of Mary Stuart in an heroic and tragic aspect. Guilt, penitence, persecution, misfortune, heightened by the charms of her beauty, the devotion of friends, the passionate self-

* Correspondence, No. 630; July 19, 1799.

sacrifice of love, are its pathetic elements. To these is
added the sharp contrast of Elizabeth, false, jealous, vengeful ; strong where Mary is weak, weak and despicable where
Mary is strong and noble. The character of Elizabeth is
drawn, indeed, in darkest colors ; yet the poet's injustice
consists rather in concealing her higher qualities as queen,
with which his drama was not concerned, than in any mis-
representation of her personal characteristics. The contrast and antagonism of these two women offer, indeed,
many striking and tragic aspects. Schiller has been criti-
cized for exaggerating the purely personal element, and for
making the final catastrophe turn upon personal passions,
aroused by a fictitious interview. But herein the author
followed a true poetic instinct. It is, after all, not *events*,
however momentous, but *persons* and the collisions of personal feeling and action, that most interest us. And it is
with infinite pathos that an interview, for which in fact Mary
had earlier begged in vain, is made the scene of the supreme
conflict and the swift occasion of her death. In a still
profounder sense, also, this interview becomes the central
point of the play ; for Mary is thus made an active agent,
provoking her own ruin. A passive martyrdom is pathetic
indeed, but not tragic. But, as already by the fiction of
her understanding with Mortimer and her intrigue with
Leicester, so especially in the bold fiction of this interview,
Mary is made to display the passionate elements of her own
character, and, goaded to desperation, becomes herself the
aggressor, thus creating the situation in which poetic justice
demands her doom. These bold fictions of Mary's relations with Mortimer and with Leicester, and of her interview with Elizabeth — which are all, in fact, part of one
purpose — are the very soul of the play, and are perhaps
Schiller's happiest achievement in dramatic invention.

17. Of his moral judgment of Mary, Schiller leaves us in no doubt. He assumes her guilt in the death of Darnley and in her marriage with Bothwell; but the one is due to bitter provocation, the other to the overmastering power of the tempter, and both have been expiated by years of penitence and suffering. As a captive queen she has sought release; but of all charges as against the queen of England she is innocent, a sacrifice to her religious faith, and the victim alike of the devotion of friends and the malice of enemies. Whatever her earlier crimes or errors, "*in England ist kein Richter über sie,*" and Elizabeth is not her lawful prosecutor. Thus her death becomes a martyrdom. Such Mary herself feels it to be, and with all the resignation and glory of a martyr she mounts the scaffold. On the other hand Elizabeth, though triumphant, is left at last alone and despised. Her character, made up of strange contrasts, is drawn with great power. Schiller's conception of her as a "*königliche Heuchlerin*" makes the adequate representation of the character only the more difficult; indeed, he thought it demanded even more ability in the actress than that of Mary.

18. Around these two principal personages, each the center of her own party, are grouped the other characters of the play. Hannah Kennedy and the other women exhibit the devoted affection with which Mary ever knew how to inspire her intimates. Paulet is the austere Puritan, faithful alike to the law and to his prisoner, and spurning overtures of treachery, even from his queen. Burleigh represents the statesmanship of England in that stormy time, holding the safety of the crown superior to all personal or even humane considerations. Kent occupies the lower and narrower plane of the mere partisan. In Shrews-

bury (Talbot), whose kindness as Mary's keeper has been remarked, is uttered the voice of a larger humanity, appealing from the passions of the hour to the final judgment of mankind. Davison is the faithful public servant, with a shrewd knowledge of Elizabeth's character, yet deceived at last by her dissimulation and punished for her crime. The arts of the French diplomacy of that day are well represented in Aubespine and Bellièvre. In Melvil are seen the serene faith and devotion of the true priest; while the fictitious character of Mortimer stands for the passionate ardor that inflamed so many enthusiasts for the liberation of Mary, and for that fascination of sensuous love which it seemed part of her unhappy destiny to inspire. In contrast with this noble if sometimes extravagant character, as a foil also to Elizabeth and, with Mortimer, the chief agent in the development of the plot, stands Leicester, the favorite of Elizabeth, yet plotting for the hand of Mary, and false to both; the ambitious yet cringing courtier and artful schemer, all whose advantages, though managed with consummate ability yet for purely selfish objects, are brought to failure and shame. All these characters are not only types true to their age, but, though sometimes with free transposition of facts, are well marked *persons* also. In none of Schiller's dramas is the characterization more distinctly marked or more consistently maintained.

19. It was in part, doubtless, Schiller's harsh picture of Elizabeth that prevented the early acceptance of this play in England. Schiller was anxious that it should be at once published and acted in English. For this purpose, as he completed the successive acts, they were submitted to Mr. Joseph Mellish, an English friend then residing in

Germany. But this project met with no success in England. The translation by Mellish (included in Bohn's Library) is, however, of great literary interest; for, besides being generally well executed, it gives the earlier (MSS.) form of the play; and in many cases, especially in the earlier Acts, shows important variations from the standard texts.

20. One further point it seems important to notice here. Schiller has been accused of showing in this play undue partiality for the Catholic religion, and, with equal zeal, of injustice to that Church. The two charges ought to show, what is the fact, that neither is true. Nothing was farther from Schiller's purpose than religious propagandism in any form. The ecclesiastical conflict he regarded as only a part, though a very important part, of the historical setting of his play. He does full justice to the solemnity and sensuous charm of the worship of the Catholic Church, and to the devotion of its true believers; yet he does not conceal the crimes committed in its name, nor the intemperate zeal of some of its adherents. The honors of probity and piety, with their opposite faults or errors, are distributed with equal hand among the confessors of either faith.

21. The language of the play is everywhere lofty and grand, perhaps too evenly so. Very great freedom is used in the construction of the verse — in the number of syllables, the verse-accent, cæsura, etc. — not from carelessness, but because the author had come to assert a larger liberty in dramatic composition. Such irregularities may best be verified in the reading. In the play also for the first time, and with delightful effect (Act III., Scene 1), the author employs lyric stanzas, of which he made so large use in his later dramas. In this, as in other respects, it seems that the author was justified in regarding this play as having first assured his mastery of the "dramatic organ," and as marking thus an epoch in his own development.

22. A more detailed criticism of the play would be out of place here, and perhaps unjust to those who are expected to read it with fresh and unbiased interest. *Maria Stuart* did not at first make the same great impression on the stage as *Wallenstein*, the *Maid of Orleans*, or *Tell*. Yet, while its success as an acting play has rather grown with the lapse of time, its literary repute has always been great. Goethe regarded it as one of the greatest of Schiller's dramas. Tieck and A. W. Schlegel gave it highest praise. Mme. de Stael declared it to be the most pathetic and the best conceived of all German tragedies. Even in England, Carlyle, though not content with its portraiture of Elizabeth, declares that "Maria Stuart is a beautiful tragedy" ... "with abundant proofs of genius." In this country, interested as we are in English history yet free from historical prejudice, its subject will always cause it to be widely read, and the reading will best reveal its power and beauty.

Maria Stuart

Personen:

Elisabeth, Königin von England.

Maria Stuart, Königin von Schottland, Gefangene in England.

Robert Dudley, Graf von Leicester.

Georg Talbot, Graf von Shrewsbury.

Wilhelm Cecil, Baron von Burleigh, Großschatz= meister.

Graf von Kent.

Wilhelm Davison, Staatssekretär.

Amias Paulet, Ritter, Hüter der Maria.

Mortimer, sein Neffe.

Graf Aubespine, französischer Gesandter.

Graf Bellievre, außerordentlicher Botschafter von Frankreich.

Okelly, Mortimers Freund.

Drugeon Drury, zweiter Hüter der Maria.

Melvil, ihr Haushofmeister.

Burgoyn, ihr Arzt.

Hanna Kennedy, ihre Amme.

Margareta Kurl, ihre Kammerfrau.

Sheriff der Grafschaft.

Offizier der Leibwache.

Französische und englische Herren.

Trabanten.

Hofdiener der Königin von England.

Diener und Dienerinnen der Königin von Schott= land.

Erster Aufzug.

—

Im Schloß zu Fotheringhay.

Ein Zimmer.

Erster Auftritt.

Hanna Kennedy, Amme der Königin von Schottland, in heftigem Streit mit **Paulet,** der im Begriff ist, einen Schrank zu öffnen. **Drugeon Drury,** sein Gehilfe, mit Brecheisen.

Kennedy.

Was macht Ihr, Sir? Welch neue Dreistigkeit!
Zurück von diesem Schrank!

Paulet.

        Wo kam der Schmuck her?
Vom obern Stock ward er herabgeworfen;
Der Gärtner hat bestochen werden sollen
Mit diesem Schmuck — Fluch über Weiberlist!
Trotz meiner Aufsicht, meinem scharfen Suchen
Noch Kostbarkeiten, noch geheime Schätze!
        (Sich über den Schrank machend.)
Wo das gesteckt hat, liegt noch mehr!

Kennedy.

          Zurück, Verwegener!
Hier liegen die Geheimnisse der Lady!

(5)

Paulet.

Die eben such' ich. (Schriften hervorziehend.)   10

Kennedy.

                              Unbedeutende
Papiere, bloße Übungen der Feder,
Des Kerkers traur'ge Weile zu verkürzen.

Paulet.

In müß'ger Weile schafft der böse Geist.

Kennedy.

Es sind französische Schriften.

Paulet.

                    Desto schlimmer!
Die Sprache redet Englands Feind.   15

Kennedy.

                              Konzepte
Von Briefen an die Königin von England.

Paulet.

Die überliefr' ich — Sieh! Was schimmert hier?
(Er hat einen geheimen Ressort geöffnet und zieht aus einem verborgenen Fach
Geschmeide hervor.)
Ein königliches Stirnband, reich an Steinen,
Durchzogen mit den Lilien von Frankreich!
                    (Er giebt es seinem Begleiter.)
Verwahrt's, Drury. Legt's zu dem übrigen! (Drury geht ab.)   20

Kennedy.

O schimpfliche Gewalt, die wir erleiden!

Paulet.

Solang sie noch besitzt, kann sie noch schaden,
Denn alles wird Gewehr in ihrer Hand.

Kennedy.

Seid gütig, Sir. Nehmt nicht den letzten Schmuck

Aus unserm Leben weg.   Die Jammervolle   25
Erfreut der Anblick alter Herrlichkeit,
Denn alles andre habt Ihr uns entrissen.

Paulet.

Es liegt in guter Hand.   Gewissenhaft
Wird es zu seiner Zeit zurückgegeben!

Kennedy.

Wer sieht es diesen kahlen Wänden an,   30
Daß eine Königin hier wohnt?   Wo ist
Die Himmeldecke über ihrem Sitz?
Muß sie den zärtlich weichgewöhnten Fuß
Nicht auf gemeinen rauhen Boden setzen?
Mit grobem Zinn — die schlechtste Edelfrau   35
Würd' es verschmähn — bedient man ihre Tafel.

Paulet.

So speiste sie zu Sterlyn ihren Gatten,
Da sie aus Gold mit ihrem Buhlen trank.

Kennedy.

Sogar des Spiegels kleine Notdurft mangelt.

Paulet.

Solang sie noch ihr eitles Bild beschaut,   40
Hört sie nicht auf, zu hoffen und zu wagen.

Kennedy.

An Büchern fehlt's, den Geist zu unterhalten.

Paulet.

Die Bibel ließ man ihr, das Herz zu bessern.

Kennedy.

Selbst ihre Laute ward ihr weggenommen.

Paulet.

Weil sie verbuhlte Lieder drauf gespielt.   45

Kennedy.

Ist das ein Schicksal für die Weicherzogne,

Die in der Wiege Königin schon war,
Am üpp'gen Hof der Medicäerin
In jeder Freuden Fülle aufgewachsen?
Es sei genug, daß man die Macht ihr nahm,   50
Muß man die armen Flitter ihr mißgönnen?
In großes Unglück lernt ein edles Herz
Sich endlich finden; aber wehe thut's,
Des Lebens kleine Zierden zu entbehren.

Paulet.

Sie wenden nur das Herz dem Eiteln zu,   55
Das in sich gehen und bereuen soll.
Ein üppig lastervolles Leben büßt sich
In Mangel und Erniedrigung allein.

Kennedy.

Wenn ihre zarte Jugend sich verging,
Mag sie's mit Gott abthun und ihrem Herzen,   60
In England ist kein Richter über sie.

Paulet.

Sie wird gerichtet, wo sie frevelte.

Kennedy.

Zum Freveln fesseln sie zu enge Bande.

Paulet.

Doch wußte sie aus diesen engen Banden
Den Arm zu strecken in die Welt, die Fackel   65
Des Bürgerkrieges in das Reich zu schleudern
Und gegen unsre Königin, die Gott
Erhalte! Meuchelrotten zu bewaffnen.
Erregte sie aus diesen Mauern nicht
Den Böswicht Parry und den Babington   70
Zu der verfluchten That des Königsmords?
Hielt dieses Eisengitter sie zurück,
Das edle Herz des Norfolk zu umstricken?

Für sie geopfert, fiel das beste Haupt
Auf dieser Insel unterm Henkerbeil —   75
Und schreckte dieses jammervolle Beispiel
Die Rasenden zurück, die sich wetteifernd
Um ihretwillen in den Abgrund stürzen?
Die Blutgerüste füllen sich für sie
Mit immer neuen Todesopfern an,   80
Und das wird nimmer enden, bis sie selbst,
Die Schuldigste, darauf geopfert ist.
— O, Fluch dem Tag, da dieses Landes Küste
Gastfreundlich diese Helena empfing.

Kennedy.

Gastfreundlich hätte England sie empfangen?   85
Die Unglückselige, die seit dem Tag,
Da sie den Fuß gesetzt in dieses Land,
Als eine Hilfeflehende, Vertriebne
Bei der Verwandten Schutz zu suchen kam,
Sich wider Völkerrecht und Königswürde   90
Gefangen sieht, in enger Kerkerhaft
Der Jugend schöne Jahre muß vertrauern —
Die jetzt, nachdem sie alles hat erfahren,
Was das Gefängnis Bittres hat, gemeinen
Verbrechern gleich, vor des Gerichtes Schranken   95
Gefordert wird und schimpflich angeklagt
Auf Leib und Leben — eine Königin!

Paulet.

Sie kam ins Land als eine Mörderin,
Verjagt von ihrem Volk, des Throns entsetzt,
Den sie mit schwerer Greuelthat geschändet.   100
Verschworen kam sie gegen Englands Glück,
Der spanischen Maria blut'ge Zeiten
Zurück zu bringen, Engelland katholisch

Zu machen, an den Franzmann zu verraten.
Warum verschmähte sie's, den Edinburger   105
Vertrag zu unterschreiben, ihren Anspruch
An England aufzugeben und den Weg
Aus diesem Kerker schnell sich aufzuthun
Mit einem Federstrich? Sie wollte lieber
Gefangen bleiben, sich mißhandelt sehn,   110
Als dieses Titels leerem Prunk entsagen.
Weswegen that sie das? Weil sie den Ränken
Vertraut, den bösen Künsten der Verschwörung,
Und unheilspinnend diese ganze Insel
Aus ihrem Kerker zu erobern hofft.   115

Kennedy.

Ihr spottet, Sir — Zur Härte fügt Ihr noch
Den bittern Hohn! Sie hegte solche Träume,
Die hier lebendig eingemauert lebt,
Zu der kein Schall des Trostes, keine Stimme
Der Freundschaft aus der lieben Heimat dringt,   120
Die längst kein Menschenangesicht mehr schaute,
Als ihrer Kerkermeister finstre Stirn,
Die erst seit kurzem einen neuen Wächter
Erhielt in Eurem rauhen Anverwandten,
Von neuen Stäben sich umgittert sieht —   125

Paulet.

Kein Eisengitter schützt vor ihrer List.
Weiß ich, ob diese Stäbe nicht durchfeilt,
Nicht dieses Zimmers Boden, diese Wände,
Von außen fest, nicht hohl von innen sind
Und den Verrat einlassen, wenn ich schlafe?   130
Fluchvolles Amt, das mir geworden ist,
Die unheilbrütend Listige zu hüten.
Vom Schlummer jagt die Furcht mich auf; ich gehe

Nachts um, wie ein gequälter Geist, erprobe
Des Schlosses Riegel und der Wächter Treu   135
Und sehe zitternd jeden Morgen kommen,
Der meine Furcht wahr machen kann.   Doch wohl mir!
Wohl! Es ist Hoffnung, daß es bald nun endet.
Denn lieber möcht' ich der Verdammten Schar
Wachstehend an der Höllenpforte hüten,   140
Als diese ränkevolle Königin.

Kennedy.

Da kommt sie selbst!

Paulet.

     Den Christus in der Hand,
Die Hoffart und die Weltlust in dem Herzen.

Zweiter Auftritt.

Maria im Schleier, ein Kruzifix in der Hand. **Die Vorigen.**

Kennedy (ihr entgegeneilend).

O Königin! Man tritt uns ganz mit Füßen,
Der Tyrannei, der Härte wird kein Ziel,   145
Und jeder neue Tag häuft neue Leiden
Und Schmach auf dein gekröntes Haupt.

Maria.

      Faß' dich!
Sag' an, was neu geschehen ist?

Kennedy.

      Sieh her!
Dein Pult ist aufgebrochen, deine Schriften,
Dein einz'ger Schatz, den wir mit Müh gerettet,   150
Der letzte Rest von deinem Brautgeschmeide

Aus Frankreich ist in seiner Hand. Du hast nun
Nichts Königliches mehr, bist ganz beraubt.

Maria.

Beruhige dich, Hanna. Diese Flitter machen
Die Königin nicht aus. Man kann uns niedrig   155
Behandeln, nicht erniedrigen. Ich habe
In England mich an viel gewöhnen lernen,
Ich kann auch das verschmerzen. Sir, Ihr habt Euch
Gewaltsam zugeeignet, was ich Euch
Noch heut zu übergeben willens war.   160
Bei diesen Schriften findet sich ein Brief,
Bestimmt für meine königliche Schwester
Von England — Gebt mir Euer Wort, daß Ihr
Ihn redlich an sie selbst wollt übergeben,
Und nicht in Burleighs ungetreue Hand.   165

Paulet.

Ich werde mich bedenken, was zu thun ist

Maria.

Ihr sollt den Inhalt wissen, Sir. Ich bitte
In diesem Brief um eine große Gunst —
— Um eine Unterredung mit ihr selbst,
Die ich mit Augen nie gesehn — Man hat mich   170
Vor ein Gericht von Männern vorgefordert,
Die ich als meinesgleichen nicht erkennen,
Zu denen ich kein Herz mir fassen kann.
Elisabeth ist meines Stammes, meines
Geschlechts und Ranges — Ihr allein, der Schwester,   175
Der Königin, der Frau kann ich mich öffnen.

Paulet.

Sehr oft, Mylady, habt Ihr Euer Schicksal
Und Eure Ehre Männern anvertraut,
Die Eurer Achtung minder würdig waren.

Maria.

Ich bitte noch um eine zweite Gunst,   180
Unmenschlichkeit allein kann mir sie weigern.
Schon lange Zeit entbehr' ich im Gefängnis
Der Kirche Trost, der Sakramente Wohlthat,
Und die mir Kron' und Freiheit hat geraubt,
Die meinem Leben selber droht, wird mir   185
Die Himmelsthüre nicht verschließen wollen.

Paulet.

Auf Euren Wunsch wird der Dechant des Orts —

Maria (unterbricht ihn lebhaft).

Ich will nichts vom Dechanten. Einen Priester
Von meiner eignen Kirche fordre ich.
— Auch Schreiber und Notarien verlang' ich,   190
Um meinen letzten Willen aufzusetzen.
Der Gram, das lange Kerkerelend nagt
An meinem Leben. Meine Tage sind
Gezählt, befürcht' ich, und ich achte mich
Gleich einer Sterbenden.   195

Paulet.

           Da thut Ihr wohl,
Das sind Betrachtungen, die Euch geziemen.

Maria.

Und weiß ich, ob nicht eine schnelle Hand
Des Kummers langsames Geschäft beschleunigt?
Ich will mein Testament aufsetzen, will
Verfügung treffen über das, was mein ist.   200

Paulet.

Die Freiheit habt Ihr. Englands Königin
Will sich mit Eurem Raube nicht bereichern.

Maria.

Man hat von meinen treuen Kammerfrauen,

Von meinen Dienern mich getrennt — Wo sind sie?
Was ist ihr Schicksal? Ihrer Dienste kann ich   205
Entraten; doch beruhigt will ich sein,
Daß die Getreu'n nicht leiden und entbehren.

Paulet.

Für Eure Diener ist gesorgt.   (Er will gehen.)

Maria.

Ihr geht, Sir? Ihr verlaßt mich abermals,
Und ohne mein geängstigt fürchtend Herz   210
Der Qual der Ungewißheit zu entladen.
Ich bin, Dank Eurer Späher Wachsamkeit,
Von aller Welt geschieden, keine Kunde
Gelangt zu mir durch diese Kerkermauern,
Mein Schicksal liegt in meiner Feinde Hand.   215
Ein peinlich langer Monat ist vorüber,
Seitdem die vierzig Kommissarien
In diesem Schloß mich überfallen, Schranken
Errichtet, schnell, mit unanständiger Eile,
Mich unbereitet, ohne Anwalts Hilfe,   220
Vor ein noch nie erhört Gericht gestellt,
Auf schlaugefaßte schwere Klagepunkte
Mich, die Betäubte, Überraschte, flugs
Aus dem Gedächtnis Rede stehen lassen —
Wie Geister kamen sie und schwanden wieder.   225
Seit diesem Tage schweigt mir jeder Mund,
Ich such' umsonst in Eurem Blick zu lesen,
Ob meine Unschuld, meiner Freunde Eifer,
Ob meiner Feinde böser Rat gesiegt.
Brecht endlich Euer Schweigen — laßt mich wissen,   230
Was ich zu fürchten, was zu hoffen habe.

Paulet (nach einer Pause).

Schließt Eure Rechnung mit dem Himmel ab.

Maria.

Ich hoff' auf seine Gnade, Sir — und hoffe
Auf strenges Recht von meinen ird'schen Richtern.

Paulet

Recht soll Euch werden.   Zweifelt nicht daran.   235

Maria,

Ist mein Prozeß entschieden, Sir?

Paulet

                    Ich weiß nicht.

Maria.

Bin ich verurteilt?

Paulet.

        Ich weiß nichts, Mylady.

Maria.

Man liebt hier rasch zu Werk zu gehn.   Soll mich
Der Mörder überfallen, wie die Richter?

Paulet.

Denkt immerhin, es sei so, und er wird Euch   240
In beßrer Fassung dann, als diese, finden.

Maria.

Nichts soll mich in Erstaunen setzen, Sir,
Was ein Gerichtshof in Westminsterhall,
Den Burleighs Haß und Hattons Eifer lenkt,
Zu urteln sich erdreiste — Weiß ich doch,   245
Was Englands Königin wagen darf zu thun.

Paulet.

Englands Beherrscher brauchen nichts zu scheuen,
Als ihr Gewissen und ihr Parlament.
Was die Gerechtigkeit gesprochen, furchtlos,
Vor aller Welt wird es die Macht vollziehn.   250

Dritter Auftritt.

Die Vorigen. Mortimer, Paulets Neffe, tritt herein und, ohne der Königin einige Aufmerksamkeit zu bezeigen, zu Paulet.

Mortimer.

Man sucht Euch, Oheim.

(Er entfernt sich auf eben die Weise. Die Königin bemerkt es mit Unwillen und wendet sich zu Paulet, der ihm folgen will.)

Maria.

Sir, noch eine Bitte.

Wenn Ihr mir was zu sagen habt — von Euch
Ertrag' ich viel, ich ehre Euer Alter.
Den Übermut des Jünglings trag' ich nicht,
Spart mir den Anblick seiner rohen Sitten.   255

Paulet.

Was ihn Euch widrig macht, macht mir ihn wert.
Wohl ist es keiner von den weichen Thoren,
Die eine falsche Weiberthräne schmelzt —
Er ist gereist, kommt aus Paris und Reims
Und bringt sein treu altenglisch Herz zurück: 260
Lady, an dem ist Eure Kunst verloren!   (Geht ab.)

Vierter Auftritt.

Maria. Kennedy.

Kennedy.

Darf Euch der Rohe das ins Antlitz sagen!
O, es ist hart!

Maria (in Nachdenken verloren).

Wir haben in den Tagen unsers Glanzes

MARIA STUART.

From the original picture by Zucchero, in the Feinbermann Collection, London.

Dem Schmeichler ein zu willig Ohr geliehn;   265
Gerecht ist's, gute Kennedy, daß wir
Des Vorwurfs ernste Stimme nun vernehmen.

Kennedy.

Wie? so gebeugt, so mutlos, teure Lady?
Wart Ihr doch sonst so froh, Ihr pflegtet mich zu trösten,
Und eher mußt' ich Euren Flattersinn,   270
Als Eure Schwermut schelten.

Maria.

           Ich erkenn' ihn.
Es ist der blut'ge Schatten König Darnleys,
Der zürnend aus dem Gruftgewölbe steigt,
Und er wird nimmer Friede mit mir machen,
Bis meines Unglücks Maß erfüllet ist.   275

Kennedy.

Was für Gedanken —

Maria.

           Du vergissest, Hanna —
Ich aber habe ein getreu Gedächtnis —
Der Jahrstag dieser unglückseligen That
Ist heute abermals zurückgekehrt,
Er ist's, den ich mit Buß' und Fasten feire.   280

Kennedy.

Schickt endlich diesen bösen Geist zur Ruh.
Ihr habt die That mit jahrelanger Reu,
Mit schweren Leidensproben abgebüßt.
Die Kirche, die den Löseschlüssel hat
Für jede Schuld, der Himmel hat vergeben.   285

Maria.

Frischblutend steigt die längst vergebne Schuld
Aus ihrem leichtbedeckten Grab empor!

2

Des Gatten racheforderndes Gespenst
Schickt keines Messedieners Glocke, kein
Hochwürdiges in Priesters Hand zur Gruft.   290

Kennedy.

Nicht Ihr habt ihn gemordet! Andre thaten's!

Maria.

Ich wußte drum.   Ich ließ die That geschehn
Und lockt' ihn schmeichelnd in das Todesnetz.

Kennedy.

Die Jugend mildert Eure Schuld.   Ihr wart
So zarten Alters noch.   295

Maria.

                    So zart — und lud
Die schwere Schuld auf mein so junges Leben.

Kennedy.

Ihr wart durch blutige Beleidigung
Gereizt und durch des Mannes Übermut,
Den Eure Liebe aus der Dunkelheit,
Wie eine Götterhand, hervorgezogen,   300
Den Ihr durch Euer Brautgemach zum Throne
Geführt, mit Eurer blühenden Person
Beglückt und Eurer angestammten Krone.
Konnt' er vergessen, daß sein prangend Los
Der Liebe großmutsvolle Schöpfung war?   305
Und doch vergaß er's, der Unwürdige!
Beleidigte mit niedrigem Verdacht,
Mit rohen Sitten Eure Zärtlichkeit,
Und widerwärtig wurd' er Euren Augen.
Der Zauber schwand, der Euren Blick getäuscht,   310
Ihr floht erzürnt des Schändlichen Umarmung
Und gabt ihn der Verachtung preis — Und er —

Verfucht' er's, Eure Gunst zurückzurufen?
Bat er um Gnade? Warf er sich bereuend
Zu Euren Füßen, Besserung versprechend?   315
Trotz bot Euch der Abscheuliche — Der Euer
Geschöpf war, Euren König wollt' er spielen,
Vor Euren Augen ließ er Euch den Liebling,
Den schönen Sänger Rizzio, durchbohren —
Ihr rächtet blutig nur die blut'ge That.   320

Maria.

Und blutig wird sie auch an mir sich rächen,
Du sprichst mein Urteil aus, da du mich tröstest.

Kennedy.

Da Ihr die That geschehn ließt, wart Ihr nicht
Ihr selbst, gehörtet Euch nicht selbst. Ergriffen
Hatt' Euch der Wahnsinn blinder Liebesglut,   325
Euch unterjocht dem furchtbaren Verführer,
Dem unglückfel'gen Bothwell — Über Euch
Mit übermüt'gem Männerwillen herrschte
Der Schreckliche, der Euch durch Zaubertränke,
Durch Höllenkünste das Gemüt verwirrend,   330
Erhitzte —

Maria.

Seine Künste waren keine andre,
Als seine Männerkraft und meine Schwachheit.

Kennedy.

Nein, sag' ich. Alle Geister der Verdammnis
Mußt' er zu Hilfe rufen, der dies Band
Um Eure hellen Sinne wob. Ihr hattet   335
Kein Ohr mehr für der Freundin Warnungsstimme,
Kein Aug' für das, was wohlanständig war.
Verlassen hatte Euch die zarte Scheu
Der Menschen; Eure Wangen, sonst der Sitz

Schamhaft errötender Bescheidenheit,   340
Sie glühten nur vom Feuer des Verlangens.
Ihr warft den Schleier des Geheimnisses
Von Euch; des Mannes keckes Laster hatte
Auch Eure Blödigkeit besiegt; Ihr stelltet
Mit dreister Stirne Eure Schmach zur Schau.   345
Ihr ließt das königliche Schwert von Schottland
Durch ihn, den Mörder, dem des Volkes Flüche
Nachschallten, durch die Gassen Edinburgs
Vor Euch hertragen im Triumph, umringtet
Mit Waffen Euer Parlament, und hier,   350
Im eignen Tempel der Gerechtigkeit,
Zwangt Ihr mit frechem Possenspiel die Richter,
Den Schuldigen des Mordes loszusprechen —
Ihr gingt noch weiter — Gott!

Maria.

                  Vollende nur!
Und reicht' ihm meine Hand vor dem Altare!   355

Kennedy.

O, laßt ein ewig Schweigen diese That
Bedecken! Sie ist schauderhaft, empörend,
Ist einer ganz Verlornen wert — Doch Ihr seid keine
Verlorene — ich kenn' Euch ja, ich bin's,
Die Eure Kindheit auferzogen. Weich   360
Ist Euer Herz gebildet, offen ist's
Der Scham — der Leichtsinn nur ist Euer Laster.
Ich wiederhol' es, es giebt böse Geister,
Die in des Menschen unverwahrter Brust
Sich augenblicklich ihren Wohnplatz nehmen,   365
Die schnell in uns das Schreckliche begehn
Und, zu der Höll' entfliehend, das Entsetzen
In dem befleckten Busen hinterlassen.
Seit dieser That, die Euer Leben schwärzt,

Habt Ihr nichts Lasterhaftes mehr begangen,   370
Ich bin ein Zeuge Eurer Besserung.
Drum fasset Mut! Macht Friede mit Euch selbst!
Was Ihr auch zu bereuen habt, in England
Seid Ihr nicht schuldig; nicht Elisabeth,
Nicht Englands Parlament ist Euer Richter.   375
Macht ist's, die Euch hier unterdrückt; vor diesen
Anmaßlichen Gerichtshof dürft Ihr Euch
Hinstellen mit dem ganzen Mut der Unschuld.

Maria.

Wer kommt? (Mortimer zeigt sich an der Thüre.)

Kennedy.

Es ist der Neffe.   Geht hinein.

Fünfter Auftritt.

Die Vorigen. Mortimer scheu hereintretend.

Mortimer (zur Amme).

Entfernt Euch, haltet Wache vor der Thür,   380
Ich habe mit der Königin zu reden.

Maria (mit Ansehn).

Hanna, du bleibst.

Mortimer.

Habt keine Furcht, Mylady.   Lernt mich kennen.
(Er überreicht ihr eine Karte.)

Maria
(sieht sie an und fährt bestürzt zurück).

Ha!   Was ist das?

Mortimer (zur Amme).

   Geht, Dame Kennedy,
Sorgt, daß mein Oheim uns nicht überfalle!   385

Maria
(zur Amme, welche zaudert und die Königin fragend ansieht).

Geh! Geh! Thu, was er sagt.
   (Die Amme entfernt sich mit Zeichen der Verwunderung.)

Sechster Auftritt.

Mortimer. Maria.

Maria.

     Von meinem Oheim,
Dem Kardinal von Lothringen aus Frankreich! (Liest.)
„Traut dem Sir Mortimer, der Euch dies bringt,
„Denn keinen treuern Freund habt Ihr in England.‟
   (Mortimern mit Erstaunen ansehend.)
Ist's möglich? Ist's kein Blendwerk, das mich täuscht? 390
So nahe find' ich einen Freund und wähnte mich
Verlassen schon von aller Welt — find' ihn
In Euch, dem Neffen meines Kerkermeisters,
In dem ich meinen schlimmsten Feind —

   Mortimer (sich ihr zu Füßen werfend).
         Verzeihung
Für diese verhaßte Larve, Königin,   395
Die mir zu tragen Kampf genug gekostet,
Doch der ich's danke, daß ich mich Euch nahen,
Euch Hilfe und Errettung bringen kann.

   Maria.

Steht auf — Ihr überrascht mich, Sir — Ich kann

So schnell nicht aus der Tiefe meines Elends   400
Zur Hoffnung übergehen — Redet, Sir —
Macht mir dies Glück begreiflich, daß ich's glaube.

Mortimer (steht auf).

Die Zeit verrinnt.   Bald wird mein Oheim hier sein,
Und ein verhaßter Mensch begleitet ihn.
Eh Euch ihr Schreckensauftrag überrascht,   405
Hört an, wie Euch der Himmel Rettung schickt.

Maria.

Er schickt sie durch ein Wunder seiner Allmacht!

Mortimer.

Erlaubt, daß ich von mir beginne.

Maria.

Redet, Sir!

Mortimer.

Ich zählte zwanzig Jahre, Königin,
In strengen Pflichten war ich aufgewachsen,   410
In finsterm Haß des Papsttums aufgesäugt,
Als mich die unbezwingliche Begierde
Hinaus trieb auf das feste Land.   Ich ließ
Der Puritaner dumpfe Predigtstuben,
Die Heimat hinter mir, in schnellem Lauf   415
Durchzog ich Frankreich, das gepriesene
Italien mit heißem Wunsche suchend.
   Es war die Zeit des großen Kirchenfests,
Von Pilgerscharen wimmelten die Wege,
Bekränzt war jedes Gottesbild, es war,   420
Als ob die Menschheit auf der Wandrung wäre,
Wallfahrend nach dem Himmelreich — Mich selbst
Ergriff der Strom der glaubenvollen Menge

Und riß mich in das Weichbild Roms —
    Wie ward mir, Königin!   425
Als mir der Säulen Pracht und Siegesbogen
Entgegenstieg, des Kolosseums Herrlichkeit
Den Staunenden umfing, ein hoher Bildnergeist
In seine heitre Wunderwelt mich schloß!
Ich hatte nie der Künste Macht gefühlt;   430
Es haßt die Kirche, die mich auferzog,
Der Sinne Reiz, kein Abbild duldet sie,
Allein das körperlose Wort verehrend.
Wie wurde mir, als ich ins Innre nun
Der Kirchen trat, und die Musik der Himmel   435
Herunterstieg, und der Gestalten Fülle
Verschwenderisch aus Wand und Decke quoll,
Das Herrlichste und Höchste, gegenwärtig,
Vor den entzückten Sinnen sich bewegte;
Als ich sie selbst nun sah, die Göttlichen,   440
Den Gruß des Engels, die Geburt des Herrn,
Die heil'ge Mutter, die herabgestiegne
Dreifaltigkeit, die leuchtende Verklärung —
Als ich den Papst drauf sah in seiner Pracht
Das Hochamt halten und die Völker segnen!   445
O, was ist Goldes, was Juwelen Schein,
Womit der Erde Könige sich schmücken!
Nur er ist mit dem Göttlichen umgeben.
Ein wahrhaft Reich der Himmel ist sein Haus,
Denn nicht von dieser Welt sind diese Formen.   450

Maria.

O, schonet mein! Nicht weiter! Höret auf,
Den frischen Lebensteppich vor mir aus=
Zubreiten — Ich bin elend und gefangen.

Mortimer.

Auch ich war's, Königin! und mein Gefängnis

Sprang auf, und frei auf einmal fühlte sich   455
Der Geist, des Lebens schönen Tag begrüßend.
Haß schwur ich nun dem engen dumpfen Buch,
Mit frischem Kranz die Schläfe mir zu schmücken,
Mich fröhlich an die Fröhlichen zu schließen.
Viel edle Schotten drängten sich an mich   460
Und der Franzosen muntre Landsmannschaften.
Sie brachten mich zu Eurem edlen Oheim,
Dem Kardinal von Guise — Welch ein Mann!
Wie sicher, klar und männlich groß! — Wie ganz
Geboren, um die Geister zu regieren!   465
Das Muster eines königlichen Priesters,
Ein Fürst der Kirche, wie ich keinen sah!

Maria.

Ihr habt sein treues Angesicht gesehn,
Des vielgeliebten, des erhabnen Mannes,
Der meiner zarten Jugend Führer war.   470
O, redet mir von ihm! Denkt er noch mein?
Liebt ihn das Glück, blüht ihm das Leben noch,
Steht er noch herrlich da, ein Fels der Kirche?

Mortimer.

Der Treffliche ließ selber sich herab,
Die hohen Glaubenslehren mir zu deuten,   475
Und meines Herzens Zweifel zu zerstreun.
Er zeigte mir, daß grübelnde Vernunft
Den Menschen ewig in der Irre leitet,
Daß seine Augen sehen müssen, was
Das Herz soll glauben, daß ein sichtbar Haupt   480
Der Kirche not thut, daß der Geist der Wahrheit
Geruht hat auf den Sitzungen der Väter.
Die Wahnbegriffe meiner kind'schen Seele,
Wie schwanden sie vor seinem siegenden
Verstand und vor der Suada seines Mundes!   485

Ich kehrte in der Kirche Schoß zurück,
Schwur meinen Irrtum ab in seine Hände.

Maria.

So seid Ihr einer jener Tausende,
Die er mit seiner Rede Himmelskraft,
Wie der erhabne Prediger des Berges,   490
Ergriffen und zum ew'gen Heil geführt!

Mortimer.

Als ihn des Amtes Pflichten bald darauf
Nach Frankreich riefen, sandt' er mich nach Reims,
Wo die Gesellschaft Jesu, fromm geschäftig,
Für Englands Kirche Priester auferzieht.   495
Den edlen Schotten Morgan fand ich hier,
Auch Euren treuen Leßley, den gelehrten
Bischof von Roße, die auf Frankreichs Boden
Freudlose Tage der Verbannung leben —
Eng schloß ich mich an diese Würdigen   500
Und stärkte mich im Glauben — Eines Tags
Als ich mich umsah in des Bischofs Wohnung,
Fiel mir ein weiblich Bildnis in die Augen
Von rührend wundersamem Reiz; gewaltig
Ergriff es mich in meiner tiefsten Seele,   505
Und, des Gefühls nicht mächtig, stand ich da.
Da sagte mir der Bischof: Wohl mit Recht
Mögt Ihr gerührt bei diesem Bilde weilen.
Die schönste aller Frauen, welche leben,
Ist auch die jammernswürdigste von allen;   510
Um unsres Glaubens willen duldet sie,
Und Euer Vaterland ist's, wo sie leidet.

Maria.

Der Redliche! Nein, ich verlor nicht alles,
Da solcher Freund im Unglück mir geblieben.

Mortimer.

Drauf fing er an, mit herzerschütternder   515
Beredsamkeit mir Euer Märtyrtum
Und Eurer Feinde Blutgier abzuschildern.
Auch Euern Stammbaum wies er mir, er zeigte
Mir Eure Abkunft von dem hohen Hause
Der Tudor, überzeugte mich, daß Euch   520
Allein gebührt, in Engelland zu herrschen,
Nicht dieser Afterkönigin, gezeugt
In ehebrecherischem Bett, die Heinrich,
Ihr Vater, selbst verwarf als Bastardtochter.
Nicht seinem einz'gen Zeugnis wollt' ich traun,   525
Ich holte Rat bei allen Rechtsgelehrten,
Viel alte Wappenbücher schlug ich nach,
Und alle Kundige, die ich befragte,
Bestätigten mir Eures Anspruchs Kraft.
Ich weiß nunmehr, daß Euer gutes Recht   530
An England Euer ganzes Unrecht ist,
Daß Euch dies Reich als Eigentum gehört,
Worin Ihr schuldlos als Gefangne schmachtet.

Maria.

O dieses unglücksvolle Recht! Es ist
Die einz'ge Quelle aller meiner Leiden.   535

Mortimer.

Um diese Zeit kam mir die Kunde zu,
Daß Ihr aus Talbots Schloß hinweggeführt
Und meinem Oheim übergeben worden —
Des Himmels wundervolle Rettungshand
Glaubt' ich in dieser Fügung zu erkennen.   540
Ein lauter Ruf des Schicksals war sie mir,
Das m e i n e n Arm gewählt, Euch zu befreien.
Die Freunde stimmen freudig bei, es giebt

Der Kardinal mir seinen Rat und Segen
Und lehrt mich der Verstellung schwere Kunst.   545
Schnell ward der Plan entworfen, und ich trete
Den Rückweg an ins Vaterland, wo ich,
Ihr wißt's, vor zehen Tagen bin gelandet.

(Er hält inne.)

Ich sah Euch, Königin — Euch selbst!
Nicht Euer Bild! — O, welchen Schatz bewahrt   550
Dies Schloß! Kein Kerker! Eine Götterhalle,
Glanzvoller als der königliche Hof
Von England — O des Glücklichen, dem es
Vergönnt ist, e i n e Luft mit Euch zu atmen!
    Wohl hat sie recht, die Euch so tief verbirgt!   555
Aufstehen würde Englands ganze Jugend,
Kein Schwert in seiner Scheide müßig bleiben,
Und die Empörung mit gigantischem Haupt
Durch diese Friedensinsel schreiten, sähe
Der Britte seine Königin!   560

Maria.

Wohl ihr,
Säh' jeder Britte sie mit Euren Augen!

Mortimer.

Wär' er, wie ich, ein Zeuge Eurer Leiden,
Der Sanftmut Zeuge und der edlen Fassung,
Womit Ihr das Unwürdige erduldet.
Denn geht Ihr nicht aus allen Leidensproben   565
Als eine Königin hervor? Raubt Euch
Des Kerkers Schmach von Eurem Schönheitsglanze?
Euch mangelt alles, was das Leben schmückt,
Und doch umfließt Euch ewig Licht und Leben.
Nie setz' ich meinen Fuß auf diese Schwelle,   570
Daß nicht mein Herz zerrissen wird von Qualen,
Nicht von der Lust entzückt, Euch anzuschauen! —

Doch furchtbar naht sich die Entscheidung, wachsend
Mit jeder Stunde dringet die Gefahr;
Ich darf nicht länger säumen — Euch nicht länger   575
Das Schreckliche verbergen —

Maria.

Ist mein Urteil
Gefällt?   Entdeckt mir's frei.   Ich kann es hören.

Mortimer.

Es ist gefällt.   Die zweiundvierzig Richter haben
Ihr S c h u l d i g ausgesprochen über Euch.   Das Haus
Der Lords und der Gemeinen, die Stadt London   580
Bestehen heftig dringend auf des Urteils
Vollstreckung; nur die Königin säumt noch
— Aus arger List, daß man sie nötige,
Nicht aus Gefühl der Menschlichkeit und Schonung.

Maria (mit Fassung).
                                                            585
Sir Mortimer, Ihr überrascht mich nicht,
Erschreckt mich nicht.   Auf solche Botschaft war ich
Schon längst gefaßt.   Ich kenne meine Richter.
Nach den Mißhandlungen, die ich erlitten,
Begreif' ich wohl, daß man die Freiheit mir
Nicht schenken kann — Ich weiß, wo man hinaus will.   590
In ew'gem Kerker will man mich bewahren,
Und meine Rache, meinen Rechtsanspruch
Mit mir verscharren in Gefängnisnacht.

Mortimer.

Nein, Königin — o nein! nein!   Dabei steht man
Nicht still.   Die Tyrannei begnügt sich nicht,   595
Ihr Werk nur halb zu thun.   Solang Ihr lebt,
Lebt auch die Furcht der Königin von England.
Euch kann kein Kerker tief genug begraben,
Nur Euer Tod versichert ihren Thron.

Maria.

Sie könnt' es wagen, mein gekröntes Haupt   600
Schmachvoll auf einen Henkerblock zu legen?

Mortimer.

Sie wird es wagen. Zweifelt nicht daran.

Maria.

Sie könnte so die eigne Majestät
Und aller Könige im Staube wälzen?
Und fürchtet sie die Rache Frankreichs nicht?   605

Mortimer.

Sie schließt mit Frankreich einen ew'gen Frieden,
Dem Duc von Anjou schenkt sie Thron und Hand.

Maria.

Wird sich der König Spaniens nicht waffnen?

Mortimer.

Nicht eine Welt in Waffen fürchtet sie,
Solang sie Frieden hat mit ihrem Volke.   610

Maria.

Den Britten wollte sie dies Schauspiel geben?

Mortimer.

Dies Land, Mylady, hat in letzten Zeiten
Der königlichen Frauen m e h r vom Thron
Herab aufs Blutgerüste steigen sehn.
Die eigne Mutter der Elisabeth   615
Ging diesen Weg und Katharina Howard,
Auch Lady Gray war ein gekröntes Haupt.

Maria (nach einer Pause).

Nein, Mortimer! Euch blendet eitle Furcht.
Es ist die Sorge Eures treuen Herzens,
Die Euch vergebne Schrecknisse erschafft.   620
Nicht das Schafott ist's, das ich fürchte, Sir.
Es giebt noch andre Mittel, stillere,
Wodurch sich die Beherrscherin von England
Vor meinem Anspruch Ruhe schaffen kann.
Eh sich ein Henker für mich findet, wird   625
Noch eher sich ein Mörder dingen lassen.
— Das ist's, wovor ich zittre, Sir! und nie
Setz' ich des Bechers Rand an meine Lippen,
Daß nicht ein Schauder mich ergreift, er könnte
Kredenzt sein von der Liebe meiner Schwester.   630

Mortimer.

Nicht offenbar, noch heimlich soll's dem Mord
Gelingen, Euer Leben anzutasten.
Seid ohne Furcht! Bereitet ist schon alles.
Zwölf edle Jünglinge des Landes sind
In meinem Bündnis, haben heute früh   635
Das Sakrament darauf empfangen, Euch
Mit starkem Arm aus diesem Schloß zu führen.
Graf Aubespine, der Abgesandte Frankreichs,
Weiß um den Bund, er bietet selbst die Hände,
Und sein Palast ist's, wo wir uns versammeln.   640

Maria.

Ihr macht mich zittern, Sir — doch nicht vor Freude.
Mir fliegt ein böses Ahnen durch das Herz.
Was unternehmt Ihr? Wißt Ihr's? Schrecken Euch
Nicht Babingtons, nicht Tichburns blut'ge Häupter,
Auf Londons Brücke warnend aufgesteckt?   645
Nicht das Verderben der Unzähligen,

Die ihren Tod in gleichem Wagstück fanden
Und meine Ketten schwerer nur gemacht?
Unglücklicher, verführter Jüngling — flieht!
Flieht, wenn's noch Zeit ist — wenn der Späher Burleigh   650
Nicht jetzt schon Kundschaft hat von Euch, nicht schon
In Eure Mitte den Verräter mischte.
Flieht aus dem Reiche schnell! Marien Stuart
Hat noch kein Glücklicher beschützt.

Mortimer.

      Mich schrecken
Nicht Babingtons, nicht Tichburns blut'ge Häupter,   655
Auf Londons Brücke warnend aufgesteckt,
Nicht das Verderben der unzähl'gen andern,
Die ihren Tod in gleichem Wagstück fanden;
Sie fanden auch darin den ew'gen Ruhm,
Und Glück schon ist's, für Eure Rettung sterben.   660

Maria.

Umsonst! Mich rettet nicht Gewalt, nicht List.
Der Feind ist wachsam, und die Macht ist sein.
Nicht Paulet nur und seiner Wächter Schar,
Ganz England hütet meines Kerkers Thore.
Der freie Wille der Elisabeth allein   665
Kann sie mir aufthun.

Mortimer.

    O, das hoffet nie!

Maria.

Ein einz'ger Mann lebt, der sie öffnen kann.

Mortimer.

O, nennt mir diesen Mann —

Maria.

    Graf Lester.

Mortimer (tritt erstaunt zurück).

Lester!

Graf Lester! — Euer blutigster Verfolger,
Der Günstling der Elisabeth — Von diesem —   670

Maria.

Bin ich zu retten, ist's allein durch ihn.
— Geht zu ihm.   Öffnet Euch ihm frei,
Und zur Gewähr, daß ich's bin, die Euch sendet,
Bringt ihm dies Schreiben.   Es enthält mein Bildnis.
(Sie zieht ein Papier aus dem Busen.   Mortimer tritt zurück und zögert, es
anzunehmen.)

Nehmt hin.   Ich trag' es lange schon bei mir,   675
Weil Eures Oheims strenge Wachsamkeit
Mir jeden Weg zu ihm gehemmt — Euch sandte
Mein guter Engel —

Mortimer.

Königin — dies Rätsel —

Erklärt es mir —

Maria.

Graf Lester wird's Euch lösen.
Vertraut ihm, er wird Euch vertrauen — Wer kommt?   680

Kennedy (eilfertig eintretend).

Sir Paulet naht mit einem Herrn vom Hofe.

Mortimer.

Es ist Lord Burleigh.   Faßt Euch, Königin!
Hört es mit Gleichmut an, was er Euch bringt.
(Er entfernt sich durch eine Seitenthür.   Kennedy folgt ihm.)

3

Siebenter Auftritt.

Maria. Lord Burleigh, Großschatzmeister von England,
und Ritter Paulet.

Paulet.

Ihr wünschet heut Gewißheit Eures Schicksals,
Gewißheit bringt Euch Seine Herrlichkeit,   685
Mylord von Burleigh.   Tragt sie mit Ergebung.

Maria.

Mit Würde, hoff' ich, die der Unschuld ziemt.

Burleigh.

Ich komme als Gesandter des Gerichts.

Maria.

Lord Burleigh leiht dienstfertig dem Gerichte,
Dem er den Geist geliehn, nun auch den Mund.   690

Paulet.

Ihr sprecht, als wüßtet Ihr bereits das Urteil.

Maria.

Da es Lord Burleigh bringt, so weiß ich es.
— Zur Sache, Sir.

Burleigh.

        Ihr habt Euch dem Gericht
Der Zweiundvierzig unterworfen, Lady —

Maria.

Verzeiht, Mylord, daß ich Euch gleich zu Anfang   695
Ins Wort muß fallen — Unterworfen hätt' ich mich
Dem Richterspruch der Zweiundvierzig, sagt Ihr?
Ich habe keineswegs mich unterworfen.

Nie konnt' ich das — ich konnte meinem Rang,
Der Würde meines Volks und meines Sohnes   700
Und aller Fürsten nicht so viel vergeben.
Verordnet ist im englischen Gesetz,
Daß jeder Angeklagte durch Geschworne
Von seinesgleichen soll gerichtet werden.
Wer in der Committee ist meinesgleichen?   705
Nur Könige sind meine Peers.

Burleigh.

                         Ihr hörtet
Die Klagartikel an, ließt Euch darüber
Vernehmen vor Gerichte —

Maria.

                         Ja, ich habe mich
Durch Hattons arge List verleiten lassen,
Bloß meiner Ehre wegen und im Glauben   710
An meiner Gründe siegende Gewalt,
Ein Ohr zu leihen jenen Klagepunkten
Und ihren Ungrund darzuthun — Das that ich
Aus Achtung für die würdigen Personen
Der Lords, nicht für ihr Amt, das ich verwerfe.   715

Burleigh.

Ob Ihr sie anerkennt, ob nicht, Mylady,
Das ist nur eine leere Förmlichkeit,
Die des Gerichtes Lauf nicht hemmen kann.
Ihr atmet Englands Luft, genießt den Schutz,
Die Wohlthat des Gesetzes, und so seid Ihr   720
Auch seiner Herrschaft unterthan!

Maria.

                         Ich atme
Die Luft in einem englischen Gefängnis.

Heißt das in England leben, der Gesetze
Wohlthat genießen? Kenn' ich sie doch kaum.
Nie hab' ich eingewilligt, sie zu halten. 725
Ich bin nicht dieses Reiches Bürgerin,
Bin eine freie Königin des Auslands.

Burleigh.

Und denkt Ihr, daß der königliche Name
Zum Freibrief dienen könne, blut'ge Zwietracht
In fremdem Lande straflos auszusäen? 730
Wie stünd' es um die Sicherheit der Staaten,
Wenn das gerechte Schwert der Themis nicht
Die schuld'ge Stirn des königlichen Gastes
Erreichen könnte, wie des Bettlers Haupt?

Maria.

Ich will mich nicht der Rechenschaft entziehn, 735
Die Richter sind es nur, die ich verwerfe.

Burleigh.

Die Richter! Wie, Mylady? Sind es etwa
Vom Pöbel aufgegriffene Verworfne,
Schamlose Zungendrescher, denen Recht
Und Wahrheit feil ist, die sich zum Organ 740
Der Unterdrückung willig dingen lassen?
Sind's nicht die ersten Männer dieses Landes,
Selbständig gnug, um wahrhaft sein zu dürfen,
Um über Fürstenfurcht und niedrige
Bestechung weit erhaben sich zu sehn? 745
Sind's nicht dieselben, die ein edles Volk
Frei und gerecht regieren, deren Namen
Man nur zu nennen braucht, um jeden Zweifel,
Um jeden Argwohn schleunig stumm zu machen?
An ihrer Spitze steht der Völkerhirte, 750
Der fromme Primas von Canterbury,

Der weise Talbot, der des Siegels wahret,
Und Howard, der des Reiches Flotten führt.
Sagt! Konnte die Beherrscherin von England
Mehr thun, als aus der ganzen Monarchie   755
Die Edelsten auslesen und zu Richtern
In diesem königlichen Streit bestellen?
Und wär's zu denken, daß Parteienhaß
Den einzelnen bestäche — können vierzig
Erlesne Männer sich in einem Spruche   760
Der Leidenschaft vereinigen?

Maria (nach einigem Stillschweigen).

Ich höre staunend die Gewalt des Mundes,
Der mir von je so unheilbringend war —
Wie werd' ich mich, ein ungelehrtes Weib,
Mit so kunstfert'gem Redner messen können! —   765
Wohl! Wären diese Lords, wie Ihr sie schildert,
Verstummen müßt' ich, hoffnungslos verloren
Wär' meine Sache, sprächen sie mich schuldig.
Doch diese Namen, die Ihr preisend nennt,
Die mich durch ihr Gewicht zermalmen sollen,   770
Mylord, ganz andre Rollen seh' ich sie
In den Geschichten dieses Landes spielen.
Ich sehe diesen hohen Adel Englands,
Des Reiches majestätischen Senat,
Gleich Sklaven des Serails den Sultanslaunen   775
Heinrichs des Achten, meines Großohms, schmeicheln —
Ich sehe dieses edle Oberhaus,
Gleich feil mit den erkäuflichen Gemeinen,
Gesetze prägen und verrufen, Ehen
Auflösen, binden, wie der Mächtige   780
Gebietet, Englands Fürstentöchter heute
Enterben, mit dem Bastardnamen schänden,
Und morgen sie zu Königinnen krönen.

Ich sehe diese würd'gen Peers mit schnell
Vertauschter Überzeugung unter vier   785
Regierungen den Glauben viermal ändern —

Burleigh.

Ihr nennt Euch fremd in Englands Reichsgesetzen,
In Englands Unglück seid Ihr sehr bewandert.

Maria.

Und das sind meine Richter! — Lord Schatzmeister!
Ich will gerecht sein gegen Euch! Seid Ihr's   790
Auch gegen mich — Man sagt, Ihr meint es gut
Mit diesem Staat, mit Eurer Königin,
Seid unbestechlich, wachsam, unermüdet —
Ich will es glauben. Nicht der eigne Nutzen
Regiert Euch, Euch regiert allein der Vorteil   795
Des Souveräns, des Landes. Eben darum
Mißtraut Euch, edler Lord, daß nicht der Nutzen
Des Staats Euch als Gerechtigkeit erscheine.
Nicht zweifl' ich dran, es sitzen neben Euch
Noch edle Männer unter meinen Richtern.   800
Doch sie sind Protestanten, Eiferer
Für Englands Wohl, und sprechen über mich,
Die Königin von Schottland, die Papistin!
Es kann der Britte gegen den Schotten nicht
Gerecht sein, ist ein uralt Wort — Drum ist   805
Herkömmlich seit der Väter grauer Zeit,
Daß vor Gericht kein Britte gegen den Schotten,
Kein Schotte gegen jenen zeugen darf.
Die Not gab dieses seltsame Gesetz;
Ein tiefer Sinn wohnt in den alten Bräuchen,   810
Man muß sie ehren, Mylord — die Natur
Warf diese beiden feur'gen Völkerschaften
Auf dieses Brett im Ozean; ungleich

Verteilte sie's und hieß sie darum kämpfen.
Der Tweede schmales Bette trennt allein	815
Die heft'gen Geister; oft vermischte sich
Das Blut der Kämpfenden in ihren Wellen.
Die Hand am Schwerte, schauen sie sich drohend
Von beiden Ufern an seit tausend Jahren.
Kein Feind bedränget Engelland, dem nicht	820
Der Schotte sich zum Helfer zugesellte;
Kein Bürgerkrieg entzündet Schottlands Städte,
Zu dem der Britte nicht den Zunder trug.
Und nicht erlöschen wird der Haß, bis endlich
Ein Parlament sie brüderlich vereint,	825
Ein Zepter waltet durch die ganze Insel.

Burleigh.

Und eine Stuart sollte dieses Glück
Dem Reich gewähren?

Maria.

Warum soll ich's leugnen?
Ja, ich gesteh's, daß ich die Hoffnung nährte,
Zwei edle Nationen unterm Schatten	830
Des Ölbaums frei und fröhlich zu vereinen.
Nicht ihres Völkerhasses Opfer glaubt' ich
Zu werden; ihre lange Eifersucht,
Der alten Zwietracht unglücksel'ge Glut
Hofft' ich auf ew'ge Tage zu ersticken,	835
Und, wie mein Ahnherr Richmond die zwei Rosen
Zusammenband nach blut'gem Streit, die Kronen
Schottland und England friedlich zu vermählen.

Burleigh.

Auf schlimmem Weg verfolgtet Ihr dies Ziel,
Da Ihr das Reich entzünden, durch die Flammen	840
Des Bürgerkriegs zum Throne steigen wolltet.

Maria.

Das wollt' ich nicht — beim großen Gott des Himmels!
Wann hätt' ich das gewollt? Wo sind die Proben?

Burleigh.

Nicht Streitens wegen kam ich her.   Die Sache
Ist keinem Wortgefecht mehr unterworfen.   845
Es ist erkannt durch vierzig Stimmen gegen zwei,
Daß Ihr die Akte vom vergangnen Jahr
Gebrochen, dem Gesetz verfallen seid.
Es ist verordnet im vergangnen Jahr:
„Wenn sich Tumult im Königreich erhübe   850
„Im Namen und zum Nutzen irgend einer
„Person, die Rechte vorgibt an die Krone,
„Daß man gerichtlich gegen sie verfahre,
„Bis in den Tod die Schuldige verfolge" —
Und da bewiesen ist —   855

Maria.

                    Mylord von Burleigh!
Ich zweifle nicht, daß ein Gesetz, ausdrücklich
Auf mich gemacht, verfaßt, mich zu verderben,
Sich gegen mich wird brauchen lassen — Wehe
Dem armen Opfer, wenn derselbe Mund,
Der das Gesetz gab, auch das Urteil spricht!   860
Könnt Ihr es leugnen, Lord, daß jene Akte
Zu meinem Untergang ersonnen ist?

Burleigh.

Zu Eurer Warnung sollte sie gereichen,
Zum Fallstrick habt Ihr selber sie gemacht.
Den Abgrund saht Ihr, der vor Euch sich aufthat,   865
Und, treu gewarnet, stürzet Ihr hinein.
Ihr wart mit Babington, dem Hochverräter,

Und seinen Mordgesellen einverstanden.
Ihr hattet Wissenschaft von allem, lenktet
Aus Eurem Kerker planvoll die Verschwörung.　　　　870

Maria.

Wann hätt' ich das gethan? Man zeige mir
Die Dokumente auf.

Burleigh.

　　　　　　Die hat man Euch
Schon neulich vor Gerichte vorgewiesen.

Maria.

Die Kopien, von fremder Hand geschrieben!
Man bringe die Beweise mir herbei,　　　　875
Daß ich sie selbst diktiert, daß ich sie so
Diktiert, gerade so, wie man gelesen.

Burleigh.

Daß es dieselben sind, die er empfangen,
Hat Babington vor seinem Tod bekannt.

Maria.

Und warum stellte man ihn mir nicht lebend　　　　880
Vor Augen? Warum eilte man so sehr,
Ihn aus der Welt zu fördern, eh' man ihn
Mir, Stirne gegen Stirne, vorgeführt?

Burleigh.

Auch Eure Schreiber, Kurl und Nau, erhärten
Mit einem Eid, daß es die Briefe seien,　　　　885
Die sie aus Eurem Munde niederschrieben.

Maria.

Und auf das Zeugnis meiner Hausbedienten
Verdammt man mich! Auf Treu und Glauben derer,
Die mich verraten, ihre Königin,

Die in demselben Augenblick die Treu   890
Mir brachen, da sie gegen mich gezeugt?

Burleigh.

Ihr selbst erklärtet sonst den Schotten Kurl
Für einen Mann von Tugend und Gewissen.

Maria.

So kannt' ich ihn — doch eines Mannes Tugend
Erprobt allein die Stunde der Gefahr.   895
Die Folter konnt' ihn ängstigen, daß er
Aussagte und gestand, was er nicht wußte!
Durch falsches Zeugnis glaubt' er sich zu retten
Und mir, der Königin, nicht viel zu schaden.

Burleigh.

Mit einem freien Eid hat er's beschworen.   900

Maria.

Vor meinem Angesichte nicht! — Wie, Sir?
Das sind zwei Zeugen, die noch beide leben!
Man stelle sie mir gegenüber, lasse sie
Ihr Zeugnis mir ins Antlitz wiederholen!
Warum mir eine Gunst, ein Recht verweigern,   905
Das man dem Mörder nicht versagt?   Ich weiß
Aus Talbots Munde, meines vor'gen Hüters,
Daß unter dieser nämlichen Regierung
Ein Reichsschluß durchgegangen, der befiehlt,
Den Kläger dem Beklagten vorzustellen.   910
Wie? Oder hab' ich falsch gehört? — Sir Paulet!
Ich hab' Euch stets als Biedermann erfunden,
Beweist es jetzo.   Sagt mir auf Gewissen,
Ist's nicht so?   Giebt's kein solch Gesetz in England?

Paulet.

So ist's, Mylady.   Das ist bei uns Rechtens.   915
Was wahr ist, muß ich sagen.

Maria.

Nun, Mylord!

Wenn man mich denn so streng nach englischem Recht
Behandelt, wo dies Recht mich unterdrückt,
Warum dasselbe Landesrecht umgehen,
Wenn es mir Wohlthat werden kann? — Antwortet! 920
Warum ward Babington mir nicht vor Augen
Gestellt, wie das Gesetz befiehlt? Warum
Nicht meine Schreiber, die noch beide leben?

Burleigh.

Ereifert Euch nicht, Lady. Euer Einverständnis
Mit Babington ist's nicht allein — 925

Maria.

Es ist's

Allein, was mich dem Schwerte des Gesetzes
Bloßstellt, wovon ich mich zu rein'gen habe.
Mylord! Bleibt bei der Sache. Beugt nicht aus.

Burleigh.

Es ist bewiesen, daß Ihr mit Mendoza,
Dem spanischen Botschafter, unterhandelt — 930

Maria (lebhaft).

Bleibt bei der Sache, Lord!

Burleigh.

Daß Ihr Anschläge

Geschmiedet, die Religion des Landes
Zu stü zen, alle Könige Europens
Zum Krieg mit England aufgeregt —

Maria.

Und wenn ich's

Gethan? Ich hab' es nicht gethan — Jedoch 935
Gesetzt, ich that's! Mylord, man hält mich hier

Gefangen wider alle Völkerrechte.
Nicht mit dem Schwerte kam ich in dies Land,
Ich kam herein, als eine Bittende,
Das heil'ge Gastrecht fordernd, in den Arm   940
Der blutsverwandten Königin mich werfend —
Und so ergriff mich die Gewalt, bereitete
Mir Ketten, wo ich Schutz gehofft — Sagt an!
Ist mein Gewissen gegen diesen Staat
Gebunden?   Hab' ich Pflichten gegen England?   945
Ein heilig Zwangsrecht üb' ich aus, da ich
Aus diesen Banden strebe, Macht mit Macht
Abwende, alle Staaten dieses Weltteils
Zu meinem Schutz aufrühre und bewege.
Was irgend nur in einem guten Krieg   950
Recht ist und ritterlich, das darf ich üben.
Den Mord allein, die heimlich blut'ge That,
Verbietet mir mein Stolz und mein Gewissen;
Mord würde mich beflecken und entehren.
Entehren, sag' ich — keineswegs mich   955
Verdammen, einem Rechtsspruch unterwerfen.
Denn nicht vom Rechte, von Gewalt allein
Ist zwischen mir und Engelland die Rede.

Burleigh (bedeutend).

Nicht auf der Stärke schrecklich Recht beruft Euch,
Mylady! Es ist der Gefangenen nicht günstig.   960

Maria.

Ich bin die Schwache, sie die Mächt'ge — Wohl!
Sie brauche die Gewalt, sie töte mich,
Sie bringe ihrer Sicherheit das Opfer.
Doch sie gestehe dann, daß sie die Macht
Allein, nicht die Gerechtigkeit geübt.   965
Nicht vom Gesetze borge sie das Schwert,

Sich der verhaßten Feindin zu entladen,
Und kleide nicht in heiliges Gewand
Der rohen Stärke blutiges Erkühnen.
Solch Gaukelspiel betrüge nicht die Welt!   970
Ermorden lassen kann sie mich, nicht richten!
Sie geb' es auf, mit des Verbrechens Früchten
Den heil'gen Schein der Tugend zu vereinen,
Und was sie ist, das wage sie zu scheinen! (Sie geht ab.)

Achter Auftritt.

Burleigh. Paulet.

Burleigh.

Sie trotzt uns — wird uns trotzen, Ritter Paulet,   975
Bis an die Stufen des Schafotts — Dies stolze Herz
Ist nicht zu brechen — Überraschte sie
Der Urtelspruch? Saht Ihr sie eine Thräne
Vergießen? Ihre Farbe nur verändern?
Nicht unser Mitleid ruft' sie an. Wohl kennt sie   980
Den Zweifelmut der Königin von England,
Und unsre Furcht ist's, was sie mutig macht.

Paulet.

Lord Großschatzmeister! Dieser eitle Trotz wird schnell
Verschwinden, wenn man ihm den Vorwand raubt.
Es sind Unziemlichkeiten vorgegangen   985
In diesem Rechtsstreit, wenn ich's sagen darf.
Man hätte diesen Babington und Tichburn
Ihr in Person vorführen, ihre Schreiber
Ihr gegenüber stellen sollen.

Burleigh (schnell).
Nein!
Nein, Ritter Paulet! Das war nicht zu wagen.   990

Zu groß ist ihre Macht auf die Gemüter
Und ihrer Thränen weibliche Gewalt.
Ihr Schreiber Kurl, ständ' er ihr gegenüber,
Käm' es dazu, das Wort nun auszusprechen,
An dem ihr Leben hängt — er würde zaghaft   995
Zurückziehn, sein Geständnis widerrufen —

Paulet.

So werden Englands Feinde alle Welt
Erfüllen mit gehässigen Gerüchten,
Und des Prozesses festliches Gepräng
Wird als ein kühner Frevel nur erscheinen.   1000

Burleigh.

Dies ist der Kummer unsrer Königin —
Daß diese Stifterin des Unheils doch
Gestorben wäre, ehe sie den Fuß
Auf Englands Boden setzte!

Paulet.

        Dazu sag' ich Amen.

Burleigh.

Daß Krankheit sie im Kerker aufgerieben!   1005

Paulet.

Viel Unglück hätt' es diesem Land erspart.

Burleigh.

Doch, hätt' auch gleich ein Zufall der Natur
Sie hingerafft — wir hießen doch die Mörder.

Paulet.

Wohl wahr. Man kann den Menschen nicht verwehren,
Zu denken, was sie wollen.   1010

Burleigh.

        Zu beweisen wär's
Doch nicht, und würde weniger Geräusch erregen —

Paulet.

Mag es Geräusch erregen! Nicht der laute,
Nur der gerechte Tadel kann verletzen.

Burleigh.

O! auch die heilige Gerechtigkeit
Entflieht dem Tadel nicht. Die Meinung hält es   1015
Mit dem Unglücklichen, es wird der Neid
Stets den obsiegend Glücklichen verfolgen.
Das Richterschwert, womit der Mann sich ziert,
Verhaßt ist's in der Frauen Hand.   Die Welt
Glaubt nicht an die Gerechtigkeit des Weibes,   1020
Sobald ein Weib das Opfer wird.   Umsonst,
Daß wir, die Richter, nach Gewissen sprachen!
Sie hat der Gnade königliches Recht,
Sie muß es brauchen! Unerträglich ist's,
Wenn sie den strengen Lauf läßt dem Gesetze!   1025

Paulet.

Und also —

Burleigh (rasch einfallend).

            Also soll sie leben? Nein!
Sie darf nicht leben! Nimmermehr! Dies, **eben**
Dies ist's, was unsre Königin beängstigt —
Warum der Schlaf ihr Lager flieht — Ich lese
In ihren Augen ihrer Seele Kampf,   1030
Ihr Mund wagt ihre Wünsche nicht zu sprechen;
Doch vielbedeutend fragt ihr stummer Blick:
Ist unter allen meinen Dienern keiner,
Der die verhaßte Wahl mir spart, in ew'ger Furcht
Auf meinem Thron zu zittern, oder grausam   1035
Die Königin, die eigne Blutsverwandte,
Dem Beil zu unterwerfen?

Paulet.

Das ist nun die Notwendigkeit, steht nicht zu ändern.

Burleigh.

Wohl stünd's zu ändern, meint die Königin,
Wenn sie nur aufmerksamre Diener hätte.   1040

Paulet.

Aufmerksamre?

Burleigh.

                    Die einen stummen Auftrag
Zu deuten wissen.

Paulet.

                    Einen stummen Auftrag!

Burleigh.

Die, wenn man ihnen eine gift'ge Schlange
Zu hüten gab, den anvertrauten Feind
Nicht wie ein heilig teures Kleinod hüten.   1045

Paulet (bedeutungsvoll).

Ein hohes Kleinod ist der gute Name,
Der unbescholtne Ruf der Königin,
Den kann man nicht zu wohl bewachen, Sir!

Burleigh.

Als man die Lady von dem Shrewsbury
Wegnahm und Ritter Paulets Hut vertraute,   1050
Da war die Meinung —

Paulet.

                    Ich will hoffen, Sir,
Die Meinung war, daß man den schwersten Auftrag
Den reinsten Händen übergeben wollte.
Bei Gott! Ich hätte dieses Schergenamt
Nicht übernommen, dächt' ich nicht, daß es   1055
Den besten Mann in England forderte.

Laßt mich nicht denken, daß ich's etwas anderm
Als meinem reinen Rufe schuldig bin.

Burleigh.

Man breitet aus, sie schwinde, läßt sie kränker
Und kränker werden, endlich still verscheiden;   1060
So stirbt sie in der Menschen Angedenken —
Und Euer Ruf bleibt rein.

Paulet.

       Nicht mein Gewissen.

Burleigh.

Wenn Ihr die eigne Hand nicht leihen wollt,
So werdet Ihr der fremden doch nicht wehren —

Paulet (unterbricht ihn).

Kein Mörder soll sich ihrer Schwelle nahn,   1065
Solang die Götter meines Dachs sie schützen.
Ihr Leben ist mir heilig, heil'ger nicht
Ist mir das Haupt der Königin von England.
Ihr seid die Richter! Richtet! Brecht den Stab!
Und wenn es Zeit ist, laßt den Zimmerer   1070
Mit Axt und Säge kommen, das Gerüst
Aufschlagen — für den Sheriff und den Henker
Soll meines Schlosses Pforte offen sein.
Jetzt ist sie zur Bewahrung mir vertraut,
Und seid gewiß, ich werde sie bewahren,   1075
Daß sie nichts Böses thun soll, noch erfahren! (Gehen ab).

Zweiter Aufzug.

Der Palast zu Westminster.

Erster Auftritt.

Der Graf von Kent und **Sir William Davison** begegnen einander.

Davison.

Seid Ihr's, Mylord von Kent? Schon vom Turnierplatz
Zurück, und ist die Festlichkeit zu Ende?

Kent.

Wie? Wohntet Ihr dem Ritterspiel nicht bei?

Davison.

Mich hielt mein Amt.   1080

Kent.

                  Ihr habt das schönste Schauspiel
Verloren, Sir, das der Geschmack ersonnen
Und edler Anstand ausgeführt — denn, wißt,
Es wurde vorgestellt die keusche Festung
Der Schönheit, wie sie vom Verlangen
Berennt wird — Der Lord Marschall, Oberrichter,   1085
Der Seneschall nebst zehen andern Rittern
Der Königin verteidigten die Festung,
Und Frankreichs Kavaliere griffen an.

Voraus erschien ein Herold, der das Schloß
Aufforderte in einem Madrigale, 1090
Und von dem Wall antwortete der Kanzler.
Drauf spielte das Geschütz, und Blumensträuße,
Wohlriechend köstliche Essenzen wurden
Aus niedlichen Feldstücken abgefeuert.
Umsonst! Die Stürme wurden abgeschlagen, 1095
Und das Verlangen mußte sich zurückziehn.

Davison.

Ein Zeichen böser Vorbedeutung, Graf,
Für die französische Brautwerbung.

Kent.

Nun, nun, das war ein Scherz — Im Ernste, denk' ich,
Wird sich die Festung endlich doch ergeben. 1100

Davison.

Glaubt Ihr? Ich glaub' es nimmermehr.

Kent.

Die schwierigsten Artikel sind bereits
Berichtigt und von Frankreich zugestanden.
Monsieur begnügt sich, in verschlossener
Kapelle seinen Gottesdienst zu halten, 1105
Und öffentlich die Reichsreligion
Zu ehren und zu schützen — Hättet Ihr den Jubel
Des Volks gesehn, als diese Zeitung sich verbreitet!
Denn dieses war des Landes ew'ge Furcht,
Sie möchte sterben ohne Leibeserben, 1110
Und England wieder Papstes Fesseln tragen,
Wenn ihr die Stuart auf dem Throne folgte.

Davison.

Der Furcht kann es entledigt sein — Sie geht
Ins Brautgemach, die Stuart geht zum Tode.

Kent.

Die Königin kommt! 1115

Zweiter Auftritt.

Die Vorigen. Elisabeth, von Leicester geführt. Graf Aubespine,
Bellievre, Graf Shrewsbury, Lord Burleigh mit noch
andern französischen und englischen Herren treten auf.

Elisabeth (zu Aubespine).

Graf! Ich beklage diese edeln Herrn,
Die ihr galanter Eifer über Meer
Hierher geführt, daß sie die Herrlichkeit
Des Hofs von St. Germain bei mir vermissen.
Ich kann so prächt'ge Götterfeste nicht   1120
Erfinden, als die königliche Mutter
Von Frankreich — Ein gesittet fröhlich Volk,
Das sich, so oft ich öffentlich mich zeige,
Mit Segnungen um meine Sänfte drängt,
Dies ist das Schauspiel, das ich fremden Augen   1125
Mit ein'gem Stolze zeigen kann.   Der Glanz
Der Edelfräulein, die im Schönheitsgarten
Der Katharina blühn, verbärge nur
Mich selber und mein schimmerlos Verdienst.

Aubespine.

Nur eine Dame zeigt Westminsterhof   1130
Dem überraschten Fremden — aber alles,
Was an dem reizenden Geschlecht entzückt,
Stellt sich versammelt dar in dieser einen.

Bellievre.

Erhabne Majestät von Engelland,
Vergönne, daß wir unsern Urlaub nehmen   1135
Und Monsieur, unsern königlichen Herrn,
Mit der ersehnten Freudenpost beglücken.
Ihn hat des Herzens heiße Ungeduld
Nicht in Paris gelassen, er erwartet

Zu Amiens die Boten seines Glücks,   1140
Und bis nach Calais reichen seine Posten,
Das Jawort, das dein königlicher Mund
Aussprechen wird, mit Flügelschnelligkeit
Zu seinem trunknen Ohre hinzutragen.

Elisabeth.

Graf Bellievre, dringt nicht weiter in mich.   1145
Nicht Zeit ist's jetzt, ich wiederhol' es Euch,
Die freud'ge Hochzeitsfackel anzuzünden.
Schwarz hängt der Himmel über diesem Land,
Und besser ziemte mir der Trauerflor,
Als das Gepränge bräutlicher Gewänder.   1150
Denn nahe droht ein jammervoller Schlag,
Mein Herz zu treffen und mein eignes Haus.

Bellievre.

Nur dein Versprechen gieb uns, Königin;
In frohern Tagen folge die Erfüllung.

Elisabeth.

Die Könige sind nur Sklaven ihres Standes,   1155
Dem eignen Herzen dürfen sie nicht folgen.
Mein Wunsch war's immer, unvermählt zu sterben,
Und meinen Ruhm hätt' ich darein gesetzt,
Daß man dereinst auf meinem Grabstein läse:
„Hier ruht die jungfräuliche Königin."   1160
Doch meine Unterthanen wollen's nicht,
Sie denken jetzt schon fleißig an die Zeit,
Wo ich dahin sein werde — Nicht genug,
Daß jetzt der Segen dieses Land beglückt,
Auch ihrem künft'gen Wohl soll ich mich opfern,   1165
Auch meine jungfräuliche Freiheit soll ich,
Mein höchstes Gut, hingeben für mein Volk,
Und der Gebieter wird mir aufgedrungen.

Es zeigt mir dadurch an, daß ich ihm nur
Ein Weib bin, und ich meinte doch, regiert   1170
Zu haben wie ein Mann und wie ein König.
Wohl weiß ich, daß man Gott nicht dient, wenn man
Die Ordnung der Natur verläßt, und Lob
Verdienen sie, die vor mir hier gewaltet,
Daß sie die Klöster aufgethan, und tausend   1175
Schlachtopfer einer falschverstandnen Andacht
Den Pflichten der Natur zurückgegeben.
Doch eine Königin, die ihre Tage
Nicht ungenützt in müßiger Beschauung
Verbringt, die unverdrossen, unermüdet   1180
Die schwerste aller Pflichten übt, d i e sollte
Von dem Naturzweck ausgenommen sein,
Der e i n e Hälfte des Geschlechts der Menschen
Der andern unterwürfig macht - -

Aubespine.

Jedwede Tugend, Königin, hast du   1185
Auf deinem Thron verherrlicht; nichts ist übrig,
Als dem Geschlechte, dessen Ruhm du bist,
Auch noch in seinen eigensten Verdiensten
Als Muster vorzuleuchten. Freilich lebt
Kein Mann auf Erden, der es würdig ist,   1190
Daß du die Freiheit ihm zum Opfer brächtest.
Doch wenn Geburt, wenn Hoheit, Heldentugend
Und Männerschönheit einen Sterblichen
D e r Ehre würdig machen, so —

Elisabeth.

                  Kein Zweifel,
Herr Abgesandter, daß ein Ehebündnis   1195
Mit einem königlichen Sohne Frankreichs
Mich ehrt. Ja, ich gesteh' es unverhohlen,

Wenn es sein muß — wenn ich's nicht ändern kann,
Dem Dringen meines Volkes nachzugeben —
Und es wird stärker sein, als ich, befürcht' ich —   1200
So kenn' ich in Europa keinen Fürsten,
Dem ich mein höchstes Kleinod, meine Freiheit,
Mit minderm Widerwillen opfern würde.
Laßt dies Geständnis Euch Genüge thun.

Bellievre.

Es ist die schönste Hoffnung; doch es ist   1205
Nur eine Hoffnung, und mein Herr wünscht mehr —

Elisabeth.

Was wünscht er?
(Sie zieht einen Ring vom Finger und betrachtet ihn nachdenkend.)
                    Hat die Königin doch nichts
Voraus vor dem gemeinen Bürgerweibe!
Das gleiche Zeichen weist auf gleiche Pflicht,
Auf gleiche Dienstbarkeit — der Ring macht Ehen,   1210
Und Ringe sind's, die eine Kette machen.
— Bringt Seiner Hoheit dies Geschenk.   Es ist
Noch keine Kette, bindet mich noch nicht;
Doch kann ein Reif draus werden, der mich bindet.

Bellievre (kniet nieder, den Ring empfangend).

In seinem Namen, große Königin,   1215
Empfang' ich knieend dies Geschenk und drücke
Den Kuß der Huldigung auf meiner Fürstin Hand.

Elisabeth.

(zum Grafen Leicester, den sie während der letzten Rede unverwandt
betrachtet hat.)
Erlaubt, Mylord!
(Sie nimmt ihm das blaue Band ab und hängt es dem Bellievre um.)
                    Bekleidet Seine Hoheit
Mit diesem Schmuck, wie ich Euch hier damit
Bekleide und in meines Ordens Pflichten nehme.   1220

Honi soit qui mal y pense! — Es schwinde
Der Argwohn zwischen beiden Nationen,
Und ein vertraulich Band umschlinge fortan
Die Kronen Frankreich und Britannien!

Aubespine.

Erhabne Königin, dies ist ein Tag   1225
Der Freude!   Möcht' er's allen sein, und möchte
Kein Leidender auf dieser Insel trauern!
Die Gnade glänzt auf deinem Angesicht,
O! daß ein Schimmer ihres heitern Lichts
Auf eine unglücksvolle Fürstin fiele,   1230
Die Frankreich und Britannien gleich nahe
Angeht —

Elisabeth.

                Nicht weiter, Graf!   Vermengen wir
Nicht zwei ganz unvereinbare Geschäfte.
Wenn Frankreich ernstlich meinen Bund verlangt,
Muß es auch meine Sorgen mit mir teilen,   1235
Und meiner Feinde Freund nicht sein —

Aubespine.

                                    Unwürdig
In deinen eignen Augen würd' es handeln,
Wenn es die Unglückselige, die Glaubens-
Verwandte und die Witwe seines Königs
In diesem Bund vergäße — Schon die Ehre,   1240
Die Menschlichkeit verlangt —

Elisabeth.

                        In diesem Sinn
Weiß ich sein Fürwort nach Gebühr zu schätzen.
Frankreich erfüllt die Freundespflicht; mir wird
Verstattet sein, als Königin zu handeln.

(Sie neigt sich gegen die französischen Herren, welche sich mit den übrigen
Lords ehrfurchtsvoll entfernen.)

Dritter Auftritt.

Elisabeth. Leicester. Burleigh. Talbot.

(Die Königin setzt sich.)

Burleigh.

Ruhmvolle Königin! Du krönest heut 1245
Die heißen Wünsche deines Volks. Nun erst
Erfreun wir uns der segenvollen Tage,
Die du uns schenkst, da wir nicht zitternd mehr
In eine stürmevolle Zukunft schauen.
Nur eine Sorge kümmert noch dies Land, 1250
Ein Opfer ist's, das alle Stimmen fordern.
Gewähr' auch dieses, und der heut'ge Tag
Hat Englands Wohl auf immerdar gegründet.

Elisabeth.

Was wünscht mein Volk noch? Sprecht, Mylord.

Burleigh.

Es fordert
Das Haupt der Stuart — Wenn du deinem Volk 1255
Der Freiheit köstliches Geschenk, das teuer
Erworbne Licht der Wahrheit willst versichern,
So muß sie nicht mehr sein — Wenn wir nicht ewig
Für dein kostbares Leben zittern sollen,
So muß die Feindin untergehn! — Du weißt es, 1260
Nicht alle deine Britten denken gleich;
Noch viele heimliche Verehrer zählt
Der röm'sche Götzendienst auf dieser Insel.
Die alle nähren feindliche Gedanken;
Nach dieser Stuart steht ihr Herz, sie sind 1265
Im Bund mit den lothringischen Brüdern,
Den unversöhnten Feinden deines Namens.
Dir ist von dieser wütenden Partei

Der grimmige Vertilgungskrieg geschworen,
Den man mit falschen Höllenwaffen führt.   1270
Zu Reims, dem Bischofssitz des Kardinals,
Dort ist das Rüsthaus, wo sie Blitze schmieden;
Dort wird der Königsmord gelehrt — von dort
Geschäftig senden sie nach deiner Insel
Die Missionen aus, entschloßne Schwärmer,   1275
In allerlei Gewand vermummt — von dort
Ist schon der dritte Mörder ausgegangen,
Und unerschöpflich, ewig neu erzeugen
Verborgne Feinde sich aus diesem Schlunde.
— Und in dem Schloß zu Fotheringhay sitzt   1280
Die Ate dieses ew'gen Kriegs, die mit
Der Liebesfackel dieses Reich entzündet.
Für sie, die schmeichelnd jedem Hoffnung giebt,
Weiht sich die Jugend dem gewissen Tod —
Sie zu befreien, ist die Losung; sie   1285
Auf deinen Thron zu setzen, ist der Zweck.
Denn dies Geschlecht der Lothringer erkennt
Dein heilig Recht nicht an, du heißest ihnen
Nur eine Räuberin des Throns, gekrönt
Vom Glück! Sie waren's, die die Thörichte   1290
Verführt, sich Englands Königin zu schreiben.
Kein Friede ist mit ihr und ihrem Stamm!
Du mußt den Streich erleiden oder führen.
Ihr Leben ist dein Tod! Ihr Tod dein Leben!

Elisabeth.

Mylord! Ein traurig Amt verwaltet Ihr.   1295
Ich kenne Eures Eifers reinen Trieb,
Weiß, daß gediegne Weisheit aus Euch redet;
Doch diese Weisheit, welche Blut befiehlt,
Ich hasse sie in meiner tiefsten Seele.

Sinnt einen mildern Rat aus — Edler Lord 1300
Von Shrewsbury! Sagt Ihr uns Eure Meinung.

Talbot.

Du gabst dem Eifer ein gebührend Lob,
Der Burleighs treue Brust beseelt — Auch mir,
Strömt es mir gleich nicht so beredt vom Munde,
Schlägt in der Brust kein minder treues Herz. 1305
Mögst du noch lange leben, Königin,
Die Freude deines Volks zu sein, das Glück
Des Friedens diesem Reiche zu verlängern.
So schöne Tage hat dies Eiland nie
Gesehn, seit eigne Fürsten es regieren. 1310
Mög' es sein Glück mit seinem Ruhme nicht
Erkaufen! Möge Talbots Auge wenigstens
Geschlossen sein, wenn dies geschieht!

Elisabeth.

Verhüte Gott, daß wir den Ruhm befleckten!

Talbot.

Nun dann, so wirst du auf ein ander Mittel sinnen, 1315
Dies Reich zu retten — denn die Hinrichtung
Der Stuart ist ein ungerechtes Mittel.
Du kannst das Urteil über die nicht sprechen,
Die dir nicht unterthänig ist.

Elisabeth.

          So irrt
Mein Staatsrat und mein Parlament, im Irrtum 1320
Sind alle Richterhöfe dieses Landes,
Die mir dies Recht einstimmig zuerkannt —

Talbot.

Nicht Stimmenmehrheit ist des Rechtes Probe,
England ist nicht die Welt, dein Parlament
Nicht der Verein der menschlichen Geschlechter. 1325

Dies heut'ge England ist das künft'ge nicht,
Wie's das vergangne nicht mehr ist — Wie sich
Die Neigung anders wendet, also steigt
Und fällt des Urteils wandelbare Woge.
Sag' nicht, du müssest der Notwendigkeit   1330
Gehorchen und dem Dringen deines Volks.
Sobald du willst, in jedem Augenblick
Kannst du erproben, daß dein Wille frei ist.
Versuch's! Erkläre, daß du Blut verabscheust,
Der Schwester Leben willst gerettet sehn;   1335
Zeig' denen, die dir anders raten wollen,
Die Wahrheit deines königlichen Zorns,
Schnell wirst du die Notwendigkeit verschwinden
Und Recht in Unrecht sich verwandeln sehn.
Du selbst mußt richten, du allein.　Du kannst dich   1340
Auf dieses unstät schwanke Rohr nicht lehnen.
Der eignen Milde folge du getrost.
Nicht Strenge legte Gott ins weiche Herz
Des Weibes — und die Stifter dieses Reichs,
Die auch dem Weib die Herrscherzügel gaben,   1345
Sie zeigten an, daß Strenge nicht die Tugend
Der Könige soll sein in diesem Lande.

Elisabeth.

Ein warmer Anwalt ist Graf Shrewsbury
Für meine Feindin und des Reichs. Ich ziehe
Die Räte vor, die meine Wohlfahrt lieben.   1350

Talbot.

Man gönnt ihr keinen Anwalt, niemand wagt's,
Zu ihrem Vorteil sprechend, deinem Zorn
Sich bloßzustellen — so vergönne mir,
Dem alten Manne, den am Grabesrand
Kein irdisch Hoffen mehr verführen kann,   1355

Daß ich die Aufgegebene beschütze.
Man soll nicht sagen, daß in deinem Staatsrat
Die Leidenschaft, die Selbstsucht eine Stimme
Gehabt, nur die Barmherzigkeit geschwiegen.
Verbündet hat sich alles wider sie,   1360
Du selber hast ihr Antlitz nie gesehn,
Nichts spricht in deinem Herzen für die Fremde.
— Nicht ihrer Schuld red' ich das Wort.   Man sagt,
Sie habe den Gemahl ermorden lassen;
Wahr ist's, daß sie den Mörder ehlichte.   1365
Ein schwer Verbrechen!   Aber es geschah
In einer finster unglückvollen Zeit,
Im Angstgedränge bürgerlichen Kriegs,
Wo sie, die Schwache, sich umrungen sah
Von heftigdringenden Vasallen, sich   1370
Dem Mutvollstärksten in die Arme warf —
Wer weiß, durch welcher Künste Macht besiegt?
Denn ein gebrechlich Wesen ist das Weib.

Elisabeth.

Das Weib ist nicht schwach. Es giebt starke Seelen
In dem Geschlecht — Ich will in meinem Beisein   1375
Nichts von der Schwäche des Geschlechtes hören.

Talbot.

Dir war das Unglück eine strenge Schule.
Nicht seine Freudenseite kehrte d i r
Das Leben zu.   Du sahest keinen Thron
Von ferne, nur das Grab zu deinen Füßen.   1380
Zu Woodstock war's und in des Towers Nacht,
Wo dich der gnäd'ge Vater dieses Landes
Zur ernsten Pflicht durch Trübsal auferzog.
Dort suchte dich der Schmeichler nicht.   Früh lernte,
Vom eitlen Weltgeräusche nicht zerstreut,   1385

Dein Geist sich sammeln, denkend in sich gehn
Und dieses Lebens wahre Güter schätzen.
— Die Arme rettete kein Gott. Ein zartes Kind
Ward sie verpflanzt nach Frankreich, an den Hof
Des Leichtsinns, der gedankenlosen Freude.   1390
Dort in der Feste ew'ger Trunkenheit
Vernahm sie nie der Wahrheit ernste Stimme.
Geblendet ward sie von der Laster Glanz
Und fortgeführt vom Strome des Verderbens.
Ihr ward der Schönheit eitles Gut zu teil,   1395
Sie überstrahlte blühend alle Weiber,
Und durch Gestalt nicht minder als Geburt — —

Elisabeth.

Kommt zu Euch selbst, Mylord von Shrewsbury!
Denkt, daß wir hier im ernsten Rate sitzen.
Das müssen Reize sondergleichen sein,   1400
Die einen Greis in solches Feuer setzen.
— Mylord von Lester! Ihr allein schweigt still?
Was ihn beredt macht, bindet's Euch die Zunge?

Leicester.

Ich schweige vor Erstaunen, Königin,
Daß man dein Ohr mit Schrecknissen erfüllt,   1405
Daß diese Märchen, die in Londons Gassen
Den gläub'gen Pöbel ängsten, bis herauf
In deines Staatsrats heitre Mitte steigen
Und weise Männer ernst beschäftigen.
Verwunderung ergreift mich, ich gesteh's,   1410
Daß diese länderlose Königin
Von Schottland, die den eignen kleinen Thron
Nicht zu behaupten wußte, ihrer eignen
Vasallen Spott, der Auswurf ihres Landes,
Dein Schrecken wird auf einmal im Gefängnis!   1415

— Was, beim Allmächt'gen! machte sie dir furchtbar?
Daß sie dies Reich in Anspruch nimmt? daß dich
Die Guisen nicht als Königin erkennen?
Kann dieser Guisen Widerspruch das Recht
Entkräften, das Geburt dir gab, der Schluß   1420
Der Parlamente dir bestätigte?
Ist sie durch Heinrichs letzten Willen nicht
Stillschweigend abgewiesen? und wird England,
So glücklich im Genuß des neuen Lichts,
Sich der Papistin in die Arme werfen?   1425
Von dir, der angebeteten Monarchin,
Zu Darnleys Mörderin hinüberlaufen?
Was wollen diese ungestümen Menschen,
Die dich noch lebend mit der Erbin quälen,
Dich nicht geschwind genug vermählen können,   1430
Um Staat und Kirche von Gefahr zu retten?
Stehst du nicht blühend da in Jugendkraft,
Welkt jene nicht mit jedem Tag zum Grabe?
Bei Gott! Du wirst, ich hoff's, noch viele Jahre
Auf ihrem Grabe wandeln, ohne daß   1435
Du selber sie hinabzustürzen brauchtest. —

Burleigh.

Lord Lester hat nicht immer so geurteilt.

Leicester.

Wahr ist's, ich habe selber meine Stimme
Zu ihrem Tod gegeben im G e r i c h t.
— Im S t a a t s r a t sprech' ich anders. Hier ist nicht   1440
Die Rede von dem Recht, nur von dem Vorteil.
Ist's jetzt die Zeit, von ihr Gefahr zu fürchten,
Da Frankreich sie verläßt, ihr einz'ger Schutz,
Da du den Königssohn mit deiner Hand
Beglücken willst, die Hoffnung eines neuen   1445

Regentenstammes diesem Lande blüht?
Wozu sie also töten? Sie ist tot!
Verachtung ist der wahre Tod. Verhüte,
Daß nicht das Mitleid sie ins Leben rufe!
Drum ist mein Rat: Man lasse die Sentenz,   1450
Die ihr das Haupt abspricht, in voller Kraft
Bestehn! Sie lebe — aber unterm Beile
Des Henkers lebe sie, und schnell, wie sich
Ein Arm für sie bewaffnet, fall' es nieder.

Elisabeth (steht auf).

Mylords, ich hab' nun eure Meinungen   1455
Gehört und sag' euch Dank für euren Eifer.
Mit Gottes Beistand, der die Könige
Erleuchtet, will ich eure Gründe prüfen
Und wählen, was das Bessere mir dünkt.

Vierter Auftritt.

Die Vorigen. Ritter Paulet mit Mortimer.

Elisabeth.

Da kommt Amias Paulet. Edler Sir,   1460
Was bringt Ihr uns?

Paulet.

          Glorwürd'ge Majestät!
Mein Neffe, der ohnlängst von weiten Reisen
Zurückgekehrt, wirft sich zu deinen Füßen
Und leistet dir sein jugendlich Gelübde.
Empfange du es gnadenvoll und laß   1465
Ihn wachsen in der Sonne deiner Gunst.

Mortimer (läßt sich auf ein Knie nieder).

Lang lebe meine köntgliche Frau,
Und Glück und Ruhm bekröne ihre Stirne!

Elisabeth.

Steht auf. Seid mir willkommen, Sir, in England.
Ihr habt den großen Weg gemacht, habt Frankreich   1470
Bereist und Rom und Euch zu Reims verweilt.
Sagt mir denn an, was spinnen unsre Feinde?

Mortimer.

Ein Gott verwirre sie und wende rückwärts
Auf ihrer eignen Schützen Brust die Pfeile,
Die gegen meine Königin gesandt sind!   1475

Elisabeth.

Saht Ihr den Morgan und den ränkespinnenden
Bischof von Roße?

Mortimer.

                    Alle schottische
Verbannte lernt' ich kennen, die zu Reims
Anschläge schmieden gegen diese Insel.
In ihr Vertrauen stahl ich mich, ob ich   1480
Etwa von ihren Ränken was entdeckte.

Paulet.

Geheime Briefe hat man ihm vertraut,
In Ziffern, für die Königin von Schottland,
Die er mit treuer Hand u n s überliefert.

Elisabeth.

Sagt, was sind ihre neuesten Entwürfe?   1485

Mortimer.

Es traf sie alle wie ein Donnerstreich,
  5

Daß Frankreich sie verläßt, den festen Bund
Mit England schließt; jetzt richten sie die Hoffnung
Auf Spanien.

Elisabeth.

So schreibt mir Walsingham.

Mortimer.

Auch eine Bulle, die Papst Sixtus jüngst   1490
Vom Vatikane gegen dich geschleudert,
Kam eben an zu Reims, als ich's verließ;
Das nächste Schiff bringt sie nach dieser Insel.

Leicester.

Vor solchen Waffen zittert England nicht mehr.

Burleigh.

Sie werden furchtbar in des Schwärmers Hand.   1495

Elisabeth (Mortimern forschend ansehend).

Man gab Euch schuld, daß Ihr zu Reims die Schulen
Besucht und Euren Glauben abgeschworen?

Mortimer.

Die Miene gab ich mir, ich leugn' es nicht,
So weit ging die Begierde, dir zu dienen!

Elisabeth (zu Paulet, der ihr Papiere überreicht).

Was zieht Ihr da hervor?   1500

Paulet.

Es ist ein Schreiben,
Das dir die Königin von Schottland sendet.

Burleigh (hastig darnach greifend).

Gebt mir den Brief.

Paulet (giebt das Papier der Königin).

Verzeiht, Lord Großschatzmeister!
In meiner Königin selbsteigne Hand

Befahl sie mir den Brief zu übergeben.
Sie sagt mir stets, ich sei ihr Feind.   Ich bin   1505
Nur ihrer Laster Feind; was sich verträgt
Mit meiner Pflicht, mag ich ihr gern erweisen.

(Die Königin hat den Brief genommen.   Während sie ihn liest, sprechen
Mortimer und Leicester einige Worte heimlich miteinander.)

Burleigh (zu Paulet).

Was kann der Brief enthalten? Eitle Klagen,
Mit denen man das mitleidsvolle Herz
Der Königin verschonen soll.   1510

Paulet.
                          Was er
Enthält, hat sie mir nicht verhehlt.   Sie bittet
Um die Vergünstigung, das Angesicht
Der Königin zu sehen.

Burleigh (schnell).
              Nimmermehr!

Talbot.
Warum nicht?   Sie erfleht nichts Ungerechtes.

Burleigh.
Die Gunst des königlichen Angesichts   1515
Hat sie verwirkt, die Mordanstifterin,
Die nach dem Blut der Königin gedürstet.
Wer's treu mit seiner Fürstin meint, der kann
Den falsch verräterischen Rat nicht geben.

Talbot.
Wenn die Monarchin sie beglücken will,   1520
Wollt Ihr der Gnade sanfte Regung hindern?

Burleigh.
Sie ist verurteilt!   Unterm Beile liegt
Ihr Haupt.   Unwürdig ist's der Majestät,

Das Haupt zu sehen, das dem Tod geweiht ist.
Das Urteil kann nicht mehr vollzogen werden,   1525
Wenn sich die Königin ihr genahet hat,
Denn Gnade bringt die königliche Nähe —

Elisabeth

(nachdem sie den Brief gelesen, ihre Thränen trocknend).

Was ist der Mensch! Was ist das Glück der Erde!
Wie weit ist diese Königin gebracht,
Die mit so stolzen Hoffnungen begann,   1530
Die auf den ältsten Thron der Christenheit
Berufen worden, die in ihrem Sinn
Drei Kronen schon aufs Haupt zu setzen meinte!
Welch andre Sprache führt sie jetzt, als damals,
Da sie das Wappen Englands angenommen,   1535
Und von den Schmeichlern ihres Hofs sich Königin
Der zwei britann'schen Inseln nennen ließ!
— Verzeiht, Mylords, es schneidet mir ins Herz,
Wehmut ergreift mich, und die Seele blutet,
Daß Irdisches nicht fester steht, das Schicksal   1540
Der Menschheit, das entsetzliche, so nahe
An meinem eignen Haupt vorüberzieht.

Talbot.

O Königin! Dein Herz hat Gott gerührt,
Gehorche dieser himmlischen Bewegung!
Schwer büßte sie fürwahr die schwere Schuld,   1545
Und Zeit ist's, daß die harte Prüfung ende!
Reich' ihr die Hand, der Tiefgefallenen!
Wie eines Engels Lichterscheinung steige
In ihres Kerkers Gräbernacht hinab —

Burleigh.

Sei standhaft, große Königin. Laß nicht   1550
Ein lobenswürdig menschliches Gefühl

Dich irre führen.   Raube dir nicht selbst
Die Freiheit, das Notwendige zu thun.
Du kannst sie nicht begnadigen, nicht retten,
So lade nicht auf dich verhaßten Tadel,   1555
Daß du mit grausam höhnendem Triumph
Am Anblick deines Opfers dich geweidet.

Leicester.

Laßt uns in unsern Schranken bleiben, Lords.
Die Königin ist weise, sie bedarf
Nicht unsers Rats, das Würdigste zu wählen.   1560
Die Unterredung beider Königinnen
Hat nichts gemein mit des Gerichtes Gang.
Englands Gesetz, nicht der Monarchin Wille,
Verurteilt die Maria.   Würdig ist's
Der großen Seele der Elisabeth,   1565
Daß sie des Herzens schönem Triebe folge,
Wenn das Gesetz den strengen Lauf behält.

Elisabeth.

Geht, meine Lords.   Wir werden Mittel finden,
Was Gnade fordert, was Notwendigkeit
Uns auferlegt, geziemend zu vereinen.   1570
Jetzt — tretet ab!
        (Die Lords gehen. An der Thüre ruft sie den Mortimer zurück.)
            Sir Mortimer!   Ein Wort!

Fünfter Auftritt.

Elisabeth. Mortimer.

Elisabeth
(nachdem sie ihn einige Augenblicke forschend mit den Augen gemessen.)
Ihr zeigtet einen kecken Mut und seltne
Beherrschung Eurer selbst für Eure Jahre.

Wer schon so früh der Täuschung schwere Kunst
Ausübte, der ist mündig vor der Zeit,   1575
Und er verkürzt sich seine Prüfungsjahre.
— Auf eine große Bahn ruft Euch das Schicksal,
Ich prophezei' es Euch, und mein Orakel
Kann ich, zu Eurem Glücke, selbst vollziehn.

Mortimer.

Erhabene Gebieterin, was ich   1580
Vermag und bin, ist deinem Dienst gewidmet.

Elisabeth.

Ihr habt die Feinde Englands kennen lernen.
Ihr Haß ist unversöhnlich gegen mich,
Und unerschöpflich ihre Blutentwürfe.
Bis diesen Tag zwar schützte mich die Allmacht;   1585
Doch ewig wankt die Kron' auf meinem Haupt,
Solang sie lebt, die ihrem Schwärmereifer
Den Vorwand leiht und ihre Hoffnung nährt.

Mortimer.

Sie lebt nicht mehr, sobald du es gebietest.

Elisabeth.

Ach, Sir! Ich glaubte mich am Ziele schon   1590
Zu sehn, und bin nicht weiter als am Anfang.
Ich wollte die Gesetze handeln lassen,
Die eigne Hand vom Blute rein behalten.
Das Urteil ist gesprochen. Was gewinn' ich?
Es muß vollzogen werden, Mortimer!   1595
Und ich muß die Vollziehung anbefehlen.
Mich immer trifft der Haß der That. Ich muß
Sie eingestehn und kann den Schein nicht retten.
Das ist das Schlimmste!

Mortimer.

Was bekümmert dich
Der böse Schein bei der gerechten Sache?　　　　1600

Elisabeth.

Ihr kennt die Welt nicht, Ritter. Was man scheint,
Hat jedermann zum Richter, was man ist, hat keinen.
Von meinem Rechte überzeug' ich niemand,
So muß ich Sorge tragen, daß mein Anteil
An ihrem Tod in ew'gem Zweifel bleibe.　　　　1605
Bei solchen Thaten doppelter Gestalt
Giebt's keinen Schutz, als in der Dunkelheit.
Der schlimmste Schritt ist, den man eingesteht,
Was man nicht aufgiebt, hat man nie verloren.

Mortimer (ausforschend).

Dann wäre wohl das Beste —　　　　1610

Elisabeth (schnell).

Freilich wär's
Das Beste — O, mein guter Engel spricht
Aus Euch. Fahrt fort, vollendet, werter Sir!
Euch ist es ernst, Ihr dringet auf den Grund,
Seid ein ganz andrer Mann, als Euer Oheim —

Mortimer (betroffen.)

Entdecktest du dem Ritter deinen Wunsch?　　　　1615

Elisabeth.

Mich reuet, daß ich's that.

Mortimer.

Entschuldige
Den alten Mann. Die Jahre machen ihn
Bedenklich. Solche Wagestücke fordern
Den kecken Mut der Jugend —

Elisabeth (schnell).

Darf ich Euch —

Mortimer.

Die Hand will ich dir leihen, rette du   1620
Den Namen, wie du kannst —

Elisabeth.

Ja, Sir! wenn Ihr
Mich eines Morgens mit der Botschaft wecktet:
Maria Stuart, deine blut'ge Feindin,
Ist heute nacht verschieden!

Mortimer.

Zähl' auf mich.

Elisabeth.

Wann wird mein Haupt sich ruhig schlafen legen?   1625

Mortimer.

Der nächste Neumond ende deine Furcht.

Elisabeth.

Gehabt Euch wohl, Sir! Laßt es Euch nicht leid thun,
Daß meine Dankbarkeit den Flor der Nacht
Entlehnen muß — Das Schweigen ist der Gott
Der Glücklichen — Die engsten Bande sind's,   1630
Die zärtesten, die das Geheimnis stiftet! (Sie geht ab.)

Sechster Auftritt.

Mortimer (allein).

Geh, falsche, gleisnerische Königin!
Wie du die Welt, so täusch' ich dich. Recht ist's,
Dich zu verraten, eine gute That!

Seh' ich aus, wie ein Mörder? Lasest du   1635
Ruchlose Fertigkeit auf meiner Stirn?
Trau' nur auf meinen Arm und halte deinen
Zurück.   Gieb dir den frommen Heuchelschein
Der Gnade vor der Welt, indessen du
Geheim auf meine Mörderhilfe hoffst,   1640
So werden wir zur Rettung Frist gewinnen!
    Erhöhen willst du mich — zeigst mir von ferne
Bedeutend einen kostbaren Preis — Und wärst
Du selbst der Preis und deine Frauengunst!
Wer bist du, Armste, und was kannst du geben?   1645
Mich locket nicht des eiteln Ruhmes Geiz!
Bei ihr nur ist des Lebens Reiz —
Um sie, in ew'gem Freudenchore, schweben
Der Anmut Götter und der Jugendlust,
Das Glück der Himmel ist an ihrer Brust,   1650
Du hast nur tote Güter zu vergeben!
Das eine Höchste, was das Leben schmückt,
Wenn sich ein Herz, entzückend und entzückt,
Dem Herzen schenkt in süßem Selbstvergessen,
Die Frauenkrone hast du nie besessen,   1655
Nie hast du liebend einen Mann beglückt!
— Ich muß den Lord erwarten, ihren Brief
Ihm übergeben.   Ein verhaßter Auftrag!
Ich habe zu dem Höflinge kein Herz,
Ich selber kann sie retten, ich allein,   1660
Gefahr und Ruhm und auch der Preis sei mein!
                    (Indem er gehen will, begegnet ihm Paulet.)

Siebenter Auftritt.

Mortimer. Paulet.

Paulet.

Was sagte dir die Königin?

Mortimer.

Nichts, Sir.
Nichts — von Bedeutung.

Paulet (fixiert ihn mit ernstem Blick).

Höre, Mortimer!
Es ist ein schlüpfrig glatter Grund, auf den
Du dich begeben.   Lockend ist die Gunst   1665
Der Könige, nach Ehre geizt die Jugend.
— Laß dich den Ehrgeiz nicht verführen!

Mortimer.

Wart Ihr's nicht selbst, der an den Hof mich brachte?

Paulet.

Ich wünschte, daß ich's nicht gethan.   Am Hofe
Ward unsers Hauses Ehre nicht gesammelt.   1670
Steh fest, mein Neffe.   Kaufe nicht zu teuer!
Verletze dein Gewissen nicht!

Mortimer.

Was fällt Euch ein?   Was für Besorgnisse!

Paulet.

Wie groß dich auch die Königin zu machen
Verspricht — trau' ihrer Schmeichelrede nicht.   1675
Verleugnen wird sie dich, wenn du gehorcht,
Und, ihren eigenen Namen rein zu waschen,
Die Blutthat rächen, die sie selbst befahl.

Mortimer.

Die Blutthat, sagt Ihr? —

Paulet.

Weg mit der Verstellung!
Ich weiß, was dir die Königin angesonnen.   1680
Sie hofft, daß deine ruhmbegier'ge Jugend
Willfähr'ger sein wird, als mein starres Alter.
Hast du ihr zugesagt? Hast du?

Mortimer.

Mein Oheim!

Paulet.

Wenn du's gethan hast, so verfluch' ich dich,
Und dich verwerfe —   1685

Leicester (kommt).

Werter Sir, erlaubt
Ein Wort mit Eurem Neffen. Die Monarchin
Ist gnadenvoll gesinnt für ihn, sie will,
Daß man ihm die Person der Lady Stuart
Uneingeschränkt vertraue — Sie verläßt sich
Auf seine Redlichkeit —   1690

Paulet.

Verläßt sich — Gut!

Leicester.

Was sagt Ihr, Sir?

Paulet.

Die Königin verläßt sich
Auf ihn, und ich, Mylord, verlasse mich
Auf mich und meine beiden offnen Augen.   (Er geht ab.)

Achter Auftritt.

Leicester. Mortimer.

Leicester (verwundert).

Was wandelte den Ritter an?

Mortimer.

Ich weiß es nicht — Das unerwartete 1695
Vertrauen, das die Königin mir schenkt —

Leicester (ihn forschend ansehend).

Verdient Ihr, Ritter, daß man Euch vertraut?

Mortimer (ebenso).

Die Frage thu' ich Euch, Mylord von Lester.

Leicester.

Ihr hattet mir was in geheim zu sagen.

Mortimer.

Versichert mir erst, daß ich's wagen darf. 1700

Leicester.

Wer giebt mir die Versicherung für Euch?
— Laßt Euch mein Mißtraun nicht beleidigen!
Ich seh' Euch zweierlei Gesichter zeigen
An diesem Hofe — Eins darunter ist
Notwendig falsch; doch welches ist das wahre? 1705

Mortimer.

Es geht mir eben so mit Euch, Graf Lester.

Leicester.

Wer soll nun des Vertrauens Anfang machen?

Mortimer.

Wer das Geringere zu wagen hat.

Leicester.

Nun! Der seid Ihr!

Mortimer.

Ihr seid es! Euer Zeugnis,
Des vielbedeutenden, gewalt'gen Lords,   1710
Kann mich zu Boden schlagen, meins vermag
Nichts gegen Euren Rang und Eure Gunst.

Leicester.

Ihr irrt Euch, Sir. In allem andern bin ich
Hier mächtig, nur in diesem zarten Punkt,
Den ich jetzt Eurer Treu preisgeben soll,   1715
Bin ich der schwächste Mann an diesem Hof,
Und ein verächtlich Zeugnis kann mich stürzen.

Mortimer.

Wenn sich der allvermögende Lord Lester
So tief zu mir herunterläßt, ein solch
Bekenntnis mir zu thun, so darf ich wohl   1720
Ein wenig höher denken von mir selbst,
Und ihm in Großmut ein Exempel geben.

Leicester.

Geht mir voran im Zutraun, ich will folgen.

Mortimer (den Brief schnell hervorziehend).

Dies sendet Euch die Königin von Schottland.

Leicester (schrickt zusammen und greift hastig darnach).

Sprecht leise, Sir — Was seh' ich! Ach! Es ist   1725
Ihr Bild! (Küßt es und betrachtet es mit stummem Entzücken.)

Mortimer (der ihn während des Lesens scharf beobachtet).

Mylord, nun glaub' ich Euch.

Leicester (nachdem er den Brief schnell durchlaufen).

Sir Mortimer! Ihr wißt des Briefes Inhalt?

Mortimer.

Nichts weiß ich.

Leicester.

Nun! Sie hat Euch ohne Zweifel

Vertraut —

Mortimer.

Sie hat mir nichts vertraut. Ihr würdet
Dies Rätsel mir erklären, sagte sie.   1730
Ein Rätsel ist es mir, daß Graf von Lester,
Der Günstling der Elisabeth, Mariens
Erklärter Feind und ihrer Richter einer,
Der Mann sein soll, von dem die Königin
In ihrem Unglück Rettung hofft — Und dennoch   1735
Muß dem so sein, denn Eure Augen sprechen
Zu deutlich aus, was Ihr für sie empfindet.

Leicester.

Entdeckt mir selbst erst, wie es kommt, daß Ihr
Den feur'gen Anteil nehmt an ihrem Schicksal,
Und was Euch ihr Vertraun erwarb.   1740

Mortimer.

Mylord,
Das kann ich Euch mit wenigem erklären.
Ich habe meinen Glauben abgeschworen
Zu Rom und steh' im Bündnis mit den Guisen.
Ein Brief des Erzbischofs zu Reims hat mich
Beglaubigt bei der Königin von Schottland.   1745

Leicester.

Ich weiß von Eurer Glaubensänderung;
Sie ist's, die mein Vertrauen zu Euch weckte.
Gebt mir die Hand. Verzeiht mir meinen Zweifel.
Ich kann der Vorsicht nicht zu viel gebrauchen,
Denn Walsingham und Burleigh hassen mich; 1750
Ich weiß, daß sie mir lauernd Netze stellen.
Ihr konntet ihr Geschöpf und Werkzeug sein,
Mich in das Garn zu ziehn —

Mortimer.

          Wie kleine Schritte
Geht ein so großer Lord an diesem Hof!
Graf, ich beklag' Euch. 1755

Leicester.

          Freudig werf' ich mich
An die vertraute Freundesbrust, wo ich
Des langen Zwangs mich endlich kann entladen.
Ihr seid verwundert, Sir, daß ich so schnell
Das Herz geändert gegen die Maria.
Zwar in der That haßt' ich sie nie — der Zwang 1760
Der Zeiten machte mich zu ihrem Gegner.
Sie war mir zugedacht seit langen Jahren,
Ihr wißt's, eh sie die Hand dem Darnley gab,
Als noch der Glanz der Hoheit sie umlachte.
Kalt stieß ich damals dieses Glück von mir; 1765
Jetzt im Gefängnis, an des Todes Pforten
Such' ich sie auf, und mit Gefahr des Lebens.

Mortimer.

Das heißt großmütig handeln!

Leicester.

          — Die Gestalt
Der Dinge, Sir, hat sich indes verändert.

Mein Ehrgeiz war es, der mich gegen Jugend   1770
Und Schönheit fühllos machte.   Damals hielt ich
Mariens Hand für mich zu klein, ich hoffte
Auf den Besitz der Königin von England.

Mortimer.

Es ist bekannt, daß sie Euch allen Männern
Vorzog —   1775

Leicester.

So schien es, edler Sir — und nun, nach zehn
Verlornen Jahren unverdroßnen Werbens,
Verhaßten Zwangs — O Sir, mein Herz geht auf!
Ich muß des langen Unmuts mich entladen —
Man preist mich glücklich — Wüßte man, was es
Für Ketten sind, um die man mich beneidet —   1780
Nachdem ich zehen bittre Jahre lang
Dem Götzen ihrer Eitelkeit geopfert,
Mich jedem Wechsel ihrer Sultanslaunen
Mit Sklavendemut unterwarf, das Spielzeug
Des kleinen grillenhaften Eigensinns,   1785
Geliebkost jetzt von ihrer Zärtlichkeit,
Und jetzt mit sprödem Stolz zurückgestoßen,
Von ihrer Gunst und Strenge gleich gepeinigt,
Wie ein Gefangener vom Argusblick
Der Eifersucht gehütet, ins Verhör   1790
Genommen wie ein Knabe, wie ein Diener
Gescholten — O, die Sprache hat kein Wort
Für diese Hölle!

Mortimer.

               Ich beklag' Euch, Graf.

Leicester.

Täuscht mich am Ziel der Preis! Ein andrer kommt,
Die Frucht des teuren Werbens mir zu rauben.   1795
An einen jungen blühenden Gemahl

Verlier' ich meine lang besessnen Rechte!
Heruntersteigen soll ich von der Bühne,
Wo ich so lange als der Erste glänzte.
Nicht ihre Hand allein, auch ihre Gunst   1800
Droht mir der neue Ankömmling zu rauben.
Sie ist ein Weib, und er ist liebenswert.

Mortimer.

Er ist Kathrinens Sohn.   In guter Schule
Hat er des Schmeichelns Künste ausgelernt.

Leicester.

So stürzen meine Hoffnungen — ich suche   1805
In diesem Schiffbruch meines Glücks ein Brett
Zu fassen — und mein Auge wendet sich
Der ersten schönen Hoffnung wieder zu.
Mariens Bild, in ihrer Reize Glanz,
Stand neu vor mir, Schönheit und Jugend traten   1810
In ihre vollen Rechte wieder ein;
Nicht kalter Ehrgeiz mehr, das Herz verglich,
Und ich empfand, welch Kleinod ich verloren.
Mit Schrecken seh' ich sie in tiefes Elend
Herabgestürzt, gestürzt durch mein Verschulden.   1815
Da wird in mir die Hoffnung wach, ob ich
Sie jetzt noch retten könnte und besitzen.
Durch eine treue Hand gelingt es mir,
Ihr mein verändert Herz zu offenbaren,
Und dieser Brief, den Ihr mir überbracht,   1820
Versichert mir, daß sie verzeiht, sich mir
Zum Preise schenken will, wenn ich sie rette.

Mortimer.

Ihr thatet aber nichts zu ihrer Rettung!
Ihr ließt geschehn, daß sie verurteilt wurde,

6

Gabt Eure Stimme selbst zu ihrem Tod!   1825
Ein Wunder muß geschehn — Der Wahrheit Licht
Muß mich, den Neffen ihres Hüters, rühren,
Im Vatikan zu Rom muß ihr der Himmel
Den unverhofften Retter zubereiten,
Sonst fand sie nicht einmal den Weg zu Euch!   1830

Leicester.

Ach, Sir, es hat mir Qualen gnug gekostet!
Um selbe Zeit ward sie von Talbots Schloß
Nach Fotheringhay weggeführt, der strengen
Gewahrsam Eures Oheims anvertraut.
Gehemmt ward jeder Weg zu ihr, ich mußte   1835
Fortfahren vor der Welt, sie zu verfolgen.
Doch denket nicht, daß ich sie leidend hätte
Zum Tode gehen lassen! Nein, ich hoffte
Und hoffe noch, das Äußerste zu hindern,
Bis sich ein Mittel zeigt, sie zu befreien.   1840

Mortimer.

Das ist gefunden — Lester, Euer edles
Vertraun verdient Erwiderung. Ich will sie
Befreien, darum bin ich hier, die Anstalt
Ist schon getroffen, Euer mächt'ger Beistand
Versichert uns den glücklichen Erfolg.   1845

Leicester.

Was sagt Ihr? Ihr erschreckt mich. Wie? Ihr wolltet—

Mortimer.

Gewaltsam aufthun will ich ihren Kerker,
Ich hab' Gefährten, alles ist bereit —

Leicester.

Ihr habt Mitwisser und Vertraute! Weh mir!

In welches Wagnis reißt Ihr mich hinein!   1850
Und diese wissen auch um mein Geheimnis?

Mortimer.

Sorgt nicht.   Der Plan ward ohne Euch entworfen,
Ohn' Euch wär' er vollstreckt, bestünde sie
Nicht drauf, Euch ihre Rettung zu verdanken.

Leicester.

So könnt Ihr mich für ganz gewiß versichern,   1855
Daß in dem Bund mein Name nicht genannt ist?

Mortimer.

Verlaßt Euch drauf!   Wie?   So bedenklich, Graf,
Bei einer Botschaft, die Euch Hilfe bringt!
Ihr wollt die Stuart retten und besitzen,
Ihr findet Freunde, plötzlich, unerwartet,   1860
Vom Himmel fallen Euch die nächsten Mittel —
Doch zeigt Ihr mehr Verlegenheit als Freude?

Leicester.

Es ist nichts mit Gewalt.   Das Wagestück
Ist zu gefährlich.

Mortimer.

Auch das Säumen ist's!

Leicester.

Ich sag' Euch, Ritter, es ist nicht zu wagen.   1865

Mortimer (bitter).

Nein, nicht für Euch, der sie besitzen will!
Wir wollen sie bloß retten und sind nicht so
Bedenklich —

Leicester.

Junger Mann, Ihr seid zu rasch
In so gefährlich dornenvoller Sache.

Mortimer.

Ihr — sehr bedacht in solchem Fall der Ehre.   1870

Leicester.

Ich seh' die Netze, die uns rings umgeben.

Mortimer.

Ich fühle Mut, sie alle zu durchreißen.

Leicester.

Tollkühnheit, Raserei ist dieser Mut.

Mortimer.

Nicht Tapferkeit ist diese Klugheit, Lord.

Leicester.

Euch lüstet's wohl, wie Babington zu enden?   1875

Mortimer.

Euch nicht, des Norfolks Großmut nachzuahmen.

Leicester.

Norfolk hat seine Braut nicht heimgeführt.

Mortimer.

Er hat bewiesen, daß er's würdig war.

Leicester.

Wenn w i r verderben, reißen wir sie nach.

Mortimer.

Wenn wir uns schonen, wird sie nicht gerettet.   1880

Leicester.

Ihr überlegt nicht, hört nicht, werdet alles
Mit heftig blindem Ungestüm zerstören,
Was auf so guten Weg geleitet war.

Mortimer.

Wohl auf den guten Weg, den J h r gebahnt?
Was habt Ihr denn gethan, um sie zu retten?　　1885
— Und wie? Wenn ich nun Bube gnug gewesen,
Sie zu e r m o r d e n, wie die Königin
Mir anbefahl, wie sie zu dieser Stunde
Von mir erwartet — Nennt mir doch die Anstalt,
Die Ihr gemacht, ihr Leben zu erhalten.　　1890

Leicester (erstaunt).

Gab Euch die Königin diesen Blutbefehl?

Mortimer.

Sie irrte sich in mir, wie sich Maria
In Euch.

Leicester.

Und Ihr habt zugesagt? Habt Ihr?

Mortimer.

Damit sie andre Hände nicht erkaufe,
Bot ich die meinen an.　　1895

Leicester.

　　　　　Ihr thatet wohl.
Dies kann uns Raum verschaffen. Sie verläßt sich
Auf Euren blut'gen Dienst, das Todesurteil
Bleibt unvollstreckt, und wir gewinnen Zeit —

Mortimer (ungeduldig).

Nein, wir verlieren Zeit!

Leicester.

　　　　　Sie zählt auf Euch,
So minder wird sie Anstand nehmen, sich　　1900
Den Schein der Gnade vor der Welt zu geben.

Vielleicht, daß ich durch List sie überrede,
Das Angesicht der Gegnerin zu sehn,
Und dieser Schritt muß ihr die Hände binden.
Burleigh hat recht. Das Urteil kann nicht mehr　　　1905
Vollzogen werden, wenn sie sie gesehn.
— Ja, ich versuch' es, alles biet' ich auf —

Mortimer.

Und was erreicht Ihr dadurch? Wenn sie sich
In mir getäuscht sieht, wenn Maria fortfährt,
Zu leben — ist nicht alles, wie zuvor?　　　1910
Frei wird sie niemals! Auch das Mildeste,
Was kommen kann, ist ewiges Gefängnis.
Mit einer kühnen That müßt Ihr doch enden,
Warum wollt Ihr nicht gleich damit beginnen?
In Euren Händen ist die Macht, Ihr bringt　　　1915
Ein Heer zusammen, wenn Ihr nur den Adel
Auf Euren vielen Schlössern waffnen wollt!
Maria hat noch viel verborgne Freunde;
Der Howard und der Percy edle Häuser,
Ob ihre Häupter gleich gestürzt, sind noch　　　1920
An Helden reich, sie harren nur darauf,
Daß ein gewalt'ger Lord das Beispiel gebe!
Weg mit Verstellung! Handelt öffentlich!
Verteidigt als ein Ritter die Geliebte,
Kämpft einen edeln Kampf um sie! Ihr seid　　　1925
Herr der Person der Königin von England,
Sobald Ihr wollt. Lockt sie auf Eure Schlösser,
Sie ist Euch oft dahin gefolgt. Dort zeigt ihr
Den Mann! Sprecht als Gebieter! Haltet sie
Verwahrt, bis sie die Stuart frei gegeben!　　　1930

Leicester.

Ich staune, ich entsetze mich — Wohin
Reißt Euch der Schwindel? — Kennt Ihr diesen Boden?

Wißt Ihr, wie's steht an diesem Hof, wie eng
Dies Frauenreich die Geister hat gebunden?
Sucht nach dem Heldengeist, der ehmals wohl   1935
In diesem Land sich regte — Unterworfen
Ist alles unterm Schlüssel eines Weibes,
Und jedes Mutes Federn abgespannt.
Folgt meiner Leitung. Wagt nichts unbedachtsam.
— Ich höre kommen, geht.   1940

Mortimer.

Maria hofft!
Kehr' ich mit leerem Trost zu ihr zurück?

Leicester.

Bringt ihr die Schwüre meiner ew'gen Liebe!

Mortimer.

Bringt ihr die selbst! Zum Werkzeug ihrer Rettung
Bot ich mich an, nicht Euch zum Liebesboten!

(Er geht ab.)

Neunter Auftritt.

Elisabeth. Leicester.

Elisabeth.

Wer ging da von Euch weg? Ich hörte sprechen.   1945

Leicester (sich auf ihre Rede schnell und erschrocken umwendend).

Es war Sir Mortimer.

Elisabeth.

Was ist Euch, Lord?
So ganz betreten?

Leicester (faßt sich).

— Über deinen Anblick!
Ich habe dich so reizend nie gesehn,
Geblendet steh' ich da von deiner Schönheit.
— Ach!   1950

Elisabeth.

Warum seufzt Ihr?

Leicester.

Hab' ich keinen Grund
Zu seufzen?   Da ich deinen Reiz betrachte,
Erneut sich mir der namenlose Schmerz
Des drohenden Verlustes.

Elisabeth.

Was verliert Ihr?

Leicester.

Dein Herz, dein liebenswürdig Selbst verlier' ich.
Bald wirst du in den jugendlichen Armen   1955
Des feurigen Gemahls dich glücklich fühlen,
Und ungeteilt wird er dein Herz besitzen.
Er ist von königlichem Blut, das bin
Ich nicht; doch Trotz sei aller Welt geboten,
Ob einer lebt auf diesem Erdenrund,   1960
Der mehr Anbetung für dich fühlt, als ich.
Der Duc von Anjou hat dich nie gesehn,
Nur deinen Ruhm und Schimmer kann er lieben,
Ich liebe dich.   Wärst du die ärmste Hirtin,
Ich als der größte Fürst der Welt geboren,   1965
Zu deinem Stand würd' ich heruntersteigen,
Mein Diadem zu deinen Füßen legen.

Elisabeth.

Beklag' mich, Dudley, schilt mich nicht! — Ich darf ja

Mein Herz nicht fragen.   Ach! das hätte anders
Gewählt.   Und wie beneid' ich andre Weiber,   1970
Die das erhöhen dürfen, was sie lieben.
So glücklich bin ich nicht, daß ich dem Manne,
Der mir vor allen teuer ist, die Krone
Aufsetzen kann! — Der Stuart ward's vergönnt,
Die Hand nach ihrer Neigung zu verschenken;   1975
Die hat sich jegliches erlaubt, sie hat
Den vollen Kelch der Freuden ausgetrunken.

Leicester.

Jetzt trinkt sie auch den bittern Kelch des Leidens.

Elisabeth.

Sie hat der Menschen Urteil nichts geachtet.
Leicht wurd' es ihr zu leben, nimmer lud sie   1980
Das Joch sich auf, dem ich mich unterwarf.
Hätt' ich doch auch Ansprüche machen können,
Des Lebens mich, der Erde Lust zu freun,
Doch zog ich strenge Königspflichten vor.
Und doch gewann sie aller Männer Gunst,   1985
Weil sie sich nur befliß, ein Weib zu sein,
Und um sie buhlt die Jugend und das Alter.
So sind die Männer.   Lüstlinge sind alle!
Dem Leichtsinn eilen sie, der Freude zu
Und schätzen nichts, was sie verehren müssen.   1990
Verjüngte sich nicht dieser Talbot selbst,
Als er auf ihren Reiz zu reden kam!

Leicester.

Vergieb es ihm.   Er war ihr Wächter einst;
Die List'ge hat mit Schmeicheln ihn bethört.

Elisabeth.

Und ist's denn wirklich wahr, daß sie so schön ist?   1995

So oft mußt' ich die Larve rühmen hören,
Wohl möcht' ich wissen, was zu glauben ist.
Gemälde schmeicheln, Schilderungen lügen,
Nur meinen eignen Augen würd' ich traun.
— Was schaut Ihr mich so seltsam an?   2000

Leicester.

                                        Ich stellte
Dich in Gedanken neben die Maria.
— Die Freude wünscht' ich mir, ich berg' es nicht,
Wenn es ganz in geheim geschehen könnte,
Der Stuart gegenüber dich zu sehn!
Dann solltest du erst deines ganzen Siegs   2005
Genießen! Die Beschämung gönnt' ich ihr,
Daß sie mit eignen Augen — denn der Neid
Hat scharfe Augen — überzeugt sich sähe,
Wie sehr sie auch an Adel der Gestalt
Von dir besiegt wird, der sie so unendlich   2010
In jeder andern würd'gen Tugend weicht.

Elisabeth.

Sie ist die Jüngere an Jahren.

Leicester.

                                        Jünger!
Man sieht's ihr nicht an. Freilich ihre Leiden!
Sie mag wohl vor der Zeit gealtert haben.
Ja, und was ihre Kränkung bittrer machte,   2015
Das wäre, dich als Braut zu sehn! Sie hat
Des Lebens schöne Hoffnung hinter sich,
Dich sähe sie dem Glück entgegenschreiten!
Und als die Braut des Königssohns von Frankreich,
Da sie sich stets so viel gewußt, so stolz   2020
Gethan mit der französischen Vermählung,
Noch jetzt auf Frankreichs mächt'ge Hilfe pocht!

Elisabeth (nachlässig hinwerfend).

Man peinigt mich ja, sie zu sehn.

Leicester (lebhaft).

Sie fordert's

Als eine Gunst, gewähr' es ihr als Strafe!
Du kannst sie auf das Blutgerüste führen,   2025
Es wird sie minder peinigen, als sich
Von deinen Reizen ausgelöscht zu sehn.
Dadurch ermordest du sie, wie sie dich
Ermorden wollte — Wenn sie deine Schönheit
Erblickt, durch Ehrbarkeit bewacht, in Glorie   2030
Gestellt durch einen unbefleckten Tugendruf,
Den sie, leichtsinnig buhlend, von sich warf,
Erhoben durch der Krone Glanz, und jetzt
Durch zarte Bräutlichkeit geschmückt — dann hat
Die Stunde der Vernichtung ihr geschlagen.   2035
Ja — wenn ich jetzt die Augen auf dich werfe —
Nie warst du, nie zu einem Sieg der Schönheit
Gerüsteter, als eben jetzt — Mich selbst
Hast du umstrahlt wie eine Lichterscheinung,
Als du vorhin ins Zimmer tratest — Wie?   2040
Wenn du gleich jetzt, jetzt, wie du bist, hinträtest
Vor sie, du findest keine schönre Stunde —

Elisabeth.

Jetzt — Nein — Nein — Jetzt nicht, Lester — Nein, das
      muß ich
Erst wohl bedenken — mich mit Burleigh —

Leicester (lebhaft einfallend).

Burleigh!

Der denkt allein auf deinen Staatsvorteil;   2045
Auch deine Weiblichkeit hat ihre Rechte,
Der zarte Punkt gehört vor dein Gericht,

Nicht vor des Staatsmanns—ja, auch Staatskunst will es,
Daß du sie siehst, die öffentliche Meinung
Durch eine That der Großmut dir gewinnest!   2050
Magst du nachher dich der verhaßten Feindin,
Auf welche Weise dir's gefällt, entladen.

Elisabeth.

Nicht wohlanständig wär' mir's, die Verwandte
Im Mangel und in Schmach zu sehn.   Man sagt,
Daß sie nicht königlich umgeben sei,   2055
Vorwerfend wär' mir ihres Mangels Anblick.

Leicester.

Nicht ihrer Schwelle brauchst du dich zu nahn.
Hör' meinen Rat.   Der Zufall hat es eben
Nach Wunsch gefügt.   Heut ist das große Jagen,
An Fotheringhay führt der Weg vorbei,   2060
Dort kann die Stuart sich im Park ergehn,
Du kommst ganz wie von ohngefähr dahin,
Es darf nichts als vorher bedacht erscheinen,
Und wenn es dir zuwider, redest du
Sie gar nicht an —   2065

Elisabeth.

                    Begeh' ich eine Thorheit,
So ist es Eure, Lester, nicht die meine.
Ich will Euch heute keinen Wunsch versagen,
Weil ich von meinen Unterthanen allen
Euch heut am wehesten gethan. (Ihn zärtlich ansehend.)
Sei's eine Grille nur von Euch.   Dadurch   2070
Giebt Neigung sich ja kund, daß sie bewilligt
Aus freier Gunst, was sie auch nicht gebilligt.
          (Leicester stürzt zu ihren Füßen, der Vorhang fällt.)

Dritter Aufzug.

Gegend in einem Park. Vorn mit Bäumen
besetzt, hinten eine weite Aussicht.

Erster Auftritt.

Maria tritt in schnellem Lauf hinter Bäumen hervor. Hanna Kennedy
folgt langsam.

Kennedy.

Ihr eilet ja, als wenn Ihr Flügel hättet,
So kann ich Euch nicht folgen, wartet doch!

Maria.

Laß mich der neuen Freiheit genießen,   2075
Laß mich ein Kind sein, sei es mit,
Und auf dem grünen Teppich der Wiesen
Prüfen den leichten, geflügelten Schritt.
Bin ich dem finstern Gefängnis entstiegen,
Hält sie mich nicht mehr, die traurige Gruft?   2080
Laß mich in vollen, in durstigen Zügen
Trinken die freie, die himmlische Luft.

Kennedy.

O meine teure Lady! Euer Kerker
Ist nur um ein klein Weniges erweitert.
Ihr seht nur nicht die Mauer, die uns einschließt,   2085
Weil sie der Bäume dicht Gesträuch versteckt.

(93)

Maria.

O Dank, Dank diesen freundlich grünen Bäumen,
Die meines Kerkers Mauern mir verstecken!
Ich will mich frei und glücklich träumen,
Warum aus meinem süßen Wahn mich wecken? 2090
Umfängt mich nicht der weite Himmelsschoß?
Die Blicke, frei und fessellos,
Ergehen sich in ungemeßnen Räumen.
Dort, wo die grauen Nebelberge ragen,
Fängt meines Reiches Grenze an, 2095
Und diese Wolken, die nach Mittag jagen,
Sie suchen Frankreichs fernen Ozean.

    Eilende Wolken, Segler der Lüfte!
    Wer mit euch wanderte, mit euch schiffte!
    Grüßet mir freundlich mein Jugendland! 2100
    Ich bin gefangen, ich bin in Banden,
    Ach, ich hab' keinen andern Gesandten!
    Frei in Lüften ist eure Bahn,
    Ihr seid nicht dieser Königin unterthan.

Kennedy.

Ach, teure Lady! Ihr seid außer Euch, 2105
Die langentbehrte Freiheit macht Euch schwärmen.

Maria.

    Dort legt ein Fischer den Nachen an.
    Dieses elende Werkzeug könnte mich retten,
    Brächte mich schnell zu befreundeten Städten.
    Spärlich nährt es den dürftigen Mann.
    Beladen wollt' ich ihn reich mit Schätzen, 2110
    Einen Zug sollt' er thun, wie er keinen gethan,
    Das Glück sollt' er finden in seinen Netzen,
    Nähm' er mich ein in den rettenden Kahn.

Kennedy.

Verlorne Wünsche! Seht Ihr nicht, daß uns 2115
Von ferne dort die Spähertritte folgen?
Ein finster grausames Verbot scheucht jedes
Mitleidige Geschöpf aus unserm Wege.

Maria.

Nein, gute Hanna. Glaub' mir, nicht umsonst
Ist meines Kerkers Thor geöffnet worden. 2120
Die kleine Gunst ist mir des größern Glücks
Verkünderin. Ich irre nicht. Es ist
Der Liebe thät'ge Hand, der ich sie danke.
Lord Lesters mächt'gen Arm erkenn' ich drin.
Allmählich will man mein Gefängnis weiten, 2125
Durch Kleineres zum Größern mich gewöhnen,
Bis ich das Antlitz dessen endlich schaue,
Der mir die Bande löst auf immerdar.

Kennedy.

Ach, ich kann diesen Widerspruch nicht reimen!
Noch gestern kündigt man den Tod Euch an, 2130
Und heute wird Euch plötzlich solche Freiheit.
Auch denen, hört' ich sagen, wird die Kette
Gelöst, auf die die ew'ge Freiheit wartet.

Maria.

Hörst du das Hifthorn? Hörst du's klingen,
Mächtigen Rufes, durch Feld und Hain? 2135
Ach, auf das mutige Roß mich zu schwingen,
An den fröhlichen Zug mich zu reihn!
Noch mehr! O, die bekannte Stimme,
Schmerzlich süßer Erinnerung voll.
Oft vernahm sie mein Ohr mit Freuden 2140
Auf des Hochlands bergichten Heiden,
Wenn die tobende Jagd erscholl.

Zweiter Auftritt.

Paulet. Die Vorigen.

Paulet.

Nun! Hab' ich's endlich recht gemacht, Mylady?
Verdien' ich einmal Euern Dank?

Maria.

     Wie, Ritter?
Seid Ihr's, der diese Gunst mir ausgewirkt?   2145
Ihr seid's?

Paulet.

   Warum soll ich's nicht sein? Ich war
Am Hof, ich überbrachte Euer Schreiben —

Maria.

Ihr übergabt es? Wirklich, thatet Ihr's?
Und diese Freiheit, die ich jetzt genieße,
Ist eine Frucht des Briefs —   2150

Paulet (mit Bedeutung).

    Und nicht die einz'ge!
Macht Euch auf eine größere noch gefaßt.

Maria.

Auf eine größere, Sir? Was meint Ihr damit?

Paulet.

Ihr hörtet doch die Hörner —

Maria (zurückfahrend, mit Ahnung).

     Ihr erschreckt mich!

Paulet.

Die Königin jagt in dieser Gegend.

Maria.

Was?

Paulet.

In wenig Augenblicken steht sie vor Euch. 2155

Kennedy

(auf Maria zueilend, welche zittert und hinzusinken droht).

Wie wird Euch, teure Lady! Ihr verblaßt.

Paulet.

Nun! Ist's nun nicht recht? War's nicht Eure Bitte?
Sie wird Euch früher gewährt, als Ihr gedacht.
Ihr wart sonst immer so geschwinder Zunge,
Jetzt bringet Eure Worte an, jetzt ist 2160
Der Augenblick, zu reden!

Maria.

O, warum hat man mich nicht vorbereitet!
Jetzt bin ich nicht darauf gefaßt, jetzt nicht.
Was ich mir als die höchste Gunst erbeten,
Dünkt mir jetzt schrecklich, fürchterlich — Komm, Hanna, 2165
Führ' mich ins Haus, daß ich mich fasse, mich
Erhole —

Paulet.

Bleibt. Ihr müßt sie hier erwarten.
Wohl, wohl mag's Euch beängstigen, ich glaub's
Vor Eurem Richter zu erscheinen.

Dritter Auftritt.

Graf Shrewsbury zu den Vorigen.

Maria.

Es ist nicht darum! Gott, mir ist ganz anders　　　2170
Zu Mut — Ach, edler Shrewsbury! Ihr kommt,
Vom Himmel mir ein Engel zugesendet!
— Ich kann sie nicht sehn! Rettet, rettet mich
Von dem verhaßten Anblick —

Shrewsbury.

Kommt zu Euch, Königin! Faßt Euren Mut　　　2175
Zusammen.　Das ist die entscheidungsvolle Stunde.

Maria.

Ich habe darauf geharret — jahrelang
Mich darauf bereitet, alles hab' ich mir
Gesagt und ins Gedächtnis eingeschrieben,
Wie ich sie rühren wollte und bewegen!　　　2180
Vergessen plötzlich, ausgelöscht ist alles,
Nichts lebt in mir in diesem Augenblick,
Als meiner Leiden brennendes Gefühl.
In blut'gen Haß gewendet wider sie
Ist mir das Herz, es fliehen alle guten　　　2185
Gedanken, und die Schlangenhaare schüttelnd,
Umstehen mich die finstern Höllengeister.

Shrewsbury.

Gebietet Eurem wild empörten Blut,
Bezwingt des Herzens Bitterkeit! Es bringt
Nicht gute Frucht, wenn Haß dem Haß begegnet.　　　2190
Wie sehr auch Euer Innres widerstrebe,
Gehorcht der Zeit und dem Gesetz der Stunde!
Sie ist die Mächtige — demütigt Euch!

Maria.

Vor ihr! Ich kann es nimmermehr.

Shrewsbury.

Thut's dennoch!
Sprecht ehrerbietig, mit Gelassenheit!   2195
Ruft ihre Großmut an, trotzt nicht, jetzt nicht
Auf Euer Recht, jetzo ist nicht die Stunde.

Maria.

Ach, mein Verderben hab' ich mir erfleht,
Und mir zum Fluche wird mein Flehn erhört!
Nie hätten wir uns sehen sollen, niemals!   2200
Daraus kann nimmer, nimmer Gutes kommen!
Eh mögen Feu'r und Wasser sich in Liebe
Begegnen und das Lamm den Tiger küssen —
Ich bin zu schwer verletzt — sie hat zu schwer
Beleidigt — Nie ist zwischen uns Versöhnung!   2205

Shrewsbury.

Seht sie nur erst von Angesicht!
Ich sah es ja, wie sie von Eurem Brief
Erschüttert war, ihr Auge schwamm in Thränen.
Nein, sie ist nicht gefühllos, hegt Ihr selbst
Nur besseres Vertrauen — Darum eben   2210
Bin ich vorausgeeilt, damit ich Euch
In Fassung setzen und ermahnen möchte.

Maria (seine Hand ergreifend).

Ach, Talbot! Ihr wart stets mein Freund — daß ich
In Eurer milden Haft geblieben wäre!
Es ward mir hart begegnet, Shrewsbury!   2215

Shrewsbury.

Vergeßt jetzt alles. Darauf denkt allein,
Wie Ihr sie unterwürfig wollt empfangen.

Maria.

Ist Burleigh auch mit ihr, mein böser Engel?

Shrewsbury.

Niemand begleitet sie als Graf von Lester.

Maria.

Lord Lester!　　　　　　　　　　　　　　　　　2220

Shrewsbury.

　　　　　Fürchtet nichts von ihm.　Nicht er
Will Euren Untergang — Sein Werk ist es,
Daß Euch die Königin die Zusammenkunft
Bewilligt.　.

Maria.

　　　　　Ach! Ich wußt' es wohl!

Shrewsbury.

　　　　　　　　　Was sagt Ihr?

Paulet.

Die Königin kommt!

(Alles weicht auf die Seite; nur Maria bleibt, auf die Kennedy gelehnt.)

Vierter Auftritt.

Die Vorigen. Elisabeth. Graf Leicester. Gefolge.

Elisabeth (zu Leicester).

Wie heißt der Landsitz?　　　　　　　　　　　　2225

Leicester.

　　　　　　　　　Fotheringhayschloß.

Elisabeth (zu Shrewsbury).

Schickt unser Jagdgefolg voraus nach London.

Das Volk drängt allzuheftig in den Straßen,
Wir suchen Schutz in diesem stillen Park.

(Talbot entfernt das Gefolge. Sie fixiert mit den Augen die Maria, indem
sie zu Leicester weiter spricht.)

Mein gutes Volk liebt mich zu sehr. Unmäßig,
Abgöttisch sind die Zeichen seiner Freude,   2230
So ehrt man einen Gott, nicht einen Menschen.

Maria

(welche diese Zeit über halb ohnmächtig auf die Amme gelehnt war, erhebt sich
jetzt, und ihr Auge begegnet dem gespannten Blick der Elisabeth. Sie schau-
dert zusammen und wirft sich wieder an der Amme Brust).

O Gott, aus diesen Zügen spricht kein Herz!

Elisabeth.

Wer ist die Lady?   (Ein allgemeines Schweigen.)

Leicester.

— Du bist zu Fotheringhay, Königin.

Elisabeth

(stellt sich überrascht und erstaunt, einen finstern Blick auf Leicestern richtend).

Wer hat mir das gethan? Lord Lester!   2235

Leicester.

Es ist geschehen, Königin — Und nun
Der Himmel deinen Schritt hieher gelenkt,
So laß die Großmut und das Mitleid siegen.

Shrewsbury.

Laß dich erbitten, königliche Frau,
Dein Aug' auf die Unglückliche zu richten,   2240
Die hier vergeht vor deinem Anblick.

(Maria rafft sich zusammen und will auf die Elisabeth zugehen, steht aber
auf halbem Wege schaudernd still; ihre Gebärden drücken den heftigsten
Kampf aus.)

Elisabeth.

Wie, Mylords?
Wer war es denn, der eine Tiefgebeugte
Mir angekündigt? Eine Stolze find' ich,
Vom Unglück keineswegs geschmeidigt.

Maria.

Sei's!
Ich will mich auch noch diesem unterwerfen.   2245
Fahr hin, ohnmächt'ger Stolz der edlen Seele!
Ich will vergessen, wer ich bin, und was
Ich litt; ich will vor ihr mich niederwerfen,
Die mich in diese Schmach herunterstieß.

(Sie wendet sich gegen die Königin.)

Der Himmel hat für Euch entschieden, Schwester!   2250
Gekrönt vom Sieg ist Euer glücklich Haupt,
Die Gottheit bet' ich an, die Euch erhöhte!

(Sie fällt vor ihr nieder.)

Doch seid auch Ihr nun edelmütig, Schwester!
Laßt mich nicht schmachvoll liegen! Eure Hand
Streckt aus, reicht mir die königliche Rechte,   2255
Mich zu erheben von dem tiefen Fall!

Elisabeth (zurücktretend).

Ihr seid an Eurem Platz, Lady Maria!
Und dankend preis' ich meines Gottes Gnade,
Der nicht gewollt, daß ich zu Euren Füßen
So liegen sollte, wie Ihr jetzt zu meinen.   2260

Maria (mit steigendem Affekt).

Denkt an den Wechsel alles Menschlichen!
Es leben Götter, die den Hochmut rächen!
Verehret, fürchtet sie, die schrecklichen,
Die mich zu Euren Füßen niederstürzen —

Um dieser fremden Zeugen willen ehrt   2265
In mir Euch selbst! entweihet, schändet nicht
Das Blut der Tudor, das in meinen Adern,
Wie in den Euren, fließt — O Gott im Himmel!
Steht nicht da, schroff und unzugänglich, wie
Die Felsenklippe, die der Strandende   2270
Vergeblich ringend zu erfassen strebt.
Mein Alles hängt, mein Leben, mein Geschick
An meiner Worte, meiner Thränen Kraft;
Löst mir das Herz, daß ich das Eure rühre!
Wenn Ihr mich anschaut mit dem Eisesblick,   2275
Schließt sich das Herz mir schaudernd zu, der Strom
Der Thränen stockt, und kaltes Grausen fesselt
Die Flehensworte mir im Busen an.

Elisabeth (kalt und streng).

Was habt Ihr mir zu sagen, Lady Stuart?
Ihr habt mich sprechen wollen.   Ich vergesse   2280
Die Königin, die schwer beleidigte,
Die fromme Pflicht der Schwester zu erfüllen,
Und meines Anblicks Trost gewähr' ich Euch.
Dem Trieb der Großmut folg' ich, setze mich
Gerechtem Tadel aus, daß ich so weit   2285
Heruntersteige — denn Ihr wißt,
Daß Ihr mich habt ermorden lassen wollen.

Maria.

Womit soll ich den Anfang machen, wie
Die Worte klüglich stellen, daß sie Euch
Das Herz ergreifen, aber nicht verletzen!   2290
O Gott, gieb meiner Rede Kraft und nimm
Ihr jeden Stachel, der verwunden könnte!
Kann ich doch für mich selbst nicht sprechen, ohne Euch
Schwer zu verklagen, und das will ich nicht.

— Ihr habt an mir gehandelt, wie nicht recht ist,　　2295
Denn ich bin eine Königin, wie Ihr,
Und Ihr habt als Gefangne mich gehalten.
Ich kam zu Euch als eine Bittende,
Und Ihr, des Gastrechts heilige Gesetze,
Der Völker heilig Recht in mir verhöhnend,　　2300
Schloßt mich in Kerkermauern ein; die Freunde,
Die Diener werden grausam mir entrissen,
Unwürd'gem Mangel werd' ich preisgegeben,
Man stellt mich vor ein schimpfliches Gericht —
Nichts mehr davon!   Ein ewiges Vergessen　　2305
Bedecke, was ich Grausames erlitt.
— Seht!   Ich will alles eine Schickung nennen,
Ihr seid nicht schuldig, i c h bin auch nicht schuldig;
Ein böser Geist stieg aus dem Abgrund auf,
Den Haß in unsern Herzen zu entzünden,　　2310
Der unsre zarte Jugend schon entzweit.
Er wuchs mit uns, und böse Menschen fachten
Der unglücksel'gen Flamme Atem zu;
Wahnsinn'ge Eiferer bewaffneten
Mit Schwert und Dolch die unberufne Hand —　　2315
Das ist das Fluchgeschick der Könige,
Daß sie, entzweit, die Welt in Haß zerreißen
Und jeder Zwietracht Furien entfesseln.
— Jetzt ist kein fremder Mund mehr zwischen uns,
　　　(nähert sich ihr zutraulich und mit schmeichelndem Ton)
Wir stehen einander selbst nun gegenüber.　　2320
Jetzt, Schwester, redet! Nennt mir meine Schuld,
Ich will Euch völliges Genügen leisten.
Ach, daß Ihr damals mir Gehör geschenkt,
Als ich so dringend Euer Auge suchte!
Es wäre nie so weit gekommen, nicht　　2325
An diesem traur'gen Ort geschähe jetzt
Die unglückselig traurige Begegnung.

Elisabeth.

Mein guter Stern bewahrte mich davor,
Die Natter an den Busen mir zu legen.
— Nicht die Geschicke, Euer schwarzes **Herz**   2830
Klagt an, die wilde Ehrsucht Eures Hauses.
Nichts Feindliches war zwischen uns geschehn,
Da kündigte mir Euer Ohm, der stolze,
Herrschwüt'ge Priester, der die freche Hand
Nach allen Kronen streckt, die Fehde an,   2835
Bethörte Euch, mein Wappen anzunehmen,
Euch meine Königstitel zuzueignen,
Auf Tod und Leben in den Kampf mit mir
Zu gehn — Wen rief er gegen mich nicht auf?
Der Priester Zungen und der Völker Schwert,   2840
Des frommen Wahnsinns fürchterliche Waffen;
Hier selbst, im Friedenssitze meines Reichs,
Blies er mir der Empörung Flammen an —
Doch Gott ist mit mir, und der stolze Priester
Behält das Feld nicht — Meinem Haupte war   2845
Der Streich gedrohet, und das Eure fällt!

Maria.

Ich steh' in Gottes Hand. Ihr werdet Euch
So blutig Eurer Macht nicht überheben —

Elisabeth.

Wer soll mich hindern? Euer Oheim gab
Das Beispiel allen Königen der Welt,   2850
Wie man mit seinen Feinden Frieden macht.
Die Sankt Barthelemi sei meine Schule!
Was ist mir Blutsverwandtschaft, Völkerrecht?
Die Kirche trennet aller Pflichten Band,
Den Treubruch heiligt sie, den Königsmord;   2855
Ich übe nur, was Eure Priester lehren.

Sagt, welches Pfand gewährte mir für Euch,
Wenn ich großmütig Eure Bande löste?
Mit welchem Schloß verwahr' ich Eure Treue,
Das nicht Sankt Peters Schlüssel öffnen kann? 2360
Gewalt nur ist die einz'ge Sicherheit,
Kein Bündnis ist mit dem Gezücht der Schlangen.

Maria.

O, das ist Euer traurig finstrer Argwohn!
Ihr habt mich stets als eine Feindin nur
Und Fremdlingin betrachtet.   Hättet Ihr 2365
Zu Eurer Erbin mich erklärt, wie mir
Gebührt, so hätten Dankbarkeit und Liebe
Euch eine treue Freundin und Verwandte
In mir erhalten.

Elisabeth.

                        Draußen, Lady Stuart,
Ist Eure Freundschaft, Euer Haus das Papsttum, 2370
Der Mönch ist Euer Bruder — Euch, zur Erbin
Erklären! Der verräterische Fallstrick!
Daß Ihr bei meinem Leben noch mein Volk
Verführtet, eine listige Armida,
Die edle Jugend meines Königreichs 2375
In Eurem Buhlernetze schlau verstricket —
Daß alles sich der neu aufgehenden Sonne
Zuwendete, und ich —

Maria.

                        Regiert in Frieden!
Jedwedem Anspruch auf dies Reich entsag' ich.
Ach, meines Geistes Schwingen sind gelähmt, 2380
Nicht Größe lockt mich mehr — Ihr habt's erreicht,
Ich bin nur noch der Schatten der Maria.
Gebrochen ist in langer Kerkerschmach

Der edle Mut — Ihr habt das Äußerste an mir
Gethan, habt mich zerstört in meiner Blüte! 2385
-— Jetzt macht ein Ende, Schwester! Sprecht es aus,
Das Wort, um dessentwillen Ihr gekommen,
Denn nimmer will ich glauben, daß Ihr kamt,
Um Euer Opfer grausam zu verhöhnen.
Sprecht dieses Wort aus! Sagt mir: „Ihr seid frei, 2390
„Maria! Meine Macht habt Ihr gefühlt,
„Jetzt lernet meinen Edelmut verehren.”
Sagt's, und ich will mein Leben, meine Freiheit
Als ein Geschenk aus Eurer Hand empfangen.
— Ein Wort macht alles ungeschehn. Ich warte 2395
Darauf. O! laßt mich's nicht zu lang erharren!
Weh Euch, wenn Ihr mit diesem Wort nicht endet!
Denn wenn Ihr jetzt nicht segenbringend, herrlich,
Wie eine Gottheit, von mir scheidet — Schwester!
Nicht um dies ganze reiche Eiland, nicht 2400
Um alle Länder, die das Meer umfaßt,
Möcht' ich vor Euch so stehn, wie Ihr vor mir!

Elisabeth.

Bekennt Ihr endlich Euch für überwunden?
Ist's aus mit Euren Ränken? Ist kein Mörder
Mehr unterweges? Will kein Abenteurer 2405
Für Euch die traur'ge Ritterschaft mehr wagen?
— Ja, es ist aus, Lady Maria. Ihr verführt
Mir keinen mehr. Die Welt hat andre Sorgen.
Es lüstet keinen, Euer — vierter Mann
Zu werden, denn Ihr tötet Eure Freier, 2410
Wie Eure Männer!

Maria (auffahrend).

Schwester, Schwester!
O Gott! Gott! Gieb mir Mäßigung!

Elisabeth (sieht sie lange mit einem Blick stolzer Verachtung an).

Das also sind die Reizungen, Lord Lester,
Die ungestraft kein Mann erblickt, daneben
Kein andres Weib sich wagen darf zu stellen!　　　　2415
Fürwahr! Der Ruhm war wohlfeil zu erlangen;
Es kostet nichts, die allgemeine Schönheit
Zu sein, als die gemeine sein für alle!

Maria.

Das ist zu viel!

Elisabeth (höhnisch lachend).

　　　　　　　Jetzt zeigt Ihr Euer wahres
Gesicht, bis jetzt war's nur die Larve.　　　　2420

Maria (von Zorn glühend, doch mit einer edeln Würde).

Ich habe menschlich, jugendlich gefehlt,
Die Macht verführte mich, ich hab' es nicht
Verheimlicht und verborgen, falschen Schein
Hab' ich verschmäht mit königlichem Freimut.
Das Ärgste weiß die Welt von mir, und ich　　　　2425
Kann sagen, ich bin besser als mein Ruf.
Weh Euch, wenn sie von Euren Thaten einst
Den Ehrenmantel zieht, womit Ihr gleißend
Die wilde Glut verstohlner Lüste deckt.
Nicht Ehrbarkeit habt Ihr von Eurer Mutter　　　　2430
Geerbt; man weiß, um welcher Tugend willen
Anna von Boulen das Schafott bestiegen.

Shrewsbury (tritt zwischen beide Königinnen).

O Gott des Himmels! Muß es dahin kommen!
Ist das die Mäßigung, die Unterwerfung,
Lady Maria?　　　　2435

Maria.

Mäßigung! Ich habe
Ertragen, was ein Mensch ertragen kann.
Fahr hin, lammherzige Gelassenheit!
Zum Himmel fliehe, leidende Geduld!
Spreng' endlich deine Bande, tritt hervor
Aus deiner Höhle, langverhaltner Groll! 2440
Und du, der dem gereizten Basilisk
Den Mordblick gab, leg' auf die Zunge mir
Den gift'gen Pfeil —

Shrewsbury.

O, sie ist außer sich!
Verzeih der Rasenden, der schwer Gereizten!
(Elisabeth, vor Zorn sprachlos, schießt wütende Blicke auf Marien.)

Leicester (in der heftigsten Unruhe, sucht die Elisabeth hinwegzuführen).

Höre
Die Wütende nicht an! Hinweg, hinweg 2445
Von diesem unglücksel'gen Ort!

Maria.

Der Thron von England ist durch einen Bastard
Entweiht, der Britten edelherzig Volk
Durch eine list'ge Gauklerin betrogen.
— Regierte Recht, so läget I h r vor mir 2450
Im Staube jetzt, denn ich bin Euer König.
(Elisabeth geht schnell ab, die Lords folgen ihr in der höchsten Bestürzung.)

Fünfter Auftritt.

Kennedy.

O, was habt Ihr gethan!   Sie geht in Wut!
Jetzt ist es aus, und alle Hoffnung schwindet.

Maria (noch ganz außer sich).

Sie geht in Wut!   Sie trägt den Tod im Herzen!

(Der Kennedy um den Hals fallend.)

O, wie mir wohl ist, Hanna!   Endlich, endlich,   2455
Nach Jahren der Erniedrigung, der Leiden,
Ein Augenblick der Rache, des Triumphs!
Wie Bergeslasten fällt's von meinem Herzen,
Das Messer stieß ich in der Feindin Brust.

Kennedy.

Unglückliche!   Der Wahnsinn reißt Euch hin,   2460
Ihr habt die Unversöhnliche verwundet.
Sie führt den Blitz, sie ist die Königin,
Vor ihrem Buhlen habt Ihr sie verhöhnt!

Maria.

Vor Lesters Augen hab' ich sie erniedrigt!
Er sah es, er bezeugte meinen Sieg!   2465
Wie ich sie niederschlug von ihrer Höhe,
Er stand dabei, mich stärkte seine Nähe!

Sechster Auftritt.

Mortimer zu den Vorigen.

Kennedy.

O Sir! Welch ein Erfolg —

Mortimer.

Ich hörte alles.

(Giebt der Amme ein Zeichen, sich auf ihren Posten zu begeben, und tritt näher.
Sein ganzes Wesen drückt eine heftige, leidenschaftliche Stimmung aus.)

Du hast gesiegt!   Du tratst sie in den Staub!
Du warst die Königin, s i e der Verbrecher. 2470
Ich bin entzückt von deinem Mut, ich bete
Dich an, wie eine Göttin groß und herrlich
Erscheinst du mir in diesem Augenblick.

Maria.

Ihr spracht mit Lestern, überbrachtet ihm
Mein Schreiben, mein Geschenk — O redet, Sir! 2475

Mortimer (mit glühenden Blicken sie betrachtend).

Wie dich der edle königliche Zorn
Umglänzte, deine Reize mir verklärte!
Du bist das schönste Weib auf dieser Erde!

Maria.

Ich bitt' Euch, Sir!   Stillt meine Ungeduld.
Was spricht Mylord? O sagt, was darf ich hoffen? 2480

Mortimer.

Wer?   Er?   Das ist ein Feiger, Elender!
Hofft nichts von ihm, verachtet ihn, vergeßt ihn!

Maria.

Was sagt Ihr?

Mortimer.

Er Euch retten und besitzen!
Er Euch! Er soll es wagen! Er! Mit mir
Muß er auf Tod und Leben darum kämpfen!   2485

Maria.

Ihr habt ihm meinen Brief nicht übergeben?
— O, dann ist's aus!

Mortimer.

Der Feige liebt das Leben.
Wer dich will retten und die Seine nennen,
Der muß den Tod beherzt umarmen können.

Maria.

Er will nichts für mich thun?   2490

Mortimer.

Nichts mehr von ihm!
Was kann er thun, und was bedarf man sein?
Ich will dich retten, ich allein!

Maria.

Ach, was vermögt Ihr!

Mortimer.

Täuschet Euch nicht mehr,
Als ob es noch wie gestern mit Euch stünde!
So wie die Königin jetzt von Euch ging,   2495
Wie dies Gespräch sich wendete, ist alles
Verloren, jeder Gnadenweg gesperrt.
Der That bedarf's jetzt, Kühnheit muß entscheiden,
Für alles werde alles frisch gewagt,
Frei müßt Ihr sein, noch eh der Morgen tagt.   2500

Maria.

Was sprecht Ihr? Diese Nacht! Wie ist das möglich?

Mortimer.

Hört, was beschlossen ist. Versammelt hab' ich
In heimlicher Kapelle die Gefährten;
Ein Priester hörte unsre Beichte an,
Ablaß ist uns erteilt für alle Schulden, 2505
Die wir begingen, Ablaß im voraus
Für alle, die wir noch begehen werden.
Das letzte Sakrament empfingen wir,
Und fertig sind wir zu der letzten Reise.

Maria.

O, welche fürchterliche Vorbereitung! 2510

Mortimer.

Dies Schloß ersteigen wir in dieser Nacht;
Der Schlüssel bin ich mächtig. Wir ermorden
Die Hüter, reißen dich aus deiner Kammer
Gewaltsam, sterben muß von unsrer Hand,
Daß niemand überbleibe, der den Raub 2515
Verraten könne, jede lebende Seele.

Maria.

Und Drury, Paulet, meine Kerkermeister?
O, eher werden sie ihr letztes Blut —

Mortimer.

Von meinem Dolche fallen sie zuerst!

Maria.

Was? Euer Oheim, Euer zweiter Vater? 2520

Mortimer.

Von meinen Händen stirbt er. Ich ermord' ihn.

Maria.

O blut'ger Frevel!

8

Mortimer.

Alle Frevel sind
Vergeben im voraus.   Ich kann das Ärgste
Begehen, und ich will's.

Maria.

O schrecklich, schrecklich!

Mortimer.

Und müßt' ich auch die Königin durchbohren,   2525
Ich hab' es auf die Hostie geschworen.

Maria.

Nein, Mortimer!   Eh so viel Blut um mich —

Mortimer.

Was ist mir alles Leben gegen dich
Und meine Liebe!   Mag der Welten Band
Sich lösen, eine zweite Wasserflut   2530
Herwogend alles Atmende verschlingen!
— Ich achte nichts mehr!   Eh ich dir entsage,
Eh nahe sich das Ende aller Tage.

Maria (zurücktretend).

Gott!   Welche Sprache, Sir, und — welche Blicke!
— Sie schrecken, sie verscheuchen mich.   2535

Mortimer (mit irren Blicken und im Ausdruck des stillen Wahnsinns).

Das Leben ist
Nur ein Moment, der Tod ist auch nur einer!
— Man schleife mich nach Tyburn, Glied für Glied
Zerreiße man mit glühnder Eisenzange,
(indem er heftig auf sie zugeht, mit ausgebreiteten Armen)
Wenn ich dich, Heißgeliebte, umfange —

Maria (zurücktretend).

Unsinniger, zurück! —   2540

Mortimer.

An dieser Brust,
Auf diesem Liebe atmenden Munde —

Maria.

Um Gotteswillen, Sir! Laßt mich hineingehn!

Mortimer.

Der ist ein Rasender, der nicht das Glück
Festhält in unauflöslicher Umarmung,
Wenn es ein Gott in seine Hand gegeben.   2545
Ich will dich retten, kost' es tausend Leben,
Ich rette dich, ich will es, doch, so wahr
Gott lebt! ich schwör's, ich will dich auch besitzen.

Maria.

O, will kein Gott, kein Engel mich beschützen!
Furchtbares Schicksal! Grimmig schleuderst du   2550
Von einem Schrecknis mich dem andern zu.
Bin ich geboren, nur die Wut zu wecken?
Verschwört sich Haß und Liebe, mich zu schrecken?

Mortimer.

Ja, glühend, wie sie hassen, lieb' ich dich!
Sie wollen dich enthaupten, diesen Hals,   2555
Den blendend weißen, mit dem Beil durchschneiden.
O, weihe du dem Lebensgott der Freuden,
Was du dem Hasse blutig opfern mußt!
Mit diesen Reizen, die nicht dein mehr sind,
Beselige den glücklichen Geliebten!   2560
Die schöne Locke, dieses seidne Haar,
Verfallen schon den finstern Todesmächten,
Gebrauch's, den Sklaven ewig zu umflechten!

Maria.

O, welche Sprache muß ich hören! Sir!

Mein Unglück sollt' Euch heilig sein, mein Leiden,   2565
Wenn es mein königliches Haupt nicht ist.

Mortimer.

Die Krone ist von deinem Haupt gefallen,
Du hast nichts mehr von ird'scher Majestät;
Versuch' es, laß dein Herrscherwort erschallen,
Ob dir ein Freund, ein Retter aufersteht.   2570
Nichts blieb dir, als die rührende Gestalt,
Der hohen Schönheit göttliche Gewalt,
Die läßt mich alles wagen und vermögen,
Die treibt dem Beil des Henkers mich entgegen —

Maria.

O, wer errettet mich von seiner Wut!   2575

Mortimer.

Verwegner Dienst belohnt sich auch verwegen!
Warum verspritzt der Tapfere sein Blut?
Ist Leben doch des Lebens höchstes Gut!
Ein Rasender, der es umsonst verschleudert!
Erst will ich ruhn an seiner wärmsten Brust —   2580
(Er preßt sie heftig an sich.)

Maria.

O, muß ich Hilfe rufen gegen den Mann,
Der mein Erretter —

Mortimer.

        Du bist nicht gefühllos;
Nicht kalter Strenge klagt die Welt dich an,
Dich kann die heiße Liebesbitte rühren,
Du hast den Sänger Rizzio beglückt,   2585
Und jener Bothwell durfte dich entführen.

Maria.

Vermessener!

Mortimer.

Er war nur dein Tyrann!
Du zittertest vor ihm, da du ihn liebtest!
Wenn nur der Schrecken dich gewinnen kann,
Beim Gott der Hölle! —   2590

Maria.

Laßt mich!   Raset Ihr?

Mortimer.

Erzittern sollst du auch vor mir!

Kennedy (hereinstürzend).

Man naht.   Man kommt.   Bewaffnet Volk erfüllt
Den ganzen Garten.

Mortimer (auffahrend und zum Degen greifend).

Ich beschütze dich!

Maria.

O Hanna! Rette mich aus seinen Händen!
Wo find ich Ärmste einen Zufluchtsort?   2595
Zu welchem Heiligen soll ich mich wenden?
Hier ist Gewalt, und drinnen ist der Mord.
(Sie flieht dem Hause zu, Kennedy folgt.)

Siebenter Auftritt.

Mortimer. Paulet und Drury, welche außer sich hereinstürzen.
Gefolge eilt über die Szene.

Paulet.

Verschließt die Pforten.   Zieht die Brücken auf!

Mortimer.

Oheim, was ist's?

Paulet.

Wo ist die Mörderin?
Hinab mit ihr ins finsterste Gefängnis!   2600

Mortimer.

Was giebt's?   Was ist geschehen?

Paulet.

Die Königin!
Verfluchte Hände!   Teuflisches Erkühnen!

Mortimer.

Die Königin!   Welche Königin?

Paulet.

Von England!
Sie ist ermordet auf der Londner Straßen!

(Eilt ins Haus.)

Achter Auftritt.

Mortimer, gleich darauf **Okelly.**

Mortimer.

Bin ich im Wahnwitz?   Kam nicht eben jemand   2605
Vorbei und rief: die Königin sei ermordet?
Nein, nein, mir träumte nur.   Ein Fieberwahn
Bringt mir als wahr und wirklich vor den Sinn,
Was die Gedanken gräßlich mir erfüllt.
Wer kommt?   Es ist Okell'.   So schreckenvoll!   2610

Okelly (hereinstürzend).

Flieht, Mortimer!   Flieht!   Alles ist verloren.

Mortimer.

Was ist verloren?

Okelly.

Fragt nicht lange.   Denkt
Auf schnelle Flucht!

Mortimer.

Was giebt's denn?

Okelly.

Sauvage führte
Den Streich, der Rasende.

Mortimer.

So ist es wahr?

Okelly.

Wahr, wahr!   O, rettet Euch!   2615

Mortimer.

Sie ist ermordet,
Und auf den Thron von England steigt Maria!

Okelly.

Ermordet!   Wer sagt das?

Mortimer.

Ihr selbst!

Okelly.

Sie lebt!
Und ich und Ihr, wir alle sind des Todes.

Mortimer.

Sie lebt!

Okelly.

Der Stoß ging fehl, der Mantel fing ihn auf,
Und Shrewsbury entwaffnete den Mörder.   2620

Mortimer.

Sie lebt!

Okelly.

Lebt, um uns alle zu verderben!
Kommt, man umzingelt schon den Park.

Mortimer.

Wer hat
Das Rasende gethan?

Okelly.

Der Barnabit'
Aus Toulon war's, den Ihr in der Kapelle
Tiefsinnig sitzen saht, als uns der Mönch   2625
Das Anathem ausdeutete, worin
 Der Papst die Königin mit dem Fluch belegt.
Das Nächste, Kürzeste wollt' er ergreifen,
Mit einem kecken Streich die Kirche Gottes
Befrein, die Martyrkrone sich erwerben;   2630
Dem Priester nur vertraut' er seine That,
Und auf dem Londner Weg ward sie vollbracht.

Mortimer
(nach einem langen Stillschweigen).

O, dich verfolgt ein grimmig wütend Schicksal,
Unglückliche! Jetzt — ja, jetzt mußt du sterben,
Dein Engel selbst bereitet deinen Fall.   2635

Okelly.

Sagt! Wohin wendet Ihr die Flucht? Ich gehe,
Mich in des Nordens Wäldern zu verbergen.

Mortimer

Flieht hin und Gott geleite Eure Flucht!
Ich bleibe. Noch versuch' ich's, sie zu retten,
Wo nicht, auf ihrem Sarge mir zu betten.   2640
(Gehen ab zu verschiedenen Seiten.)

Vierter Aufzug.

Vorzimmer.

Erster Auftritt.

Graf Aubespine, Kent und Leicester.

Aubespine.

Wie steht's um Ihro Majestät? Mylords,
Ihr seht mich noch ganz außer mir vor Schrecken.
Wie ging das zu? Wie konnte das in Mitte
Des allertreuesten Volks geschehen?

Leicester.

                  Es geschah
Durch keinen aus dem Volke. Der es that,   2645
War Eures Königs Unterthan, ein Franke.

Aubespine.

Ein Rasender gewißlich!

Kent.

               Ein Papist,
Graf Aubespine!

Zweiter Auftritt.

Vorige. Burleigh im Gespräch mit **Davison.**

Burleigh.

Sogleich muß der Befehl
Zur Hinrichtung gefaßt und mit dem Siegel
Versehen werden — Wenn er ausgefertigt,   2650
Wird er der Königin zur Unterschrift
Gebracht.   Geht!   Keine Zeit ist zu verlieren.

Davison.

Es soll geschehn.   (Geht ab.)

Aubespine (Burleigh entgegen.)

Mylord, mein treues Herz
Teilt die gerechte Freude dieser Insel.
Lob sei dem Himmel, der den Mörderstreich   2655
Gewehrt von diesem königlichen Haupt!

Burleigh.

Er sei gelobt, der unsrer Feinde Bosheit
Zu schanden machte!

Aubespine.

Mög' ihn Gott verdammen,
Den Thäter dieser fluchenswerten That!

Burleigh.

Den Thäter und den schändlichen Erfinder.   2660

Aubespine (zu Kent).

Gefällt es Eurer Herrlichkeit, Lordmarschall,
Bei Ihro Majestät mich einzuführen,
Daß ich den Glückwunsch meines Herrn und Königs
Zu ihren Füßen schuldigst niederlege —

Burleigh.

Bemüht Euch nicht, Graf Aubespine.   2665

Aubespine (offiziös).

                                            Ich weiß,
Lord Burleigh, was mir obliegt.

Burleigh.

                                    Euch liegt ob,
Die Insel auf das schleunigste zu räumen.

Aubespine (tritt erstaunt zurück.)

Was!   Wie ist das?

Burleigh.

                            Der heilige Charakter
Beschützt Euch heute noch, und morgen nicht mehr.

Aubespine.

Und was ist mein Verbrechen?   2670

Burleigh.

                                    Wenn ich es
Genannt, so ist es nicht mehr zu vergeben.

Aubespine.

Ich hoffe, Lord, das Recht der Abgesandten —

Burleigh.

Schützt — Reichsverräter nicht.

Leicester und Kent.

                        Ha! Was ist das!

Aubespine.

                                            Mylord!
Bedenkt Ihr wohl —

Burleigh.

                    Ein Paß, von Eurer Hand
Geschrieben, fand sich in des Mörders Tasche.   2675

Kent.

Ist's möglich?

Aubespine.

Viele Pässe teil' ich aus,
Ich kann der Menschen Innres nicht erforschen.

Burleigh.

In Eurem Hause beichtete der Mörder.

Aubespine.

Mein Haus ist offen.

Burleigh.

Jedem Feinde Englands.

Aubespine.

Ich fordre Untersuchung.　　　　　　　　　　　　　2680

Burleigh.

Fürchtet sie!

Aubespine.

In meinem Haupt ist mein Monarch verletzt,
Zerreißen wird er das geschloßne Bündnis.

Burleigh.

Zerrissen schon hat es die Königin,
England wird sich mit Frankreich nicht vermählen.
Mylord von Kent!　Ihr übernehmet es,　　　　　　　2685
Den Grafen sicher an das Meer zu bringen.
Das aufgebrachte Volk hat sein Hotel
Gestürmt, wo sich ein ganzes Arsenal
Von Waffen fand; es droht, ihn zu zerreißen,
Wie er sich zeigt; verberget ihn, bis sich　　　　　　2690
Die Wut gelegt — Ihr haftet für sein Leben!

Aubespine.

Ich gehe, ich verlasse dieses Land,

Wo man der Völker Recht mit Füßen tritt
Und mit Verträgen spielt — doch mein Monarch
Wird blut'ge Rechenschaft —   2695

Burleigh.

Er hole sie!
(Kent und Aubespine gehen ab.)

Dritter Auftritt.

Leicester und **Burleigh.**

Leicester.

So löst Ihr selbst das Bündnis wieder auf,
Das Ihr geschäftig unberufen knüpftet.
Ihr habt um England wenig Dank verdient,
Mylord, die Mühe konntet Ihr Euch sparen.

Burleigh.

Mein Zweck war gut. Gott leitete es anders.   2700
Wohl dem, der sich nichts Schlimmeres bewußt ist!

Leicester.

Man kennt Cecils geheimnisreiche Miene,
Wenn er die Jagd auf Staatsverbrechen macht.
— Jetzt, Lord, ist eine gute Zeit für Euch.
Ein ungeheurer Frevel ist geschehn,   2705
Und noch umhüllt Geheimnis seine Thäter.
Jetzt wird ein Inquisitionsgericht
Eröffnet. Wort und Blicke werden abgewogen,
Gedanken selber vor Gericht gestellt.
Da seid Ihr der allwicht'ge Mann, der Atlas   2710
Des Staats, ganz England liegt auf Euren Schultern.

Burleigh.

In Euch, Mylord, erkenn' ich meinen Meister;
Denn solchen Sieg, als Eure Rednerkunst
Erfocht, hat meine nie davongetragen.

Leicester.

Was meint Ihr damit, Lord?   2715

Burleigh.

Ihr wart es doch, der hinter meinem Rücken
Die Königin nach Fotheringhayschloß
Zu locken wußte?

Leicester.

                     Hinter Eurem Rücken!
Wann scheuten meine Thaten Eure Stirn?

Burleigh.

Die Königin hättet Ihr nach Fotheringhay   2720
Geführt? Nicht doch! Ihr habt die Königin
Nicht hingeführt! — Die Königin war es,
Die so gefällig war, Euch hinzuführen.

Leicester.

Was wollt Ihr damit sagen, Lord?

Burleigh.

                                 Die edle
Person, die Ihr die Königin dort spielen ließt!   2725
Der herrliche Triumph, den Ihr der arglos
Vertrauenden bereitet — Güt'ge Fürstin!
So schamlos frech verspottete man dich,
So schonungslos wardst du dahingegeben!
— Das also ist die Großmut und die Milde,   2730
Die Euch im Staatsrat plötzlich angewandelt!

Darum ist diese Stuart ein so schwacher,
Verachtungswerter Feind, daß es der Müh'
Nicht lohnt, mit ihrem Blut sich zu beflecken!
Ein feiner Plan! Fein zugespitzt! Nur schade,   2735
Zu fein geschärfet, daß die Spitze brach!

Leicester.

Nichtswürdiger! Gleich folgt mir! An dem Throne
Der Königin sollt Ihr mir Rede stehn.

Burleigh.

Dort trefft Ihr mich — Und sehet zu, Mylord,
Daß Euch dort die Beredsamkeit nicht fehle! (Geht ab.)   2740

Vierter Auftritt.

Leicester allein, darauf **Mortimer.**

Leicester.

Ich bin entdeckt, ich bin durchschaut — Wie kam
Der Unglückselige auf meine Spuren!
Weh mir, wenn er Beweise hat! Erfährt
Die Königin, daß zwischen mir und der Maria
Verständnisse gewesen — Gott! Wie schuldig   2745
Steh' ich vor ihr! Wie hinterlistig treulos
Erscheint mein Rat, mein unglückseliges
Bemühn, nach Fotheringhay sie zu führen!
Grausam verspottet sieht sie sich von mir,
An die verhaßte Feindin sich verraten!   2750
O, nimmer, nimmer kann sie das verzeihn!
Vorherbedacht wird alles nun erscheinen,
Auch diese bittre Wendung des Gesprächs,
Der Gegnerin Triumph und Hohngelächter,

Ja, selbst die Mörderhand, die blutig, schrecklich, 2755
Ein unerwartet ungeheures Schicksal,
Dazwischen kam, werd' ich bewaffnet haben!
Nicht Rettung seh' ich, nirgends! Ha! Wer kommt!

Mortimer
(kommt in der heftigsten Unruhe und blickt scheu umher).

Graf Lester! Seid Ihr's? Sind wir ohne Zeugen?

Leicester.

Unglücklicher, hinweg! Was sucht Ihr hier? 2760

Mortimer.

Man ist auf unsrer Spur, auf Eurer auch;
Nehmt Euch in acht!

Leicester.
Hinweg, hinweg!

Mortimer.
Man weiß,

Daß bei dem Grafen Aubespine geheime
Versammlung war —

Leicester.
Was kümmert's mich! 2765

Mortimer.
Daß sich der Mörder

Dabei befunden —

Leicester.
Das ist Eure Sache!

Verwegener! Was unterfangt Ihr Euch,
In Euren blut'gen Frevel m i c h zu flechten?
Verteidigt Eure bösen Händel selbst!

Mortimer.

So hört mich doch nur an. 2770

Leicester (in heftigem Zorn).

Geht in die Hölle!

Was hängt Ihr Euch, gleich einem bösen Geist,
An meine Fersen! Fort! Ich kenn' Euch nicht,
Ich habe nichts gemein mit Meuchelmördern.

Mortimer.

Ihr wollt nicht hören.   Euch zu warnen komm' ich;
Auch Eure Schritte sind verraten —   2775

Leicester.

Ha!

Mortimer.

Der Großschatzmeister war zu Fotheringhay
Sogleich, nachdem die Unglücksthat geschehn **war,**
Der Königin Zimmer wurden streng durchsucht,
Da fand sich —

Leicester.

Was?

Mortimer.

Ein angefangner Brief
Der Königin an Euch —   2780

Leicester.

Die Unglücksel'ge!

Mortimer.

Worin sie Euch auffordert, Wort zu halten,
Euch das Versprechen ihrer Hand erneuert,
Des Bildnisses gedenkt —

Leicester.

Tod und Verdammnis!

Mortimer.

Lord Burleigh hat den Brief.

Leicester.

      Ich bin verloren!

(Er geht während der folgenden Rede Mortimers verzweiflungsvoll auf und
nieder.)

Mortimer.

Ergreift den Augenblick! Kommt ihm zuvor!   2785
Errettet Euch, errettet sie — Schwört Euch
Heraus, ersinnt Entschuldigungen, wendet
Das Ärgste ab! Ich selbst kann nichts mehr thun.
Zerstreut sind die Gefährten, auseinander
Gesprengt ist unser ganzer Bund. Ich eile   2790
Nach Schottland, neue Freunde dort zu sammeln.
An Euch ist's jetzt, versucht, was Euer Ansehn,
Was eine kecke Stirn vermag!

Leicester

(steht still, plötzlich besonnen).

      Das will ich.

(Er geht nach der Thüre, öffnet sie und ruft.)

He da! Trabanten!

(Zu dem Offizier, der mit Bewaffneten hereintritt.)

     Diesen Staatsverräter
Nehmt in Verwahrung und bewacht ihn wohl!   2795
Die schändlichste Verschwörung ist entdeckt,
Ich bringe selbst der Königin die Botschaft.

(Er geht ab.)

Mortimer

(steht anfangs starr vor Erstaunen, faßt sich aber bald und sieht Leicestern mit
einem Blick der tiefsten Verachtung nach.)

Ha, Schändlicher! — Doch ich verdiene das!
Wer hieß mich auch dem Elenden vertrauen?
Weg über meinen Nacken schreitet er,   2800

Mein Fall muß ihm die Rettungsbrücke bauen.
— So rette dich! Verschlossen bleibt mein Mund,
Ich will dich nicht in mein Verderben flechten.
Auch nicht im Tode mag ich deinen Bund,
Das Leben ist das einz'ge Gut des Schlechten.   2805
(Zu dem Offizier der Wache, der hervortritt, um ihn gefangen zu nehmen.)
Was willst du, feiler Sklav der Tyrannei?
Ich spotte deiner, ich bin frei! (Einen Dolch ziehend.)

Offizier.

Er ist bewehrt — Entreißt ihm seinen Dolch!
(Sie bringen auf ihn ein, er erwehrt sich ihrer.)

Mortimer.

Und frei im letzten Augenblicke soll
Mein Herz sich öffnen, meine Zunge lösen!   2810
Fluch und Verderben euch, die ihren Gott
Und ihre wahre Königin verraten!
Die von der irdischen Maria sich
Treulos, wie von der himmlischen, gewendet,
Sich dieser Bastardkönigin verkauft —   2815

Offizier.

Hört ihr die Lästrung! Auf! Ergreifet ihn!

Mortimer.

Geliebte! Nicht erretten konnt' ich dich,
So will ich dir ein männlich Beispiel geben.
Maria, heil'ge, bitt' für mich
Und nimm mich zu dir in dein himmlisch Leben!   2820
(Er durchsticht sich mit dem Dolch und fällt der Wache in die Arme.)

Zimmer der Königin.

Fünfter Auftritt.

Elisabeth, einen Brief in der Hand. Burleigh.

Elisabeth.

Mich hinzuführen! Solchen Spott mit mir
Zu treiben! Der Verräter! Im Triumph
Vor seiner Buhlerin mich aufzuführen!
O, so ward noch kein Weib betrogen, Burleigh!

Burleigh.

Ich kann es noch nicht fassen, wie es ihm, 2825
Durch welche Macht, durch welche Zauberkünste
Gelang, die Klugheit meiner Königin
So sehr zu überraschen.

Elisabeth.

O, ich sterbe
Vor Scham! Wie mußt' er meiner Schwäche spotten!
S i e glaubt' ich zu erniedrigen und war, 2830
Ich selber, ihres Spottes Ziel!

Burleigh.

Du siehst nun ein, wie treu i c h dir geraten!

Elisabeth.

O, ich bin schwer dafür gestraft, daß ich
Von Eurem weisen Rate mich entfernt!
Und sollt' ich i h m nicht glauben? In den Schwüren 2835
Der treusten Liebe einen Fallstrick fürchten?
Wem darf ich trau'n, wenn e r mich hinterging?
Er, den ich groß gemacht vor allen Großen,

Der mir der Nächste stets am Herzen war,
Dem ich verstattete, an diesem Hof 2840
Sich wie der Herr, der König zu betragen!

Burleigh.

Und zu derselben Zeit verriet er dich
An diese falsche Königin von Schottland!

Elisabeth.

O, sie bezahle mir's mit ihrem Blut!
— Sagt! Ist das Urteil abgefaßt? 2845

Burleigh.

                                   Es liegt
Bereit, wie du befohlen.

Elisabeth.

                       Sterben soll sie!
Er soll sie fallen sehn und nach ihr fallen.
Verstoßen hab' ich ihn aus meinem Herzen,
Fort ist die Liebe, Rache füllt es ganz.
So hoch er stand, so tief und schmählich sei 2850
Sein Sturz! Er sei ein Denkmal meiner Strenge,
Wie er ein Beispiel meiner Schwäche war.
Man führ' ihn nach dem Tower; ich werde Peers
Ernennen, die ihn richten. Hingegeben
Sei er der ganzen Strenge des Gesetzes. 2855

Burleigh.

Er wird sich zu dir drängen, sich rechtfert'gen —

Elisabeth.

Wie kann er sich rechtfert'gen? Überführt
Ihn nicht der Brief? O, sein Verbrechen ist
Klar, wie der Tag!

Burleigh.

Doch du bist mild und gnädig;
Sein Anblick, seine mächt'ge Gegenwart —　　　　2860

Elisabeth.

Ich will ihn nicht sehn.　Niemals, niemals wieder!
Habt Ihr Befehl gegeben, daß man ihn
Zurückweist, wenn er kommt?

Burleigh.

So ist's befohlen!

Page (tritt ein).

Mylord von Lester!

Königin.

Der Abscheuliche!
Ich will ihn nicht sehn.　Sagt ihm, daß ich ihn　　　2865
Nicht sehen will.

Page.

Das wag' ich nicht dem Lord
Zu sagen, und er würde mir's nicht glauben.

Königin.

So hab' ich ihn erhöht, daß meine Diener
Vor seinem Ansehn mehr als meinem zittern!

Burleigh (zum Pagen).

Die Königin verbiet' ihm, sich zu nahn!　　　　2870
(Page geht zögernd ab.)

Königin (nach einer Pause).

Wenn's dennoch möglich wäre — Wenn er sich
Rechtfert'gen könnte! — Sagt mir, könnt' es nicht
Ein Fallstrick sein, den mir Maria legte,

Mich mit dem treusten Freunde zu entzwein?
O, sie ist eine abgefeimte Bübin! 2875
Wenn sie den Brief nur schrieb, mir gift'gen Argwohn
Ins Herz zu streun, ihn, den sie haßt, ins Unglück
Zu stürzen —

Burleigh.

Aber, Königin, erwäge —

Sechster Auftritt.

Vorige. Leicester.

Leicester

(reißt die Thüre mit Gewalt auf und tritt mit gebieterischem Wesen herein).

Den Unverschämten will ich sehn, der mir
Das Zimmer meiner Königin verbietet. 2880

Elisabeth.

Ha, der Verwegene!

Leicester.

Mich abzuweisen!
Wenn sie für einen Burleigh sichtbar ist,
So ist sie's auch für mich!

Burleigh.

Ihr seid sehr kühn, Mylord,
Hier wider die Erlaubnis einzustürmen.

Leicester.

Ihr seid sehr frech, Lord, hier das Wort zu nehmen. 2885
Erlaubnis! Was! Es ist an diesem Hofe
Niemand, durch dessen Mund Graf Lester sich
Erlauben und verbieten lassen kann!

(Indem er sich der Elisabeth demütig nähert.)

Aus meiner Königin eignem Mund will ich —

Elisabeth (ohne ihn anzusehen).

Aus meinem Angesicht, Nichtswürdiger!   2890

Leicester.

Nicht meine gütige Elisabeth,
Den Lord vernehm' ich, meinen Feind, in diesen
Unholden Worten — Ich berufe mich auf m e i n e
Elisabeth — du liehest i h m dein Ohr,
Das Gleiche fordr' ich.   2895

Elisabeth.

         Redet, Schändlicher!
Vergrößert Euren Frevel! Leugnet ihn!

Leicester.

Laßt diesen Überlästigen sich erst
Entfernen — Tretet ab, Mylord — Was ich
Mit meiner Königin zu verhandeln habe,
Braucht keinen Zeugen. Geht.   2900

Elisabeth (zu Burleigh).

         Bleibt.   Ich befehl' es!

Leicester.

Was soll der dritte zwischen dir und mir!
Mit meiner angebeteten Monarchin
Hab' ich's zu thun — Die Rechte meines Platzes
Behaupt' ich — Es sind heil'ge Rechte!
Und ich bestehe drauf, daß sich der Lord   2905
Entferne!

Elisabeth.

Euch geziemt die stolze Sprache!

Leicester.

Wohl ziemt sie mir, denn ich bin der Beglückte,

Dem deine Gunst den hohen Vorzug gab;
Das hebt mich über ihn und über alle!
Dein Herz verlieh mir diesen stolzen Rang,   2910
Und was die Liebe gab, werd' ich, bei Gott!
Mit meinem Leben zu behaupten wissen.
Er geh' — und zweier Augenblicke nur
Bedarf's, mich mit dir zu verständigen.

Elisabeth.

Ihr hofft umsonst, mich listig zu beschwatzen.   2915

Leicester.

Beschwatzen konnte dich der Plauderer,
Ich aber will zu deinem Herzen reden,
Und was ich im Vertraun auf deine Gunst
Gewagt, will ich auch nur vor deinem Herzen
Rechtfertigen — Kein anderes Gericht   2920
Erkenn' ich über mir, als deine Neigung!

Elisabeth.

Schamloser! Eben diese ist's, die Euch zuerst
Verdammt — Zeigt ihm den Brief, Mylord!

Burleigh.

Hier ist er!

Leicester

(durchläuft den Brief, ohne die Fassung zu verlieren).

Das ist der Stuart Hand!

Elisabeth.

Lest und verstummt!

Leicester (nachdem er gelesen, ruhig).

Der Schein ist gegen mich; doch darf ich hoffen,   2925
Daß ich nicht nach dem Schein gerichtet werde!

Elisabeth.

Könnt Ihr es leugnen, daß Ihr mit der Stuart
In heimlichem Verständnis wart, ihr Bildnis
Empfingt, ihr zur Befreiung Hoffnung machtet?

Leicester.

Leicht wäre mir's, wenn ich mich schuldig fühlte,   2930
Das Zeugnis einer Feindin zu verwerfen!
Doch frei ist mein Gewissen; ich bekenne,
Daß sie die Wahrheit schreibt!

Elisabeth.

     Nun denn,
Unglücklicher!

Burleigh.

   Sein eigner Mund verdammt ihn.

Elisabeth.

Aus meinen Augen! In den Tower — Verräter!   2935

Leicester.

Der bin ich nicht. Ich hab' gefehlt, daß ich
Aus diesem Schritt dir ein Geheimnis machte;
Doch redlich war die Absicht, es geschah,
Die Feindin zu erforschen, zu verderben.

Elisabeth.

Elende Ausflucht! —   2940

Burleigh.

    Wie, Mylord? Ihr glaubt —

Leicester.

Ich habe ein gewagtes Spiel gespielt,
Ich weiß, und nur Graf Lester durfte sich

An diesem Hofe solcher That erkühnen.
Wie ich die Stuart hasse, weiß die Welt.
Der Rang, den ich bekleide, das Vertrauen, 2945
Wodurch die Königin mich ehrt, muß jeden Zweifel
In meine treue Meinung niederschlagen.
Wohl darf der Mann, den deine Gunst vor allen
Auszeichnet, einen eignen kühnen Weg
Einschlagen, seine Pflicht zu thun. 2950

Burleigh.

                Warum,
Wenn's eine gute Sache war, verschwiegt Ihr?

Leicester.

Mylord! Ihr pflegt zu schwatzen, eh Ihr handelt,
Und seid die Glocke Eurer Thaten. Das
Ist Eure Weise, Lord. Die meine ist,
Erst handeln und dann reden! 2955

Burleigh.

Ihr redet jetzo, weil Ihr müßt.

Leicester

(ihn stolz und höhnisch mit den Augen messend).

               Und Ihr
Berühmt Euch, eine wundergroße That
Ins Werk gerichtet, Eure Königin
Gerettet, die Verrätherei entlarvt
Zu haben — Alles wißt Ihr, Eurem Scharfblick 2960
Kann nichts entgehen, meint Ihr — Armer Prahler!
Trotz Eurer Spürkunst war Maria Stuart
Noch heute frei, wenn ich es nicht verhindert.

Burleigh.

Ihr hättet —

Leicester.

Ich, Mylord.   Die Königin
Vertraute sich dem Mortimer, sie schloß   2965
Ihr Innerstes ihm auf, sie ging so weit,
Ihm einen blut'gen Auftrag gegen die Maria
Zu geben, da der Oheim sich mit Abscheu
Von einem gleichen Antrag abgewendet —
Sagt! Ist es nicht so?   2970
           (Königin und Burleigh sehen einander betroffen an.)

Burleigh.

                    Wie gelangtet Ihr
Dazu? —

Leicester.

           Ist's nicht so? — Nun, Mylord! Wo hattet
Ihr Eure tausend Augen, nicht zu sehn,
Daß dieser Mortimer Euch hinterging?
Daß er ein wütender Papist, ein Werkzeug
Der Guisen, ein Geschöpf der Stuart war,   2975
Ein keck entschloßner Schwärmer, der gekommen,
Die Stuart zu befrein, die Königin
Zu morden —

Elisabeth (mit dem äußersten Erstaunen).

           Dieser Mortimer!

Leicester.

                    Er war's, durch den
Maria Unterhandlung mit mir pflog,
Den ich auf diesem Wege kennen lernte.   2980
Noch heute sollte sie aus ihrem Kerker
Gerissen werden, diesen Augenblick
Entdeckte mir's sein eigner Mund; ich ließ ihn
Gefangen nehmen, und in der Verzweiflung,
Sein Werk vereitelt, sich entlarvt zu sehn,   2985
Gab er sich selbst den Tod!

Elisabeth.

　　　　　　O, ich bin unerhört
Betrogen — dieser Mortimer!

Burleigh.

　　　　　　　Und jetzt
Geschah das? Jetzt, nachdem ich Euch verlassen?

Leicester.

Ich muß um meinetwillen sehr beklagen,
Daß es dies Ende mit ihm nahm. Sein Zeugnis,　　2990
Wenn er noch lebte, würde mich vollkommen
Gereinigt, aller Schuld entledigt haben.
Drum übergab ich ihn des Richters Hand.
Die strengste Rechtsform sollte meine Unschuld
Vor aller Welt bewähren und besiegeln.　　2995

Burleigh.

Er tötete sich, sagt Ihr. Er sich selber? Oder
Ihr ihn?

Leicester.

　　　　Unwürdiger Verdacht! Man höre
Die Wache ab, der ich ihn übergab!
(Er geht an die Thür und ruft hinaus. Der Offizier der Leibwache tritt herein.)
Erstattet Ihrer Majestät Bericht,
Wie dieser Mortimer umkam!　　3000

Offizier.

　　　　　　Ich hielt die Wache
Im Vorsaal, als Mylord die Thüre schnell
Eröffnete und mir befahl, den Ritter
Als einen Staatsverräter zu verhaften.
Wir sahen ihn hierauf in Wut geraten,
Den Dolch ziehn unter heftiger Verwünschung　　3005
Der Königin und, eh wir's hindern konnten,

Ihn in die Brust sich stoßen, daß er tot
Zu Boden stürzte —

Leicester.

Es ist gut. Ihr könnt
Abtreten, Sir! Die Königin weiß genug!

(Offizier geht ab.)

Elisabeth.

O, welcher Abgrund von Abscheulichkeiten!   3010

Leicester.

Wer war's nun, der dich rettete? War es
Mylord von Burleigh? Wußt' er die Gefahr,
Die dich umgab? War e r's, der sie von dir
Gewandt? — Dein treuer Lester war dein Engel!

Burleigh.

Graf! Dieser Mortimer starb Euch sehr gelegen.   3015

Elisabeth.

Ich weiß nicht, was ich sagen soll. Ich glaub' Euch,
Und glaub' Euch nicht. Ich denke, Ihr seid schuldig,
Und seid es nicht! O, die Verhaßte, die
Mir all dies Weh bereitet!

Leicester.

Sie muß sterben.
Jetzt stimm' ich selbst für ihren Tod. Ich riet   3020
Dir an, das Urteil unvollstreckt zu lassen,
Bis sich aufs neu ein Arm für sie erhübe.
Dies ist geschehn — und ich bestehe drauf,
Daß man das Urteil ungesäumt vollstrecke.

Burleigh.

Ihr rietet dazu! Ihr!   3025

Leicester.

So sehr es mich
Empört, zu einem Äußersten zu greifen,
Ich sehe nun und glaube, daß die Wohlfahrt
Der Königin dies blut'ge Opfer heischt;
Drum trag' ich darauf an, daß der Befehl
Zur Hinrichtung gleich ausgefertigt werde! 3030

Burleigh (zur Königin).

Da es Mylord so treu und ernstlich meint,
So trag' ich darauf an, daß die Vollstreckung
Des Richterspruchs ihm übertragen werde.

Leicester.

Mir!

Burleigh.

Euch. Nicht besser könnt Ihr den Verdacht,
Der jetzt noch auf Euch lastet, widerlegen, 3035
Als wenn Ihr s i e, die Ihr geliebt zu haben
Beschuldigt werdet, selbst enthaupten lasset.

Elisabeth (Leicestern mit den Augen fixierend).

Mylord rät gut. So sei's, und dabei bleib' es.

Leicester.

Mich sollte billig meines Ranges Höh'
Von einem Auftrag dieses traur'gen Inhalts 3040
Befrein, der sich in jedem Sinne besser
Für einen Burleigh ziemen mag als mich.
Wer seiner Königin so nahe steht,
Der sollte nichts Unglückliches vollbringen.
Jedoch, um meinen Eifer zu bewähren, 3045
Um meiner Königin genugzuthun,
Begeb' ich mich des Vorrechts meiner Würde
Und übernehme die verhaßte Pflicht.

Elisabeth.

Lord Burleigh teile sie mit Euch! (Zu diesem.)

Tragt Sorge,

Daß der Befehl gleich ausgefertigt werde. 3050

(Burleigh geht. Man hört draußen ein Getümmel.)

Siebenter Auftritt.

Graf von Kent zu den Vorigen.

Elisabeth.

Was giebt's, Mylord von Kent? Was für ein Auflauf
Erregt die Stadt — Was ist es?

Kent.

Königin,

Es ist das Volk, das den Palast umlagert;
Es fordert heftig dringend, dich zu sehn.

Elisabeth.

Was will mein Volk? 3055

Kent.

Der Schrecken geht durch London,
Dein Leben sei bedroht, es gehen Mörder
Umher, vom Papste wider dich gesendet.
Verschworen seien die Katholischen,
Die Stuart aus dem Kerker mit Gewalt
Zu reißen und zur Königin auszurufen. 3060
Der Pöbel glaubt's und wütet. Nur das Haupt
Der Stuart, das noch heute fällt, kann ihn
Beruhigen.

Elisabeth.

Wie? Soll mir Zwang geschehn?

Kent.

Sie sind entschlossen, eher nicht zu weichen,
Bis du das Urteil unterzeichnet hast. 3065

Achter Auftritt.

Burleigh und **Davison** mit einer Schrift. **Die Vorigen.**

Elisabeth.

Was bringt Ihr, Davison?

Davison (nähert sich, ernsthaft).

Du hast befohlen,

O Königin —

Elisabeth.

Was ist's?

(Indem sie die Schrift ergreifen will, schauert sie zusammen und fährt zurück.)

O Gott!

Burleigh.

Gehorche

Der Stimme des Volks, sie ist die Stimme Gottes.

Elisabeth (unentschlossen mit sich selbst kämpfend).

O meine Lords! Wer sagt mir, ob ich wirklich
Die Stimme meines ganzen Volks, die Stimme   3070
Der Welt vernehme! Ach, wie sehr befürcht' ich,
Wenn ich dem Wunsch der Menge nun gehorcht,
Daß eine ganz verschiedne Stimme sich
Wird hören lassen — ja, daß eben die,
Die jetzt gewaltsam zu der That mich treiben,   3075
Mich, wenn's vollbracht ist, strenge tadeln **werden**!

Neunter Auftritt.

Graf Shrewsbury zu den Vorigen.

Shrewsbury (kommt in großer Bewegung).

Man will dich übereilen, Königin!

10

O halte fest, sei standhaft!

(Indem er Davison mit der Schrift gewahr wird.

Oder ist es

Geschehen? Ist es wirklich? Ich erblicke
Ein unglückselig Blatt in dieser Hand.　　　　　　　3080
Das komme meiner Königin jetzt nicht
Vor Augen.

Elisabeth.

Edler Shrewsbury! Man zwingt mich.

Shrewsbury.

Wer kann dich zwingen? Du bist Herrscherin,
Hier gilt es, deine Majestät zu zeigen!
Gebiete Schweigen jenen rohen Stimmen,　　　　　　3085
Die sich erdreisten, deinem Königswillen
Zwang anzuthun, dein Urteil zu regieren.
Die Furcht, ein blinder Wahn bewegt das Volk,
Du selbst bist außer dir, bist schwer gereizt,
Du bist ein Mensch, und jetzt kannst du nicht richten.　3090

Burleigh.

Gerichtet ist schon längst. Hier ist kein Urteil
Zu fällen, zu vollziehen ist's.

Kent

(der sich bei Shrewsburys Eintritt entfernt hat, kommt zurück).

Der Auflauf wächst, das Volk ist länger nicht
Zu bändigen.

Elisabeth (zu Shrewsbury).

Ihr seht, wie sie mich drängen!

Shrewsbury.

Nur Aufschub fordr' ich. Dieser Federzug　　　　　3095
Entscheidet deines Lebens Glück und Frieden.

Du haſt es jahrelang bedacht, ſoll dich
Der Augenblick im Sturme mit ſich führen?
Nur kurzen Aufſchub. Sammle dein Gemüt,
Erwarte eine ruhigere Stunde.   3100

Burleigh (heftig).

Erwarte, zögre, ſäume, bis das Reich
In Flammen ſteht, bis es der Feindin endlich
Gelingt, den Mordſtreich wirklich zu vollführen.
Dreimal hat ihn ein Gott von dir entfernt;
Heut hat er n a h e dich berührt; noch einmal   3105
Ein Wunder hoffen, hieße Gott verſuchen.

Shrewsbury.

Der Gott, der dich durch ſeine Wunderhand
Viermal erhielt, der heut dem ſchwachen Arm
Des Greiſen Kraft gab, einen Wütenden
Zu überwält'gen — er verdient Vertrauen!   3110
Ich will die Stimme der Gerechtigkeit
Jetzt nicht erheben, jetzt iſt nicht die Zeit,
Du kannſt in dieſem Sturme ſie nicht hören.
Dies Eine nur vernimm! Du zitterſt jetzt
Vor dieſer lebenden Maria. Nicht   3115
Die Lebende haſt du zu fürchten. Zittre vor
Der Toten, der Enthaupteten. Sie wird
Vom Grab erſtehen, eine Zwietrachtsgöttin,
Ein Rachegeiſt in deinem Reich herumgehn,
Und deines Volkes Herzen von dir wenden.   3120
Jetzt h a ß t der Britte die Gefürchtete,
Er wird ſie r ä c h e n, wenn ſie nicht mehr iſt.
Nicht mehr die Feindin ſeines Glaubens, nur
Die Enkeltochter ſeiner Könige,
Des Haſſes Opfer und der Eiferſucht   3125
Wird er in der Bejammerten erblicken!

Schnell wirst du die Veränderung erfahren.
Durchziehe London, wenn die blut'ge That
Geschehen, zeige dich dem Volk, das sonst
Sich jubelnd um dich her ergoß, du wirst   3130
Ein andres England sehn, ein andres Volk,
Denn dich umgiebt nicht mehr die herrliche
Gerechtigkeit, die alle Herzen dir
Besiegte! Furcht, die schreckliche Begleitung
Der Tyrannei, wird schaudernd vor dir herziehn,   3135
Und jede Straße, wo du gehst, veröden.
Du hast das Letzte, Äußerste gethan,
Welch Haupt steht fest, wenn dieses heil'ge fiel!

Elisabeth.

Ach, Shrewsbury! Ihr habt mir heut das Leben
Gerettet, habt des Mörders Dolch von mir   3140
Gewendet — Warum ließet Ihr ihm nicht
Den Lauf? So wäre jeder Streit geendigt,
Und alles Zweifels ledig, rein von Schuld,
Läg' ich in meiner stillen Gruft! Fürwahr,
Ich bin des Lebens und des Herrschens müd'!   3145
Muß eine von uns Königinnen fallen,
Damit die andre lebe — und es ist
Nicht anders, das erkenn' ich — kann denn ich
Nicht die sein, welche weicht? Mein Volk mag wählen,
Ich geb' ihm seine Majestät zurück.   3150
Gott ist mein Zeuge, daß ich nicht für mich,
Nur für das Beste meines Volks gelebt.
Hofft es von dieser schmeichlerischen Stuart,
Der jüngern Königin, glücklichere Tage,
So steig' ich gern von diesem Thron und kehre   3155
In Woodstocks stille Einsamkeit zurück,
Wo meine anspruchlose Jugend lebte,
Wo ich, vom Tand der Erdengröße fern,

Die Hoheit in mir selber fand — Bin ich
Zur Herrscherin doch nicht gemacht! Der Herrscher   3160
Muß hart sein können, und mein Herz ist weich.
Ich habe diese Insel lange glücklich
Regiert, weil ich nur brauchte zu beglücken.
Es kommt die erste schwere Königspflicht,
Und ich empfinde meine Ohnmacht —   3165

Burleigh.

                              Nun, bei Gott!
Wenn ich so ganz unkönigliche Worte
Aus meiner Königin Mund vernehmen muß,
So wär's Verrat an meiner Pflicht, Verrat
Am Vaterlande, länger still zu schweigen.
— Du sagst, du liebst dein Volk, mehr als dich selbst,   3170
Das zeige jetzt! Erwähle nicht den Frieden
Für dich und überlaß das Reich den Stürmen.
— Denk' an die Kirche! Soll mit dieser Stuart
Der alte Aberglaube wiederkehren?
Der Mönch aufs neu hier herrschen, der Legat   3175
Aus Rom gezogen kommen, unsre Kirchen
Verschließen, unsre Könige entthronen?
— Die Seelen aller deiner Unterthanen,
Ich fordre sie von dir — Wie du jetzt handelst,
Sind sie gerettet oder sind verloren.   3180
Hier ist nicht Zeit zu weichlichem Erbarmen,
Des Volkes Wohlfahrt ist die höchste Pflicht;
Hat Shrewsbury das Leben dir gerettet,
So will ich England retten — das ist mehr!

Elisabeth.

Man überlasse mich mir selbst! Bei Menschen ist
Nicht Rat noch Trost in dieser großen Sache.   3185
Ich trage sie dem höhern Richter vor.

Was der mich lehrt, das will ich thun — Entfernt euch,
Mylords! (Zu Davison.)

Ihr, Sir, könnt in der Nähe bleiben!

(Die Lords gehen ab. Shrewsbury allein bleibt noch einige Augenblicke vor
der Königin stehen mit bedeutungsvollem Blick, dann entfernt er sich langsam
mit einem Ausdruck des tiefsten Schmerzes.)

Zehnter Auftritt.

Elisabeth (allein).

O Sklaverei des Volksdiensts! Schmähliche   3190
Knechtschaft — Wie bin ich's müde, diesem Götzen
Zu schmeicheln, den mein Innerstes verachtet!
Wann soll ich frei auf diesem Throne stehn!
Die Meinung muß ich ehren, um das Lob
Der Menge buhlen, einem Pöbel muß ich's   3195
Recht machen, dem der Gaukler nur gefällt.
O, der ist noch nicht König, der der Welt
Gefallen muß! Nur der ist's, der bei seinem Thun
Nach keines Menschen Beifall braucht zu fragen.

   Warum hab' ich Gerechtigkeit geübt,   3200
Willkür gehaßt mein Leben lang, daß ich
Für diese erste unvermeidliche
Gewaltthat selbst die Hände mir gefesselt!
Das Muster, das ich selber gab, verdammt mich!
War ich tyrannisch, wie die spanische   3205
Maria war, mein Vorfahr auf dem Thron, ich könnte
Jetzt ohne Tadel Königsblut verspritzen!
Doch war's denn meine eigne freie Wahl,
Gerecht zu sein? Die allgewaltige
Notwendigkeit, die auch das freie Wollen   3210
Der Könige zwingt, gebot mir diese Tugend.
   Umgeben rings von Feinden, hält mich nur

Die Volksgunst auf dem angefochtnen Thron.
Mich zu vernichten, streben alle Mächte
Des festen Landes. Unversöhnlich schleudert   3215
Der röm'sche Papst den Bannfluch auf mein Haupt,
Mit falschem Bruderkuß verrät mich Frankreich,
Und offnen, wütenden Vertilgungskrieg
Bereitet mir der Spanier auf den Meeren.
So steh' ich kämpfend gegen eine Welt,   3220
Ein wehrlos Weib! Mit hohen Tugenden
Muß ich die Blöße meines Rechts bedecken,
Den Flecken meiner fürstlichen Geburt,
Wodurch der eigne Vater mich geschändet.
Umsonst bedeck' ich ihn — Der Gegner Haß   3225
Hat ihn entblößt und stellt mir diese Stuart,
Ein ewig drohendes Gespenst, entgegen.
    Nein, diese Furcht soll endigen!
Ihr Haupt soll fallen. Ich will Frieden haben!
— Sie ist die Furie meines Lebens! Mir   3230
Ein Plagegeist, vom Schicksal angeheftet.
Wo ich mir eine Freude, eine Hoffnung
Gepflanzt, da liegt die Höllenschlange mir
Im Wege. Sie entreißt mir den Geliebten,
Den Bräut'gam raubt sie mir! Maria Stuart   3235
Heißt jedes Unglück, das mich niederschlägt!
Ist sie aus den Lebendigen vertilgt,
Frei bin ich, wie die Luft auf den Gebirgen.
                (Stillschweigen.)
Mit welchem Hohn sie auf mich niedersah,
Als sollte mich der Blick zu Boden blitzen!   3240
Ohnmächtige! Ich führe beßre Waffen,
Sie treffen tödlich, und du bist nicht mehr!
(Mit raschem Schritt nach dem Tische gehend und die Feder ergreifend.)
Ein Bastard bin ich dir? — Unglückliche!
Ich bin es nur, so lang du lebst und atmest.
Der Zweifel meiner fürstlichen Geburt,   3245

Er ist getilgt, so bald ich dich vertilge.
Sobald den Britten keine Wahl mehr bleibt,
Bin ich im echten Ehebett geboren!

(Sie unterschreibt mit einem raschen, festen Federzug, läßt dann die Feder
fallen und tritt mit einem Ausdruck des Schreckens zurück. Nach einer
Pause klingelt sie.)

Elfter Auftritt.

Elisabeth. Davison.

Elisabeth.

Wo sind die andern Lords?

Davison.

                Sie sind gegangen,   3250
Das aufgebrachte Volk zur Ruh zu bringen.
Das Toben war auch augenblicks gestillt,
Sobald der Graf von Shrewsbury sich zeigte.
„Der ist's! Das ist er!" riefen hundert Stimmen,
„Der rettete die Königin! Hört ihn,   3255
Den bravsten Mann in England!" Nun begann
Der edle Talbot und verwies dem Volk
In sanften Worten sein gewaltsames
Beginnen, sprach so kraftvoll überzeugend,
Daß alles sich besänftigte und still
Vom Platze schlich.   3260

Elisabeth.

               Die wankelmüt'ge Menge,
Die jeder Wind herumtreibt! Wehe dem,
Der auf dies Rohr sich lehnet! — Es ist gut,
Sir Davison. Ihr könnt nun wieder gehn.

(Wie sich jener nach der Thüre gewendet.)

Und dieses Blatt — Nehmt es zurück — Ich leg's
In Eure Hände.   3265

From the picture in the new Palace of Westminster.

Davison

(wirft einen Blick in das Papier und erschrickt).

Königin! Dein Name!
Du hast entschieden?

Elisabeth.

— Unterschreiben sollt' ich.
Ich hab's gethan. Ein Blatt Papier entscheidet
Noch nicht, ein Name tötet nicht.

Davison.

Dein Name, Königin, unter dieser Schrift
Entscheidet alles, tötet, ist ein Strahl   3270
Des Donners, der geflügelt trifft — Dies Blatt
Befiehlt den Kommissarien, dem Sheriff,
Nach Fotheringhayschloß sich stehenden Fußes
Zur Königin von Schottland zu verfügen,
Den Tod ihr anzukündigen und schnell,   3275
Sobald der Morgen tagt, ihn zu vollziehn.
Hier ist kein Aufschub: jene hat gelebt,
Wenn ich dies Blatt aus meinen Händen gebe.

Elisabeth.

Ja, Sir! Gott legt ein wichtig, groß Geschick
In Eure schwachen Hände. Fleht ihn an,   3280
Daß er mit seiner Weisheit Euch erleuchte.
Ich geh' und überlaß' Euch Eurer Pflicht.

(Sie will gehen.)

Davison (tritt ihr in den Weg).

Nein, meine Königin! Verlaß mich nicht,
Eh du mir deinen Willen kund gethan.
Bedarf es hier noch einer andern Weisheit,   3285
Als dein Gebot buchstäblich zu befolgen?
— Du legst dies Blatt in meine Hand, daß ich
Zu schleuniger Vollziehung es befördere?

Elisabeth.

Das werdet Ihr nach Eurer Klugheit —

Davison (schnell und erschrocken einfallend).

Nicht

Nach meiner! Das verhüte Gott! Gehorsam   3290
Ist meine ganze Klugheit.   Deinem Diener
Darf hier nichts zu entscheiden übrig bleiben.
Ein klein Versehen wär' hier Königsmord,
Ein unabsehbar, ungeheures Unglück.
Vergönne mir, in dieser großen Sache   3295
Dein blindes Werkzeug willenlos zu sein.
In klare Worte fasse deine Meinung,
Was soll mit diesem Blutbefehl geschehn?

Elisabeth.

— Sein Name spricht es aus.

Davison.

So willst du, daß er gleich vollzogen werde?   3300

Elisabeth (zögernd).

Das sag' ich nicht und zittre, es zu denken.

Davison.

Du willst, daß ich ihn länger noch bewahre?

Elisabeth (schnell).

Auf Eure Gefahr! Ihr haftet für die Folgen.

Davison.

Ich? Heil'ger Gott! — Sprich, Königin! Was willst du?

Elisabeth (ungeduldig).

Ich will, daß dieser unglücksel'gen Sache   3305
Nicht mehr gedacht soll werden, daß ich endlich
Will Ruhe davor haben und auf ewig.

Davison.

Es kostet dir ein einzig Wort.   O sage,
Bestimme, was mit dieser Schrift soll werden!

Elisabeth.

Ich hab's gesagt, und quält mich nun nicht weiter. 3310

Davison.

Du hättest es gesagt? Du hast mir nichts
Gesagt — O, es gefalle meiner Königin,
Sich zu erinnern.

Elisabeth (stampft auf den Boden).

Unerträglich!

Davison.

Habe Nachsicht

Mit mir! Ich kam seit wenig Monden erst
In dieses Amt! Ich kenne nicht die Sprache 3315
Der Höfe und der Könige — in schlicht
Einfacher Sitte bin ich aufgewachsen.
Drum habe du Geduld mit deinem Knecht!
Laß dich das Wort nicht reun, das mich belehrt,
Mich klar macht über meine Pflicht — 3320

(Er nähert sich ihr in flehender Stellung, sie kehrt ihm den Rücken zu, er steht
in Verzweiflung, dann spricht er mit entschloßnem Ton.)

Nimm dies Papier zurück! Nimm es zurück!
Es wird mir glühend Feuer in den Händen.
Nicht mich erwähle, dir in diesem furchtbaren
Geschäft zu dienen.

Elisabeth.

Thut was Eures Amts ist! (Sie geht ab.)

Zwölfter Auftritt.

Davison, gleich darauf Burleigh.

Davison.

Sie geht! Sie läßt mich ratlos, zweifelnd stehn   3325
Mit diesem fürchterlichen Blatt — Was thu' ich?
Soll ich's bewahren? Soll ich's übergeben?

(Zu Burleigh, der hereintritt.)

O gut, gut, daß Ihr kommt, Mylord! Ihr seid's,
Der mich in dieses Staatsamt eingeführt.
Befreiet mich davon! Ich übernahm es,   3330
Unkundig seiner Rechenschaft. Laßt mich
Zurückgehn in die Dunkelheit, wo Ihr
Mich fandet, ich gehöre nicht auf diesen Platz —

Burleigh.

Was ist Euch, Sir? Faßt Euch. Wo ist das Urteil?
Die Königin ließ Euch rufen.   3335

Davison.

Sie verließ mich

In heft'gem Zorn. O ratet mir! Helft mir!
Reißt mich aus dieser Höllenangst des Zweifels!
Hier ist das Urteil — es ist unterschrieben.

Burleigh (haftig).

Ist es? O gebt! Gebt her!

Davison.

Ich darf nicht.

Burleigh.

Was?

Davison.

Sie hat mir ihren Willen noch nicht deutlich —   3340

Burleigh.

Nicht deutlich! Sie hat unterschrieben. Gebt!

Davison.

Ich soll's vollziehen lassen — soll es nicht
Vollziehen lassen — Gott! Weiß ich, was ich soll?

Burleigh (heftiger dringend).

Gleich, augenblicks sollt Ihr's vollziehen lassen.
Gebt her! Ihr seid verloren, wenn Ihr säumt.   3345

Davison.

Ich bin verloren, wenn ich's übereile.

Burleigh.

Ihr seid ein Thor, Ihr seid von Sinnen! Gebt!
(Er entreißt ihm die Schrift und eilt damit ab.)

Davison (ihm nacheilend).

Was macht Ihr? Bleibt! Ihr stürzt mich ins Verderben!

Fünfter Aufzug.

Die Szene ist das Zimmer des ersten Aufzugs.

Erster Auftritt.

Hanna Kennedy, in tiefe Trauer gekleidet, mit verweinten Augen und einem großen, aber stillen Schmerz, ist beschäftigt, Pakete und Briefe zu versiegeln. Oft unterbricht sie der Jammer in ihrem Geschäft, und man sieht sie dazwischen still beten. **Paulet und Drury,** gleichfalls in schwarzen Kleidern, treten ein; ihnen folgen viele **Bediente,** welche goldene und silberne Gefäße, Spiegel, Gemälde und andere Kostbarkeiten tragen und den Hintergrund des Zimmers damit anfüllen. Paulet überliefert der Amme ein Schmuckkästchen nebst einem Papier und bedeutet ihr durch Zeichen, daß es ein Verzeichnis der gebrachten Dinge enthalte. Beim Anblick dieser Reichtümer erneuert sich der Schmerz der Amme; sie versinkt in ein tiefes Trauern, indem jene sich still wieder entfernen. **Melvil** tritt ein.

Kennedy
(schreit auf, sobald sie ihn gewahr wird).

Melvil! Ihr seid es! Euch erblick' ich wieder!

Melvil.

Ja, treue Kennedy, wir sehn uns wieder!　　　　　3350

Kennedy.

Nach langer, langer, schmerzenvoller Trennung!

Melvil.

Ein unglückselig schmerzvoll Wiedersehn!

Kennedy.

O Gott! Ihr kommt —

Melvil.

Den letzten, ewigen

Abschied von meiner Königin zu nehmen.

Kennedy.

Jetzt endlich, jetzt, am Morgen ihres Todes,   3355
Wird ihr die langentbehrte Gegenwart
Der Ihrigen vergönnt — O teurer Sir,
Ich will nicht fragen, wie es Euch erging,
Euch nicht die Leiden nennen, die wir litten,
Seitdem man Euch von unsrer Seite riß.   3360
Ach, dazu wird wohl einst die Stunde kommen!
O Melvil! Melvil! Mußten wir's erleben,
Den Anbruch dieses Tags zu sehn!

Melvil.

Laßt uns

Einander nicht erweichen! Weinen will ich,
So lang noch Leben in mir ist; nie soll   3365
Ein Lächeln diese Wangen mehr erheitern,
Nie will ich dieses nächtliche Gewand
Mehr von mir legen! Ewig will ich trauern!
Doch heute will ich standhaft sein — Versprecht
Auch Ihr mir, Euren Schmerz zu mäßigen —   3370
Und wenn die andern alle der Verzweiflung
Sich trostlos überlassen, lasset uns
Mit männlich edler Fassung ihr vorangehn
Und ihr ein Stab sein auf dem Todesweg!

Kennedy.

Melvil! Ihr seid im Irrtum, wenn Ihr glaubt,   3375
Die Königin bedürfe unsers Beistands,
Um standhaft in den Tod zu gehn! Sie selber ist's,
Die uns das Beispiel edler Fassung giebt.

Seid ohne Furcht! Maria Stuart wird
Als eine Königin und Heldin sterben.   3380

Melvil.

Nahm sie die Todespost mit Fassung auf?
Man sagt, daß sie nicht vorbereitet war.

Kennedy.

Das war sie nicht. Ganz andre Schrecken waren's,
Die meine Lady ängstigten.   Nicht vor dem Tod,
Vor dem Befreier zitterte Maria.   3385
— Freiheit war uns verheißen.   Diese Nacht
Versprach uns Mortimer von hier wegzuführen,
Und zwischen Furcht und Hoffnung, zweifelhaft,
Ob sie dem kecken Jüngling ihre Ehre
Und fürstlich? Person vertrauen dürfe,   3390
Erwartete die Königin den Morgen.
— Da wird ein Auflauf in dem Schloß, ein Pochen
Schreckt unser Ohr und vieler Hämmer Schlag.
Wir glauben, die Befreier zu vernehmen,
Die Hoffnung winkt, der süße Trieb des Lebens   3395
Wacht unwillkürlich, allgewaltig auf —
Da öffnet sich die Thür — Sir Paulet ist's,
Der uns verkündigt — daß — die Zimmerer
Zu unsren Füßen das Gerüst aufschlagen!
(Sie wendet sich ab, von heftigem Schmerz ergriffen.)

Melvil.

Gerechter Gott! O, sagt mir, wie ertrug   3400
Maria diesen fürchterlichen Wechsel?

Kennedy
(nach einer Pause, worin sie sich wieder etwas gefaßt hat).

Man löst sich nicht allmählich von dem Leben!
Mit einemmal, schnell, augenblicklich muß

Der Tausch geschehen zwischen Zeitlichem
Und Ewigem, und Gott gewährte meiner Lady   3405
In diesem Augenblick, der Erde Hoffnung
Zurück zu stoßen mit entschloßner Seele,
Und glaubenvoll den Himmel zu ergreifen.
Kein Merkmal bleicher Furcht, kein Wort der Klage
Entehrte meine Königin — Dann erst,   3410
Als sie Lord Lesters schändlichen Verrat
Vernahm, das unglückselige Geschick
Des werten Jünglings, der sich ihr geopfert,
Des alten Ritters tiefen Jammer sah,
Dem seine letzte Hoffnung starb durch sie,   3415
Da flossen ihre Thränen; nicht das eigne Schicksal,
Der fremde Jammer preßte sie ihr ab.

Melvil.

Wo ist sie jetzt? Könnt Ihr mich zu ihr bringen?

Kennedy.

Den Rest der Nacht durchwachte sie mit Beten,
Nahm von den teuern Freunden schriftlich Abschied   3420
Und schrieb ihr Testament mit eigner Hand.
Jetzt pflegt sie einen Augenblick der Ruh,
Der letzte Schlaf erquickt sie.

Melvil.

Wer ist bei ihr?

Kennedy.

Ihr Leibarzt Burgoyn und ihre Frauen,

11

Zweiter Auftritt.

Margareta Kurl zu den Vorigen.

Kennedy.

Was bringt Ihr, Mistreß?   Ist die Lady wach?   3425

Kurl (ihre Thränen trocknend).

Schon angekleidet — Sie verlangt nach Euch.

Kennedy.

Ich komme. (Zu Melvil, der sie begleiten will.)

                    Folgt mir nicht, bis ich die Lady
Auf Euren Anblick vorbereitet.   (Geht hinein.)

Kurl.

                    Melvil!
Der alte Haushofmeister!

Melvil.

                    Ja, der bin ich!

Kurl.

O, dieses Haus braucht keines Meisters mehr!   3430
— Melvil! Ihr kommt von London, wißt Ihr mir
Von meinem Manne nichts zu sagen?

Melvil.

Er wird auf freien Fuß gesetzt, sagt man,
Sobald —

Kurl.

                    Sobald die Königin nicht mehr ist!
O der nichtswürdig schändliche Verräter!   3435
Er ist der Mörder dieser teuren Lady;
Sein Zeugnis, sagt man, habe sie verurteilt.

Melvil.

So ist's.

Kurl.

O, seine Seele sei verflucht
Bis in die Hölle!   Er hat falsch gezeugt —

Melvil.

Mylady Kurl! Bedenket Eure Reden!   3440

Kurl.

Beschwören will ich's vor Gerichtes Schranken,
Ich will es ihm ins Antlitz wiederholen,
Die ganze Welt will ich damit erfüllen.
Sie stirbt unschuldig —

Melvil.

O, das gebe Gott!

Dritter Auftritt.

Burgoyn zu den Vorigen. Hernach Hanna Kennedy.

Burgoyn (erblickt Melvil).

O Melvil!   3445

Melvil (ihn umarmend).

Burgoyn!

Burgoyn (zur Margareta Kurl).

Besorget einen Becher
Mit Wein für unsre Lady! Machet hurtig! (Kurl geht ab.)

Melvil.

Wie? Ist der Königin nicht wohl?

Burgoyn.

Sie fühlt sich stark, sie täuscht ihr Heldenmut,
Und keiner Speise glaubt sie zu bedürfen;
Doch ihrer wartet noch ein schwerer Kampf,   3450
Und ihre Feinde sollen sich nicht rühmen,
Daß Furcht des Todes ihre Wangen bleiche,
Wenn die Natur aus Schwachheit unterliegt.

Melvil (zur Amme, die hereintritt).

Will sie mich sehn?

Kennedy.

    Gleich wird sie selbst hier sein.
— Ihr scheint Euch mit Verwundrung umzusehn,   3455
Und Eure Blicke fragen mich: Was soll
Das Prachtgerät in diesem Ort des Todes?
— O Sir! Wir litten Mangel, da wir lebten,
Erst mit dem Tode kommt der Überfluß zurück.

Vierter Auftritt.

**Vorige. Zwei andre Kammerfrauen der Maria, gleichfalls in Trauer-
kleidern. Sie brechen bei Melvils Anblick in laute Thränen aus.**

Melvil.

Was für ein Anblick! Welch ein Wiedersehn!   3460
Gertrude, Rosamund!

Zweite Kammerfrau.

    Sie hat uns von sich
Geschickt! Sie will zum letztenmal allein
Mit Gott sich unterhalten!

(Es kommen noch zwei weibliche Bediente, wie die Vorigen in Trauer, die mit
stummen Gebärden ihren Jammer ausdrücken.)

Fünfter Auftritt.

Margareta Kurl zu den Vorigen. Sie trägt einen goldnen Becher mit Wein und setzt ihn auf den Tisch, indem sie sich bleich und zitternd an einem Stuhl hält.

Melvil.

Was ist Euch, Mistreß? Was entsetzt Euch so?

Kurl.

O Gott!   3465

Burgoyn.

     Was habt Ihr?

Kurl.

          Was mußt' ich erblicken!

Melvil.

Kommt zu Euch! Sagt uns, was es ist!

Kurl.

               Als ich
Mit diesem Becher Wein die große Treppe
Heraufstieg, die zur untern Halle führt,
Da that die Thür sich auf — ich sah hinein —
Ich sah — o Gott! —   3470

Melvil.

     Was saht Ihr? Fasset Euch!

Kurl.

Schwarz überzogen waren alle Wände,
Ein groß Gerüst, mit schwarzem Tuch beschlagen,
Erhob sich von dem Boden, mitten drauf
Ein schwarzer Block, ein Kissen und daneben
Ein blankgeschliffnes Beil — Voll Menschen war   3475

Der Saal, die um das Mordgerüst sich drängten
Und, heiße Blutgier in dem Blick, das Opfer
Erwarteten.

Die Kammerfrauen.

O Gott, sei unsrer Lady gnädig!

Melvil.

Faßt euch! Sie kommt!

Sechster Auftritt.

Die Vorigen. Maria. Sie ist weiß und festlich gekleidet, am Halse trägt
sie an einer Kette von kleinen Kugeln ein Agnus Dei, ein Rosenkranz hängt
am Gürtel herab, sie hat ein Kruzifix in der Hand und ein Diadem in den
Haaren, ihr großer schwarzer Schleier ist zurückgeschlagen. Bei ihrem Eintritt weichen die Anwesenden zu beiden Seiten zurück und drücken den heftigsten Schmerz aus. Melvil ist mit einer unwillkürlichen Bewegung auf die
Kniee gesunken.

Maria
(mit ruhiger Hoheit im ganzen Kreise herumsehend).

Was klagt ihr? Warum weint ihr? Freuen solltet   3480
Ihr euch mit mir, daß meiner Leiden Ziel
Nun endlich naht, daß meine Bande fallen,
Mein Kerker aufgeht und die frohe Seele sich
Auf Engelsflügeln schwingt zur ew'gen Freiheit.
Da, als ich in die Macht der stolzen Feindin   3485
Gegeben war, Unwürdiges erduldend,
Was einer freien, großen Königin
Nicht ziemt, da war es Zeit, um mich zu weinen!
— Wohlthätig, heilend nahet mir der Tod,
Der ernste Freund! Mit seinen schwarzen Flügeln   3490
Bedeckt er meine Schmach — Den Menschen adelt,
Den tiefstgesunkenen, das letzte Schicksal.
Die Krone fühl' ich wieder auf dem Haupt,

Den würd'gen Stolz in meiner edlen Seele!
(Indem sie einige Schritte weiter vortritt.)
Wie? Melvil hier? — Nicht also, edler Sir!　3495
Steht auf! Ihr seid zu Eurer Königin
Triumph, zu ihrem Tode nicht gekommen.
Mir wird ein Glück zu teil, wie ich es nimmer
Gehoffet, daß mein Nachruhm doch nicht ganz
In meiner Feinde Händen ist, daß doch　3500
Ein Freund mir, ein Bekenner meines Glaubens,
Als Zeuge dasteht in der Todesstunde.
— Sagt, edler Ritter, wie erging es Euch
In diesem feindlichen, unholden Lande,
Seitdem man Euch von meiner Seite riß?　3505
Die Sorg' um Euch hat oft mein Herz bekümmert.

Melvil.

Mich drückte sonst kein Mangel, als der Schmerz
Um dich, und meine Ohnmacht, dir zu dienen.

Maria.

Wie steht's um Didier, meinen alten Kämmrer?
Doch der Getreue schläft wohl lange schon　3510
Den ew'gen Schlaf, denn er war hoch an Jahren.

Melvil.

Gott hat ihm diese Gnade nicht erzeigt,
Er lebt, um deine Jugend zu begraben.

Maria.

Daß mir vor meinem Tode noch das Glück
Geworden wäre, ein geliebtes Haupt　3515
Der teuren Blutsverwandten zu umfassen!
Doch ich soll sterben unter Fremdlingen,
Nur eure Thränen soll ich fließen sehn!
— Melvil, die letzten Wünsche für die Meinen

Leg' ich in Eure treue Brust — Ich segne   3520
Den allerchristlichsten König, meinen Schwager,
Und Frankreichs ganzes königliches Haus —
Ich segne meinen Ohm, den Kardinal,
Und Heinrich Guise, meinen edlen Vetter.
Ich segne auch den Papst, den heiligen   3525
Statthalter Christi, der mich wieder segnet,
Und den kathol'schen König, der sich edelmütig
Zu meinem Retter, meinem Rächer anbot —
Sie alle stehn in meinem Testament,
Sie werden die Geschenke meiner Liebe,   3530
Wie arm sie sind, darum gering nicht achten.

(Sich zu ihren Dienern wendend.)

Euch hab' ich meinem königlichen Bruder
Von Frankreich anempfohlen, er wird sorgen
Für euch, ein neues Vaterland euch geben.
Und ist euch meine letzte Bitte wert,   3535
Bleibt nicht in England, daß der Britte nicht
Sein stolzes Herz an eurem Unglück weide,
Nicht die im Staube seh', die mir gedient.
Bei diesem Bildnis des Gekreuzigten
Gelobet mir, dies unglücksel'ge Land   3540
Alsbald, wenn ich dahin bin, zu verlassen!

Melvil (berührt das Kruzifix).

Ich schwöre dir's im Namen dieser aller.

Maria.

Was ich, die Arme, die Beraubte, noch besaß,
Worüber mir vergönnt ist frei zu schalten,
Das hab' ich unter euch verteilt; man wird,   3545
Ich hoff' es, meinen letzten Willen ehren.
Auch was ich auf dem Todeswege trage,
Gehöret euch — Vergönnet mir noch einmal
Der Erde Glanz auf meinem Weg zum Himmel!

(Zu den Fräulein.)

Dir, meine Alix, Gertrud, Rosamund,   3550
Bestimm' ich meine Perlen, meine Kleider,
Denn eure Jugend freut sich noch des Putzes.
Du, Margareta, hast das nächste Recht
An meine Großmut, denn ich lasse dich
Zurück als die Unglücklichste von allen.   3555
Daß ich des Gatten Schuld an dir nicht räche,
Wird mein Vermächtnis offenbaren — Dich,
O meine treue Hanna, reizet nicht
Der Wert des Goldes, nicht der Steine Pracht,
Dir ist das höchste Kleinod mein Gedächtnis.   3560
Nimm dieses Tuch! Ich hab's mit eigner Hand
Für dich gestickt in meines Kummers Stunden,
Und meine heißen Thränen eingewoben.
Mit diesem Tuch wirst du die Augen mir verbinden,
Wenn es so weit ist — diesen letzten Dienst   3565
Wünsch' ich von meiner Hanna zu empfangen.

Kennedy.

O Melvil! Ich ertrag' es nicht!

Maria.

Kommt alle!
Kommt und empfangt mein letztes Lebewohl!

(Sie reicht ihre Hände hin, eins nach dem andern fällt ihr zu Füßen und
küßt die dargebotene Hand unter heftigem Weinen.)

Leb' wohl, Margreta — Alix, lebe wohl —
Dank, Burgoyn, für Eure treuen Dienste —   3570
Dein Mund brennt heiß, Gertrude — Ich bin viel
Gehasset worden, doch auch viel geliebt!
Ein edler Mann beglücke meine Gertrud,
Denn Liebe fordert dieses glühnde Herz —
Bertha! Du hast das beßre Teil erwählt,   3575
Die keusche Braut des Himmels willst du werden.

O, eile, dein Gelübde zu vollziehn!
Betrüglich sind die Güter dieser Erden,
Das lern' an deiner Königin! — Nichts weiter!
Lebt wohl! Lebt wohl! Lebt ewig wohl!   3580

(Sie wendet sich schnell von ihnen; alle bis auf Melvil entfernen sich.)

Siebenter Auftritt.

Maria. Melvil.

Maria.

Ich habe alles Zeitliche berichtigt
Und hoffe, keines Menschen Schuldnerin
Aus dieser Welt zu scheiden — Eins nur ist's,
Melvil, was der beklemmten Seele noch
Verwehrt, sich frei und freudig zu erheben.   3585

Melvil.

Entdecke mir's. Erleichtre deine Brust,
Dem treuen Freund vertraue deine Sorgen.

Maria.

Ich stehe an dem Rand der Ewigkeit;
Bald soll ich treten vor den höchsten Richter,
Und noch hab' ich den Heil'gen nicht versöhnt.   3590
Versagt ist mir der Priester meiner Kirche.
Des Sakramentes heil'ge Himmelspeise
Verschmäh' ich aus den Händen falscher Priester.
Im Glauben meiner Kirche will ich sterben,
Denn der allein ist's, welcher selig macht.   3595

Melvil.

Beruhige dein Herz. Dem Himmel gilt
Der feurig fromme Wunsch statt des Vollbringens.

Tyrannenmacht kann nur die Hände fesseln,
Des Herzens Andacht hebt sich frei zu Gott;
Das Wort ist tot, der Glaube macht lebendig. 3600

The letter killeth, but the spirit giveth life

Maria.

Ach, Melvil! Nicht allein genug ist sich
Das Herz, ein irdisch Pfand bedarf der Glaube,
Das hohe Himmlische sich zuzueignen.
Drum ward der Gott zum Menschen und verschloß
Die unsichtbaren himmlischen Geschenke 3605
Geheimnisvoll in einem sichtbarn Leib.
— Die Kirche ist's, die heilige, die hohe,
Die zu dem Himmel uns die Leiter baut;
Die allgemeine, die kathol'sche heißt sie,
Denn nur der Glaube aller stärkt den Glauben. 3610
Wo Tausende anbeten und verehren,
Da wird die Glut zur Flamme, und beflügelt
Schwingt sich der Geist in alle Himmel auf.
— Ach, die Beglückten, die das froh geteilte
Gebet versammelt in dem Haus des Herrn! 3615
Geschmückt ist der Altar, die Kerzen leuchten,
Die Glocke tönt, der Weihrauch ist gestreut,
Der Bischof steht im reinen Meßgewand,
Er faßt den Kelch, er segnet ihn, er kündet
Das hohe Wunder der Verwandlung an, 3620
Und niederstürzt dem gegenwärt'gen Gotte
Das gläubig überzeugte Volk — Ach! Ich
Allein bin ausgeschlossen, nicht zu mir
In meinen Kerker bringt der Himmelssegen.

Melvil.

Er bringt zu dir! Er ist dir nah! Vertraue 3625
Dem Allvermögenden — der dürre Stab
Kann Zweige treiben in des Glaubens Hand!
Und der die Quelle aus dem Felsen schlug,

Kann dir im Kerker den Altar bereiten,
Kann diesen Kelch, die irdische Erquickung,   3630
Dir schnell in eine himmlische verwandeln.

(Er ergreift den Kelch, der auf dem Tische steht.)

Maria.

Melvil! Versteh' ich Euch! Ja! Ich versteh' Euch!
Hier ist kein Priester, keine Kirche, kein
Hochwürdiges — Doch der Erlöser spricht:
Wo Zwei versammelt sind in meinem Namen,   3635
Da bin ich gegenwärtig unter ihnen.
Was weiht den Priester ein zum Mund des Herrn?
Das reine Herz, der unbefleckte Wandel.
— So seid Ihr mir, auch ungeweiht, ein Priester,
Ein Bote Gottes, der mir Frieden bringt.   3640
Euch will ich meine letzte Beichte thun,
Und Euer Mund soll mir das Heil verkünden.

Melvil.

Wenn dich das Herz so mächtig dazu treibt,
So wisse, Königin, daß dir zum Troste
Gott auch ein Wunder wohl verrichten kann.   3645
Hier sei kein Priester, sagst du, keine Kirche,
Kein Leib des Herrn? — Du irrest dich. Hier ist
Ein Priester, und ein Gott ist hier zugegen.

(Er entblößt bei diesen Worten das Haupt; zugleich zeigt er ihr eine Hostie
in einer goldenen Schale.)

— Ich bin ein Priester; deine letzte Beichte
Zu hören, dir auf deinem Todesweg   3650
Den Frieden zu verkündigen, hab' ich
Die sieben Weihn auf meinem Haupt empfangen,
Und diese Hostie überbring' ich dir
Vom heil'gen Vater, die er selbst geweihet.

Maria.

O, so muß an der Schwelle selbst des Todes   3655

Mir noch ein himmlisch Glück bereitet sein!
Wie ein Unsterblicher auf goldnen Wolken
Herniederfährt, wie den Apostel einst
Der Engel führte aus des Kerkers Banden,
Ihn hält kein Riegel, keines Hüters Schwert,   3660
Er schreitet mächtig durch verschloßne Pforten,
Und im Gefängnis steht er glänzend da,
So überrascht mich hier der Himmelsbote,
Da jeder ird'sche Retter mich getäuscht!
— Und Ihr, mein Diener einst, seid jetzt der Diener   3665
Des höchsten Gottes und sein heil'ger Mund!
Wie Eure Kniee sonst vor mir sich beugten,
So lieg' ich jetzt im Staub vor Euch.

(Sie sinkt vor ihm nieder.)

Melvil.

(indem er das Zeichen des Kreuzes über sie macht).

Im Namen

Des Vaters und des Sohnes und des Geistes!
Maria, Königin!   Hast du dein Herz   3670
Erforschet, schwörst du und gelobest du,
Wahrheit zu beichten vor dem Gott der Wahrheit?

Maria.

Mein Herz liegt offen da vor dir und ihm.

Melvil.

Sprich, welcher Sünde zeiht dich dein Gewissen,
Seitdem du Gott zum letztenmal versöhnt?   3675

Maria.

Von neid'schem Hasse war mein Herz erfüllt,
Und Rachgedanken tobten in dem Busen.
Vergebung hofft' ich Sünderin von Gott,
Und konnte nicht der Gegnerin vergeben.

Melvil.

Bereuest du die Schuld, und ist's dein ernster   3680
Entschluß, versöhnt aus dieser Welt zu scheiden?

Maria.

So wahr ich hoffe, daß mir Gott vergebe.

Melvil.

Welch andrer Sünde klagt das Herz dich an?

Maria.

Ach, nicht durch Haß allein, durch sünd'ge Liebe
Noch mehr hab' ich das höchste Gut beleidigt.   3685
Das eitle Herz ward zu dem Mann gezogen,
Der treulos mich verlassen und betrogen!

Melvil.

Bereuest du die Schuld, und hat dein Herz
Vom eiteln Abgott sich zu Gott gewendet?

Maria.

Es war der schwerste Kampf, den ich bestand,   3690
Zerrissen ist das letzte ird'sche Band.

Melvil.

Welch andrer Schuld verklagt dich dein Gewissen?

Maria.

Ach, eine frühe Blutschuld, längst gebeichtet,
Sie kehrt zurück mit neuer Schreckenskraft
Im Augenblick der letzten Rechenschaft,   3695
Und wälzt sich schwarz mir vor des Himmels Pforten.
Den König, meinen Gatten, ließ ich morden,
Und dem Verführer schenkt' ich Herz und Hand!
Streng büßt' ich's ab mit allen Kirchenstrafen,
Doch in der Seele will der Wurm nicht schlafen.   3700

Melvil.

Verklagt das Herz dich keiner andern Sünde,
Die du noch nicht gebeichtet und gebüßt?

Maria.

Jetzt weißt du alles, was mein Herz belastet.

Melvil.

Denk' an die Nähe des Allwissenden!
Der Strafen denke, die die heil'ge Kirche   3705
Der mangelhaften Beichte droht! Das ist
Die Sünde zu dem ew'gen Tod, denn das
Ist wider seinen heil'gen Geist gefrevelt.

Maria.

So schenke mir die ew'ge Gnade Sieg
Im letzten Kampf, als ich dir wissend nichts verschwieg. 3710

Melvil.

Wie? Deinem Gott verhehlst du das Verbrechen,
Um dessentwillen dich die Menschen strafen?
Du sagst mir nichts von deinem blut'gen Anteil
An Babingtons und Parrys Hochverrat?
Den zeitlichen Tod stirbst du für diese That,   3715
Willst du auch noch den ew'gen dafür sterben?

Maria.

Ich bin bereit, zur Ewigkeit zu gehn:
Noch eh sich der Minutenzeiger wendet,
Werd' ich vor meines Richters Throne stehn;
Doch wiederhol' ich's: Meine Beichte ist vollendet. 3720

Melvil.

Erwäg' es wohl. Das Herz ist ein Betrüger.
Du hast vielleicht mit list'gem Doppelsinn

Das Wort vermieden, das dich schuldig macht,
Obgleich der Wille das Verbrechen teilte.
Doch wisse, keine Gaukelkunst berückt   3725
Das Flammenauge, das ins Innre blickt!

Maria.

Ich habe alle Fürsten aufgeboten,
Mich aus unwürd'gen Banden zu befrein,
Doch nie hab' ich durch Vorsatz oder That
Das Leben meiner Feindin angetastet!   3730

Melvil.

So hätten deine Schreiber falsch gezeugt?

Maria.

Wie ich gesagt, so ist's.   Was jene zeugten,
Das richte Gott!

Melvil.

            So steigst du, überzeugt
Von deiner Unschuld, auf das Blutgerüste?

Maria.

Gott würdigt mich, durch diesen unverdienten Tod   3735
Die frühe schwere Blutschuld abzubüßen.

Melvil. (macht den Segen über sie).

So gehe hin und sterbend büße sie!
Sink, ein ergebnes Opfer, am Altare!
Blut kann versöhnen, was das Blut verbrach,
Du fehltest nur aus weiblichem Gebrechen,   3740
Dem sel'gen Geiste folgen nicht die Schwächen
Der Sterblichkeit in die Verklärung nach.
Ich aber künde dir, kraft der Gewalt,
Die mir verliehen ist, zu lösen und zu binden,
Erlassung an von allen deinen Sünden!   3745

Wie du geglaubet, so geschehe dir!

(Er reicht ihr die Hostie.)

Nimm hin den Leib, er ist für dich geopfert.

(Er ergreift den Kelch, der auf dem Tische steht, konsekriert ihn mit stillem
Gebet, dann reicht er ihr denselben. Sie zögert, ihn anzunehmen, und weist
ihn mit der Hand zurück.)

Nimm hin das Blut, es ist für dich vergossen!

Nimm hin! Der Papst erzeigt dir diese Gunst!

Im Tode noch sollst du das höchste Recht   3750

Der Könige, das priesterliche, üben!

Und wie du jetzt dich in dem ird'schen Leib

Geheimnisvoll mit deinem Gott verbunden,

So wirst du dort in seinem Freudenreich,

Wo keine Schuld mehr sein wird und kein Weinen,   3755

Ein schön verklärter Engel, dich

Auf ewig mit dem Göttlichen vereinen.

(Er setzt den Kelch nieder. Auf ein Geräusch, das gehört wird, bedeckt er sich
das Haupt und geht an die Thüre; Maria bleibt in stiller Andacht auf den
Knieen liegen.)

Melvil (zurückkommend).

Dir bleibt ein harter Kampf noch zu bestehn.

Fühlst du dich stark genug, um jede Regung

Der Bitterkeit, des Hasses zu besiegen?   3760

Maria.

Ich fürchte keinen Rückfall. Meinen Haß

Und meine Liebe hab' ich Gott geopfert.

Melvil.

Nun; so bereite dich, die Lords von Lester

Und Burleigh zu empfangen. Sie sind da.

Achter Auftritt.

Die Vorigen. Burleigh. Leicester und **Paulet.** Leicester bleibt ganz in der Entfernung stehen, ohne die Augen aufzuschlagen. Burleigh, der seine Fassung beobachtet, tritt zwischen ihn und die Königin.

Burleigh.

Ich komme, Lady Stuart, Eure letzten   3765
Befehle zu empfangen.

Maria.

                    Dank, Mylord!

Burleigh.

Es ist der Wille meiner Königin,
Daß Euch nichts Billiges verweigert werde.

Maria.

Mein Testament nennt meine letzten Wünsche.
Ich hab's in Ritter Paulets Hand gelegt,   3770
Und bitte, daß es treu vollzogen werde.

Paulet.

Verlaßt Euch drauf.

Maria.

Ich bitte, meine Diener ungekränkt
Nach Schottland zu entlassen oder Frankreich,
Wohin sie selber wünschen und begehren.   3775

Burleigh.

Es sei, wie Ihr es wünscht.

Maria.

                    Und weil mein Leichnam
Nicht in geweihter Erde ruhen soll,

So dulde man, daß dieser treue Diener
Mein Herz nach Frankreich bringe zu den Meinen.
— Ach! Es war immer dort!   3780

Burleigh.

Es soll geschehn!
Habt Ihr noch sonst —

Maria.

Der Königin von England
Bringt meinen schwesterlichen Gruß — Sagt ihr,
Daß ich ihr meinen Tod von ganzem Herzen
Vergebe, meine Heftigkeit von gestern
Ihr reuevoll abbitte — Gott erhalte sie   3785
Und schenk' ihr eine glückliche Regierung!

Burleigh.

Sprecht! Habt Ihr noch nicht bessern Rat erwählt?
Verschmäht Ihr noch den Beistand des Dechanten?

Maria.

Ich bin mit meinem Gott versöhnt — Sir Paulet!
Ich hab' Euch schuldlos vieles Weh bereitet,   3790
Des Alters Stütze Euch geraubt — O, laßt
Mich hoffen, daß Ihr meiner nicht mit Haß
Gedenket —

Paulet (giebt ihr die Hand).

Gott sei mit Euch! Gehet hin in Frieden!

Neunter Auftritt.

Die Vorigen. Hanna Kennedy und die anderen **Frauen** der Königin bringen herein mit Zeichen des Entsetzens; ihnen folgt der **Sheriff**, einen weißen Stab in der Hand, hinter demselben sieht man durch die offen bleibende Thüre **gewaffnete Männer**.

Maria.

Was ist dir, Hanna? — Ja, nun ist es Zeit!
Hier kommt der Sheriff, uns zum Tod zu führen.   3795
Es muß geschieden sein! Lebt wohl! Lebt wohl!
(Ihre Frauen hängen sich an sie mit heftigem Schmerz; zu Melvil.)
Ihr, werter Sir, und meine treue Hanna
Sollt mich auf diesem letzten Gang begleiten.
Mylord, versagt mir diese Wohlthat nicht.

Burleigh.

Ich habe dazu keine Vollmacht.   3800

Maria.

                                             Wie?
Die kleine Bitte könntet Ihr mir weigern?
Habt Achtung gegen mein Geschlecht! Wer soll
Den letzten Dienst mir leisten! Nimmermehr
Kann es der Wille meiner Schwester sein,
Daß mein Geschlecht in mir beleidigt werde,   3805
Der Männer rohe Hände mich berühren!

Burleigh.

Es darf kein Weib die Stufen des Gerüstes
Mit Euch besteigen — Ihr Geschrei und Jammern —

Maria.

Sie soll nicht jammern! Ich verbürge mich
Für die gefaßte Seele meiner Hanna!   3810
Seid gütig, Lord. O, trennt mich nicht im Sterben

Von meiner treuen Pflegerin und Amme!
Sie trug auf ihren Armen mich ins Leben,
Sie leite mich mit sanfter Hand zum Tod.

Paulet (zu Burleigh).

Laßt es geschehn!

3815

Burleigh.

Es sei.

Maria.

Nun hab' ich nichts mehr

Auf dieser Welt — (Sie nimmt das Kruzifix und küßt es.)

Mein Heiland! Mein Erlöser!

Wie du am Kreuz die Arme ausgespannt,
So breite sie jetzt aus, mich zu empfangen.

(Sie wendet sich zu gehen. In diesem Augenblick begegnet ihr Auge dem
Grafen Leicester, der bei ihrem Aufbruch unwillkürlich aufgefahren und nach
ihr hingesehen. — Bei diesem Anblick zittert Maria, die Kniee versagen ihr,
sie ist im Begriff hinzusinken; da ergreift sie Graf Leicester und empfängt
sie in seinen Armen. Sie sieht ihn eine Zeitlang ernst und schweigend an,
er kann ihren Blick nicht aushalten, endlich spricht sie.)

Ihr haltet Wort, Graf Lester — Ihr verspracht
Mir Euren Arm, aus diesem Kerker mich
Zu führen, und Ihr leihet mir ihn jetzt!

3820

(Er steht wie vernichtet. Sie fährt mit sanfter Stimme fort.)

Ja, Lester, und nicht bloß
Die Freiheit wollt' ich Eurer Hand verdanken.
Ihr solltet mir die Freiheit t e u e r machen,
An Eurer Hand, beglückt durch Eure Liebe,

3825

Wollt' ich des neuen Lebens mich erfreun.
Jetzt, da ich auf dem Weg bin, von der Welt
Zu scheiden und ein sel'ger Geist zu werden,
Den keine ird'sche Neigung mehr versucht,
Jetzt, Lester, darf ich ohne Schamerröten

3830

Euch die besiegte Schwachheit eingestehn —
Lebt wohl, und wenn Ihr könnt, so lebt beglückt!
Ihr durftet werben um zwei Königinnen;

Ein zärtlich liebend Herz habt Ihr verschmäht,
Verraten, um ein stolzes zu gewinnen. 3835
Kniet zu den Füßen der Elisabeth!
Mög' Euer Lohn nicht Eure Strafe werden!
Lebt wohl! — Jetzt hab' ich nichts mehr auf der Erden!

(Sie geht ab, der Sheriff voraus, Melvil und die Amme ihr zur Seite. Burleigh und Paulet folgen, die übrigen sehen ihr jammernd nach, bis sie ver-
schwunden ist; dann entfernen sie sich durch die zwei andern Thüren.)

Zehnter Auftritt.

Leicester (allein zurückbleibend).

Ich lebe noch! Ich trag' es, noch zu leben!
Stürzt dieses Dach nicht sein Gewicht auf mich! 3840
Thut sich kein Schlund auf, das elendeste
Der Wesen zu verschlingen! Was hab' ich
Verloren! Welche Perle warf ich hin!
Welch Glück der Himmel hab' ich weggeschleudert!
— Sie geht dahin, ein schon verklärter Geist, 3845
Und mir bleibt die Verzweiflung der Verdammten.
— Wo ist mein Vorsatz hin, mit dem ich kam,
Des Herzens Stimme fühllos zu ersticken?
Ihr fallend Haupt zu sehn mit unbewegten Blicken?
Weckt mir ihr Anblick die erstorbne Scham? 3850
Muß sie im Tod mit Liebesbanden mich umstricken?
— Verworfener, dir steht es nicht mehr an,
In zartem Mitleid weibisch hinzuschmelzen;
Der Liebe Glück liegt nicht auf deiner Bahn,
Mit einem ehrnen Harnisch angethan 3855
Sei deine Brust, die Stirne sei ein Felsen!
Willst du den Preis der Schandthat nicht verlieren,
Dreist mußt du sie behaupten und vollführen!
Verstumme, Mitleid! Augen, werdet Stein!

Ich seh' sie fallen, ich will Zeuge sein.   3860

(Er geht mit entschlossenem Schritt der Thüre zu, durch welche Maria gegangen, bleibt aber auf der Mitte des Weges stehen.)

Umsonst! Umsonst! Mich faßt der Hölle Grauen,
Ich kann, ich kann das Schreckliche nicht schauen,
Kann sie nicht sterben sehen — Horch! Was war das?
Sie sind schon unten — Unter meinen Füßen
Bereitet sich das fürchterliche Werk.   3865
Ich höre Stimmen — Fort! Hinweg! Hinweg
Aus diesem Haus des Schreckens und des Todes!

(Er will durch eine andre Thür entfliehen, findet sie aber verschlossen und fährt zurück.)

Wie? Fesselt mich ein Gott an diesen Boden?
Muß ich anhören, was mir anzuschauen graut?
Die Stimme des Dechanten — Er ermahnet sie —   3870
— Sie unterbricht ihn — Horch! — Laut betet sie —
Mit fester Stimme — Es wird still — Ganz still!
Nur schluchzen hör' ich und die Weiber weinen —
Sie wird entkleidet — Horch! Der Schemel wird
Gerückt — Sie kniet aufs Kissen — legt das Haupt —   3875

(Nachdem er die letzten Worte mit steigender Angst gesprochen und eine Weile inne gehalten, sieht man ihn plötzlich mit einer zuckenden Bewegung zusammen= fahren und ohnmächtig niedersinken; zugleich erschallt von unten herauf ein dumpfes Getöse von Stimmen, welches lange forthallt.)

Das zweite Zimmer des vierten Aufzugs.

Elfter Auftritt.

Elisabeth

tritt aus einer Seitenthüre, ihr Gang und ihre Gebärden drücken die heftigste Unruhe aus.

Noch niemand hier — Noch keine Botschaft — Will es
Nicht Abend werden? Steht die Sonne fest
In ihrem himmlischen Lauf? — Ich soll noch länger

Auf dieser Folter der Erwartung liegen!
— Ist es geschehen? Ist es nicht? — Mir graut   3880
Vor beidem, und ich wage nicht, zu fragen!
Graf Lester zeigt sich nicht, auch Burleigh nicht,
Die ich ernannt, das Urteil zu vollstrecken.
Sind sie von London abgereist — dann ist's
Geschehen; der Pfeil ist abgedrückt, er fliegt,   3885
Er trifft, er hat getroffen; gält's mein Reich,
Ich kann ihn nicht mehr halten — Wer ist da?

Zwölfter Auftritt.

Elisabeth. Ein Page.

Elisabeth.

Du kommst allein zurück — Wo sind die Lords?

Page.

Mylord von Lester und der Großschatzmeister —

Elisabeth (in der höchsten Spannung).

Wo sind sie?   3890

Page.

Sie sind nicht in London.

Elisabeth.

Nicht?

Wo sind sie denn?

Page.

Das wußte niemand mir zu sagen.
Vor Tagesanbruch hätten beide Lords
Eilfertig und geheimnisvoll die Stadt
Verlassen.

Elisabeth (lebhaft ausbrechend).

Ich bin Königin von England!
(Auf- und niedergehend in der höchsten Bewegung.)

Geh! Rufe mir — nein, bleibe — Sie ist tot!   3895
Jetzt endlich hab' ich Raum auf dieser Erde.
— Was zittr' ich? Was ergreift mich diese Angst?
Das Grab deckt meine Furcht, und wer darf sagen,
Ich hab's gethan! Es soll an Thränen mir
Nicht fehlen, die Gefallne zu beweinen!   3900
(Zum Pagen.)

Stehst du noch hier? — Mein Schreiber Davison
Soll augenblicklich sich hierher verfügen.
Schickt nach dem Grafen Shrewsbury — Da ist
Er selbst!   (Page geht ab.)

Dreizehnter Auftritt.

Elisabeth. Graf Shrewsbury.

Elisabeth.

Willkommen, edler Lord! Was bringt Ihr?
Nichts Kleines kann es sein, was Euren Schritt   3905
So spät hierher führt.

Shrewsbury.

Große Königin,
Mein sorgenvolles Herz, um deinen Ruhm
Bekümmert, trieb mich heute nach dem Tower,
Wo Kurl und Nau, die Schreiber der Maria,
Gefangen sitzen; denn noch einmal wollt' ich   3910
Die Wahrheit ihres Zeugnisses erproben.
Bestürzt, verlegen weigert sich der Leutnant
Des Turms, mir die Gefangenen zu zeigen

Durch Drohung nur verschafft' ich mir den Eintritt.
— Gott, welcher Anblick zeigte sich mir da!   3915
Das Haar verwildert, mit des Wahnsinns Blicken,
Wie ein von Furien Gequälter, lag
Der Schotte Kurl auf seinem Lager — Kaum
Erkennt mich der Unglückliche, so stürzt er
Zu meinen Füßen — schreiend, meine Knie   3920
Umklammernd, mit Verzweiflung, wie ein Wurm
Vor mir gekrümmt — fleht er mich an, beschwört mich,
Ihm seiner Königin Schicksal zu verkünden;
Denn ein Gerücht, daß sie zum Tod verurteilt sei,
War in des Towers Klüfte eingedrungen.   3925
Als ich ihm das bejahet nach der Wahrheit,
Hinzu gefügt, daß es sein Zeugnis sei,
Wodurch sie sterbe, sprang er wütend auf,
Fiel seinen Mitgefangnen an, riß ihn
Zu Boden mit des Wahnsinns Riesenkraft,   3930
Ihn zu erwürgen strebend.   Kaum entrissen wir
Den Unglücksel'gen seines Grimmes Händen.
Nun kehrt' er gegen sich die Wut, zerschlug
Mit grimm'gen Fäusten sich die Brust, verfluchte sich
Und den Gefährten allen Höllengeistern: 3935
Er habe falsch gezeugt, die Unglücksbriefe
An Babington, die er als echt beschworen,
Sie seien falsch, er habe andre Worte
Geschrieben, als die Königin diktiert,
Der Böswicht Nau hab' ihn dazu verleitet.   3940
Drauf rannt' er an das Fenster, riß es auf
Mit wütender Gewalt, schrie in die Gassen
Hinab, daß alles Volk zusammen lief,
Er sei der Schreiber der Maria, sei
Der Böswicht, der sie fälschlich angeklagt;   3945
Er sei verflucht, er sei ein falscher Zeuge!

Elisabeth.

Ihr sagtet selbst, daß er von Sinnen war.
Die Worte eines Rasenden, Verrückten
Beweisen nichts.

Shrewsbury.

Doch dieser Wahnsinn selbst
Beweiset desto mehr! O Königin,   3950
Laß dich beschwören, übereile nichts.
Befiehl, daß man von neuem untersuche!

Elisabeth.

Ich will es thun — weil Ihr es wünschet, Graf,
Nicht, weil ich glauben kann, daß meine Peers
In dieser Sache übereilt gerichtet.   3955
Euch zur Beruhigung erneure man
Die Untersuchung — Gut, daß es noch Zeit ist!
An unsrer königlichen Ehre soll
Auch nicht der Schatten eines Zweifels haften.

Vierzehnter Auftritt.

Davison zu den Vorigen.

Elisabeth.

Das Urteil, Sir, das ich in Eure Hand   3960
Gelegt — wo ist's?

Davison (im höchsten Erstaunen).

Das Urteil?

Elisabeth.

Das ich gestern
Euch in Verwahrung gab —

Davison.

Mir in Verwahrung!

Elisabeth.

Das Volk bestürmte mich, zu unterzeichnen,
Ich mußt' ihm seinen Willen thun, ich that's,
Gezwungen that ich's, und in Eure Hände   3965
Legt' ich die Schrift, ich wollte Zeit gewinnen.
Ihr wißt, was ich Euch sagte! — Nun! Gebt her!

Shrewsbury.

Gebt, werter Sir! Die Sachen liegen anders,
Die Untersuchung muß erneuert werden.

Davison.

Erneuert? — Ewige Barmherzigkeit!   3970

Elisabeth.

Bedenkt Euch nicht so lang.   Wo ist die Schrift?

Davison (in Verzweiflung).

Ich bin gestürzt, ich bin ein Mann des Todes!

Elisabeth (hastig einfallend).

Ich will nicht hoffen, Sir —

Davison.

Ich bin verloren!

Ich hab' sie nicht mehr.

Elisabeth.

Wie? Was?

Shrewsbury.

Gott im Himmel!

Davison.

Sie ist in Burleighs Händen — schon seit gestern.   3975

Elisabeth.

Unglücklicher! So habt Ihr mir gehorcht?
Befahl ich Euch nicht streng, sie zu verwahren?

Davison.

Das hast du nicht befohlen, Königin.

Elisabeth.

Willst du mich Lügen strafen, Elender?
Wann hieß ich dir die Schrift an Burleigh geben?   3980

Davison.

Nicht in bestimmten, klaren Worten — aber —

Elisabeth.

Nichtswürdiger! Du wagst es, meine Worte
Zu deuten? deinen eignen blut'gen Sinn
Hinein zu legen? — Wehe dir, wenn Unglück
Aus dieser eigenmächt'gen That erfolgt!   3985
Mit deinem Leben sollst du mir's bezahlen.
— Graf Shrewsbury, Ihr sehet, wie mein Name
Gemißbraucht wird.

Shrewsbury.

       Ich sehe — o mein Gott!

Elisabeth.

Was sagt Ihr?

Shrewsbury.

       Wenn der Squire sich dieser That
Vermessen hat auf eigene Gefahr,   3990
Und ohne deine Wissenschaft gehandelt,

So muß er vor den Richterstuhl der Peers
Gefordert werden, weil er deinen Namen
Dem Abscheu aller Zeiten preisgegeben.

———

Letzter Auftritt.

Die Vorigen. Burleigh, zuletzt Kent.

Burleigh (beugt ein Knie vor der Königin).

Lang lebe meine königliche Frau,　　　　　　　　3995
Und mögen alle Feinde dieser Insel
Wie diese Stuart enden!
(Shrewsbury verhüllt sein Gesicht, Davison ringt verzweiflungsvoll die
Hände.)

Elisabeth.

Redet, Lord!
Habt Ihr den tödlichen Befehl von mir
Empfangen?

Burleigh.

Nein, Gebieterin! Ich empfing ihn
Von Davison.　　　　　　　　　　　　　　4000

Elisabeth.

Hat Davison ihn Euch
In meinem Namen übergeben?

Burleigh.

Nein!
Das hat er nicht —

Elisabeth.

Und Ihr vollstrecktet ihn,
Rasch, ohne meinen Willen erst zu wissen?
Das Urteil war gerecht, die Welt kann uns

Nicht tadeln; aber Euch gebührte nicht, 4005
Der Milde unsers Herzens vorzugreifen —
Drum seid verbannt von unserm Angesicht!
(Zu Davison.)

Ein strengeres Gericht erwartet Euch,
Der seine Vollmacht frevelnd überschritten,
Ein heilig anvertrautes Pfand veruntreut. 4010
Man führ' ihn nach dem Tower! Es ist mein Wille,
Daß man auf Leib und Leben ihn verklage.
— Mein edler Talbot! Euch allein hab' ich
Gerecht erfunden unter meinen Räten;
Ihr sollt fortan mein Führer sein, mein Freund — 4015

Shrewsbury.

Verbanne deine treusten Freunde nicht,
Wirf sie nicht ins Gefängnis, die für dich
Gehandelt haben, die jetzt für dich schweigen!
— Mir aber, große Königin, erlaube,
Daß ich das Siegel, das du mir zwölf Jahre 4020
Vertraut, zurück in deine Hände gebe.

Elisabeth (betroffen).

Nein, Shrewsbury! Ihr werdet mich jetzt nicht
Verlassen, jetzt —

Shrewsbury.

Verzeih, ich bin zu alt,
Und diese grade Hand, sie ist zu starr,
Um deine neuen Thaten zu versiegeln. 4025

Elisabeth.

Verlassen wollte mich der Mann, der mir
Das Leben rettete?

Shrewsbury.

Ich habe wenig

Gethan — Ich habe deinen eblern Teil
Nicht retten können.　　Lebe, herrsche glücklich!
Die Gegnerin ist tot.　　Du hast von nun an　　　　　4030
Nichts mehr zu fürchten, brauchst nichts mehr zu achten.

(Geht ab.)

Elisabeth
(zum Grafen Kent, der hereintritt).

Graf Lester komme her!

Kent.

Der Lord läßt sich
Entschuldigen, er ist zu Schiff nach Frankreich.

(Sie bezwingt sich und steht mit ruhiger Fassung da.　Der Vorhang fällt.)

NOTES.

*The figures in black-faced type refer to lines, which are numbered continuously from the beginning; * is used to mark notes on the stage-directions, not counted in the lines.*

ACT I., SCENE 1.

The first scene gives a dramatic and spirited opening. It is held at Fotheringhay Castle (afterwards destroyed by James I.), where Mary Stuart, already condemned to death, is kept under the guardianship of Sir Amias Paulet, a zealous bigot, and his assistant Sir Drue (Drugeon) Drury. (See Introduction, §§ 12, 13.) The dialogue between Paulet and Hanna Kennedy, Mary's faithful attendant and early nurse [the name is elsewhere given as Jane Kennedy], skillfully depicts the opening situation.

2. der Schmuck, which Paulet holds in his hand — found in the garden under Mary's window — gives immediate occasion to this scene. — **Schrank,** cabinet, or chest of drawers, including a writing-desk.

4. hat ... sollen, was to have been bribed; it is supposed, to convey a letter to Lord Leicester — of which hereafter.

6. meinem Suchen refers to the fact that Mary's papers, etc., had been seized at the time of Babington's conspiracy. (See Intr., § 12.)

* sich ... machend, going to work on — continuing his search.

10. Die eben, just these: They are just what I am looking for.

13. Like our "An idle brain is the devil's workshop."

15. Die, emphatic, *that* language. For word-order see note, *l*. 25. **Konzepte** means unfinished outlines or rough drafts — which may, however, have since been finished.

* Ressort (French, *ressortir*) is properly *a spring* — here, compartment opened by a spring. — **Fach,** drawer, or "pigeon-hole."

193

19. den Lilien, the *fleur-de-lys,* royal emblem of France, which Mary had worn as Queen of France. Legend attributes its origin to a shield sent by an angel to King Clovis. It is thought, however, that the device at first represented the head of a javelin.

22. besitzt, used absolutely — possesses anything — has anything left; that is, as a means of bribery, etc. — **Gewehr,** here poetic for **Waffe.**

25. Die Jammervolle: note emphatic position of object, as *l.* 15. In such case the emphasis is often best retained by taking the object as subject, and then adapting the verb; as: delights in the sight of, etc. Often, as *l.* 15, the verb will best be rendered as passive.

29. zu seiner Zeit, phrase: in due time — has here an ominous meaning (as will appear Act V.), which Kennedy does not suspect. — **Wird . . . zurückgegeben** (werden) — the frequent present for future, as *l.* 17.

30. sieht . . . an, sees from — by looking at. — **es** anticipates the following.

32. Himmeldecke, canopy — bearing the arms of Scotland, as symbol of Mary's royal rank. On the announcement of Mary's condemnation — which, however, Kennedy is here not presumed to know — Paulet had been ordered to remove this canopy, and Mary put a crucifix in its place. In other respects also her confinement had been made more severe.

33. zärtlich, in this sense more usually **zart,** is not adverb, but uninflected adjective, construed before another adj. as if forming a compound — a poetic form, which Schiller very often employs. — **weichgewöhnt** (soft-accustomed, used to softness) is an occasional compound such as, so often, English cannot imitate. [Such examples may at once usefully illustrate the frequent inadequacy of translation — all the better, if thereby the student is made to feel the limitations of his own idiom, and to *think* the original.]

35. schlechtste, here in the earlier — now poetic — sense of *humble, poor.*

37. Sterlyn, Stirling (Castle) — for the French spelling see Intr., § 15 — on the Forth, was an important fortress and a favorite abode of Scotch royalty. The time referred to was after the murder of Rizzio, when Darnley was said to have lacked at times almost the necessaries of life. — **Buhlen,** Bothwell; see Intr., § 9.

44. ihre Laute. Mary was an accomplished musician, especially on the lute. — **verbuhlte,** wanton. But we must remember Paulet was a bigot.

47. **in der Wiege Königin,** is literally true. See Intr., § 5. — **Weicherzogene,** we may say: for one so tenderly reared. See note, *l.* 33, at end.

48. **der Medicäerin,** Catherine de Medici, of the famous Florentine family, daughter of Lorenzo de Medici, wife and widow of Henry II. of France, mother of the kings Francis II. (Mary's first husband), Charles IX., and Henry III., and during the minority of Charles, Queen-Regent, was distinguished for ability and unscrupulousness, as well as for the splendor and gayety of her court (Intr., § 5). The phrase, however, is not here strictly accurate; for during Mary's youth in France, Catherine's husband was still living, and her own position at court not yet prominent.

49. **Freuden,** rare weak gen. sing., though more frequent in poetry; as also is the weak dative.

52. **lernt** is now the usual reading, from the early stage copies; but **lehrt** is the reading of the earliest editions. Note the accus. **in . . . .** implying *progress:* to reconcile itself to (gradually). — The phrase **wehe thut's** is very expressive — as of physical pain.

56. **soll,** is to — is intended to; that is, as shown by the treatment referred to. — **in sich gehen,** look into — examine itself. — **dem Eiteln,** to vanity.

61. Because Mary was not an English subject; moreover, the sins of her youth, which alone Kennedy here admits, were not committed in England. Paulet's reply refers to later charges.

63. **Zum Frevel,** dep. on **zu enge:** too narrow for . . .

64. **Aus diesen,** etc., refers in a general way to Mary's imprisonment, not literally to Fotheringhay, where Mary was not confined till later. — **Bürgerkrieges** refers to the uprising in the North under Northumberland (Intr., § 11), and **Meuchelrotten** to the following (Intr., § 12).

70. **Parry . . . Babington.** Parry was executed in 1585. It was the conspiracy of Babington (1586) which gave immediate occasion for Mary's trial. Both of them were charged with seeking the life of Elizabeth (Intr., § 12).

73. **Norfolk.** Thomas Howard, Duke of Norfolk, not only sought Mary's release but aspired to her hand. He was executed in 1572. His high rank and character, with his earlier well-tried fidelity, justify

Paulet's epithet, **das beſte Haupt,** etc.　See Intr., §§ 11, 12. — **zu um-
ſtricken,** from ensnaring; note infin. idiom.

77. wetteifernd, contending, as for a wager: with eager zeal.
Paulet's strong language hardly exaggerates the facts.　Scott says of
Mary, in *The Abbot:* "She is like an isle on the ocean, surrounded
with shelves and quicksands; its verdure fair and inviting to the eye,
but the wreck of many a goodly vessel."

78. Um ihretwillen.　The earlier **ihrentwillen** stands in all the
oldest editions.　For the forms, see Grammar.

84. Helena.　The Grecian Helen — herself a faithless woman —
whose coming to Troy brought war and ruin; so that the expression
conveys both personal and public reproach.　The phrase **dieſes Landes
Küſte** is not literally true of Mary's escape into England (Intr., § 9).

85. hätte, subj. indirect, referring to an actual or supposed statement — here ironically : England, you say, received, etc.　See Grammar.

86, etc.　The involved and elliptical constructions well express
Kennedy's passionate indignation; **die,** *l.* 86, is subject to **ſieht** . . .
muß vertrauen; while **da ſie,** *l.* 87, belongs to **geſetzt (hat)** . . . **kam**
— and, in both cases, the double clauses are without connecting conjunction.

89. Verwandten.　For the relationship see Introduction, § 5.
Kennedy's charge is perfectly true.

91, etc. ſieht . . . muß, construed with **ſeit,** *l.* 86 = *has seen . . .
has had to.*　Mary, now (1587) nearly forty-five years old, was only
twenty-six when, in 1568, she took refuge in England.

94. Bittres, *has of bitterness* — all the bitterness of imprisonment.
Compare **Eiteln,** *l.* 55.

97. Auf Leib und Leben, alliterative phrase, applied to indictment
of capital crime : on penalty of death. — **eine Königin,** she — a queen !

100. Greuelthat refers to the murder of Darnley (Intr., § 9),
after which Mary had been compelled to abdicate her throne.

102.　Mary, commonly known as "Bloody Mary," was daughter
of a Spanish mother and　wife of a Spanish husband (Intr., § 6). —
Verſchworen (note emphatic position), *as a conspirator against,* etc.

103. Engelland . . . Franzman are both earlier forms, the former
used here for the verse; the latter, contemptuously.

106-7. den Edinburger Vertrag, by the terms of which Mary was
"to abstain from using and bearing the title and arms of the kingdom
of England" (Intr., § 7).　The phrase **aus dieſem Kerker** is used with

the same freedom as heretofore, *l.* 64, etc. At the time of this **treaty** (1560) Mary was, of course, not in prison; but it was the claim which she then refused to renounce that afterwards held her in captivity. She claimed, however, that she had acted under her husband's compulsion, and that since his death she had never borne the arms of England.

111. **leerem Prunk,** empty show — as Paulet, of course, regards it.

114. **unheilspinnend,** mischief-plotting: by plotting schemes of mischief.

117. **hegte,** subj. indirect, as *l.* 85.

121. **kein ... mehr,** no other ... than. Note tense of **schaute**: *has beheld* — the indefinite past.

124. **Anverwandten,** Mortimer, Sc. 3, etc. Usually **Verwandten,** as *l.* 89.

128-9. **Nicht ... nicht,** emphatic repetition, for **ob ... nicht.** Note also the poetic (Saxon) gen.: **dieses Zimmers,** as often hereafter.

131. **mir geworden,** has fallen to me — become mine. For **unheilbrütend Listige,** see note, *l.* 33, end. Sometimes a conversion of terms may help; as here: artful brooder of mischief.

134. **Nachts,** by night, o'nights. For the form, see Grammar. — **Treu** (or **Treu'**) for **Treue,** as frequently for the verse.

138. **endet,** for fut., as heretofore. Paulet has in mind Mary's sentence, which, as we have seen, Kennedy is supposed not yet to know.

140. **Wachstehend = Wache stehend.** As often, a distinct verb will best translate the participle: stand guard ... and keep.

142. **Christus,** here, crucifix — descriptive accus. absolute. — **Hoffart,** from older **Hochfart** (=fahrt, from fahren).

ACT I., SCENE 2.

Mary's appearance, thus impressively announced, is made more impressive by her calm repose, in contrast with Kennedy's excitement, and by the dignity with which she meets Paulet's rude reproaches. The letter to Elizabeth, here mentioned, becomes of interest hereafter. Mary's hopeless condition is impressively pictured. In vain she asks intelligence of her fate; but is met only by Paulet's rude denial and still ruder insinuations.

145. **wird,** here implies the future sense; there is to be no limit to, etc.

148. **was neu = was neues.** Note that in her excitement, Kennedy, as if forgetful of Paulet's presence, uses **du,** etc.; elsewhere, **Ihr,** etc.

150. **gerettet,** that is, when her papers, etc., were seized. See note, *l.* 6. — She refers to the **Stirnband,** *l.* 18.

155-6. **niedrig . . . erniedrigen ;** the like relation of form should be preserved in translation. — For **gewöhnen lernen** (not *gelernt*), see Grammar.

160. **willens,** was of will — intended — to; see Grammar. — **noch heut** (like **Treu,** *l.* 135), this very day.

162. **Schwester,** in official or diplomatic sense, as often between sovereigns, etc.

165. **Burleigh,** William Cecil, Lord Burleigh, Elizabeth's prime minister. Throughout this play he is her chief adviser and Mary's most bitter enemy (Intr., § 18). Hume says he was "the most vigilant, active and prudent minister ever known in England." — Paulet's hesitation is skillfully made the occasion for the fuller exposition of the situation.

169. **Unterredung.** Mary had before vainly sought such interview.

172. **meinesgleichen** (also **meines Gleichen**), my equals. For the form, see Grammar. — **zu denen,** etc., towards whom I can feel no confidence — **mir,** the *ethical* dat.

178. **Männern** refers especially to Bothwell. Mary does not notice the sarcasm.

184. **die** = **diejenige die,** as frequently. — **Schon . . . entbehr' ich,** *l.* 182, tense as *l.* 91.

187. **der Dechant** (also **Decan'**, our *Dean*), of course a Protestant, was here Dr. Fletcher of Peterborough, who was also present at Mary's execution. — **Ich will,** etc., *I want nothing from — nothing to do with.*

190. **Notar'ien,** the regular plural is now **Notar'e.** Compare **Kleinodien, Kleinode.** In *l.* 192, note singular verb, as often hereafter.

197. **eine schnelle Hand** indicates assassination, or poison, which Mary is known to have dreaded — and with reason. She is here supposed (see note, *l.* 138) to be ignorant of her condemnation — which, in fact, had been communicated to her some months before.

200. **Verfügung treffen,** make disposition — dispose of. In next line, **die** as *l.* 18.

202. **mit Eurem Raube,** objective : with what is robbed from you; by robbing you.

206. **Entraten,** rare — here perhaps on account of **entbehren** below, which here stands absolutely = to want.

207. Mary actually made this request — as well as that in *l.* 189 —

in a letter to Elizabeth, after the first news of her condemnation. Some of her servants had been taken at the time of Norfolk's arrest, and still more when Babington's conspiracy was discovered (*l.* 70).

210. **geängſtigt fürchtend.** Here, with neuter noun, both adjs. are left uninflected. See note, *l.* 33. For gen. **der Qual,** see Grammar.

217. **die vierzig Kommiſſarien** (see **Notarien,** *l.* 190). This number is given elsewhere (*ll.* 578, 697) as forty-two. In fact, thirty-six had been present at Fotheringhay, forty at Westminster (Intr., § 13). The time here intervening was really much more than a month (Oct. 9–Feb. 6); but the shorter period gives color to the fiction that Mary is yet ignorant of the result (Int., § 2). She does not here exaggerate the facts.

221. **noch nie erhört,** "such as was never before heard of," truly describes the circumstances of Mary's trial. "Alas," she said, "how many learned counselors are here, and yet not one for me."

222. **Auf,** etc., depends on **Rede ſtehen** — compelled me to answer. The aux. **haben** is implied with all the verbs, *ll.* 218–224. Note again the emphatic and elliptical forms, expressing passion, as *l.* 86, etc.

223. **Mich,** emphatic repetition ; **die Betäubte,** also emphatic for **betäubt :** stunned and surprised as I was. — **Aus dem Gedächtnis,** because all her papers had been taken from her.

229. **Ob** would regularly be **oder (ob).**

235. **Euch werden,** as *l.* 131; in this sense = **zu Teil werden.** The form occurs in other sense, *l.* 425, etc.

236–7. Paulet knows, of course; only refuses to answer.

241. **als dieſe,** i. e. **die Richter :** than they did. Mary means the assassin; Paulet's answer refers to the executioner.

244. **Hatton,** Sir Christopher Hatton, Vice-Chamberlain and afterwards Lord Chancellor — one of the chief directors of the prosecution. See hereafter, Scene 7. — **Weſtminſterhall,** to which the court had been removed, for its final session — held in the Star Chamber, which, on other grounds, afterwards acquired infamous notoriety. — Note again sing. verb, as *l.* 192.

245. **urteln** = **urteilen,** for sake of the verse; — **erdreiſte,** potential subj.: might assume. — **Weiß ich doch,** emphatic inversion, as often with **doch.**

249. **geſprochen,** decided; **es** here repeats **foregoing.** Compare opposite use, *l.* 30 — both often called *expletive.*

ACT I., SCENE 3.

The character of Mortimer is wholly fictitious, yet he plays an important part in the drama (Intr., § 18). His appearance now serves to remove Paulet, and prepares a fine dramatic surprise hereafter.

* **auf eben die Weise,** in the same way; that is, without noticing the queen, which justifies her following remark. — **will,** is about to.

254. trage here = ertrage ; like cases are frequent in poetry. — **was,** *l.* 252 = etwas.

257. Wohl ist es keiner, as we say : Truly he is none of your, etc. Note use of **es.** Note also contrasted position of pron. objects : **ihn Euch . . . mir ihn.**

259. With **gereist,** thus used absolutely, we might expect **hat** ; but **ist** gives rather the *effect* than the fact merely. — The special significance of Rheims — where, if anywhere, Mortimer's fidelity might have been corrupted — will appear hereafter. Schiller had first written **Rom.**

261. dem, emphatic, as *l.* 10; — **ist,** for future, as heretofore. For the adjs. *l.* 260, see *l.* 210.

Paulet's concluding words — which will receive striking commentary hereafter — show also the harshest side of his character. Its better elements will appear later.

ACT I., SCENE 4.

The following scene is an important part of the exposition. Mary confesses her guilt in the murder of Darnley and in her marriage with Bothwell — as assumed by Schiller (Intr., § 17) — though in fact denied by Mary. There is thus laid the moral basis of the play. The form of the confession, through Kennedy's affectionate apology, is highly artistic. It may be added that the frank confession here attributed to Mary strengthens her protestations of innocence on other charges hereafter.

262. Euch . . . ins Antlitz, to your face.

269. Wart Ihr doch, as *l.* 245. — **Flattersinn,** 'ievity,' conveys only gentle reproach, as might be expected from Kennedy's affection.

272. Ich erkenn' ihn. These words Mary speaks to herself, as if seeing a vision. — **König Darnleys** ; see Intr., §§ 7, 9.

274. Friede, older (strong) form for **Frieden.** Note **erfüllet,** for the metre; also **blut'ge,** *l.* 272. Such enlargement or abridgment of form — especially by omission or use of *e* — is very common in German poetry.

278. There is here only slight error of date. Darnley was murdered Feb. 9, 1567; this date is Feb. 6, 1587. But, as we have seen, Schiller deals freely with such details.

282. **Reu** (or **Reu'**, as *l.* 126 — the use of the apostrophe varies), meaning (inward) *repentance,* has its counterpart in **Leidesproben,** (outward or actual) *sufferings.*

284. **Löseschlüffel,** key of absolution — as Kennedy and Mary believed. — In next line, note sing. verb, as *l.* 244, also below, *l.* 289, etc. This form occurs with great freedom, especially when the subjects follow the verb.

286. **vergebne** (see note, *l.* 274) implies, *though* long forgiven. — **leichtbedeckt,** a highly poetical epithet: lightly covered — too lightly to bury such a crime.

289-90. Referring to the services of the Catholic Church: to the bell rung by the acolyte during mass; and the host, or consecrated wafer, of the eucharist.

292. It may be questioned whether **ließ** here means *let, allowed,* or *caused* — probably the former. See note, *l.* 323. — **schmeichelnd,** by my enticements (Intr., § 9).

295. **zarten Alters,** predicate gen., as *l.* 160. Mary was really twenty-five years old at that date; but, as will be seen hereafter, Schiller represents both her and Elizabeth as much younger than they actually were.

297. **blutige** has here probably only the general sense, *brutal.*

303. **ungeſtammt,** hereditary. — **zum Throne.** Mary gave to Darnley the title of King.

312. **gabt . . . preis** (**Preis**), to give as a prize, surrender, expose. The orthography of such forms varies, as to the use of the capital letter — now less usual.

316. **der,** like **die,** *l.* 184, while **er** is emphatic repetition. — **spielen,** play (the part of). — Darnley's worthlessness and arrogance are here not exaggerated.

318. **Euch,** the ethical dat. — often untranslated — may here be rendered as possessive. — For Rizzio, see Intr., § 8. The epithet **schön** is only by poetic license, for Rizzio was not handsome. — In **Liebling** no criminal relation is here implied; none, indeed, probably existed.

323. See *l.* 292. Here — and hence probably there — the sense

seems to be *let*. Mellish (Intr., § 19) translates: "When you consented to this deed." For the true *causative* sense, see *l.* 318. — **ba,**
l. 322 = *while*, implying *even while*.

325. **hatte** belongs also to **unterjocht,** the word-order being irregular, from the emphatic position of **ergriffen.** Note the -s in **Liebesglut.** Compare **Nachts,** *l.* 134.

327. Bothwell; see Intr., § 9. — The epithet **unglückselig** probably
= **unglückbringend,** with reference to his influence on Mary.

329. **Zaubertränke,** magic potions, philters — which Bothwell himself afterwards confessed to have used. Darker means, even actual
violence, were hinted. The idea here expressed was, moreover, in
accord with the ideas of that time. As we read in *Othello* I., 1 : —

> " Are there not charms
> By which the property of youth and maidenhood
> May be abused ? "

and further also in I., 2.

331. **keine andre.** This form is more usual in Schiller's poetry
than the weak **keine andern,** which is now the rule. Earlier usage
varied. — Mary's reply testifies her magnanimity.

334. **mußte,** had to call — must have called. — **hell,** clear, keen.

336. **der Freundin ;** K. refers to herself. This picture is the more
intense because drawn by a friendly hand.

339. **der Menschen,** objective gen., *for men ;* that is, their opinion.

344. **stelltet . . . zur Schau,** exposed (to view) — phrase, as *ll.* 312,
316, etc.

346, etc. **ließt . . . hertragen,** etc., is not fact. Mary took no part
in the trial of Bothwell. He was tried, moreover, not by Parliament,
but by the High Court — so far, indeed, as tried at all — though the
acquittal was afterwards confirmed by Parliament. The event here
referred to occurred at the meeting of Parliament following the trial.

348. **dem . . . nachschallten,** followed by, etc., as *l.* 25. The
people believed in Bothwell's guilt, and largely also in Mary's collusion.
— **durch ihn,** i. e. as your representative. — **hertragen,** the prefix implies, in solemn procession.

352. **Possenspiel,** farce; such, in fact, was Bothwell's trial; yet
not (not openly at least) by Mary's connivance. But Schiller here
purposely darkens the colors for sake of the contrast hereafter.

358. **Verlornen,** if rendered by a noun, **ganz** will require an adj.,
as : a complete castaway — a perfect reprobate.

359. The force of **ja**, emphasizing usually what is assumed as known, or as matter of course, may here perhaps be rendered : don't I know you? — **ich bin's**, in English, the opposite form : *it is I;* or *I am she.*

363. **Ich wiederhol' es** refers to *l.* 333, etc. The belief in "evil spirits" has belonged to every age. See many instances in the Bible of demoniacal possession.

365. **Sich ... ihren ;** this use of the possessive (for the article, as *l.* 318), along with the dative, is unusual.

368. **befleckt,** polluted — by the consciousness and influence of sin, though committed under demoniac temptation.

372. **Friede,** as *l.* 274. Schiller represents Mary as atoning, by long penitence, for early guilt. Kennedy recognizes no other crime; as *l.* 61.

375. See note, *l.* 61. In the following Kennedy speaks as if the trial were not yet ended. See note, *l.* 138. So Mary, *l.* 236, etc.

ACT I., SCENE 5.

Mortimer reappears (see note *, Scene 3). In the next scene the situation is further unfolded, especially in its religious aspects. Mary learns her sentence, yet refuses to believe in its execution. Mortimer's plan for her release, and her final commission to him of a letter for Leicester, connect closely with the central action of the play hereafter.

382. **du bleibst** is a strong form of command. Note the broken line; so, *l.* 263, and hereafter.

385. **überfalle,** that he shall not, etc. — a common and obvious use of the subjunctive; though frequently, in such cases, the indic. is used instead.

ACT I., SCENE 6.

387. Charles de Guise, Cardinal de Lorraine, Mary's uncle (Intr., § 5), a powerful and zealous enemy of Protestantism, had been her early guardian, and always her close friend and adviser. He had died, however, in 1574, prior to the present date. The title was now borne by his nephew, Louis de Lorraine, who was Mary's cousin. This is another example of Schiller's free treatment of historical facts.

388. **Sir Mortimer ;** Mellish has : Sir Edward Mortimer. — The weak form **Mortimern,** below, was formerly quite common in proper names in –e, –er ; as **Goethen, Schillern, Petern,** etc.

394. Supply zu sehen glaubte, or ahnte.

396. mir (more usually mich) . . . gekostet, which to wear has cost . . ., i. e. which it has cost me . . . to wear, yet to which, etc.

403. die Zeit verrinnt is, under the circumstances, surely a proper caution, yet Mortimer forgets it directly. This scene, though rich in poetic beauty, is extended beyond all dramatic propriety. — The verhaßte Mensch is Lord Burleigh (Scene 7); the Schreckensauftrag, which here, strangely, does not arouse Mary's curiosity, will be made known by Mortimer himself — after a time.

412. die . . . Begierde, the art. implies that this feeling is well known to Mary. — das feste Land, the continent.

414. dumpfe Predigtstuben refers to preaching in private houses or "conventicles," as frequently among the Puritans. The term *Puritans* was adopted first in reproach; and these people were for a time almost as obnoxious to the English Church as to the Catholic.

416. gepriesen. As the home of art, culture, etc., Italy was then, relatively far more than now, the favorite resort of travel.

418. des g. Kirchenfests : no such festival occurred near this date. It is supposed that Schiller had in mind the jubilee year 1575, when Pope Gregory XIII. held a council at Rome.

420. Gottesbild, sacred image (of the Crucifix, the Virgin, etc.), such as are still to be seen on roadsides, in Catholic countries.

424. Weichbild (Eng. -*wick*, Lat. *vicus*), the immediate *precinct*, or limit of jurisdiction, of a town. — glaubenvoll ; usually glaubens-, as *l.* 475, etc.

425. wie ward mir, what feelings came over me. See, in difft. sense, *ll.* 131, 235. The broken line is here expressive of emotion.

426. Construe : der Säulen und (der) Siegesbogen Pracht, and note poetic freedom of word-order. Columns, triumphal arches and the Colosseum are among the monuments of ancient (pagan) Rome. The splendors of Christian Rome are mentioned later on.

428. den Staunenden. We cannot imitate the freedom of the German participle. See note, *ll.* 33, 223. Perhaps: wrapt me in astonishment. — Bildnergeist, artistic, or creative, spirit. Note accus., as *into* a new world; and see *l.* 52.

433. körperlos, unembodied, incorporeal, — without visible symbol. Note introductory (expletive) es, *l.* 431.

436. der Gestalten Fülle, the wealth of images streamed lavishly, etc. — referring to frescoes and other paintings in Catholic churches.

439. **gegenwärtig,** in living presence; **das H. und H.** means Divinity itself.

440. **die Göttlichen,** the divine forms — or scenes — of which those named are the most common: **den Gruß,** the Annunciation (Luke i. 23); **Verklärung,** Transfiguration (Matt. xvii. 2; Mark ix. 2) — though some suppose the Ascension to be here meant; **die herabg. Dreifaltigkeit** probably refers to the visible descent of the Spirit (Matt. iii. 16).

445. **das Hochamt,** High Mass, which at certain times the Pope himself celebrated in St. Peter's Cathedral (**sein Haus,** *l.* 449), and afterwards publicly blessed the people.

452. **Lebensteppich,** tapestry — as if embroidered with bright figures. Note the divided word — a license allowed only in compounds; — also the poetic gen. **mein** (for **meiner**). An accus. would be now more usual.

458. **zu schmücken** connects with **Haß** (as if **zu haffen**). — **dem ... Buch,** the Bible (*l.* 433). — **die Schläfe,** etc., as type of joy.

461. **Landsmannschaft,** properly an associated body; here, in a more general sense, groups, or companies. At such a time (*l.* 418) Rome was of course the resort of the faithful from all countries.

463. **Dem K. von Guise** is the same person as *l.* 387, though this title does not properly belong to him. Yet Schiller, as we have seen, is not careful about such details.

467. **Fürst.** The cardinals, who are next in rank to the Pope, are often styled Princes of the Church. — **wie ...,** etc., such as I have never seen; **sah,** as *l.* 121.

469. **des Mannes** expands **sein** : his face ... the man's.

472. **liebt ... blüht** ; **noch** belongs to both verbs: is he still favored of fortune, still in the flower of life? — **mein,** as *l.* 451. Here, as there, another form would be now usual, in prose.

475. **Glaubenslehren,** doctrines, dogmas. See *l.* 423.

478. **in der Irre leitet** ; phrase: leads astray. Compare **Irrlicht,** our *jack-o'-lantern.* — **grübelnde,** is a diminutive — here contemptuous — of **graben,** and implies minute search after trifles.

482. **Sitzungen,** sessions — or councils — of the Fathers (of the Church), by which creeds were settled, etc. — **not thut** (or **Not thut,** see *l.* 312), is necessary for.

485. **Suada,** persuasiveness. The word, now hardly used, seems to be from Italian (Lat. *suadere*), and is, possibly, a reminiscence of M.'s travels.

487. in feine Hände, phrase — before him — as if his hands received the oath. In kehrte . . . zurück, M., who was a Protestant from birth (*l.* 410, etc.), implies, as the Catholic Church holds, that other forms of faith are departures from the true Church.

490. des Berges, allusion to the Sermon on the Mount.

493. Reims, seat of the Catholic seminary for the education of priests — founded first at Douay by Dr. Allen, an eminent English Catholic. From this school came missionaries back to England, full of zeal for Mary. — Jefu (gen.), Society of Jesus — the Jesuits — a powerful order, founded by Ignatius Loyola — especially zealous for education.

496. Morgan, Thomas Morgan was a Welshman, not a Scotchman. A devoted friend of Mary, he was implicated in Parry's conspiracy and took refuge in France. His surrender was demanded and refused; yet he was confined in the Bastille, where he still continued to plot against Elizabeth.

498. John Lesley, Bishop of Ross, an eminent Scotch prelate, was one of Mary's most powerful supporters — was concerned in Norfolk's plot — first imprisoned, then banished (Intr., § 12). Note the dissyllable, Roße, which is hardly justifiable.

503. Fiel . . . Augen, phrase: struck my eye. — wundersam, poetic, like our *wondrous.*

506. mächtig, with gen., master of — able to control. — Bischof, i. e. of Ross.

513. verlor, like sah, *l.* 467: have lost.

518. Stammbaum, genealogical tree. See Intr., § 5.

522. Afterkönigin, spurious or pretended queen. See Intr., § 6. At one time Henry VIII. had excluded Elizabeth from the throne, as illegitimate — an exclusion which he afterwards revoked. Apart from this, however, in the Catholic view, E.'s claims were invalid, because Henry's marriage with Anne Boleyn was itself unlawful. — Engelland, as *l.* 103.

527. Wappenbücher, escutcheon books, books of heraldry — as if to investigate the question of title by descent. Note the form viel alte — also alle Kundige, as *l.* 331.

534. Mary speaks the truth. For this reason she was detained prisoner, and her life sought.

537. Talbot's Schloß. For many years Mary had been in the keeping of Talbot (Shrewsbury), whose kindness to her gave rise to

suspicion, and even to scandal. She did not, however, pass directly
from his hands into Paulet's nor to Fotheringhay; yet Schiller neglects
such details.

548. zehen, see note, *l.* 274. Note rapid play of tense: warb . . .
trete, etc.

553. O des, the gen. marking the cause of the emotion: O, happy
he, etc. Mary's beauty and personal charm, which so inspire Mortimer — by Schiller represented as her chief offence against Elizabeth
— have been often celebrated. See a charming description in Scott's
Abbot, II., 1.

556. Aufstehen, emphatic position; würde belongs to all the
infins., as *l.* 325.

558. Empörung schreiten reminds us of Virgil's description of
Fame, Æn. IV., *l.* 176, etc. — Britte (or Brite), in the narrower sense
of Engländer.

562. Continues the foregoing condition, dep. on Wohl (wär' es)
ihr. For word-order in next line, see *l.* 426.

566. Raubt . . . von (also gen.). The more usual form is seen
l. 184. For Leidesproben, see *l.* 283.

578. Die Zweiundvierzig. See note, *l.* 217. Reference is here
made to the final session at Westminster (Intr., § 13).

580. die Gemeinen, the Commons; the statement is true — probably also the motive attributed to Elizabeth. Mary is right in adding,
also, that her judges dared not give her liberty: they were themselves
too deeply involved.

590. wo . . . hinaus will, where they mean to end — what they
are aiming at. In fact Mary did not believe that Elizabeth would dare
to execute upon her the sentence of death, but dreaded rather other
means — and with reason, as we shall see.

594. Dabei, etc., they will not stop at that.

600. könnte, as *l.* 117, etc. Do you suppose, etc.

604. und aller Könige, her own . . . and that of all, etc. See
l. 469. König is often used for monarch, without regard to sex.

607. Duc von Anjou, formerly d'Alençon, youngest brother of
Mary's first husband, was in fact dead at this date. The affair referred
to really took place in 1581–2. See Act II., 1, 2.

608. der König Spaniens, Philip II., formerly husband of Queen
Mary of England, from whom, as a Catholic sovereign, Mary expected
promised help.

613. mehr, in sense of mehrere, more than one, several. Note the gen. Elizabeth's mother, Anne Boleyn, and Catherine Howard, wives of Henry VIII., were both beheaded on the charge of unchastity. Lady Jane Grey, proclaimed Queen of England by Northumberland according to the will of Edward VI., though not actually crowned, was beheaded in 1554. She was "royal" also by descent from Henry VII.

622. andre Mittel ; see note, *l.* 590. We shall see hereafter that such means were not only advised, but actually intended by Elizabeth herself.

626. noch eher, emphatic repetition : far sooner.

629. er könnte, dep. on Schauder — lest it might be. — **Kredenzt,** accredited — as if prepared and *foretasted.*

636. darauf refers to following : upon their vow to, etc. — For **Aubespine,** see Act IV., Scene 2. — **bietet die Hände,** offers aid.

645. warnend, as a warning. Such exposure, though not unknown, did not actually occur in this case. Tichburn was beheaded as one of Babington's accomplices. — **Wagstück** is usually **Wagestück.**

647. See note, *l.* 77. — **der Unzähligen** is of course exaggeration; yet Mary's lot was actually embittered by the attempts of her friends, as well as by such rumors, industriously circulated by her foes.

652. mischte, tense as *l.* 513, etc. Mary here refers to plans more than once adopted by Elizabeth's ministers.

It may be added that Walsingham — whom, however, Schiller mentions only casually — deserved, rather than Burleigh, the epithet **Späher.** But Schiller, with true poetic instinct, frequently thus violates historical accuracy, to avoid multiplication of personages and to concentrate the dramatic interest.

654. kein Glücklicher is here used as if adverbial : no one has with good fortune — without disaster — defended, etc.; or as if in predicate : Mary Stuart has had no fortunate defender.

This sentiment, alike true and touching, is said to have been often uttered by Mary. Scott, in *The Abbot,* attributes it to her repeatedly; as when, looking on the dying Douglas, she says : "Look there, and tell me if she who ruins all who love her ought to fly a foot farther to save her wretched life."

655-8. This repetition of Mary's words marks M.'s passionate emphasis. It is, however, rather in epic than dramatic style.

668. Lester (Leicester) is spelled by Schiller so as to show the English pronunciation. This nobleman was one of the most brilliant and ambitious, and at the same time unscrupulous, of Elizabeth's courtiers. He is made to play a central and characteristic part in this play, which, however, is wholly fictitious. He was, indeed, one of Mary's bitter enemies, and even advised poison as a means of getting rid of her. His relations to Elizabeth gave rise to repeated scandal; and he was even accused of being privy to the murder of his first wife (Amy Robsart) to open the way to marriage with the Queen (see Scott's *Kenilworth*).

671. bin idj, conditional: if I am to be saved, it is, etc.

673. ſendet, that it is I that *send* you. For alternative form, see Grammar.

675. trage . . . ſdjon, as *l.* 91, implying that she had been seeking opportunity to send it. Hence the conjecture, *l.* 4, note.

683. Again Burleigh appears in his representative character (Intr., § 18; *l.* 652, note). He was not really the messenger of this intelligence, which, indeed, had been brought long ago. It may be added, also, that Mary's earnest dissuasion of Mortimer's plot serves also the purpose of substantiating her plea of innocence hereafter. — **mit Gleidj= mut** has reference to Mortimer's assurances, *l.* 631, etc.

ACT I., SCENE 7.

In this Scene the exposition is skillfully continued. Instead of the simple ceremony of the actual announcement to Mary, the author makes it the occasion of reviewing, in vivid dialogue, the chief points of accusation in Mary's trial, the constitution of the Court, the laws under which it assumed to act, and Mary's dignified and eloquent plea of defense.

690. den Geiſt . . . den Mund, spirit . . . tongue; that is, communicates the sentence which he inspired — as Elizabeth's prime minister. Note, *l.* 686, the form **von Burleigh,** after German analogy (French *de*); so, often, in earlier English phrase: my lord of Burleigh, etc.

693. Zur Sadje, (proceed) to business. It must be remembered that Mary has already heard the sentence from Mortimer.

696. Ins Wort . . . fallen, phrase: interrupt. — **hätte,** as *l.* 85.

701. ſo viel vergeben, so far forfeit, or impugn. This is the only place where Mary mentions her son (James VI., afterwards James I. of England), now twenty years old. His actual relation to his mother had become so remote, in some respects so unnatural, that Schiller does

no⁺ make him a party to this play. It has been therefore justly supposed that this allusion is an oversight of the author.

703. **Geſchworne,** our *jurors,* with same meaning. — **von ſeines-
gleichen,** of his peers (equals); see *l.* 172.

705. **Committee** (here = **Commiſſion**), has English spelling, but
as the verse shows, French pronunciation (*comité*). The fem. is perhaps due to final –*ee* (Fr. *le comité*). **Peers** is English.

707. **lieſt . . . vernehmen,** submitted to examination. — **vor Gerichte,** technical phrase, without article.

709. **Hatton,** see note, *l.* 244. Mary had steadily refused to appear before the Commission, whose authority she did not acknowledge.
Hatton persuaded her that, if innocent, she had nothing to fear, but, by
refusing to answer, would confess guilt, and stain her reputation with
eternal infamy. To this argument she yielded.

716. **Ob . . . ob,** as *l.* 229. The sentiment of the following lines
(719, etc.) was expressed in Elizabeth's own letter to the Commission.
Mary asked the Lord Chancellor to explain it, who replied, that it was
not for subjects to interpret their sovereign's letters!

723. **Heißt das,** is that, do you call that, living, etc. For **kenne,**
etc., see *l.* 269, etc.

729. **zum Freibrief,** as a license; literally, a letter, or patent, of
privilege.

732. **Themis,** Greek goddess of Justice. — **ſtünde,** old form; see
Grammar.

737. **Sind es etwa,** are they, forsooth, wretches (see **Verlorne,** *l.*
359) picked up from the populace. — **Pöbel** is contemptuous. —
Zungendreſcher, tongue-threshers, pettifoggers, 'shysters.'

741. **Dingen laſſen,** can be hired as, etc.

750. **Völkerhirte,** shepherd of the people. The Archbishop of
Canterbury is the Primate, or chief bishop, of England.

752. **Talbot** (Earl Shrewsbury), was not really keeper of the Great
Seal, but Lord Marshal. See note, *l.* 652. Note poetic gen. **Siegels,**
as heretofore, *ll.* 451, 471. — Charles Howard, Lord Admiral, who afterwards commanded the English fleet against the Spanish Armada. He
was urgent in inducing Elizabeth to sign the death warrant.

It is remarkable, however, that none of those mentioned were at the
trial at Fotheringhay, nor was Shrewsbury at Westminster. Special
efforts were made to secure afterwards his signature to the sentence.
His kindness to Mary, as her keeper, has been noted already.

758. **Und wär's,** etc. And if it could be imagined that partisan

hate should corrupt an individual (that is, one by himself). — **vierzig,**
see *l.* 846, where the vote is quoted (incorrectly) as forty against two.

763. **von je** (her), ever, of old. — **war,** pret. indef. *has been,* as
heretofore. — **ungelehrt,** is modesty only; Mary was far from **ungelehrt,** at least in womanly culture, as regarded in those days.

766. **Lords,** like **Peers,** *l.* 706. — **müßte,** I should have to, etc.

770. **sollen,** as *l.* 56: are intended to (as you allege).

776. **Großohms** (**Oheims**). Mary was granddaughter of the
sister of Henry VIII. — **Sultanslaunen,** sultanic (despotic) humors.

779. **prägen,** stamp (as coins); here, enact. Mary's charges are
true. The reference is, of course, to Henry's marriages and divorces,
and to the disinheritance of his daughters, Mary and Elizabeth, which
was afterwards revoked.

786. **vier ... viermal.** True. In Mellish's Translation (Intr.
§ 19) stands: —

> "renounce the Pope
> With Henry, yet retain the old belief;
> Reform themselves with Edward; hear the mass
> Again with Mary; with Elizabeth,
> Who governs now, reform themselves again."

790. **Seid Ihr's,** emphatic form: be you also (**es = gerecht**). —
meint es gut, phrase: mean well.

796. **Eben darum,** for this very reason. Mary's argument, addressed to B.'s self-love, is very artful. It is also true; Elizabeth's
ministers recognized no other rule, in their dealings with Mary. — **erscheine,** as *l.* 385.

799. **dran,** as **darauf,** *l.* 636. — **noch edle Männer,** other, etc.

804. **Britte,** as *l.* 560. — **Wort,** here = proverb.

806. **grauer,** by an obvious symbolism, for *ancient.*

809. **Gesetz.** Such law could hardly have existed; yet this plea is
said to have been made (though vainly) by the Bishop of Ross, on his
trial before an English court. The next line (810) is a favorite quota-
tion.

813. **Brett,** plank, as if too narrow for both. — **ungleich,** un
equally, England being much larger than Scotland.

815. **Tweede,** with –e, is here fem. — **Bette,** old form, whence the
plural **Betten.**

818. **drohend,** like **warnend,** *l.* 645; **schauen sich an,** have been
watching each other.

826. Mary's prophetic words, to which Burleigh replies with such bitter scarcasm, were fulfilled in the person of her own son. She may well herself have cherished such a hope. — **brüderlich,** factitive: in brotherhood.

831. **Ölbaums,** the olive tree, symbol of peace. — **frei und fröhlich,** also factitive: in freedom and happiness.

837. Mary was great-granddaughter of Henry VII., Earl of Richmond, of the House of Lancaster, first of the Tudor kings, who, after the victory at Bosworth over Richard III., united the White and the Red Roses, and so ended civil war, by marrying Elizabeth of York, daughter of Edward IV. The allusion is therefore specially apt in Mary's mouth. — **Schottland,** etc., in apposition, as if **Kronen = Reiche.**

844. **Streitens wegen,** not for disputation. Burleigh may well seek to end a discussion in which he gains no laurels.

846. "By forty votes against two" is not historically correct. Two of the Commissioners, Shrewsbury and Warwick, were absent. One only, Lord Zouch, refused to concur in the sentence, believing her innocent of the charge of intended assassination.

847. The omission of **habt,** followed by **seid,** is unusual.

849. Burleigh now begins to read the sentence. The Act referred to is not quite correctly given. It provided that any person in whose behalf rebellion should be excited, should be excluded from all rights to the throne, and that all persons charged with plotting against the Queen should be tried for life by a Commission, etc. The Act was manifestly aimed against Mary, and held her responsible for plots in her behalf.

853. **sie . . . die schuldige,** refer to **Person;** hence, in English, *him . . . the guilty one* (in general). — For **erhübe,** compare **stünde,** *l.* 731.

858. **Sich . . . lassen,** can be used, etc. Here, as elsewhere in this scene, Mary's own utterances at her trial are closely followed.

863. **Zu Eurer Warnung;** so said Elizabeth in her address to Parliament, replying to Mary's charge above.

869. **Wissenschaft,** here in the earlier sense of *knowledge.* (See Intr., § 12.) — **planvoll,** perhaps, 'artfully.' See *l.* 114.

871. **Wann hätte,** as heretofore: When do you say I did that?

874. **Kopien.** Right here is the crucial question of Mary's guilt or innocence of the charge of conspiring against the life of Elizabeth. The letters to Babington, produced at her trial and alleged to have been found among her papers, clearly proved such guilt. But these

were not the originals, and Mary contended that the alleged copies
had been falsified and interpolated by the agents of Walsingham.
Babington attested the letters shown to him; but they may not have
been the same; and he was executed without giving opportunity to
test the question.   The secretaries, Kurl and Nau, also testified without
actual sight of the documents in question (and later, moreover, declared Mary's innocence).   The question is too long for discussion
here; but it is, perhaps, not too much to say, that the general verdict
of historical criticism sustains Mary's defense, that the letters relied on
to prove her guilt had been falsified by her enemies; or, at least, that
their genuineness was not proved.   Some of the grounds of this belief,
as adduced by Mary on her trial, are stated in this scene.   The
„frembe Hand" was one Philips, notoriously an agent and instrument
of Walsingham.   Mary herself accused Walsingham of the fraud,
which, in great agitation, he denied, but did not attempt to disprove.

876. diktiert. Much of Mary's large correspondence was dictated to
her secretaries, then transcribed, sometimes in cipher.

883. Stirne gegen Stirne, face to face. Burleigh does not answer, because he *could* not.

884. Kurl und Nau, the former a Scotchman, the latter a Frenchman who wrote Mary's cipher letters. It was upon such letters — de
ciphered, moreover, not by Nau but by Philips — that the evidence
against Mary was based.

889. verraten (haben). This argument is sound, and applies, in
general, to all such testimony. — The phrase auf Treu und Glauben
is idiomatic, like vor Augen, *l.* 881, vor Gerichte, etc.

892, etc. Here is implied Mary's distrust of Nau, which was first
more fully expressed (as in Mellish's Trans.) a few lines below. The
suspicion, later here omitted, that Kurl had been corrupted by Nau,
recurs Act V., Scene 13.

896. konnte . . . ängstigen, *may have*, so that, etc. Note the
idioms. The word ängstigen implies fear of torture, not actual torture,
which was not administered, because it was not necessary!

899. Because he believed her, as a queen, to be above the danger
of punishment.

903. stelle . . . gegenüber, let them be brought before me; mir
ins Antlitz, see *l.* 262. Mary's plea is the more striking when she
appeals to a law passed in Elizabeth's own reign — still more striking
is it, that the refusal to confront Mary with her secretaries was sup-

ported by Elizabeth's own letter to Burleigh, "that she considered it
unnecessary"!

905. **verweigern,** the absolute infin., as in English: why deny?

909. **Reichsſchluß,** Act of Parliament. — **durchgegangen** is an
expressive phrase for 'passed.'

912. **als Biedermann;** = to be, etc. — **jeßo,** old form for **jeßt;**
here with emphasis.

915. **Rechtens,** old gen., now technical: according to law. See *l*. 160.

924. Mary's question is unanswerable; Burleigh seeks refuge in
other charges.

928. **Bleibt,** etc., stick to the point. — **Beugt,** now usually transitive; here intrans., as older form of **biegt**: do not evade the question.
Mary means, truly, that this is the sole ground of her actual trial.

929. **Mendoza,** ambassador of Philip II., was implicated in
Throckmorton's conspiracy, 1584, and — though he denied the impu-
tation — was forced to leave England; was afterwards ambassador to
France, where he continued active efforts against Elizabeth, and in
Mary's behalf.

932. **Anſchläge geſchmiedet (haben),** laid plots, etc.   Burleigh, not
minding Mary's haughty interruption, continues to refer to her alleged
complicity with Mendoza.

935. **Gethan (hätte);** in next line the indic., **ich that's,** concedes
the supposition, for argument's sake: suppose I did.

942. **Und ſo,** And so — under these circumstances.   Mary's assertion is unanswerably true.

946. **Zwangsrecht,** right under compulsion: right of self-defense.
— **da ich . . . ſtrebe,** in striving to free myself from; — verb of motion
implied.

950. **Was irgend nur,** emphatically indefinite: whatsoever. —
guten, lawful.

955. **Entehren, ſag' ich,** is an expression of personal pride.

958. **iſt . . . die Rede,** is the question, is it a question of; —
because, as above seen, Mary denied responsibility to English law; so
also at her trial.   Her statement, **von Gewalt allein,** seems justified
by the facts.

960. **der Gefangenen,** though by the form referring to Mary, is
yet general in sense = a prisoner. — * **bedeutend,** significantly.

963. **bringe . . . das Opfer,** let her make this sacrifice to.   Note
ſi. — avoiding, contemptuously, the use of Elizabeth's name.

968. in heiliges Gewand (note accus.), in holy garb — implying deceitful disguise. — Gaukelspiel, compare Possenspiel, *l.* 352.

971. Ermorden laſſen; note strong emphasis of position. That Mary feared such attempt has been seen already, and will appear more fully hereafter.

972. es anticipates, as heretofore. We may render: let her give up the attempt to, etc. Note the introduction of rhyme, as frequently — especially at close of a scene or speech — to mark with lyric effect the emphasis of passion or sentiment.

It is to be remarked that Burleigh does not complete the announcement for which he had come. Whether this is an oversight, or whether Schiller meant thereby to show how far Burleigh was disconcerted by Mary's eloquent defense, or whether finally her sudden and passionate withdrawal prevented it, must be left to conjecture. From an earlier text, Mellish has the stage-direction, *l.* 970, *returning the verdict;* but it nowhere appears that this was handed to Mary.

Mary's cause has now been presented by herself with utmost force. The next scene will further unveil the picture.

ACT I., SCENE 8.

This scene unfolds the dark purposes of Mary's enemies. Burleigh, staggered by her unshaken courage, hints at the secret purposes of the Queen; but is met by Paulet's sturdy honesty. Such means are known to have been suggested to Paulet, at the Queen's instance, in a letter from Walsingham and Davison (see *l.* 1095, note). The fact that this was known to Davison is alleged as one reason for the severity of his punishment (Act V.).

978. Urtelſpruch ; compare urteln, *l.* 245.

980. ruft', so all the earliest editions, rufte being rare weak form for rief. But the present ruft gives equally good sense.

981. Zweifelmut, indecision, a trait which (whether real or assumed) Elizabeth often showed at critical times, to the alarm and cost of her ministers. Hence unſere Furcht, our timidity; that is, our hesitation, based on this trait of the queen.

987. The mention of Tichburn here is striking. Though executed with Babington (*l.* 645), he gave no testimony against Mary. Mellish (Translation) has "Ballard." He was a young priest from Rheims, who co-operated with Savage (Intr., § 12). But see note, *l.* 652.

990. This line expresses truly the fear of Elizabeth's ministers: *they dared not*, though a false ground is here alleged.

994. dazu, like darauf, *l.* 636, etc. B. here designates Kurl, for reasons, *l.* 884, etc.

997. So, emphatic, *then, therefore.* — festliches Gepräng. The trial had been conducted with great pomp, all the more because so extraordinary. See *l.* 221.

1003. Daß . . . doch . . . wäre, optative sub., *would that,* etc.

1008. doch, at any rate. Hence, he means, no use to try to save appearances.

1012. Mag es, let it, etc.; that is, the open procedure, which B. would avoid.

1015. hält es mit, holds (it), sides, with; es, as *l.* 791. — den obsiegend Glücklichen, the fortunate victor, as *l.* 132, etc.

1019. der Frauen is shown by der Mann to be here singular; as *l.* 49.

1021. Umsonst, daß, ellipsis for: es ist umsonst, etc. — nach Gewissen, phrase, without art., as heretofore.

1026. Und also is spoken inquiringly, as B.'s interruption shows.

1032. vielbedeutend, with deep significance.

1038. steht . . . ändern, cannot be helped. For stünde, see *l.* 731.

1042. wissen; we should expect wüßten, and *l.* 1045, hüteten: who knew how, etc. — yet the present implies, with more emphasis: *as you do.*

1050. See note 537. Schiller, as usual, simplifies the history.

1055. dächte implies that he still holds the opinion. — Schergenamt, is contemptuous, as if unworthy of Paulet's rank.

1057. es dep. on schuldig bin : owe it; perhaps an old gen.; see Grammar.

1059. Man breitet aus . . . läßt. B. speaks as if describing a supposed case, a softened form for breite aus, etc. — Sie schwinde, that she is in a decline (Cf. Schwindsucht, consumption). — läßt, i. e., by report. The suggestion, here artfully hinted, was more plainly communicated by letter to Paulet (see Intr. to this scene). His reply is worth quoting: "My goods and life are at her Majesty's disposition, and I am ready to lose them to-morrow, if it shall please her. But God forbid that I should make so foul a shipwreck of my conscience, or leave so great a blot to my poor posterity, as to shed blood without law or warrant"; a reply the more remarkable in an age in which human life and official conscience were held so cheap.

1066. die Götter is in classical phrase, reminding of the Roman *Lares et Penates*.

1069. den Stab. The breaking of a staff, symbolical of the death-penalty.

Note the concluding rhyme, as at end of Scene 7, and hereafter. The harsh traits of Paulet's character now appear in better light. The full extent of Mary's peril, and the nature of the designs against her life, are now disclosed. She passes for a time from the scene, not appearing at all in the next Act; but already she has the deep sympathy of the spectator, and all that concerns her fate will be followed with the keenest interest. On the other hand the character of Elizabeth, in advance of her appearance, has been already projected in darkest colors. The exposition, excepting only the undue length of Scene 6, has been full of dramatic interest.

ACT II., SCENE 1.

The time of action is the morning following the first Act. Kent describes to Davison a spectacle which had just taken place, typical of the Duke of Anjou's suit for Elizabeth's hand. (See next scene.) Such tournaments we know to have actually occurred during this courtship. Elizabeth's love of public display is, moreover, well known. (See Scott's *Kenilworth.*)

1077. Turnierplatz (Fr., *tournoi ;* Eng., tourney).

1085. berennt, more usually, **berannt.** The idea of Love, attacking the fortress of Beauty, is familiar in the old chivalry, though it seems not to be known from what source Schiller drew this description. In part, however, it is supposed to be imitated from the first scene in Shakespeare's Henry VIII.

The officials following are to be understood as only represented, not as really appearing in person: **Oberrichter,** Chief Justice; **Seneschal,** Lord Steward; and below, **Kanzler,** Lord Chancellor.

1088. Kavaliere, properly, horsemen, knights; here *cavaliers,* or gentlemen.

1090. aufforderte, challenged, summoned to surrender. The challenge by a herald, or by one of the contestants, was the usual mode of opening the lists. — **Madrigal** is a short song, usually amatory.

1094. **Feldstücken,** Eng., field-pieces; here, mimic cannon.

1100. **doch,** after all. But Davison's more intimate knowledge of Elizabeth's character causes him to doubt.

1102. **Die ... Artikel,** i. e. concerning religion, Anjou being a Catholic. At one time, E. had required that he should become a Protestant; later, the plan here named was agreed on.

1104. **Monsieur,** the official title of the eldest brother of a French king.

1107. **Hättet,** etc.; as we say: Had you only seen, etc.—**Zeitung,** here = news.

1110. **Sie möchte,** dep. on **Furcht,** *that,* etc. Such was really the fear of the people and of the government; and so, the cause of Mary's persecution. See *l.* 534. Hence the perpetual projects concerning Elizabeth's marriage.

ACT II., SCENE 2.

Audience of the French Ambassadors, with reference to Anjou's suit. Elizabeth is surrounded by her court. Some of the striking features of her character are shown in contrast with the polished arts of the French diplomat. The action of this scene stirs Leicester's jealousy, and so prepares the way for what is to follow. — As usual, Schiller deals very freely with the historical facts. For many years Elizabeth had been dallying with marriage proposals from the youngest son of Catherine de Medicis, formerly d'Alençon, since the accession of Henry III. known as Duc d'Anjou. After repeated embassies (the last, here referred to, in 1581), and an earlier visit *incognito,* the Duke at last came himself to receive her promised troth. The incidents of this visit are in part used in this scene. It seemed at last that the Virgin Queen would yield; but once more her own indecision and the resistance of her counselors triumphed, and Anjou was dismissed, though on her part with appearance of deep reluctance, and even with love-sick protestations. Anjou, who, as we have seen, was dead at the date of this play, was at that time 28 and Elizabeth 49 years old. He was, moreover, so unattractive in person and in mind and character that it is difficult to conceive how, even as an old maid, she could have seemed to love him. But the affair, strange as it was, was no greater puzzle than are other puzzles in Elizabeth's strange character.

1116. **Graf;** the real name was l'Aubespine, comte de Châteauneuf. See *l.* 638; and further Act IV., Scene 2.

1119. **St. Germain** (en Laye), a pretty town near Paris, where Francis I. had built a palace — a favorite resort of the French court. — **Götterfeste,** that is, fit for the gods, of divine splendor.

1124. **Sänfte,** sedan chair, in which ladies of quality were borne in those days. Elizabeth's well-known vanity here takes the form of affected self-depreciation.

* **Bellievre** (pron. as Fr. *Bellièvre*), here represented as ambassador extraordinary, was not really a member of Anjou's mission; but was sent later (1586) to intercede on behalf of Mary Stuart.

1135. **Urlaub** (rel. to **erlauben**), usually *furlough;* here, *leave.* Bellièvre refers to the object of the mission as practically accomplished. See *l.* 1102, etc.

1141. **Posten,** relays — at successive *posts.*

1147. **Hochzeitsfackel,** a familiar classical allusion. Hymen bears a lighted torch, in mythology.

1149. **ziemte,** subj. Elizabeth's allusion to Mary, and pretended sympathy with her, are here characteristic. She often recurred to this subject, in discussing the French marriage. — **Könige,** *l.* 1155, as *l.* 604.

1159. **hätte . . . läse,** condit. subj. — **darein . . . daß,** in the fact that, implies an accus. with **in** (after **setzte**). This sentiment was once expressed by Elizabeth in a letter to Parliament, and in various forms frequently.

1163. **dahin,** *gone.* — **Nicht genug,** elliptical, as **umsonst,** *l.* 1021. E. had been often urged to marry, in order to settle the succession, and especially in order to exclude Mary.

1169. **ihm,** the ethical dat., to them, in their opinion.

1175. Referring to her father, and to her brother Edward VI.; — **daß,** for having, etc.

1179. **Beschauung,** that is, as in a cloister.

1188. **vorzuleuchten,** to shine before, as a guiding light: be a shining example to. — **Jedwede** is an archaic — here emphatic — form.

1190. **es würdig ist,** see *l.* 1057. — For **zum Opfer bringen,** see *l.* 963.

1193. This description is in strong contrast with the actual Anjou. His natural ugliness was further disfigured by small-pox.

1198. **es,** anticipative : cannot do otherwise, cannot help yielding to.

1207. **nichts voraus vor,** no advantage over. — **hat . . . doch,** as *l.* 245, etc.

1212. The ring was in fact presented by E. to Anjou himself, on his visit in 1581. When, soon after, she withdrew her promise, he left the room in anger, and throwing down the ring, he exclaimed that the women of England were as changeable and capricious as their climate, or as the waves that encircled their island.

1217. meiner Fürstin, as if already the wife of his prince.

* unverwandt, fixedly — to see what effect this would produce upon her favorite and lover.

* das blaue Band, the broad blue ribbon, or sash, extending over the left shoulder and around the right hip; a silken garter was also clasped below the left knee — both bearing the motto of the Order. A silver star was also on the breast. E. had herself invested Leicester with this Order. This preliminary ceremony promises the complete investiture of the Duke hereafter.

1221. Honi soit, etc., the motto of the Order of the Garter. These gallant words, usually rendered " Evil to him that evil thinks," were spoken by Edward III. as he handed to the Countess of Salisbury the garter she had dropped. Hence the origin of this Order — one of the proudest marks of royal favor. As President of the Order, E. calls it **meines Ordens.**

1224. Frankreich, etc., as *l.* 838; note also use of **Britannien** for *England,* as *l.* 560, etc. — **beiden,** the two.

1232. Vermengen, subj., let us not. Elizabeth's characteristic jealousy of her royal prerogative is here finely indicated.

1237. es = Frankreich ; hence, *she.* For the divided compound, see *l.* 452.

1242. In diesem Sinn, that is, without political intent. Again she asserts her royal dignity — with an implied message of warning to France.

ACT II., SCENE 3.

Elizabeth with her Councillors of State. Burleigh (Intr., § 18) seizes the opportunity to urge, on grounds of public safety, the execution of Mary Stuart. Shrewsbury (here called by his family name, Talbot) makes a noble plea in her behalf, in which more than once his candor and zeal wound Elizabeth's vanity. Leicester, less sincere than either and with more selfish motives, meets Talbot's frankness with artful flattery and urges delay. Elizabeth reserves her decision. The scene sets the political situation, as well as the character of the actors, in the strongest light. Its length, however, might be criticised, since it does not directly forward the action, and is, moreover, in part repeated hereafter

1246. **Wünsche,** that is, for her marriage, which might give an heir to the throne. Note the solemn **Du** ; Elizabeth replies with **Ihr,** as usual.

1249. **Zukunft** refers to the possibility of E.'s death without an heir.

1257. **der Wahrheit** refers to religious truth — the Reformation; **Freiheit,** to political independence — both imperiled by Mary's claims.

1265. **Nach . . . steht,** their hearts are turned towards . . . look to. The term **Götzendienst** was commonly used as a reproach to Catholicism.

1266. The "Lorraine brothers" are Mary's cousins, Henry, Duke of Guise, and Louis, Cardinal of Guise, sons of Francis, Duke of Guise. They were, as Mary's uncles had been, the powerful and inveterate enemies of the Reformation and of Elizabeth.

1271. Louis, the Cardinal, was Archbishop of Rheims, as also the Cardinal, his uncle, had been. See *l.* 493.

1273. **der Königsmord,** that is, of an excommunicated sovereign like Elizabeth.

1275. **Missionen,** here, missionaries ; — **Gewand,** disguise, as *l.* 968.

1277. **der dritte Mörder,** Ballard, a young priest from Rheims, had been implicated in Babington's conspiracy. The other two are not clearly indicated; but probably Throckmorton and Parry are meant. See Intr., § 12.

1281. **Ate,** goddess of Discord. Shakespeare, King John, II., 1 speaks of :

> . . . the mother queen,
> An Ate, stirring him to blood and strife.

See also Julius Caesar, III., 1, "Caesar's spirit, with Ate by his side"; and Spenser, in the *Faerie Queene*, introduces "the old hag, Ate."

1288. **ihnen,** as **ihm,** *l.* 1169 — because, in the view of all true Catholics, Elizabeth was illegitimate.

1291. **zu schreiben,** to sign, or style, herself — when wife of Francis, after death of Queen Mary of England. It is true that the Guises, Mary's uncles, were active in urging her husband and herself to this course. See *l.* 106.

1297. **aus Euch,** we should say, *in you.* Elizabeth claimed to be — perhaps really was — averse to the execution of Mary.

1304. **strömt es . . . gleich,** as *l.* 671, for **wenn . . . gleich,** etc. The impersonal often requires a different form in English; as : Though such eloquence streams not . . . yet, etc

1310. regieren, have ruled, as *l.* 91, etc. The term **eigen Fürstin** is meant to include the whole period of national indepen-dence.

1315. Nun dann, so, emphatic, Well, then; **wirst** is also em-phatic. See *l.* 382. For **beflecken,** that *we should*, see *l.* 1149.

1319. So, again emphatic, *then*. Note sing. verb, as *l.* 284, etc. — **Richterhöfe** (usually **Gerichtshöfe**), etc., is an exaggeration.

1323. An oft-quoted line; **Probe,** proof, test. The same senti-ment is expressed by Schiller in his *Demetrius*, beginning and ending thus:

> Was ist die Mehrheit? Mehrheit ist der Unsinn,
> Verstand ist stets bei wen'gen nur gewesen.
>
> .   .   .   .
>
> Der Staat muß untergehn, früh oder spät,
> Wo Mehrheit siegt und Unverstand entscheidet.

and Mary herself warned the Commissioners: "Remember, the theatre of the world is wider than the realm of England."

1328. anders wendet, changes (its direction).

1337. die Wahrheit, the reality, implies the indecision of her pre-vious conduct.

1341. unstät . . . Rohr, that is, public opinion. Compare Act IV., Scene 10.

1347. Könige, as *l.* 604. In most countries of Europe women were excluded from the throne; Elizabeth in her reply resents the re-flection upon her sex. See her words 1170–1.

1351. Keinen Anwalt replies to E.'s **ein warmer Anwalt;** per-haps, too, with implied reference to Mary's trial. See *l.* 220.

1360. alles, everybody. Note the boldness of Talbot's plea. E. had always refused to grant Mary an interview.

1363. Nicht ihrer Schuld, her guilt I do not excuse. He here presumes the same guilt as was confessed by Mary, Act I., Scene 4, and repeats the same excuses.

1368. b. Krieges — rather the act itself precipitated the civil war. See Intr. § 9. — **umrungen,** more usually umringt. See *l.* 349.

1371. Mutvollstärksten, we cannot imitate: bravest *and* strongest. — **wer weiß,** etc., of who knows what arts. See *l.* 330, etc. The next line is very fine. In his self-forgetful zeal, Talbot again touches E.'s vanity; yet he does not notice her sharp retort.

1379. keinen Thron, because disinherited by her father,

1382. **der g. Vater** is by some taken to refer to Henry VIII. But *l.* 1388 clearly shows that God is meant. Moreover, it was not by Henry, but by her sister Mary, that in 1554, after Wyatt's rebellion, E. was sent first to the Tower, and afterwards to Wocdstock. See Intr., § 6.

1386. **in sich gehen,** see *l.* 56. For the following, see *l.* 48; also Intr., § 5.

1395. **ward . . . zu teil** (or **zu Teil,** *l.* 312), was allotted. Again he offends E.'s vanity, here in its most tender point, as we shall see hereafter.

1400. **sondergleichen,** without parallel. See **meinesgleichen,** *l.* 172.

1403. **Was,** etc. here insinuates *those unequaled charms,* an implication of special significance from Elizabeth to Leicester.

1406. **Märchen,** idle stories, i. e. of danger from Mary. — **ängften =** **ängstigen.**

1414. **Auswurf,** outcast, for Mary had been deprived of her throne and driven from Scotland by her own people (Intr., § 9). — **machte,** subj., *could make.*

1421. Parliament had by special act confirmed the will of Henry VIII., by which, should his son Edward die without issue, the succession should descend to his daughters, and after them, if dying without issue, to the line of his younger sister Mary, countess of Suffolk (grandmother of Lady Jane Gray); thus ignoring (**stillschweigend**) the descendants of his sister Margaret (Mary Stuart's grandmother). But Mary's claim, as has been seen, rested on other grounds.

1424. **des neuen Lichts,** of the Reformation.

1429. **Mit der Erbin;** for after all, the provisions of Henry's will being exhausted, Mary's claim would still accrue.

1432. **Jugendkraft.** Elizabeth was now actually fifty years, Mary forty-five years old. But, in pursuance of his purpose to make Elizabeth's jealousy of Mary's beauty a prominent motive, as well as for other obvious reasons of stage interest, Schiller supposes both to be in the prime of life; Mary, as he says, about twenty-five, Elizabeth about thirty — an age at which both flattery and jealousy are supposed to be especially sweet to woman.

1435. **ohne . . . brauchtest,** without yourself needing to, etc. **brauchtest** is subj., as **machte,** *l.* 1416, etc.

1440. The explanation of Leicester's inconsistency, though he alleges another, is to be found in the fact that the alliance with Anjou puts an end to his hope of Elizabeth's hand; and his restless ambition is again secretly turned to Mary (Intr., § 7).

1449. **Verhüte ... daß nicht,** take care that . . . not (*lest*) etc. For **töten,** *l.* 1447, see *l.* 905. Leicester's object is only to gain time for his own possible schemes.

1457. For the order see *l.* 298. It will appear hereafter how far this pious reliance is sincere. E.'s habitual indecision as to Mary is here illustrated. Compare Burleigh's words, *l.* 981.

ACT II., SCENE 4.

Paulet appears, with Mortimer, and delivers to Elizabeth the letter entrusted to him by Mary, *l.* 160, etc. Elizabeth keenly questions Mortimer. The reading of the letter exhibits another view of Elizabeth's character, and renews the discussions of the preceding scene, not without some loss of dramatic interest.

With the last scene, the exposition may be said to be concluded, and with the present scene the development of the action begins.

1462. **ohnlängst** is more usually **unlängst.**

1470 **den großen Weg** corresponds to our "the grand tour."

1476. **Morgan ... Roße;** see 496, 498. — **ränkespinnend;** see *l.* 114; such occasional compounds are frequent in poetry.

1478. Rheims (see note *l.* 493) was naturally the resort of Mary's banished friends. — For the form **alle schottische,** see *l.* 331.

1481. **ob ... entdeckte,** (to see) whether I might perchance discover something of, etc. — **was,** for **etwas** — here on account of **etwa.** The frequent use of this subj. form — less usual in prose when identical with the indic. — has been already noted.

1483. **Ziffern.** Much of Mary's correspondence was in cipher — a fact which naturally increased suspicion. Such were her letters to Babington, which she claimed had been falsely deciphered and perverted.

1489. Walsingham was in fact not in France now, though he had been earlier ambassador there. He is in this play only casually mentioned (also *l.* 1750), though really, even more than Burleigh, he had been Mary's chief enemy. See note, *l.* 652; also *l.* 874.

1490. The Bull of excommunication against Elizabeth was uttered by Pope Pius V. in 1570, and had lately been circulated anew (Intr., § 11). The Vatican is the official residence of the Pope. — **Bulle,** Lat. *bulla;* from the official seal attached.

1496. **gab ... schuld, daß,** accused you of having, etc. For **die Schulen,** see note, *l.* 493.

1503. **selbsteigene;** the emphasis of the compound can be ex-pressed only by the *tone* — which often in English supplies the place of form. Observe that Paulet's act is better than his word, *l.* 166.

1509. **mit denen ... soll,** which we must spare — with which we must not afflict, etc. **soll** gives a more direct and personal force than **sollte;** see *l.* 56.

1518. **Wer's ... meint;** see *l.* 791. Admittance to the presence of royalty implied favor, or grace, as will be seen hereafter.

1529. **Wie weit,** how low. What is the meaning of these tears? The reader may better judge hereafter.

1531. **den ältesten Thron,** that of France, by her first marriage. — **drei,** France, Scotland, England.

1534. **welch andre:** "what a different ... from when," etc. See *l.* 106, note.

1540. **Irdisches,** abstract, usually with art., **das Irdische.** In **das entsetzliche** we must repeat the noun: the awful fate. German has much more freedom than English in its use of adjectives — a natural consequence of their inflection. Hence idiomatic forms need atten-tion.

1545. **büßte,** as *l.* 513, etc. **der Tiefgefallenen,** see preceding note, and *l.* 46, 223, etc.

1560. **zu wählen,** = um ... zu wählen; dep. on **bedarf.**

1562. **nichts gemein mit,** nothing in common — nothing to do — with.

1567. **Wenn,** emphatic — even if, although.

1569. **was,** for und was. — **Wir** is here the *official* plural. Note that here, as at end of Scenes 2, 3, Elizabeth closes with the assertion of her royal dignity, which, in form and in fact, she was always careful to maintain. See also note, *l.* 1457.

ACT II., SCENE 5.

Elizabeth detains Mortimer, and seeks artfully to sound him. With equal art he leads her on, until she confides to him her inmost thought and purpose. This scene is masterly, in both content and form.

1573. **Beherrschung Eurer** (usually **Euer**) **selbst** = Selbstbeherr-schung.

1575. mündig, properly under one's own protection or control — of age, *a man.* (Compare Vormund, guardian, from old die Mund ; not from der Mund, *mouth.*)

1589. Mortimer speaks of the legal sentence; but his words mean more, and Elizabeth knows it.

1592. handeln, operate, take their course.

1602. zum Richter, as judge — every one judges it. E. speaks the truth; only her inference is wrong.

1606. doppelt, ambiguous, questionable.

1608. (der) **den . . . eingesteht** — see *l.* 184 — is that which is confessed, i. e. confession is the greatest of mistakes. Elizabeth here, as indeed in her actual character, shows keen knowledge of the world.

1610. wär's. Thinking to read Mortimer's thought, E. exposes her own. For aus Euch, compare *l.* 1297.

1613. Euch (*dat.*) **ist es ernst,** phrase: you are in earnest. — **. . . auf den Grund,** to the bottom — no half-measures.

1616. See note, *l.* 1059. In fact, after receiving Paulet's letter, E. called him 'a dainty fellow.'

1619. Darf ich Euch, some such word implied as trauen. — **den Namen,** etc., refers to Elizabeth's fears above, *l.* 1598, etc.

1624. heute nacht, usually, to-night; here, last night. The orthography nacht or Nacht is unsettled; as *l.* 1395, etc.

1627. Laßt, etc. Be not grieved, etc. The dramatic form of these lines corresponds to the thought suggested. Schiller is, indeed, severe upon Elizabeth. Does she mean what she insinuates? or is she only deceiving Mortimer too?

ACT II., SCENE 6.

Mortimer, in passionate soliloquy, expresses his contempt for Elizabeth and his love for Mary — also his hope of gaining time for Mary's rescue while Elizabeth awaits the fulfilment of his promise.

1636. Fertigkeit, readiness — for crime: unscrupulousness.

1643. Bedeutend, see *l.* 1032 — refers to E.'s hints, at end of last scene. — **Und,** emphatic, *and even.* — **deine Frauengunst** expresses, euphemistically, what was implied in E.'s words, *l.* 1627, etc. — favor as woman, not as queen. We may render, perhaps, *love.*

1646. Ruhmes, again poetic use of "Saxon gen." — here objective = Geiz nach, etc.

1649. **der Jugendlust,** as *l.* 426. Note also recurrence of rhyme, marking the rise of lyric passion.

1653. **ein Herz ... dem Herzen;** we should say: heart ... to heart. — **Wenn,** etc., defines the foregoing: when (namely), etc.

1656. **liebend,** as *l.* 656, etc., by loving — with your love.

1659. **habe ... Herz;** see *l.* 173.

ACT II., SCENE 7.

Paulet, apprehensive about Elizabeth's interview with Mortimer, returns, and remembering the proposals made to himself, warns him in earnest language. The scene is interrupted by Leicester, of whom Mortimer (after *l.* 1507) had secretly asked an interview.

1669. **wünschte ... gethan (hätte),** I could wish — subj. of softened statement — yet often with full indicative force.

1679. **Weg mit,** as in English: away with, etc. **angesonnen,** suggested — asked of you.

1686. **verwerfe,** supply **Gott;** see *l.* 1314.

1690. Leicester's words confirm Paulet's suspicions. His reply shows that he will hereafter watch Mortimer, whose plans for Mary's release are thereby impeded.

ACT II., SCENE 8.

Mortimer and Leicester meet at first with mutual distrust. Finally Mortimer delivers Mary's letter, which L. receives with great rapture. Mutual explanations follow. Leicester depicts the humiliating life he has so long led, and declares that his heart now turns again to his early love for Mary. Mortimer reveals his plans for her rescue, and asks Leicester's assistance. Leicester takes alarm, and refuses, thereby incurring Mortimer's contempt; but declares his hope of gaining time, and, further, of secretly effecting an interview between the two queens and thus rendering Mary's execution impossible. The scene — though too long — is full of dramatic power.

1694. **wandelte ... an,** what was the matter with; — the phrase is used of any sudden attack. — **Ritter,** here as title only.

1699. **in geheim;** so in earliest eds.; others give **ingeheim.** — **von Lester,** as *l.* 686. In *l.* 1700 **mir,** more usually **mich** — Schiller uses both forms. See *l* 396.

1703. **zweierlei** = two different — one to Elizabeth, one to himself (as implied by asking this interview). Mortimer's reply refers to L.'s relations with Elizabeth and with Mary (as known to himself).

1709. Note contrasted order, with changed emphasis: *That* is you. No, 'tis *you*. — For the gen., *l.* 1710, see *l.* 469.

1714. **zarten Punkt,** his relations with Mary — hence, also, with Elizabeth.

1719. **So tief . . . zu thun,** so . . . as to, etc.

1729. **würdet . . . erklären,** is here subj. indirect.

1733. **ihrer Richter,** etc. was not the fact. L. had not been present at Mary's trial; yet not the less was he her declared enemy, who from his post in Holland had written to recommend the "sure but silent agency of poison," and had even sent a divine (!) to persuade Walsingham to adopt it.

1736. **dem,** idiomatic dat., dep. on **so**: that must be so.

1741. **mit wenigem,** adv. phrase, as *l.* 1699: briefly, in few words.

1746. **Glaubensänderung,** as described Act I., sc. 6, was known also to Elizabeth, *l.* 1497 — hence, was notorious. L., practiced courtier as he was, disregards Mortimer's excuses to the queen, *l.* 1498.

1750. It is true that Elizabeth's ministers regarded Leicester with well-founded distrust and dislike. — **lauernd,** secretly, as *l.* 656.

1762. **zugedacht,** intended — by Elizabeth (Intr., § 7). But the offer was hardly sincere; nor was L. willing to surrender his hope of marriage with Elizabeth.

1767. All this, as we have seen (note *l.* 668), is purely fictitious. For **das heißt,** that is — that is what I call — see *l.* 723.

1775. **zehn Jahren.** The time was really much longer — more than twenty years. But Schiller shortens the interval, in conformity with his purpose to make Elizabeth and Mary much younger than they were.

1779. **Wüßte,** as *l.* 1107. — **zehen,** as *l.* 548.

1785. **grillenhaft,** humorsome — capricious — willfulness; a true description of Elizabeth's changeful temper.

1790. **ins Verhör genommen,** we say: taken to task. The "Argus" of mythology had a hundred eyes. — If anything could arouse sympathy for such a character, surely this eloquent and truthful description would move our pity. We may compare Spenser, *Mother Hubberd's Tale,* describing the court of Elizabeth:

" Full little knowest thou, that hast not tride,
    What hell it is in suing long to bide :
    To lose good dayes that might be better spent ;
    To waste long nights in pensive discontent ;
    To speed to-day, to be put back to-morrow ;
    To feed on hope, to pine with feare and sorrow ;
    To fret thy soule with crosses and with cares ;
    To eate thy heart through comfortlesse dispaires ;
    To fawne, to crowche, to waite, to ride, to ronne,
    To spend, to give, to want, to be undonne."

1794. **Täuſcht mich,** etc. Leicester concludes, not heeding the interruption nor his own digressions, as if in immediate connection with
nachdem, etc., *l.* 1781. For the broken and passionate style, we may
compare *ll.* 85, etc., 216, etc.

1797. **Verliere . . . an,** lose . . . to, means : they are won from me
by . . .

1810. **ſtand neu :** not, of course, the picture just delivered by Mortimer, but her image, in his heart ; **ich ſuche,** *l.* 1805, etc., being the
historical present, as appears more clearly below.

1812. **verglich,** that is, Mary and Elizabeth.

1816. **ob . . . könnte,** for **daß,** etc., because the hope is so doubtful ;
that I might yet perchance. — The **treue Hand,** etc., implies, prior to
the opening of this play ; thus justifying Mary's expectations, Act I.

1824. **ließt . . . daß,** etc., allowed her to be, etc.

1830. **Sonſt fand** = hätte gefunden, würde gefunden haben — the
form expressing the certainty of the assumed result, as if *a fact.* Compare : else she *had* not even found, etc.

1832. **ſelbe** = dieſelbe. See note, *l.* 537.

1837. **leidend,** refers to Leicester, ' passively,' would have let her
go, etc. In **das Äußerſte,** etc., L. confesses the motive of his advice,
l. 1450, etc.

1846. **wolltet ;** subj. as *l.* 117, etc., ' you intend, you say . . .'

1853. **wär' er vollſtreckt,** sc. worden. For **beſtünde,** see *l.* 731.

1855. **mich verſichern.** Compare note, *l.* 1699 ; also *l.* 1845.

1863. **Es iſt nichts,** etc., phrase : nothing can be done. — **nächſten,**
l. 1861, readiest.

1866. **der . . . will.** See note, *l.* 673. Note the following rapid
dialogue in single lines — a form much used in the Greek drama.

1874. Strong inversion for emphasis.

1878.   es, i. e. to do so.   See note, *l.* 1190.   In *l.* 1876, **des Nor-folfs** would be, more regularly, **Norfolfs,** or **des Norfolf.**   For the matter, see *l.* 73.

1883.   auf . . . geleitet, started on so good a track — moving on so well.   In the following **Wohl auf,** etc., Mortimer continues scorn-fully the same thought: Yes, forsooth! on the good track that *you* have laid!

1886.   Bube, here in bad sense — *scoundrel.*

1900.   So minder = um so —, so much the less. — **Anstand nehmen,** hesitate.

1905.   Burleigh, etc., see *l.* 1527. — **Vielleicht, daß,** as *l.* 1021.

1915.   Ihr bringt.   Such resources were easily in the power of the great nobles of England, who still had the following of feudal lords.

1919.   der Howard . . . der Percy, gen. pl.   Howard was the family name of the duke of Norfolk; Percy, that of the Earl of North-umberland — both of whom had been executed (Intr., § 12); yet had left powerful connections.

1924.   Ritter, knight, champion — referring to the ancient chivalry.

1928.   ist . . . gefolgt.   See the famous description in Scott's *Kenilworth* of Elizabeth's visit to Leicester — founded on fact.

1934.   Frauenreich, woman's rule; as *l.* 1644. — **eng . . . ge-bunden,** contracted.

1938.   Federn, springs — as in a watch; that is: every heroic im-pulse relaxed. — True enough, from Leicester's point of view, of Eliza-beth's immediate courtiers; but by no means true, of course, of her influence in general, as a sovereign — which is not here intended.

1944.   Note emphatic change of form, as *l.* 1709, etc.; also **bringen,** as *l.* 674 — our *carry, take;* and **Die,** emphatic, *that.* — *l.* 1940, **kom-men,** abstract; i. e. some one coming.

ACT II., SCENE 9.

Leicester and Elizabeth.   By artful flattery and sinister suggestion, addressed to Elizabeth's worst impulses — which he knows so well — Leicester persuades her to see Mary, and arranges a plan for their seemingly accidental meeting.   This is in accordance with his own scheme, to procure delay.   The scene is a masterpiece of portraiture. The two characters — each practicing dissimulation — unveil themselves completely, while the action hastens to its climax.

1947. **betreten,** confused — as he might well be, at E.'s sudden appearance. — **Über deinen Anblick,** objective: at the sight of you!

1953. E.'s questions invite the flattery she loves so much.

1959. **Trotz sei.** Let me bid defiance, etc. — **Erdenrund,** globe; or we may say: this round earth.

1962. **nie gesehen** is not fact. As we have seen already, Anjou did — in fact twice — come to England to press his suit. See **intr.** to Act II., Scene 2.

1968. **Dudley,** note the affectionate name, also the singular pronoun. She is not less insincere, only less artful, than he. — **ja,** you know.

1971. **das ... was,** for, him ... whom, by a sort of euphemism like: the object of their love.

1974, etc. Her irrepressible jealousy of Mary opens in advance the way that Leicester meant to prepare.

1983. **mich ... zu freun** includes both objects. Note unusual order. — **das Joch.** She means of self-sacrifice as sovereign. — **Hätte ich doch,** as heretofore: yet I too might have, etc.

1991. **dieser,** here contemptuous: that (old) T. L.'s reply refers to suspicions noted *l.* 537.

1996. **Larve,** contemptuous, implying artificial show.

2002. **wünschte,** as *l.* 1669. — **was,** *l.* 2000 = warum. — **in geheim,** as *l.* 1699; a more modern form is also **insgeheim.**

2013. **sieht's ... an,** as *l.* 30 = she does not show it. — **Freilich,** etc., elliptical, as in English: Indeed, her sufferings! is artfully spoken to confirm the truth by suggesting a probable explanation.

2021. **gewußt ... gethan** express respectively *feeling* and *conduct:* has been so proud and boastful of, etc. Note the coolness with which L. now speaks of a marriage which, a while ago (1950), caused him to sigh so deeply. But his sighs are like Elizabeth's tears!

2023. **peinigt** refers especially to Talbot's urgency, Scene 4 of this Act, where Leicester, though more artfully, had suggested the same advice. Now he presses it, by arguments welcome to Elizabeth's vanity and malice alike.

2032. **leichtsinnig buhlend,** by frivolous coquetry: yet the words mean worse.

2034. **Bräutlichkeit,** perhaps, *bridehood* (Mellish has *tender bridal graces*), but **Braut** is not = *bride.* — **hat ... geschlagen** (= wird geschlagen haben) assumes the condition as already real. Compare *l.* 1830.

2042. **findeſt** does not belong to foregoing condition, but is independent = future, by a sudden and passionate ellipsis.

2045. **denkt . . . auf** is more than **denken an**, and implies a purpose, or object in view. — **der 3. Punkt,** *that,* etc.; see *l.* 1714. Note accus., **vor dein Gericht.**

2051. **Magſt du,** condition, though you may, etc. L. here hints at means which he knew would be not unacceptable to Elizabeth, by way of removing the scruples indicated by himself, *l.* 1905, etc.

2055. See *l.* 30, etc. **Vorwerfend,** a reproach to me; at present she may plead ignorance.

2060. Schiller here locates Fotheringhay much nearer to London than it actually was. — **kann ſich . . . ergehen,** can be walking, implying that he will so arrange it, by secret orders.

2062. **von ohngefähr** (= **ungefähr**), as if by accident — referring to Elizabeth's known fondness for the chase.

2069. **am wehſten gethan,** have pained you most — as if superlative of **weh thun;** see *l.* 53.

2071. **Dadurch . . . daß,** in that — by granting, etc. — **Grille,** figurative, as *l.* 1785, whim, caprice; that is, I do it only to please you. — The words, though insincere, are in themselves innocent enough. But, interpreted in the light of 1210, etc., and of 1628, etc., they complete a picture of utter heartlessness, and worse. The sympathies of the spectator are now fully engaged — alike for Mary and against Elizabeth.

ACT III., SCENE I.

The time is the afternoon of the second day. In this Act the crisis of the play is reached in the meeting of the two queens, which results disastrously and precipitates the catastrophe that Leicester sought to avert. See Intr., § 16.

In the first scene Mary is found walking in the park, as had been arranged by Leicester. In lyric stanzas of irregular form and of great beauty, she expresses her joy, her longing and her new-born hope. Schiller, following the example of the Greek chorus, makes use here, for the first time in his dramatic writings, of the lyric form, which he used so freely in later plays. The effect in this instance is very fine, especially in contrast with the prevailing gloom of the play.

2074. **So,** that is, so rapidly. — **doch,** I pray, *do wait.*

2076. **ſei es mit,** be one with me, is parenthetical. Note gen. with

genießen, as *l.* 752, etc. — Note also the effect of the rapid dactylic movement.

2084. **um . . . Weniges,** by a very little, as we say: *a little bit.*

2091. **Himmelsschoß,** we say: canopy of heaven.

2097. **Ozean,** here poetic, for the sea that washes France. The "misty mountains" were of course not actually in sight; but Schiller deals freely with geography, as with history.

2099. **Wer . . . wanderte** an elliptical form: (happy) who should, etc., for: would that I might, etc. Mary's heart ever turned to France, where she had spent her happy youth. The well-known lines: —

> Adieu, plaisant pays de France!
> O ma patrie
> La plus chérie,
> Qui a nourri ma jeune enfance!

etc. (even if not her own) beautifully express this sentiment, and have long been associated with her name.

2107. **legt . . . an** (= **ans Land**). In **befreundeten Städten** she again has in mind France, rather than Scotland, where her enemies were now in power. It has been also aptly suggested that she here remembers her rescue in a small boat by Douglas, from her imprisonment in Lochleven. See Intr., § 9.

2131. **wird,** as *l.* 235, etc. — **noch gestern,** only yesterday; usually **erst gestern. — denen,** emphatic: *their* chains too, I have heard say.

2135. **Mächtigen Rufes,** adv. gen., *with,* etc. — **zu schwingen,** as in English: O, to spring . . .! — an absolute use of infin.

2138. **Noch mehr,** once more! (she hears the sound again). — In next line **schmerzlich,** is probably adverb: painfully sweet.

2141. **bergicht,** is usually **bergig.**

This conception of the hunting horn, at once announcing to the spectator the approach of Elizabeth, and in the unsuspecting Mary arousing the tenderest recollections and longings — and so uniting both dramatic and lyric elements — is infinitely beautiful.

It may be added that imprisonment was really all the more bitter to Mary, from her hardy and joyous temperament. "O land," she is made to say in Scott's *Abbot,* while prisoner at Lochleven, on looking at the map of Scotland: "O land, which my fathers have so long ruled! of the pleasures which you extend so freely, your Queen is now deprived, and the poorest beggar, who may wander free from one landward town to another, would scorn to change fates with Mary of Scotland."

ACT III., SCENE 2.

Paulet announces to Mary the approach of the Queen, supposing it
to be the result of the letter delivered by himself. Mary is overcome
with surprise, and shrinks from the interview — yet not for fear.

2143-4. **endlich . . . einmal** have reference to his former severity.
— For **seid Ihr's**, see *l.* 359.— Paulet does not know of Leicester's
intrigue — nor, of course, does Mary.

2156. **Wie wird Euch,** what is the matter with you?

2160. These words imply that Paulet would willingly see Mary
pardoned, if consistent with the royal will; yet his severer judgment
appears below, *l.* 2168.

2165. **Dünkt mir,** as *l.* 1459. The accus. is also used.

ACT III., SCENE 3.

Shrewsbury, whose sympathy for Mary has been already shown,
hastens on ahead of the hunting party to warn her. He seeks to prepare her mind for the coming interview — informs her also that it is
due to Leicester. — These two short scenes serve to give time for the
Queen's arrival.

2170. **nicht darum,** not on that account — not for fear; my feeling is a wholly different one. Note the emphatic accent. **dar'um.**

2175. **Faßt . . . zusammen,** compose your mind.

2184. **gewendet,** compare zugesendet, *l.* 2172, weak forms.

2187. **Höllengeister,** spirits of hell — the Furies, in mythology.
In Goethe's *Iphigenie* they are called die Immerwachen ; around the
guilty criminal, „steigen sie, die Schlangenhäupter schüttelnd, auf."
It is thought that Schiller here had conscious reference to this passage.

2192. **dem Gesetz,** the law — that is, the necessity, of the hour.

2196. **trotzt . . . auf:** insist not defiantly upon. — **jetzo,** see *l.* 913.

2202. **Eh** (or eh'), here = eher.

2206. **von Angesicht,** face to face. — **nur erst,** only just — that is,
before despairing. — **ja,** hardly translatable, refers to *l.* 1528, etc.

2210. **Darum eben,** for that very reason; as *l.* 10. For the emphatic **hegt Ihr,** see *l.* 1620.

2215. **Es ward . . . begegnet,** impers. idiom : I have been hardly
treated. — For the optative subj. **geblieben wäre,** see *l.* 1003. — For
darauf denkt, *l.* 2216, see note, *l.* 2045.

2221. **Will,** here as simple verb : desires, seeks. — Note emphatic **nicht er.** Mary's reply, which nearly betrays her to Shrewsbury, marks a sudden revulsion of feeling, and prepares us for the submissive spirit which she manifests directly. Her faith in Leicester gives her strength.

ACT III., SCENE 4.

In this splendid scene the drama reaches the crisis of its action and of its interest. With noble self-control, yet with an agitation which discloses the agony of the struggle — and with an eloquence which this struggle makes only the more touching — Mary pleads with her haughty sister. She is met first with scornful contempt, then with bitter reproaches, and finally with base and cruel insult — in which, especially in Leicester's presence, personal hate and jealousy are seen to move Elizabeth more deeply than all political or religious antagonism. — Goaded at last to desperation, Mary answers insult with insult, and with the might of a long-restrained resentment, crushes her proud persecutor in the dust. Elizabeth, trembling with rage and shame, is led away by her terrified courtiers. Mary, still beside herself with passion, glories in her triumph, which, however, is the knell of her own doom. Thus her long-sought interview and Leicester's cunning scheme hasten the catastrophe they were intended to avert.

The scene is as dramatic as it is eloquent, and calls for the highest powers of the actors on the stage; as it marks, perhaps, the acme of the author's achievement.

2225. See note, *l.* 2060; the ignorance is, of course, feigned, as an expression of contempt for Mary. The following lines are also intended to wound her.

* **stellt sich,** pretends to be. — For **Leicestern,** see note, *l.* 388.

2236. **nun,** here illative : now that, since (= **da nun**).

2243. **eine Stolze.** Elizabeth interprets Mary's struggle according to her own mind.

2245. **diesem,** here absolute ' this.' — **litt,** *l.* 2248, ' have suffered,' as heretofore. These words are spoken, of course, aside.

2252. **die Gottheit.** Mary's piety, as well as self-respect, would forbid her kneeling to a person. Yet eloquently, in the next line, she turns the invocation : **auch Ihr,** you too — as God has been generous to you.

2262. **Götter . . . die schrecklichen,** the plural is only the common phrase, with unconscious classical allusion.

The dash, *l.* 2264, etc., indicates pause, thus increasing the emphasis -- as also hereafter, and elsewhere.

2267. Tudor, the family name of Henry VII. — the common ancestor of Mary and Elizabeth.

2270. der Strandende, stranding, i. e. shipwrecked, or *drowning.* — The figure, though familiar, is here especially apt and expressive.

2275. dem, *that,* etc. — **Schließt . . . zu,** continues the figure, **Löst,** etc., above.

2280. habt . . . sprechen wollen, refers to Mary's letter, *l.* 169. The title, Lady Stuart, ignores Mary's claims as Queen of Scotland.

2285. daß, etc., as *l.* 1175. The following was the specific charge against Mary. Mary replies without noticing this accusation.

2293. Kann ich doch, as *l.* 245, etc., expresses truly, and unfortunately, the situation.

2306. was . . . Grausames, as *l.* 94. Mary here rapidly reviews the ground covered in Act I., Scenes 1, 2, 7.

2307. eine Schickung, a fate — *sent* from God (cf. **Schicksal, Geschick**). For the following, compare *l.* 363, etc.

2315. unberufen, uncalled — hence, presumptuous, lawless.

2323. daß . . . geschenkt (hättet), as *l.* 2214, etc. The time referred to — if indeed definite reference may be alleged, in view of Schiller's free treatment of the history — is probably 1568, at the time of the meeting of the commissioners of the two queens at York.

2328. davor . . . zu legen, from laying, as *l.* 73. The reference is to the well-known fable.

2333. Da, thus often tr. as dept. *when.* — **kündigte mir . . . an,** declared . . . against me. — **Ohm,** see *l.* 387, also *l.* 106. Observe that the Cardinal, as *l.* 387, is spoken of as still living. — **herrschwütige,** mad with ambition — a strong term, yet hardly too strong.

2343. blies . . . an; compare **sachte . . . zu,** *l.* 2312.

2348. Euch . . . (gen.) überheben, presume upon — **über** implying *excess* (above).

2352. Die Sankt Barthelemi (Nacht), imitating the French *la (fête de) St. Barthélemy* — German, **Bartholomäusnacht**. This massacre of French Huguenots — beginning in the night, Aug. 24–25, 1572 — was really the result of the fears and duplicity of the weak and timid Charles IX., under the influence of his mother Catherine de

Medicis. But Mary's uncle, the Cardinal, was largely responsible for the conditions which led to it, and her cousin, the Duke de Guise, was one of its chief agents. It may be added — as justifying Elizabeth's allusion — that this event alarmed the English Protestants, and increased their efforts against Mary.

2360. **Sankt Peters Schlüssel,** see **Löseschlüssel,** *l.* 284. The Popes claim to be lineal successors of St. Peter, first Bishop of Rome — to whom were promised "the Keys of the Kingdom of Heaven," with power to bind and to loose, in heaven and on earth. See St. Matt. xvi. 19. — As to Elizabeth's accusations against the Catholic Church, see Intr., § 20.

2362. **Gezücht der Schlangen,** the serpent brood — refers to the Guises, who, besides being most zealous Catholics, had ever been Elizabeth's most active enemies. Compare *l.* 1287, etc.

2366. **zu Eurer Erbin.** On this condition Mary had, indeed, offered to withdraw her actual claims to the throne. — But see Intr., § 7. — **Gebührt,** that is, by actual right of succession, Elizabeth dying without heirs.

2369. **Draußen,** abroad, in foreign lands, where in fact Mary had sought allies.

2374. **Verführtet,** etc., subj. *might*, etc. — **Armida,** a character in Tasso's epic, *Jerusalem Delivered*, employed to seduce Christian knights from duty — here typical of a wicked and seductive woman.

2376. **Buhlernetze,** cannot be fully rendered without indelicacy: Elizabeth meant the term to convey insult. See *l.* 38, 2032.

2381. **habt's erreicht,** have gained your end. — **jedwedem,** as *l.* 1185 — includes here even the right of succession.

2387. **um dessentwillen,** see note, *l.* 78 — for the sake of which — which you came to speak. Mary still hopes that E. comes with this purpose. See *l.* 2125, etc.

2395. **macht . . . ungeschehen,** undoes all; makes as if it had not been.

2404. **Ist's aus mit,** is it all over with. The truth and force and eloquence of Mary's last appeal, — to which Elizabeth can find no answer, — stir only the deeper her scorn and hate. Hence she seeks terms of bitterest insult. — **kein . . . mehr,** no other.

2407. **Mir,** the ethical dative, here only sharpens the satire (= " I ween ") — though perhaps best left untranslated.

2410. **Eure Freier** refers to Norfolk, as **Eure Männer** to Darnley.

— For the phrase **traurige Ritterſchaft**, compare Mary's words, *l.* 654.

2414. daneben = neben welche. It is the thought and the sight of Mary's beauty which, more than all else, arouses Elizabeth's bitterest venom.   See Intr., § 16.

2417. nichts . . . als, nothing, but (to be). These terrible words cannot be rendered in their full force, for want of a compound corresponding to **all-gemein**, all-common, universal.

2421. menſchlich, jugendlich, can hardly be given without paraphrase : mine were the sins of nature and of youth.

2428. gleißend, hypocritically. See *ll.* 972, etc., 1632. There were rumors and suspicions enough on this subject to give point to Mary's words.

2432. Schiller follows the French spelling for Anne Boleyn : the charge was adultery. **Ehrbarkeit** here = chastity.

2433. dahin, to *this*. **Mäßigung**, etc., with reference to his own exhortations, Scene 3.

2440. aus deiner Höhle, as of a long imprisoned beast.

The *basilisk* (little-king — so-called from the semblance of a crown on its head) was fabled to kill by a glance ; called also *cockatrice*.

2451. König ; compare *l.* 1155.   But here the word has special force.

ACT III., SCENE 5.

The sudden and complete change in the situation, so fatal to Mary's hopes, is seen and announced by Kennedy.   Mary, still beside herself, glories in her triumph, reckless of consequences.

2455. Wie mir wohl iſt ; compare *l.* 2156.   English: how good I feel !

2462. führt den Blitz, wields the thunderbolt. Kennedy knew nothing of Leicester's transactions with Mary ; but she knew the common report of his relations with Elizabeth.   Hence she sees the fatal significance of Leicester's presence ; but Mary glories in it, come what may !

Is Schiller right, in depicting the supreme conflict between two royal women, to set personal jealousy and rivalry for a man's love above politics, religion, crown, life itself ?   On the answer to this question must depend the judgment of this play.   See Intr., § 16.

ACT III., SCENE 6.

The following scene, though on a distinctly lower plane, is scarcely less passionate than Scene 4. Mortimer has overheard the conclusion of that scene, and fired with ardor and with renewed contempt for Leicester, he hurries in. Mary in vain seeks information from him; he regards only her dazzling charms. At last he reveals his plan for her immediate rescue, at which she recoils with terror: but he will dare all for her love. With rising passion, he presses his suit. In vain does Mary seek defense or escape, when suddenly Kennedy appears and announces the approach of armed men. Mortimer draws his sword to defend the queen, but she rushes away, filled with terror. — The scene brings to Mary the deepest humiliation — as if the supreme penance for the errors of her youth — while it sets in strongest light (almost too strong for the stage) the sensuous passion inspired by her beauty, and the fanatical ardor of her devotees. Conformably with its passionate character, the scene abounds in rhymes.

2469, etc. Mortimer, like Kennedy, *l.* 147, begins with the passionate **Du**, then recollecting himself uses **Ihr**, but soon returns to **Du**. Unfortunately, English offers no equivalent forms.

2475. **Geſchenk**, see *l.* 675.

2480. **Mylord**, Leicester. **das**, like **es**, *l.* 257 — here with contemptuous emphasis.

2484. **Er ſoll — wagen**: let him dare! Note strong ellipsis preceding, also the exclamatory infin., as heretofore.

2491. **ſein**, for **ſeiner**, as *l.* 471, etc. Note rhyme on end of broken line, *l.* 2492, as if in lyric form.

2505-6. **Ablaß** here stands in the double sense of *absolution* and *indulgence*. Catholic readers have taken umbrage at this passage; but it has been well remarked that Schiller is here describing the excesses of fanaticism. See Intr., § 20. — The **heimliche Kapelle** is in Aubespine's palace, *l.* 640.

2512. **mächtig**, with gen., as *l.* 506. Note the strong inversion, *l.* 2514.

2525. **müßte ich**, though I should have to. — **die Hoſtie**, the *Holy Host*, symbolic of the body of the Lord — hence the most solemn oath.

2529. **Mag**, let, etc. The language is extravagant, but true to the situation and to the character. — **Herwagend**, surging on, swallow every living creature. — *l.* 2533, **Eh** = eher, as *l.* 2202.

2537. **Tyburn**, place of execution at London. These words hardly exaggerate forms of torture employed at this time.

2544. Umarmung, etc. These words imply that Mortimer here embraces, or seeks to embrace, Mary — as indicated also by **um= fange.**

2547. doch, here very emphatic, implies: in spite of all.

2553. Wut, madness — the singular verb in next line is remarkable. The sentiment is pathetically true of Mary's history.

2556. blendend weiß, dazzling white — emphatic form, as *l.* 223, while the phrase **diesen Hals** shows that Mortimer continues his efforts to embrace Mary. — The scene is justly censured as passing the bounds of dramatic propriety, and is modified in the acting.

2557. Lebensgott, in contrast with the idea of death, below: the living God of joy. — **Freuden,** as *l.* 49, etc.

2562. verfallen, as *l.* 848.

2569. laß, etc. parenthetical — expanding **versuch' es.**

2573. läßt . . . vermögen. We may render: enables me to dare and do. — **blieb,** *l.* 2571, has been — is — left you.

2578. Ist Leben doch, etc. Life, that is, the enjoyment of life, is, after all, etc. — **seiner,** i. e. des Lebens = the warmest living breast — by a strong figure. — **umsonst,** for naught — without reward.

2587. jener, contemptuous. — **durfte** implies Mary's connivance — one of the gravest of the charges against her (Intr., § 8). The implication concerning Rizzio is probably unfounded. See note, *l.* 318. — Mortimer here proceeds from violence to insult, subjecting Mary, in the name of love, to the deepest humiliation.

2588. da, here = *though* — even while. See *l.* 322.

2597. drinnen, i. e., in the castle, this scene having taken place in the park. — **der Mord,** shows that Mary fears immediate death, as consequence of Scene 4.

ACT III., SCENE 7.

On the return to London an attempt has been made on Elizabeth's life, which Paulet supposes to have been successful. Attributed, of course, to Mary, it renders her situation still more desperate.

2598. die Brücken, drawbridges — as then common at fortified places.

2603. Mortimer's question shows that his mind is wandering — **Straßen,** old weak dat. See *l.* 2557 etc. For **Londner (Londoner),** indecl., see Grammar. Translate: on the road to London.

ACT III., SCENE 8.

One of Mortimer's confederates comes and tells him the true state of facts. He advises flight, but Mortimer, though recognizing the hope-lessness of Mary's situation, resolves to stay and attempt her release.

2610. **O'Kell'** (O'Kelly), a fictitious name; an Irishman — hence a Catholic.

2613. **Sauvage,** French form for Savage. A person of this name had shared in Babington's conspiracy, and was executed with him. He was, however, an English soldier, not a French monk (Int., § 12).

2618. **sind des Todes** ; we are dead men. Compare *l.* 295, etc.

2623. **das Rasende,** this mad deed : — it destroys Mortimer's plans. The Barnabites were an order of monks, first founded at Milan, where they took their name from the Church of St. Barnabas, which was assigned to them.

2626. **Anathem'** refers to the Pope's bull of excommunication against Elizabeth, *l.* 1490. — **Kapelle** ; see *l.* 2503.

2628. **das Nächste** ; see *l.* 1861. — **dem L. Weg,** the road to Lon-don — that is, on the return from Fotheringhay.

2635. That is, she perishes through her own friends.

2640. **Wo nicht,** phrase : if not. — **mir zu betten,** *to make my bed* — to die. The modern usage is **mich betten.**

ACT IV.

The action is at Westminster, during late afternoon or evening of the second day. The unhappy events of the last Act bear their fruit. The catastrophe begins. The French alliance is broken off. Leicester, caught in his own snares, betrays Mortimer, who slays himself — thus ending the last hope of Mary's rescue. Elizabeth orders Mary's death warrant to be prepared, which — as punishment and as test of his fidelity — Leicester shall execute. After hesitation she signs it, and delivers it to Davison, without instructions. Burleigh snatches it from him, and hurries to its execution. — Mary does not appear in this Act, but in every scene we see the approach of her doom.

ACT IV., SCENES 1, 2.

The French ambassador is informed by Burleigh of the evidence against him, and is required to leave England. — Davison is ordered to prepare the death-warrant.

2641. **Jhro,** an archaic form, used only in titles. For **steht's um,** see *l.* 731.

2643. **in Mitte,** for **in der Mitte.** Below, *l.* 2646, **Franke** for **Franzose.** The "Franks" were the German conquerors of Gaul.

ACT IV., SCENE 2.

2651. **wird . . . gebracht,** as *l.* 29 — here with imperative sense.

2658. **zu schanden** (or **zu Schanden**) **machen,** to bring to grief, or shame.

2661. The title **Lordmarschall** is here applied to Kent by oversight. See *l.* 1085, where also it is written in two words.

2664. **schuldigst,** most dutifully — as is my duty. The term **officiös,** below, means *formally,* with official dignity.

2669. **der h. Charakter,** i. e. of ambassador.

2679. **offen,** because of its official character. For B.'s charge, see *l.* 2624.

2681. **In m. Haupt,** in my person — officially.

2687. **Hotel,** here in the French sense: mansion, palace.

2695. Burleigh's answer anticipates the final word, **holen.**

The dismissal of L'Aubespine, and the ground here alleged for the breach of the royal marriage, are fictitious. This minister was indeed involved about this time in a probably pretended charge of conspiracy against Elizabeth; but after Mary's execution this was withdrawn, and he was again restored to favor.

ACT IV., SCENE 3.

Leicester, deeply embittered by the failure of his schemes, would vent his spleen on Burleigh, but is soon made to understand that the latter suspects his agency in leading the queen to Fotheringhay; and this fills him with alarm.

2697. **geschäftig unberufen,** with officious presumption. See *l.* 2315. — **konntet . . . sparen,** might *have* — as heretofore.

2701. **Schlimmeres,** see *l.* 1057. — The name **Cecil** is here contemptuous. Note the French accent **Cecil'.**

2707. **Inquisitionsgericht** refers to the Catholic courts of Inquisition in Spain, etc., for detection of heresy. — **Wort** here = **Worte.**

2710. **Atlas,** in mythology, bore the world on his shoulders.

2714. **davongetragen,** carried off — as from a field of battle.   Fr. *l'emporter.*

2720. **hättet** as *l.* 85, etc., yet in slightly different sense : You led — did I say? — **Nicht doch,** No, indeed !

2724. **wollt . . . sagen,** phrase : what do you mean by that?   B.'s irony, which implies full knowledge of L.'s deception, justly excites the latter's alarm — which is ill-concealed by his blustering, below.

2725. **Person,** here in original sense of *character, part.*

2727. **der . . . Vertrauenden.** Such forms often require a clause in English : *for her who,* etc. — **bereitet (habt).**

2731. **angewandelt,** came over you, as *l.* 1694.   B. refers to Act II., Scene 3, *l.* 1404, etc.

2735. **schade** (or **Schade**), as we say : Pity ! — **Fein,** i. e. to a fine point.

2738. **Rede stehen,** as *l.* 224.   L.'s answer can only be intended to gain time — he dares not press Burleigh for explanation.

ACT IV., SCENE 4.

Leicester is tortured with apprehension — all the more because he does not know the full extent of Burleigh's information.   Mortimer appears and, after vainly urging him to action in Mary's behalf, informs him that his correspondence with her is discovered.   This drives Leicester to despair, when suddenly a bold and brilliant thought offers him, through the betrayal of Mortimer, a last hope of escape.   Mortimer, surrounded by the guard, slays himself, while Leicester hastens to the queen.

2742. **Unglückselig,** here and *l.* 2747 = **Unglück bringend,** as *l.* 327.

2750. **sich,** i. e. **sieht sich** : note the strongly contrasted order.

2757. **Dazwischen kam,** intervened; — **werd' ich . . . haben.**   I shall (in her opinion) — shall be thought to have armed.

2765. **Kümmert,** compare **bekümmert,** *l.* 1599; and note, as heretofore, the frequent interchange of like forms, with and without prefix.

2767. **Was unterfangt,** why do you presume — **was** as *l.* 2000.

2770. **So . . . doch nur,** note the crowded particles, expressing earnest entreaty.

2777. **Unglücksthat,** the attempted assassination. — **Großschatzmeister,** Burleigh.

2780. **angefangener Brief.** This letter must have been begun between Act I., Scene 1, when Mary's papers were seized, and the surprise, Act III., Scene 7.

2783. **gedenkt,** mentions; gen. as *l.* 471, etc.

2787. **heraus,** out of it — by false oaths. — **das Ärgste,** as *l.* 1839.

2790. Mortimer's purpose has changed since end of Act III. — doubtless in consequence of this new information.

2792. **An Euch ist's,** it is your turn.

2794. **Trabant'en,** guards. The word is from Italian, though originally from German **traben** — applied to troops acting as body guards. — This brilliant stroke is worthy of Leicester: it is also highly dramatic.

2804. **mag,** not even in death will I have, etc. He prefers even death to confessing an alliance with Leicester. With next line is often compared Lessing, *Emilia Galotti,* V., 7: „Dieses Leben ist alles, was die Lasterhaften haben."

2809. **frei . . . sich** belong to both verbs, as *l.* 2750. — **er wehrt sich ihrer,** against them. Note gen. as *l.* 2348, etc.

2811. **euch . . . ihren,** we should expect euren.

2814. **der himmlischen,** the heavenly (Virgin) Mary — referring to their religious apostasy from the Catholic faith. — This tirade — at swords' point — violates, of course, all dramatic possibility, yet is consistent with Mortimer's character. See note, *l.* 403.

2818. **Beispiel,** how to die — anticipating her own death. Note, as heretofore, the lyric rhymes; and also, *ll.* 2807, 2819, at end of broken lines.

With the death of Mortimer vanishes the last hope for Mary; — he has fulfilled also his own dramatic destiny.

ACT IV., SCENE 5.

Burleigh has shown Elizabeth Mary's intended letter to Leicester (*l.* 2780). In bitterest mortification and anger, which Burleigh skillfully irritates, she declares her purpose that both of them shall die. A page announces Leicester; the Queen refuses to see him — yet not without a struggle.

2824. **Kein Weib.** This expression shows that it is as *woman* that E. most feels her humiliation; — hence jealousy and personal resentment are still uppermost in her mind.

2829. **mußte—ſpotten**, must *have*, etc.; also gen., as heretofore.

2844. **ſie bezahle.** This is true to nature; "and pity 'tis, 'tis true." See *l.* 1020, etc.—**Urteil** is here death-warrant. See *l.* 2650, etc.

2850. **So . . . ſo**, here correlative.

2854. **die ihn richten**, the sense is: *who shall*, or *to*, etc. But the form may be either subjunctive or indicative.

2863. **Zurückweiſt;** we might expect subj., as *l.* 385, etc. See last note.

2870. **verbiete**, indirect: say, the Queen forbids, etc.

2875. **abgefeimt**, with the foam off — undisguised, arrant. **Bübin** see *l.* 1886.

Elizabeth suggests possible excuses for Leicester, at Mary's cost — again true to nature. — **den ſie haßt**, because, as she would believe, of his love for herself.

ACT IV., SCENE 6.

Leicester rushes in with well assumed defiance, knowing that for him all is at stake. His knowledge of Mortimer's plans and of his understanding with Elizabeth (*ll.* 1886, etc.) gives him an advantage which he uses with shameless skill, until at last Elizabeth knows not what to believe. He now urges Mary's execution, and on Burleigh's suggestion the Queen orders that he shall himself have charge of it — a commission which he does not hesitate to accept. The scene is full of dramatic vigor.

2884. **wider die Erlaubnis** = ohne Erlaubnis.

2891. **meine . . . E.** appeals to the woman — not to the queen.

2901. **Was ſoll**, what business has — what is the use of — a third person, etc.?

2903. **Hab' ich's zu thun**, I have to deal — my business is with.

2909. **Das**, *that*, refers to all the foregoing; yet the connection seems hardly natural. — Note the boldness of Leicester's game.

2921. **Über mir**, compare the accus. *l.* 61. — **Neigung**, as *l.* 2071.

2936. **Der bin ich nicht;** we should rather expect das — i. e. ein Verräter.

2943. **durfte . . . erkühnen**, could have ventured such a deed. See *l.* 246; and note again gen., as *l.* 2348, etc.

2947. Note **Zweifel in**, with accus.; usually an, with dat.

2953. **Glocke;** we would say *trumpet*. **verſchwiegt**, *l.* 2951, is usually transitive.

2958. **Ins Werk gerichtet,** to have arranged, set on foot. — **berühmt,** more usually rühmt. Compare **kümmert, bekümmert,** *ll.* 2765, 1599, etc.

2962. **war,** as *l.* 1830. For **Spürkunst,** compare *ll.* 2703, 650.

2967. **so weit ... zu geben,** so far *as to* give, etc. Leicester here strikes home. The Queen fears that he knows still more. See *ll.* 1630, etc.

2979. **pflog:** pflegen is now usually weak, except in a few phrases.

2982. Note accus. of time. — **sollte,** etc.; see *l.* 4.

2985. **zu sehen,** *at seeing,* dep. on **Verzweiflung.** — **unerhört,** *l.* 2987, in an unheard-of way, beyond example.

2993. **des Richters,** that is, by ordering his arrest, for trial.

3015. Burleigh, though confounded, is not convinced — he knows Leicester too well. Elizabeth, as usual, solves her doubts by blaming Mary.

3022. **erhübe:** see *l.* 850. Leicester refers to Act II., Scene 3. — In **Ihr rietet,** etc., *l.* 3025: You advise that (you say)! Burleigh still shows his distrust.

3025. **So sehr,** however much. Compare *l.* 2850. — **zu einem Äußersten,** to an extreme measure. Usually as *l.* 1839, etc.

3031. **es ... meint:** see *l.* 791. Burleigh hits hard; but Leicester's shamelessness stands even this!

3038. **dabei bleib' es,** let it rest there — let that end it. E. accepts the suggestion as a test of L.'s fidelity — also (?) as a new torture to Mary.

3047. **Begeb' ich mich,** forego, waive. Compare **vergeben,** *l.* 701.

3049. **teile sie,** etc. Shows Elizabeth's remnant of distrust. Perhaps also she would mitigate the severity of her command to Leicester. In fact, not Burleigh and Leicester, but Shrewsbury and Kent, were entrusted with the execution of Mary.

ACT IV., SCENE 7.

Kent announces the uprising of the people to urge Mary's execution, in consequence of the late attempt upon the Queen's life and of wild rumors abroad. Elizabeth pretends to resent and resist such pressure — without regard to the orders just given.

3056. **sei,** etc.; the subjunctives depend on **Schrecken,** the alarm, that, etc. — It is true that such rumors were used to force Elizabeth's compliance — yet not exactly as here represented.

3062. **das noch heute fällt,** emphatic for: which must fall, etc. — **zur Königin,** factitive, as *l.* 783, etc. Note that in such cases the plural is without article. See Grammar.

3065. **eher nicht . . . bis** is pleonastic: not . . . until. — **Sie** refers to the people.

ACT IV., SCENE 8.

Davison returns with the death-warrant, which he had been ordered to prepare, Act IV., Scene 2. Elizabeth hesitates.

3066. **Du,** etc. The order came from Burleigh, *l.* 2648, etc.; but officially, in the Queen's name.

3068. Burleigh makes use, for his own purposes, of the adage *Vox populi, vox Dei.*

3072. **gehorcht (habe,** for fut.), when I shall have, etc.

ACT IV., SCENE 9.

Shrewsbury, warned by the public tumult and justly fearing the consequences, comes to beg the Queen to stand firm against the pressure brought upon her. Burleigh urges. In conclusion the Queen, after a display of emotion, still hesitates.

3079. **Geschehen,** meaning: have you signed already?

3084. **Hier gilt es,** 'tis question of: Now is the time to . . .

3090. **Ein Mensch,** that is, human. — With **außer dir** compare our *beside yourself* (in both cases implying *other than yourself*).

* 3097. **jahrelang** seems strange here, when sentence was pronounced only a few months before. But the matter had been for years considered as a probable question, which might arise at any time.

3099. **Kurzen Aufschub,** i. e. **fordre ich,** connecting with *l.* 3095.

3104. **Dreimal,** referring to the conspiracies of Throckmorton, Parry, Babington; below, **viermal,** *l.* 3108, includes the present attempt. —See also *l.* 1277.

3106. **hieße ;** compare *l.* 1768.

3109. **Greifen,** now usually **Greifes;** but here probably adjective.

3118. **Zwietrachtsgöttin ;** compare *l.* 2318; **Ein Rachegeist,** *as* an avenging spirit.

3121. **die Gefürchtete** implies: hates her because he fears her. The participle has in German a far more flexible use than in English. See *l.* 2727, etc.

3125.   For word-order compare *l*. 426.

3132.   **umgiebt,** this sudden change to present is emphatic.   So, especially, **Du haft,** etc., *l*. 3137.

3138.   **heil'ge.**   The person of sovereigns was held to be sacred.

3141.   **ließet,** etc., let it take its course.

3144.   **Läg' ich,** I should be lying.—**Gruft,** poetic for **Grab.**   It is in this speech that Mme. de Staël accuses Elizabeth of " une coquetterie sanguinaire."

3150.   **Majestät,** its sovereignty—as if conferred upon her by the people.

3156.   **Woodstock,** etc.   See *l*. 1381, etc.   How far E. is sincere will appear hereafter.

3159.   **Hoheit,** dignity—my true worth.—For **bin ich doch,** see *l*. 245, etc.—**Zur Herrscherin,** not as *l*. 3060; here: *for a ruler.*

3172.   **und überlaß; nicht** belongs to both verbs.   Mme. de Staël says: " Burleigh lui reproche tout ce dont elle veut être blâmée," and " demande ce qu'elle désire en secret, plus que lui-même."

3175.   **gezogen,** come marching—with pompous procession.   B. refers to the Papal Legate who dethroned King John (Lackland) in 1213, and took possession of the kingdom in the name of Pope Innocent III.   See also *l*. 1175, etc.

3182.   Burleigh again (as *l*. 3068) refers to a well-known maxim, *Salus populi suprema lex.*

3187.   Elizabeth's pious words, as well as her emotion above, receive a bitter commentary in the next scene.   •

[The foregoing scene, both in situation and in sentiment, is too nearly like Act II., Scenes 3, 4, to appear as other than an undramatic repetition at this point—all the more so, as the action should now be hastening to its inevitable conclusion.]

ACT IV., SCENE 10.

Elizabeth, in a remarkable monologue, lays bare her heart.   Here Schiller allows her keen political insight to appear for once; but it is soon hidden by that resentment and personal hatred of Mary which are here represented as her controlling motive.   In this scene these sentiments drive the Queen to end her indecision by signing the death-warrant.

3091.   **bin ich's müde,** etc.; **es** (see *l*. 1057, note) refers forward: *tired of,* etc.

                                                  •

3194. die Meinung, as *l.* 1015. — muß es recht machen, must satisfy — must account to.

3201. daß, etc., so that — she means that by deference to public opinion heretofore she has now tied her own hands. Compare *l.* 3160, etc.

3205. war ich = wär' ich gewesen, as *l.* 2962, 1830, etc. — but here the form occurs, as more rarely, in the protasis. — For die spanische Maria, see Intr., § 6. — Vorfahr, here = Vorgänger. See note, *l.* 102.

3213. angefochtnen finds its explanation in the following lines: Bannfluch is the excommunication referred to, *l.* 1490, etc.; Bruderkuß is the offer of marriage, which she interprets as treacherous; Vertilgungskrieg, this threat soon found its attempted realization in the Spanish Armada.

3222. Blöße ... Flecken ... geschändet. These historical points are referred to, *l.* 780, etc. Schiller represents Elizabeth — consistently with his portraiture of her character — as consciously seeking to cover these defects by the affectation of „hohen Tugenden."

3227. drohendes, because if her claim is disallowed, Mary's claim becomes legitimate.

3230. die Furie, *the curse* — as if a pursuing demon. — wo, here = *wherever.*

3236. heißt, is the name of; den Geliebten, Leicester; Bräutigam, Anjou; see *l.* 2683, etc. — a result here attributed to Mary.

3240. blitzen, crush — like lightning. — beßre, better, i. e. than yours. See *l.* 2462.

3245. For more usual form, see note, *l.* 2947. Compare getilgt, vertilge, the latter with stronger — moral — force.

Undoubtedly Elizabeth here tells the truth as to her own motives, and those of her advisers, in causing Mary's death. It is again the „allgewaltige Notwendigkeit," *l.* 3210.

ACT IV., SCENE 11.

Elizabeth delivers the warrant to Davison, but refuses further instructions and leaves him in despair. This scene, while it ends all hope for Mary, prepares the way for Elizabeth's later efforts to avoid the responsibility of her death, and is, so far, historically justified.

3251. augenblicks, here = augenblicklich, *l.* 365.

3256. **verwies,** etc., reproved . . . for. — **Beginnen,** purpose — as explained by Kent, *ll.* 3061, 3093.

3261. **Wehe dem,** etc., because she is thus robbed of her own pretext. Compare her words, *ll.* 3075-6.

3266. **sollt' ich,** I was to — was expected to; as had been urged by Parliament, by her Council, and by the people. Thus she disclaims responsibility.

3271. **geflügelt** may be a reminiscence of classical epithets, as ἔπεα πτερόεντα, etc. — or simply a metaphor, as *l.* 2078, — which we may here translate : like a winged arrow.

3273. **stehenden Fußes,** adv. gen., immediately (Lat. *stante pede*); as *l.* 2135.

3277. **hat gelebt** (Lat. *vixit*), has lived — euphemism for "is (will be) dead."

3292. **Darf,** etc., nothing must be left. — **unabsehbar,** immeasurable — beyond which the eye cannot reach; so applied to great spaces, multitudes, etc.

3305. **Ich will . . . daß ich will.** There is no redundancy, but only emphatic use of **will** (= **ich will sagen**), I *mean* that, as *l.* 2724.

3306. **nicht mehr gedacht,** no more mention shall be made of — as *l.* 2783. — **davor,** as *l.* 2328.

3309. **mit . . . werden,** shall be done with.

3314. **Monden,** poetic for **Monaten.** Davison had long been in public service, yet not long in his present office.

3318. **Knecht** here expresses deep humiliation, as **habe du** earnest entreaty.

3324. **Eures Amts,** what belongs to — the duty of; gen. as, *l.* 2618 etc.

ACT IV., SCENE 12.

Davison meets Burleigh, to whom he appeals for help. Burleigh snatches the warrant from him, and proceeds to its execution.

3329. **eingeführt . . . in,** appointed to.

3347. **von Sinnen,** out of (= away from) your senses. See note, *l.* 3090.

With the warrant in Burleigh's hands, the spectator is already prepared for the final act.

The preceding scenes present only in abridged and more dramatic form the actual facts. Elizabeth after long hesitation had signed the death-warrant and — with a jest — gave it to **Davison** to be sealed. Yet at the same time she renewed her request that he and Walsingham should write to Paulet, to see if by private means she might not be relieved of this responsibility. The letter was written, and Paulet's answer (see note, *l.* 1059) was received. Meantime, learning from Davison that the warrant had already been sealed, she rebuked his haste, yet gave no further instructions. Her ministers, dreading her indecision, determined to despatch the warrant without further consultation with her. She still seemed to indulge the hope of private murder — indeed, spoke of the subject again to Davison on the very day of Mary's execution; — so that, after all, it was doubtless with real astonishment that she learned what had been done. Thus, too, she gave color to her own professions of innocence.

The soliloquy in Scene 10 is doubtless suggested by the accounts of the Queen's mental struggles at this time. Says Camden: She sate many times melancholy and mute, and frequently sighing, muttered: *Aut fer aut feri*, " Either bear (the blow) or strike," and *Ne feriari feri*, " Strike, lest thou be stricken."

ACT V.

The action begins on the morning of the third day. The evening before, the commissioners (here Burleigh and Leicester — see *l.* 3049) had brought the fatal news to Fotheringhay, which — as we have seen, *l.* 2060, etc., Schiller locates within easy reach of London. Here are enacted Scenes 1–10; the remainder in Elizabeth's palace at Westminster.

ACT V., SCENE 1.

Kennedy and Melvil. Melvil (Sir Andrew), Mary's faithful steward, had been in fact separated from her only since her removal to Fotheringhay, and met her again only on her way to the scaffold. His *rôle* here is therefore fictitious. Kennedy depicts to him the situation, which is thus graphically brought before the spectator.

* **Pakete und Briefe.** Mary's property, which Paulet, *l.* 29, had significantly promised should be returned zu seiner Zeit. This applies also to the **Gefäße**, etc., below. Tradition, which still in part remains, required that nothing should be denied a criminal on the eve of execution. For the same reason, Melvil and other servants, formerly separated from Mary (*l.* 207), are now allowed access to her.

3362. Mußten wir's, etc. — exclamatory: That we have had to live to see! etc.

3367. nächtliche, sable — of mourning.

3381. Todespost, fatal news. Compare **Freudenpost,** *l.* 1137; and note to *l.* 1141.

3385, etc. See Act III., Scene 6, *l.* 2502, etc.

3394. Wir glauben . . . zu vernehmen, we think *we hear.* Note infin. idiom, which in English would here give different sense.

3397. Sir Paulet, etc. For the poetic effect of a more sudden surprise Schiller adopts this method, instead of the more formal and more natural (as well as actual) announcement through the commissioners.

3403. Mit einemmal (= einem Mal), suddenly. The meaning is that as Mary was unprepared, there was no gradual struggle, but a prompt courage. For **Zeitlichem und Ewigem,** temporal and eternal things, compare *l.* 1540.

3408. glaubenvoll, as *l.* 423.

3416. Da, refers back to **dann erst,** *l.* 3410. These facts Mary is supposed to have learned through Paulet, and thus to have witnessed his grief — also in Kennedy's presence.

3422. pflegt . . . der Ruh, enjoys rest (for a moment) — is enjoying a moment's rest. As in like cases heretofore, the accus. is usual in prose.

3424. Burgoyn must be read in three syllables — not as in English. In this scene, though with some departure from the facts, Schiller does not exaggerate the heroic courage with which Mary received the news of her doom. Other features are introduced later.

ACT V., SCENE 2.

The wife of the Secretary Kurl (Act I., Scene 7, *l.* 884, etc.) is introduced, partly to exhibit Mary's magnanimity in retaining her in service, partly to use her testimony to her husband's treachery. [Her real name — doubtless unknown to Schiller — was Elizabeth.] For the latter purpose opportunity is skillfully provided (*l.* 3427).

3430. Meisters = Hofmeisters. Note, as before, poetic gen. — usually accus.

3433. auf freien Fuß gesetzt, phrase: set free (= gesetzt werden, as *l.* 29, etc.).

3441. Vor Gerichtes Schranken; compare *l.* 708. — **ins Antlitz,** *l.* 262.

ACT V., SCENE 3.

In this scene a cup of wine is ordered — for seemingly natural reasons — which, however, serves a more important purpose hereafter.

3446. **Machet hurtig,** phrase: make haste. The expression **einen Becher (mit) Wein** is unusual.

3447. **der Königin;** compare *l.* 2455. Also Goethe, **Der Fischer:**

„Wie's Fischlein ist
So wohlig auf dem Grund."

3450. **ihrer,** again poet. gen. — with **bedürfen,** *l.* 3449, the gen. is still usual.

3456. **Was soll;** see *l.* 2902; here: what means? — **da,** *l.* 3458, *while.*

ACT V., SCENE 4.

This scene serves only to continue the dramatic suspense, until Kennedy's return, and to add increased solemnity to Mary's coming.

ACT V., SCENE 5.

Mistress Kurl, under deep emotion, describes the scaffold which she has seen. This description is skillfully introduced, with fine dramatic effect.

3465. **Was habt Ihr** (French: qu'avez-vous), what is the matter with you? — For **Was ist Euch,** see *l.* 2156.

3468. **zur untern Halle,** the same in which the trial had been held.

3471. **Schwarz überzogen,** draped in black. — **mitten drauf,** on the center of it.

3477. **heiße Blutgier,** descriptive accus., as heretofore. — *with . . . in their looks* — English plural, as usual.

Every circumstance of solemn impressiveness is now provided for Mary's appearance in the next scene.

ACT V., SCENE 6.

In this beautiful and pathetic scene Mary's character, as Schiller intended it to be conceived, is touchingly exhibited. Her piety, her long-suffering and noble dignity, her unselfishness and tenderness of heart, enhanced by her beauty, her solemn costume and the certainty of her impending fate — all these impress the spectator only the more profoundly because of the interval since her last appearance, and especially because of the contrast between those scenes (Act III.) and this. Even the question of guilt or innocence is forgotten, in sympathy and tragic pity.

* **weiß,** her dress was really black; — **festlich;** we may say: magnificently dressed in white.

* **Kugeln,** balls, or *beads.* — **Agnus Dei** — Lamb of God — a trinket or medallion of wax (from the candles of the altar) or of metal, with figure of the Lamb bearing the banner of the cross. The wearing of these had been specifically forbidden by Act of Parliament.

* **Rosenkranz,** rosary — of beads originally in the form of roses.

3480. Was, as *l.* 2000, etc. The following words are almost the same as were actually spoken by Mary on hearing her death-warrant.

3487. Was, etc., expands **Unwürdiges.**

3492. Den tiefstgesunkenen (not **tiefgesunkenen**) seems to be the better reading; so in the earliest texts. Mellish gives: The most degraded criminal. Compare *l.* 1547.

3495. Nicht also, that is, on your knees.

3498. wird ... zu teil, as *l.* 1395. — **wie ... es,** such as, etc. See *l.* 467.

In a letter to Elizabeth, soon after her condemnation, Mary had expressed solicitude as to the witnesses who should attend her execution.

3507. sonst kein, no other.

3510. wohl, doubtless. Her old servant, Didier Sifflard, is mentioned as actually present at the execution.

3515. Daß ... geworden wäre, as *l.* 2215. — **geworden** (zu teil), as *l.* 3498.

3521. allerchristlichen, "most Christian." By this title, of papal origin, the kings of France had long been called. The actual king was now Henry III., successor of Charles IX., both brothers of Mary's husband, Francis II. In early life a somewhat indifferent suitor for Elizabeth's hand, he had lately made earnest intercession for Mary, in terms which, in one of her most remarkable letters, Elizabeth sharply resented. He was assassinated in 1589.

3523. Ohm (= **Oheim**). See note, *l.* 387. Henry, now Duke of Guise, Mary's cousin, was now leader of the French Catholics. He was assassinated in 1588 by order of Henry III. Mary's letter, written to him at this time, is still extant.

3526. **Statthalter,** vicegerent, vicar. Mary had received the papal blessing.

3527. **kathol'schen,** title of the kings of Spain, also of papal origin. Philip II. had threatened war in Mary's behalf. See *l.* 3219.

3531. **wie** = wie . . . **auch,** however. — **darum,** therefore. Observe that the message actually entrusted by Mary to Melvil for her son is here omitted; and compare note, *l.* 701.

3535. **euch** . . . **wert,** if . . . is valued by you — avails with you. For **weide,** see *l.* 1557.

3541. **dahin,** as *l.* 1163.

3547. **Todeswege** = Weg zum Tode. Mary actually apologized to her maids for wearing her best dress on this occasion.

3550. **Dir,** we should expect **Euch**; but she speaks first to each severally. The names here given are historically unknown, though several of her women were present.

3553. **Margareta (Kurl).** Even to Kurl himself, in her will, Mary left a small legacy.

3565. **Wenn es so weit ist,** when it comes to that. This touching incident is only slightly changed from the actual fact.

* **eins,** including both sexes.

3571. **brennt heiß,** thus suggesting her own warm heart, and the following eloquent line, in which she epitomizes her own life and character.

3576. **Braut des Himmels,** that is, in a convent. So in Schiller's Toggenburg:

> „Die Ihr suchet, trägt den Schleier,
> Ist des Himmels Braut."

3579. **an,** by — the example of . . . Compare **sieht . . . an,** *l.* 30. — **Erben,** *l.* 2557, etc.

ACT V., SCENE 7.

In this scene, of utmost grandeur of poetic conception and expression, Schiller intended to resume his portraiture of Mary's life of guilt and penitence, heroism and piety, and to complete her preparation for a peaceful and glorious death. For this purpose, in her character of devout Catholic, he felt the solemn offices of Confession and of Communion to be necessary; and, in terms of deepest piety, he wrought them into his tragedy — which was thus rehearsed for the stage. But objection was taken to the exhibition of such a scene, and the Duke of Weimar, Schiller's friend and patron, made known to him through Goethe his wish that it might be avoided. Such a request was equivalent to a command, and with deep reluctance Schiller so altered the scene as to remove the Communion entirely, and to change the Confession (Beichte) to a simple acknowledgment (Bekenntnis), substituting for Melvil's appearance as a priest his promise to become one and thus to consecrate his act. Yet with true poetic instinct, Schiller retained the scene unaltered in his printed work, of which it is a unique ornament, quite unparalleled in literature.*

The changes thus made necessary will be indicated hereafter. At the same time, as the use for the cup of wine fails, Scenes 3 and 5 relating to it were omitted on the stage.

On this scene there has been much controversy as to the accuracy of Schiller's presentation of the Confession and the Communion in the Catholic Church, as well as to his conception of some points of doctrine. But as these questions interest only the critical student, they will not be noticed here.

3590. versöhnt, that is, formally, by confession and absolution, as required by the Catholic Church.

3592. Himmelspeise (usually Himmelsspeise). Compare in Schiller's Der Graf von Habsburg:

> „Ich walle zu einem sterbenden Mann,
> Der nach der Himmelskost schmachtet."

The notion of *spiritual food* is implied in the sacrament. [Some early eds. give Himmelsspeise; others, Himmelsegen, *l.* 3624.]

3600. II. Corinthians, iii. 6: "The letter killeth, but the spirit giveth life."

---

* It seems worth while here to quote the words of Mme. de Staël on this scene. While not expressly approving of its presentation on the stage, she says : "Il me semble que, sans manquer au respect qu'on doit à la religion chrétienne, on pourrait se permettre de la faire entrer dans la poésie et les beaux-arts, dans tout ce qui élève l'âme et embellit la vie . . . Il y a de la religion dans tout ce qui nous cause une émotion désintéressée ; la poésie, l'amour, la nature et la Divinité se réunissent dans notre cœur, quelques efforts qu'on fasse pour les séparer; et si l'on interdit au génie de faire résonner toutes les cordes à la fois, l'harmonie complète de l'âme ne se fera jamais sentir." — *L'Allemagne*, Ch. xviii.

3602. **Pfand** is here *symbol*, as *l.* 479. Note accus. with **bedarf,** for the more usual gen. — **allein,** refers to **Herz,** the heart alone.

3604. **der Gott zum Menschen,** the doctrine of the Incarnation — **der** is unusual.

3612. **beflügelt,** compare geflügelt, *l.* 3271; here: borne on wings.

3614. **froh geteilt.** Mellish gives: "the glad communion of pious prayer." Compare the English: *common* prayer.

3617. **Die Glocke,** as *l.* 289. — **Weirauch,** incense, swung in the censer. — **der Bischof** seems natural here; Mary recurs to what she had often witnessed. — **Meßgewand,** the chasuble. — It has been conjectured, yet without good reason, that **rein** should here be **reich.**

3620. **Verwandlung,** transubstantiation — the Catholic doctrine of the *real presence* ("This is my body").

3625. For the changes introduced here for the stage, see Appendix, also introduction to this scene.

3627–8. Allusion to Aaron's rod and to Moses striking the rock; Numbers xvii. 8; xx. 11.

3634. **Hochwürdiges;** see *l.* 290. For the following, see Matthew xviii. 20.

3642. **das Heil,** salvation, through forgiveness of sins, or *absolution,* which can be pronounced only by an ordained priest.

* **entblößt . . . das Haupt,** thus showing his priestly tonsure. — **Hostie** is the consecrated wafer. It is recorded that Mary actually had such a wafer, which had been blessed for her by the Pope.

3652. The **sieben Weihen** of the Catholic Church are the four *minor orders:* porter, or doorkeeper; lector, or reader; exorcist, and acolyte, or attendant; and three *holy orders:* subdeacon, deacon, priest. These follow in succession, after the *tonsure.*

3657. **Ein Unsterblicher,** an immortal spirit — this figure is frequent both in the Old and in the New Testament. See Matt. xxiv. 30; xxvi. 64; Mark xiii. 26; xiv. 62, etc.

3659, etc. **der Engel;** see Acts xii., 7, etc. — **ihn,** i. e. **den Engel.** Note vivid change to present tense.

3675. **versöhnt,** meaning since your last confession, as *l.* 3590. The verb **zeihen** is of unusual and formal phrase.

3685. **das höchste Gut** here stands for the Law of God, or God himself. — Note the solemn effect of the rhyme, as heretofore.

3696. **wälzt sich . . . mir:** confronts me. Compare Act I., Scene 4; also note to *l.* 292.

3700. der Wurm, of remorse — a common figure; see also Is. lxvi. 24; Mark ix. 44.

3707. "The sin unto death." (1 John v. 16); see also Matt. xii. 31, 32. Note, above, the two forms with denke; also double objects with droht.

3710. wissend, knowingly, consciously. The lengthened line here adds to the solemnity of the statement.

3714. Babingtons und Parrys; see note *l.* 70. The two are here spoken of as one (diese That). It is true that Mary was charged with complicity in both; yet only for the latter was she tried. For dessentwillen, see note *l.* 78.

3718. Minutenzeiger . . . wendet; minute-hand comes around — poetic for: within an hour.

3722. Doppelsinn, see doppelt, *l.* 1606.

3727. See *l.* 946, etc. Mary's declarations repeat Act. I., Scenes 4 and 7, with the added solemnity of a dying confession. See Intr., § 17.

3735. unverdient, that is, as to the grounds on which she was condemned. Thus the death is presented as a martyrdom and an expiation, not a penalty — and as such she accepts it. In fact, to the commissioners she thanked God that she was permitted to die for her religion.

3737. sterbend, by your death. * — den Segen, the sign of the cross. For changes here made, see introduction to this scene and Appendix I.

3739. Blut has here the double suggestion of *bloodshed* and *hot blood*, or passion. See Mary's words, *l.* 2421. — Altar is here figurative.

3744. künde . . . an. See Matt. xvi., 19. — Erlassung = absolution. See *l.* 2505.

3746. "According to your faith, be it unto you," Matt. ix. 29.

3749. diese Gunst, because in the Catholic Church the cup is not allowed to the laity. This privilege was allowed the kings of France at their coronation, also when at point of death. — das höchste Recht . . . das priesterliche, may be intended to refer to the union, in the earliest times, of royalty and priesthood. See Heb. vii. 1.

3753. verbunden, by partaking of His body and blood.

ACT V., SCENE 8.

Burleigh and Leicester, with Paulet, appear, to prepare for the final scene. See note, *l.* 3049.

* **Faſſung** (Leicester's) : condition — state of mind.

3775. **Wohin,** whithersoever — Mary had requested this, in a letter to Elizabeth.

3777. **geweihter,** consecrated — because she dies under penalty of treason.

3779. **den Meinen,** her husband, her mother, etc. See note *l.* 2099. — **Diener,** Melvil.

3785. **abbitte,** apologise for. The following wish was actually uttered by Mary in her prayer on the scaffold.

3788. **Dechanten,** see *l.* 187. Yet the Dean insisted upon his office, even on the scaffold.

3791. **Euch geraubt,** as *l.* 184. She generously assumes the blame of Mortimer's death. Paulet's answer fully redeems his earlier official harshness, and (with *l.* 3815) completes the consistent picture of his character.

ACT V., SCENE 9.

Appearance of the sheriff — the final preparations for the execution — Mary's last requests — her reproachful leave-taking of Leicester.

Historians — of whatever opinion — have vied with each other in describing this solemn scene, and Mary's heroic courage. Hume — by no means a partial judge — says : "No one was so steeled against all sentiments of humanity as not to be moved, when he reflected on her royal dignity, considered the surprising train of her misfortunes, beheld her mild but inflexible constancy, recalled her amiable accomplishments, or surveyed her beauties, which, though faded by years and yet more by her afflictions, still discovered themselves in this fatal moment."

3796. **Es muß geschieden sein,** impers. idiom : we must part. The use of **uns** for **mich,** addressed to Kennedy, finds explanation below.

3800. In fact, Kent refused a like request, but yielded at last to Mary's appeal, which is given almost literally in the following lines.

3814. **Sie leite,** let her, etc. The lines 3817–18 are almost as spoken by Mary on the scaffold : "As Thy arms, O Jesus, were extended on the cross, so stretch out the arms of Thy mercy and forgive my sins " (the form varies slightly in different authors).

* **bei ihrem Aufbruch . . . aufgefahren,** at her movement . . . starts, etc. See stage direction for Scene 8. Of this passage Mme de Staël says : " Les adieux de Marie au comte de Leicester me paraissent l'une des plus belles situations qui soient au théâtre."

3821. For some lines in earliest MS., afterwards omitted by Schiller, see Appendix I. The omission is an undoubted improvement. The line 3822, originally only part of a line, is thus left fragmentary, yet with fine effect.

3824. solltet, were to make — should have made.

3827. auf dem Weg . . . zu, about to. — **An eurer Hand** (holding by), i. e. hand in hand with you.

3833. Ihr durftet, etc. Much objection has been taken to the following lines, as inconsistent with the situation, and unworthy of Mary's last hour, after her confession, etc. To this writer (without discussion) it seems that Schiller knew the heart of woman better than his critics. These lines may, indeed, impair the pious solemnity of the scene; but they are intensely natural, and "true womanly" — and Mary was, above all, *a woman.*

This scene fully exposes Leicester's relations with Mary, and so — far more than any scruple of conscience or sentiment — prepares for his final step (last Scene).

ACT V., SCENE 10.

The execution could not be exhibited on the stage, but, in most dramatic manner, Schiller describes it by the remorseful words of Leicester, who is made its unwilling witness. With like skill, also, some of its incidents have already been wrought into the text.

3847. Wo ist . . . hin, whither has gone — what has become of. Note the rhymes.

3852. steht . . . an, becomes — befits. — **ehrnen Harnisch** reminds of Horace, *æs triplex,* Odes I., 3.

3860. sehe = will sehen.

3864. unten, below — where the scaffold was erected, *l.* 3467.

3870. The description follows nearly the actual facts. — **Schemel,** on which Mary was to kneel.

With this scene — or even with the preceding — the action of the play on the stage usually ends. And justly — for this closes the tragedy of Mary; what follows is the tragedy of Elizabeth. Yet it belongs, inseparably, to the drama, which was intended to include the doom of Elizabeth also.

ACT V., SCENES 11–12.

The scene shifts to Westminster Palace; time, the afternoon of the day of execution. Elizabeth is anxiously awaiting news from Fotheringhay. Dreading to expose herself by inquiries, she has sent a page to summon Burleigh and Leicester, as if still in London.

3881. **beidem,** either (alternative). See the pl., *l.* 1222.

3886. **gält's mein Reich,** though it should cost my kingdom— were my kingdom at stake. Note the vivid and passionate language, and see *l.* 3271. It is a fine stroke of the poet by which E. thus comforts her own indecision.

3891. **wußte ... zu,** could. — **hätten,** indirect (as I heard — it was said).

3894. This involuntary exclamation is superb; as are the following lines. See *l.* 3247.

3897. **was,** as *l.* 3480.—**Es soll,** etc., I shall not lack tears, etc. This is the harshest stroke of all, in Schiller's picture of Elizabeth— yet it is hardly without justification in her actual conduct at this time. As to her tears, see note, *l.* 1529.

3901. **Stehst du,** etc., also a fine stroke; she had forgotten his presence.

ACT V., SCENE 13.

Shrewsbury appears—relates what he had witnessed in the Tower, and begs for reconsideration of Mary's sentence. Elizabeth promises it!

3906. **So spät,** implying late afternoon or evening—after business hours.

3912. **Leutnant,** French *lieutenant*—the officer in charge.

3916. **verwildert,** dishevelled, wildly torn—absol. accus. as heretofore.

3919. **Kaum ... so** are correlative: hardly . . . when, etc.

3927. **Hinzu gefügt,** participle clause: adding that (now more usually in one word, **hinzugefügt**—as in other examples).

3935. **allen H.,** cursed himself to; we should say *by*.

3937. **als echt beschworen,** had sworn to as genuine. So Mary claimed on her trial. See note, *l.* 874; also *l.* 892. It is with reference to this testimony that Voltaire (Essai sur les mœurs) writes: "Jamais jugement ne fut plus incompétent, et jamais procédure ne fut plus irrégulière"—an opinion confirmed later by the most eminent British jurists. Mary accused Nau of her death. Kurl, in his dying words, declared her innocence.

3943. **daß alles Volk,** so that all the people — an artful stroke at Elizabeth, who valued nothing so much as public opinion. See *l.* 3190, etc. For **zusammen lief,** see note, *l.* 3927.

3954. **meine Peers,** the nobles constituting the commission to try Mary.

3956. **erneure,** her purpose to plead ignorance, etc. is here already manifest. The „Königliche Heuchlerin" speaks as if forgetful of Scene 12.

ACT V., SCENE 14.

Davison appears, in answer to the summons, *l.* 3901. Elizabeth seeks to convict him of disobedience of orders. See note at end of Act IV.

3963. **Das Volk** refers to *l.* 3053, etc. — though in fact she had learned, *l.* 3250, etc., that the uproar had ceased.

3967. **sagte,** Act IV., Scene 11.

3972. **ein M. des Todes,** a dead man. See *l.* 2618. — The phrase, **ich will nicht hoffen** is idiomatic: let me not suppose — meaning, she hopes the opposite.

3976. **So,** emphatic; *thus.* — **mich Lügen strafen,** phrase: give me the lie. Davison's loyalty binds his tongue — as Shrewsbury recognizes, *l.* 4018.

3983. **zu deuten,** to interpret, i. e. beyond their literal meaning, as the next line shows. — It has been supposed that Shakespeare had this case in mind, and thus meant to flatter Elizabeth, when he wrote (King John IV., 2) :

> " It is the curse of kings to be attended
> By slaves, who take their humors for a warrant
> To break into the bloody house of life,
> And, on the winking of authority,
> To understand a law, to know the meaning
> Of dangerous majesty, etc.

3988. **O mein Gott!** implies, God knows what! Elizabeth notes the implication, and sharply asks: **Was sagt Ihr?** which S. skillfully evades.

3990. **der Squire,** here used simply as English title, less than der Ritter, *l.* 1694. — **dieser That vermessen,** compare *l.* 2943. — **Wissenschaft.** as *l.* 860.

ACT V., SCENE 15.

Burleigh enters with news of the execution; **is severely rebuked by Elizabeth** and banished from her presence.   Davison is ordered to the Tower.   Shrewsbury resigns the Great Seal.   The Queen orders Leicester to be called, and learns from Kent that he has sailed for France. She is thus left alone.

3996. Burleigh uses almost the **very** words uttered by Dean Fletcher at the moment of Mary's execution.

4006. vorzugreifen, here, to forestall (and thus prevent). — Burleigh was actually banished for a time from Court.

4009. Euch feine ; change of person, as *l.* 2811 — here as mark of severity: she will not even speak to him.

4012. Auf Leib und Leben, as *l.* 97.   Davison was actually imprisoned in the Tower, and sentenced to pay a fine of £10,000, which reduced him to poverty.   He afterwards wrote a full account of the transaction, in which, however, he loyally forbore to accuse the Queen.

4018. für dich, for your sake.   See note, 3976. — It has been already remarked that S. had never held the Seal.

4024. grabe ... starr imply *unbending, inflexible.* — **versiegeln,** here more than siegeln (*l.* 3246) implies; *with approval.*

4026. wollte is subj., as heretofore: do you mean to say that, etc.

4031. zu fürchten ... zu achten imply a logical sequence and climax: have nothing more to fear; need have no more scruples — because she has already dared and done the worst.

4032. It is of course as a last resort, after all that has passed, that E. calls for Leicester, and the announcement of his desertion — to France, the home of Mary's friends — is, under the circumstances, the heaviest blow that could befall her. — **läßt ... entschuldigen,** begs to be excused — as if he had actually sent the message.

* The words in the final stage-direction, **mit ruhiger Fassung,** which have usually escaped notice, seem to be full of significance.   Elizabeth is guilty, convicted, deserted; yet she proudly controls herself, and as the curtain falls, she stands alone indeed, but still a queen !   This last highly poetic touch, while true to her historic character, only adds to the tragic dignity of the situation.

APPENDIX I.

Although textual criticism does not properly fall within the scope of this edition, yet it may be interesting to note the changes in the text in consequence of the removal of the Confession and the Communion from the stage editions. See Intr. to Act. V., Scene 7. It will be easily conceded that the poetry of the scene was not thereby improved.

1. The lines 3625–3631 are substituted by the following:

> Er dringt zu dir, er ist dir nah, ihn schließt
> Kein Tempel ein, kein Kerker schließt ihn aus.
> Nicht in der Formel ist der Geist enthalten,
> Den Ewigen begränzt kein irdisch Haus.
> Das sind nur Hüllen, nur die Scheingestalten
> Der unsichtbaren Himmelskraft:
> Es ist der Glaube. der den Gott erschafft.

Mary's reply remains unchanged, but then follows:

2. Instead of 3643–3672, thus:

> Wenn mich dein Herz dafür erklärt, so bin ich
> Für dich ein Priester, diese Kerzen sind
> Geweihet, und wir stehn an heil'ger Stätte.
> Ein Sakrament ist jegliches Bekenntnis,
> Das du der ew'gen Wahrheit thust. Spricht doch
> Im Beichtstuhl selbst der Mensch nur zu dem Menschen,
> Es spricht der Sündige den Sünder frei;
> Und eitel ist des Priesters Lösewort,
> Wenn dich der Gott nicht löst in deinem Busen.
> Doch kann es dich beruhigen, so schwör' ich dir,
> Was ich jetzt noch nicht b i n, ich will es w e r d e n.
> Ich will die Weih'n empfangen, die mir fehlen.
> Dem Himmel widm' ich künftig meine Tage;
> Kein irdisches Geschäft soll diese Hände
> Fortan entweihn, die dir den Segen gaben,
> Und dieses Priesterrecht, das ich voraus
> Mir nehme, wird der Papst bestätigen.

Das ist die Wohlthat unsrer heil'gen Kirche,
Daß sie ein sichtbar Oberhaupt verehrt,
Dem die Gewalt inwohnet, das Gemeine
Zu heil'gen und den Mangel zu ergänzen;
Drum wenn der Mangel nicht in deinem Herzen,
Nicht in dem Priester ist er — diese Handlung
Hat volle Kraft, sobald du daran glaubst.

    (Maria kniet vor ihm nieder.)

Hast du dein Herz erforscht, schwörst du, gelobst du,
Wahrheit zu reden vor dem Gott der Wahrheit?

3. Instead of 3738–3757, as follows:

So gehe hin, und sterbend büße sie!
Du fehltest nur aus weiblichen Gebrechen;
Blut kann versöhnen, was das Blut verbrach.
Dem sel'gen Geiste folgen nicht die Schwächen
Der Sterblichkeit in die Verklärung nach.
Sink, ein ergebnes Opfer, am Altar,
Gieb hin dem Staube was vergänglich war,
Die irdische Schönheit und die irdische Krone!
Und als ein schöner Engel schwinge dich
In seines Lichtes freudenreiche Zone,
Wo keine Schuld mehr sein wird und kein Weinen,
Gereinigt in den Schoß des Ewigreinen.

4. After line 3821 stood originally the following **(see note)**

Gekommen ist der lang ersehnte Tag,
Und in Erfüllung gehet was ich mir
In süßen Träumen gaukelnd vorgebildet.
Mylord von Lester, der erwartete,
Der heiß ersehnte Freund, er ist erschienen
In Fotheringhayschloß, ich seh' ihn mitten
In meinem Kerker stehen; alles ist
Bereit zum Aufbruch, alle Pforten offen;
Ich schreite endlich über diese Schwelle
An seiner Hand, und hinter mir auf ewig
Bleibt dieses traurige Gefängnis. — Alles
Erfüllet sich, Mylord, und Eure Ehre
Habt Ihr gelöst — — —

GENEALOGICAL TABLE — QUEEN ELIZABETH AND MARY STUART.

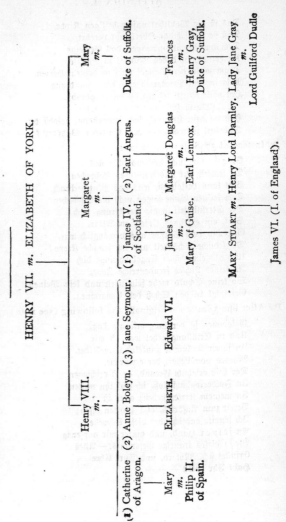

HENRY VII. m. ELIZABETH OF YORK.

Henry VIII. m.

(1) Catherine of Aragon. (2) Anne Boleyn. (3) Jane Seymour.

Mary m. Philip II. of Spain.

ELIZABETH.

Edward VI.

Margaret m.

(1) James IV. of Scotland. (2) Earl Angus.

James V. m. Mary of Guise.

Margaret Douglas m. Earl Lennox.

MARY STUART m. Henry Lord Darnley.

James VI. (I. of England).

Mary m.

Duke of Suffolk.

Frances m. Henry Gray, Duke of Suffolk.

Lady Jane Gray m. Lord Guilford Dudley.

VOCABULARY.

As Professor Joynes has noted in his Preface, a play like "Maria Stuart" is likely to be among the first read in the German classic drama. At a certain stage of the student's progress the time employed in consulting a general dictionary of sufficient size to supply his needs is better utilized in extending his vocabulary. To aid toward this end, this Vocabulary has been made. When it is noted that it contains more than four thousand words, the advantage to be gained by the reading of Schiller's drama, aside from recommendations of subject and style, is quite apparent.

The Vocabulary contains all the words in the text of the drama except proper names that belong in the list of *dramatis personae*. References are to the line-numbers in the case of speeches, but to the page in the case of stage-directions, and the number is then preceded by an asterisk. Reference is rarely made to words that occur only once or with a single meaning. In the case of words that occur with different meanings, the usual or obvious meaning is frequently not noted with line-reference; the less familiar meanings have been given with the proper reference in each case. As the Vocabulary has been made for this particular edition, free use has been made of Professor Joynes's notes, and to them the student has sometimes been sent for additional information respecting an idiom or grammatical form, *cf. N.* being then added to the line-number. He will understand, however, that literary and historical comments are not included in such references, and that the Vocabulary does not make the Notes less indispensable to his proper understanding of the play.

As "Maria Stuart" is frequently read in preparatory schools, — and with advantage when a proper amount of prose has previously been covered, — where this Vocabulary will, perhaps, be chiefly useful, considerable assistance has been given in the discrimination of synonyms. It is believed that with younger students, for whom the translation exercise is — or should be — an important aid to the cultivation of a correct English idiom, such exactness of expression may be indicated with advantage, provided they be required to use the information intelligently. With these conditions in view, derivative forms, such as participial adjectives, verbal substantives etc., have frequently been given in their alphabetical place, where they will first be sought; knowing the derivative and its meaning, the student will more readily find and better understand the root-word. In the case of adjectives used substantively, the reference is frequently given under the adjective; the student should be required to supply a suitable noun in English, to complete the sense. Adjectives and participial adjectives that are in effect substantives and are translated by English substantives are given independently in their alphabetical order. Such, e.g., are Fremde, Gefangene, Heilige.

Of nouns, the gender, the genitive singular (except of feminines), and the nominative plural, if the word has a plural, are indicated. Thus Abbild, n. -$, -er, neuter noun, genitive singular Abbilds, nominative plural Abbilder. In the case of monosyllabic masculine and neuter nouns it should be noted that the genitive singular ending –es may always be reduced to –$ unless the noun ends in f, ß, sch, z, tz. Owing to metrical requirements the –es ending is frequently employed in poetry when a speaker or a prose writer would use –$.

Of verbs the principal parts and other necessary forms are given whenever they are strong (old) or irregular. Verbs are otherwise understood to be weak (new) and regular. Verbs are to be conjugated with haben unless the auxiliary is indicated by f. (fein) or by h. and f. (haben and fein). Verbs are also marked as tr. (transitive), intr. (intransitive), or refl. (reflexive). Compound verbs are marked sep. (separable) or insep. (inseparable) when the prefix is doubtful (i. e. durch, über, um, unter, wieder); otherwise they are understood to be sep., unless marked insep. The unaccented inseparable prefixes be=, ent= (emp=), er=, ge=, ver=, zer=, however, are not so marked. Thus abbitten, bat, gebeten, tr., is a separable, transitive strong verb with auxiliary haben; abeilen, intr. f., is a separable, intransitive weak verb with auxiliary fein.

For the other parts of speech and other grammatical information customary abbreviations are used as given in the following list. The comparative and superlative of adjectives are given whenever they take umlaut or are irregular. As the superlative of adjectives does not occur in the uninflected form (except when used adverbially), the stem is followed by a dash. Thus, alt, (älter, ältest–). Since most adjectives may also be used in the uninflected form as adverbs, no mention is made of this use except when clearness requires it. Similarly the use of a participle adverbially is sometimes noted.

Accents are marked wherever it seems necessary for the student's information. A dash (—) indicates the repetition of the title-word or its uninflected part in a quoted phrase or an inflected form.

W. A. H.

Columbia University, New York, August, 1900.

ABBREVIATIONS.

acc., accusative.
act., active (voice).
adj., adjective.
adv., adverb.
art., article.
aux., auxiliary.
cf., confer (compare).
collect., collective(ly).
comp., comparative.
conj., conjunction.
dat., dative.
decl., declined.
def., definite.
demon., demonstrative.
dep., dependent.
Eng., English.
exclam., exclamation.
f., fem., feminine.
fig., figurative(ly).
Fr., French.
gen., genitive.
Ger., German.
ḥ., ḥaben.
imper., imperative.
impers., impersonal.
ind., indicative.
indecl., indeclinable.
indef., indefinite.
inf., infinitive.
insep., inseparable.
interj., interjection.
interrog., interrogative.
intr., intransitive.

irreg., irregular.
Lat., Latin.
lit., literally.
m., masc., masculine.
n., neut., neuter.
N., Note.
neg., negative.
nom., nominative.
num., numeral.
obj., object.
part., participle *or* participial.
pass., passive (voice).
pers., person *or* personal.
pl., plural.
poet., poetical.
poss., possessive.
prec., preceding.
pref., prefix.
prep., preposition.
pres., present.
pret., preterite.
pron., pronoun.
recip., reciprocal.
refl., reflexive.
reg., regular.
rel., relative.
ſ., ſein.
sep., separable.
sing., singular.
subj., subjunctive.
subst., substantive(ly).
superl., superlative.
tr., transitive.

VOCABULARY.

A.

ab, *adv. and sep. pref.*, off, away, down.

Abbild, *n.*, -8, -er, image.

abbitten, bat, gebeten, *tr.*, apologize for.

abbüßen, *tr.*, atone for.

abdrücken, *tr.*, *lit.* press off; let fly (an arrow), release, 3885.

abeilen, *intr.* f., hurry off, hasten away.

Abend, *m.*, -8, -e, evening.

Abenteurer, *n.*, -8, —, adventurer.

Aberglaube, *m.*, -n8, superstition.

abermals, *adv.*, once more, again.

abfassen, *tr.*, draw up (in writing).

abfeuern, *tr.*, fire off, discharge.

abgefeimt, *adj.*, arrant, crafty.

abgehen, ging, gegangen, *intr.*, f., go off *or* away, depart; *in stage directions*, exit, *pl.*, exeunt.

Abgesandte, *m.* (*decl. like adj.*), envoy, ambassador.

Abgott, *m.*, -8, -götter, idol.

abgöttisch, *adj.*, idolatrous.

Abgrund, *m.*, -8, -ünde, abyss, chasm; *fig.*, destruction, 78.

abhören, *tr.*, hear *or* question (a witness).

Abkunft, *f.* descent.

Ablaß, *m.*, -sses, -lässe, indulgence, absolution, 2505, *et N.*

abnehmen, nahm, genommen nimmt, *tr.*, take off.

abpressen, *tr.*, force *or* wring from.

abreisen, *intr.* f., leave, depart.

Abscheu, *m.*, -8, abhorrence.

abscheulich, *adj.*, abominable, horrible; *as subst.*, 316, 2864.

Abscheulichkeit, *f.*, -en, horror, atrocity.

Abschied, *m.*, -8, -e, leave, farewell.

abschildern, *tr.*, depict.

abschlagen, schlug, geschlagen, schlägt, *tr.*, beat off, repulse.

abschließen, schloß, geschlossen, *tr.*, close.

abschwören, schwor *and* schwur, geschworen, *tr.*, abjure, forswear.

Absicht, *f.*, -en, purpose.

abspannen, *tr.*, slacken, relax.

absprechen, sprach, gesprochen, spricht, *tr.*, deprive of, declare forfeit (*dat. of pers.*).

abthun, that, gethan, *tr.*, do thoroughly, complete; settle arrange, 60.

abtreten, trat, getreten, tritt, *intr.* f., step off; retire. withdraw.

abweisen, wies, gewiesen, *tr.*, dismiss, put aside, 1423; refuse admittance to, 2881.

abwenden, wandte *and* wendete gewandt *and* gewendet. *tr.*,

avert; *refl.*, turn away (*intr.*),
*160.

abwägen, wog, gewogen, *tr.*,
weigh, consider carefully.

ach, *interj.*, ah! oh! alas!

Acht, *f.*, care, attention; fich in
— nehmen, take care, 2762.

achten, *tr.*, deem, regard, look
upon (as), 194; heed, care for,
2532, 4031; nichts —, disre-
gard, 1979; gering —, value
lightly, despise, 3531.

Achtung, *f.*, -en, respect, regard.

Adel, *m.*, -$, nobility, 2009;
collect., 773; nobles, 1916.

adeln, *tr.*, ennoble.

Ader, *f.*, -n, vein.

Affekt', *m.*, -$, -e, passion,
emotion.

Afterkönigin, *f.*, -innen, spurious
or pretended queen, pretender,
522, *cf. N.*

Agnus Dei (*Lat.*), Agnus Dei,
an image or representation of
a lamb as emblematical of
Christ; *166, *cf. N.*

Ahnen (*verbal subst.*), *n.*, -$,
foreboding.

Ahnherr, *m.*, -n, -en, ancestor.

Ahnung, *f.*, -en, foreboding, mis-
giving.

Akte, *f.*, -n, Act (of Parliament).

Alix, *f.*, Alice, the name given
by Schiller to one of Mary
Stuart's women; 3550, *cf. N.*

all, *adj. and indef. pron.*, all,
whole, entire; each, every;
alles, *neut. sing.*, all, everything; *collect. of persons*, all,
everybody, 1360.

allein', *indec. adj.*, alone; *adv.*,
only, alone, 671; *conj.*, but.

allerchristlich, *adj.*, most Christian, 3521, *cf. N.*

allerlei, *indec. adj.*, of all sorts
or kinds.

allertreu, *adj.*, most faithful *or*
loyal.

allgemein', *adj.*, universal, 3609;
common, 2417; general, *101.

allgewaltig, *adj.*, all-powerful.

Allmacht, *f.*, omnipotence; the
Almighty, 1585.

allmächtig, *adj.*, almighty; der
A—e, the Almighty, 1416.

allmählich, *adj.*, gradual.

allvermögend, *adj.*, all-powerful,
omnipotent; der A—e, the
Omnipotent, Almighty God.

allwichtig, *adj.*, all-important.

allwissend, *adj.*, all-knowing; der
A—e, the Omniscient.

allzuheftig, *adv.*, quite too violently.

als, *conj.*, as, when; *after comp.*,
than.

alsbald, *adv.*, forthwith, immediately.

also, *adv.*, so, thus; *conj.*, then,
so.

alt (älter, ältest-), *adj.*, old, aged;
ancient, 834; former, 3174.

Altar', *m.*, -$, -e *and* -äre,
altar.

altenglisch, *adj.*, old English.

Alter, *n.*, -$, —, age, 295; old
age, 253, 1987, 3791.

altern, *intr.* h. *and* f., age, grow
old.

Amen (*Hebrew*), *interj.*, amen,
so be it.

Amiens. Amiens (*pronounce*
ä-mē-an'), a city in France.

Amme, *f.*, -n, nurse, attendant.

Amt, *n.*, -(e)$, Ämter, office;
duty, 1295; *pred. gen.*, 3324,
cf. N.

an, *prep.* (*dat. and acc.*), *adv.*
and sep. pref., at, on, to, by,
near; in, 18; an Euch ist's,
it's your turn, 2792.

Anathem', *n.*, -$, -e, anathema,

(ecclesiastical) ban *or* curse, 2626, *cf. N.*

anbefehlen, befahl, befohlen, befiehlt, *tr.* (*dat. of pers.*), command, enjoin, 1888; order, authorize, 1596.

anbeten, *tr.*, adore, worship; kneel to *or* before, 2252; angebetet, *part. adj.*, adored, 1426.

Anbetung, *f.*, -en, adoration, worship.

anbieten, bot, geboten, *tr.*, offer; *refl.*, offer oneself, volunteer, 1944, 3528.

anblasen, blies, geblasen, bläst, *tr.*, blow upon, set ablaze; fan (*as a flame*), 2343.

Anblick, *m.*, -s, -e, sight; *frequently objective*, sight of, 1947, *cf. N.*; look, glance, 2241, 2860.

anbringen, brachte, gebracht, *tr.*, make use of, suit, adapt.

Anbruch, *m.*, -s, -üche, break, dawning.

Andacht, *f.*, -en, devotion.

ander, *adj.*, other, else; different, 1534, 1614.

ändern, *tr.*, change.

anders, *adv.*, otherwise, differently.

anempfehlen, empfahl, empfohlen, empfiehlt, *tr.*, recommend to.

anerkennen, erkannte, erkannt, *tr.*, acknowledge, 1287; recognize, 716.

anfallen, fiel, gefallen, fällt, *tr.*, attack.

Anfang, *m.*, -s, -änge, beginning.

anfangen, fing, gefangen, fängt, *tr. and intr.*, begin, commence.

anfangs, *adv.* (*gen.*), in the beginning; at first, *130.

anfechten, focht, gefochten, ficht, *tr.*, combat, contest, dispute.

anfesseln, *tr.*, chain fast, confine.

anflehen, *tr.*, beseech, implore.

anfüllen, *tr.*, fill up; *refl.*, fill up; (*intr.*), be filled up.

angebetet, *part. adj.*, adored, 1426, 2902.

Angedenken, *n.*, -s, remembrance, memory.

angefangen, *part. adj.*, begun; partly written, 2779.

angefochten, *part.adj.*, contested, disputed.

angehen, ging, gegangen, *tr.*, concern.

Angeklagte, *m. and f.* (*decl. like adj.*), accused person, defendant.

Angesicht, *n.*, -s, face, 468, 1228, 1512; sight, 2890; presence, 901, 4007; von —, face to face, 2206.

angestammt, *part. adj.*, ancestral, hereditary.

angreifen, griff, gegriffen, *tr.*, attack.

Angst, *f.*, Ängste, anguish, anxiety.

ängsten, *see* ängstigen.

Angstgedränge, *n.*, -s, anxious stress, dilemma.

ängstigen, *tr.*, alarm, distress, 3384; torture, 896.

anheften, *tr.*, fasten to.

anhören, *tr.*, hear, listen to.

Anjou, Anjou, a former province of France, and the title of a reigning family; 607 *cf., N.*

anklagen, *tr.*, accuse; accuse of (*gen.*), 3683.

ankleiden, *tr.*, dress.

ankommen, kam, gekommen, *intr.* f., arrive.

Ankömmling, *m.*, -s, -e, arrival.

ankünden, *tr.*, announce; declare, 3743.

ankündigen, *tr.*, announce; inform *or* tell of, 2243; declare, 2333.

anlegen, *tr.,* bring ashore (*a boat*); moor, make fast, 2107.

anmaßlich, *adj.,* presumptuous.

Anmut, *f.,* grace, charm.

annehmen, nahm, genommen, nimmt, *tr.,* assume, 1535, 2336; take, accept, *33, *177.

anraten, riet, geraten, rät, *tr* (*dat. of pers.*), recommend, advise.

anreden, *tr.,* speak to, address.

anrufen, rief, gerufen, *tr.,* appeal to, invoke.

ansagen, *tr.,* speak, tell, say on.

anschauen, *tr.,* look at; watch, 818.

Anschlag, *m.,* -s, -äge, plan.

ansehen, sah, gesehen, sieht, *tr.,* look at; einem (etwas) —, perceive (something) in one; see from, 30, *cf. N.*; 2013, *cf. N.*

Ansehen, *n.,* -s, sight, appearance; authority, 2792, 2869, *21.

ansinnen, sann, gesonnen, *tr.* (*dat. of pers.*), expect *or* require of.

Anspruch, *m.,* -s, -üche, claim; in — nehmen, lay claim to, 1417.

anspruchlos, *adj.,* unassuming, unambitious.

Anstalt, *f.,* -en, preparation, provision.

Anstand, *m.,* -s, -ände, grace, propriety, 1082; delay, pause; — nehmen, hesitate, 1900.

anstehen, stand, gestanden, *intr.* (*with dat.*), befit.

antasten, *tr.,* lay finger on, harm.

Anteil, *m.,* -s, -e, share, part (in, an *and dat.*); interest, 1739.

anthun, that, gethan, *tr.,* put on; impose, 3087; angethan sein, be clad, 3855.

Antlitz, *n.,* -es, -e, face; einem ins —, to one's face, 262, 904.

Antrag, *m.,* -s, -äge, offer, proposition, 2969.

antragen, trug, getragen, trägt, *tr.,* propose, move.

antreten, trat, getreten, tritt, *tr.,* enter upon.

antworten, *tr. and intr.,* answer.

anvertrauen, *tr.,* entrust to (*dat.*); anvertraut, *part. adj.,* 1044, 4010.

Anverwandte, *m.* (*and f.*), (*decl. like adj.*), relative, kinsman, 124, *cf. N.*

Anwalt, *m.,* -s, -e (-älte), attorney; advocate, 1348.

anwandeln, *tr.,* befall, come over.

anwesend, *part. adj.,* present; die A—en, those present, *166.

anzeigen, *tr.* (*dat. of pers.*), inform, 1169; point out, indicate, 1346.

anzünden, *tr.,* light, kindle.

Apostel, *m.,* -s, —, apostle.

arg (ärger, ärgst-), *adj.,* bad, wicked; arrant, 583; *superl. as subst.,* the worst, 2425.

arglos, *adj.,* guileless, unsuspecting.

Argwohn, *m.,* -s, suspicion.

Argusblick, *m.,* -s, -e, Argus glance, vigilance; *cf. N.* 1790.

Arm, *m.,* -es, -e, arm.

arm (ärmer, ärmst-), *adj.,* poor; *superl. as subst.,* 1645.

Armida, Armi'da *or* Armide (-mēd), an enchantress in Tasso's "Jerusalem Delivered," 2374, *cf. N.*

Arsenal', *n.,* -s, -e, arsenal.

Arti'kel, *m.,* -s, —, article.

Arzt, *m.,* -es, Ärzte, physician.

Ate (*Gr.*), Ate (2 *syll.*), the goddess of Discord, 1281, *cf. N.*

Atem, *m.*, -ŝ, breath.

Atlas (*Gr.*), Atlas, "the supporter"; in mythology, one of the Titans; 2710, *cf. N.*

atmen, *intr.*, breathe; *part.* as *subst.*, (all) things that breathe, 2531.

auch, *conj.*, also; wie ... auch, however.

auf, *prep.* (*dat. and acc.*), *adv. and sep. pref.*, on, upon, at, to.

aufbieten, bot, geboten, *tr.*, call upon; alles —, make every effort, 1907.

aufbrechen, brach, gebrochen, bricht, *tr.*, break open.

aufbringen, brachte, gebracht, *tr.*, provoke, exasperate.

Aufbruch, *m.*, -ŝ, -üche, start, movement.

aufdringen, drang, gedrungen, *tr.*, urge *or* thrust upon.

auferlegen, *tr.*, lay *or* impose upon.

auferstehen, erstand, erstanden, *intr.* ſ., rise, arise.

auferziehen, erzog, erzogen, *tr.*, bring up, rear; train up, 495, 1383.

auffahren, fuhr, gefahren, fährt, *intr.* ſ., start (*with surprise, alarm, anger, etc.*).

auffangen, fing, gefangen, fängt, *tr.*, catch, intercept.

auffordern, *tr.*, challenge, summon, 1090; call upon, 2781.

aufführen, *tr.*, lead, conduct; parade, 2823.

aufgeben, gab, gegeben, giebt, *tr.*, give up; *part. as subst.*, deserted, helpless, 1356.

aufgebracht, *part. adj.*, excited. 2687.

aufgehen, ging, gegangen, *intr.*

ſ., go up, rise; open, 1777, 3483; aufgehend, *part. adj.*, rising, 2377.

aufgreifen, griff, gegriffen, *tr.*, seize, pick up.

aufhören, *intr.*, stop, cease.

aufjagen, *tr.*, start up, rouse.

aufladen, lud, geladen, lädt, *tr.*, load upon; burden; ſich (*dat.*) —, take upon oneself, 1980.

Auflauf, *m.*, -ŝ, -äuſe, uproar, tumult.

auflösen, *tr.*, unloose; dissolve, 2696; annul, 780.

aufmerksam, *adj.*, attentive, observant.

Aufmerksamkeit, *f.*, -en, attention, notice; — bezeigen, take notice of, *16.

aufnehmen, nahm, genommen, nimmt, *tr.*, receive.

aufregen, *tr.*, arouse, excite.

aufreiben, rieb, gerieben, *tr.*, consume, waste.

aufreißen, riß, gerissen, *tr.*, tear *or* fling open.

aufrufen, rief, gerufen, *tr.*, call upon, summon.

aufrühren, *tr.*, stir up, arouse.

aufsäugen, *tr.*, suckle, nurse.

aufschlagen, schlug, geschlagen, schlägt, *tr.*, put up, erect, 1072, 3399; raise, *178.

aufschließen, schloß, geschlossen, *tr.*, disclose.

aufschreien, schrie, geschrieen, *tr.*, cry out, scream.

Aufschub, *m.*, -ŝ, delay, postponement.

aufschwingen, schwang, geschwungen, *tr.*, swing up; *refl.*, soar, 3484.

aufsetzen, *tr.*, put *or* place upon, 1974; set down (in writing), draw up, 191.

Aufsicht, *f.*, -en, care, custody.

aufspringen, sprang, gesprungen, *intr.* f., spring *or* jump up, 3928; spring open.

aufstecken, *tr.,* stick *or* set up.

aufstehen, stand, gestanden, *intr.* f., stand up, rise.

aufsteigen, stieg, gestiegen, *intr.* f., rise, ascend.

aufsuchen, *tr.,* seek out.

aufthun, that, gethan, *tr.,* open, 108, 1175; *refl.,* open (*intr.*), be opened, 865, 3469.

Auftrag, *m.,* –s, –äge, order, charge, 1041; commission, 2967, 3040; task, 1052; errand, 1658.

auftreten, trat, getreten, tritt, *intr.* f., enter, appear.

Auftritt, *m.,* –s, –e, entrance, appearance; scene.

aufwachen, *intr.,* awake.

aufwachsen, wuchs, gewachsen, wächst, *intr.* f., grow up.

aufzeigen, *tr.,* show, produce.

aufziehen, zog, gezogen, *tr.,* draw up.

Aufzug, *m.,* –s, –üge, drawing up (of the curtain), act.

Auge, *n.* –s, –n, eye; in die —n fallen, strike the eye, 503.

Augenblick, *m.,* –s, –e, moment, instant.

augenblicklich, *adj.,* momentary; *adv.,* momentarily, temporarily, 365; in a moment, instantaneously, 3403.

augenblicks, *adv.* (*gen.*), instantly.

aus, *prep.* (*dat.*), *adv. and sep. pref.,* out, out of, from; over, at an end, 2404, 2453.

ausbeugen, *intr.,* evade, 928 *cf. N.*

ausbrechen, brach, gebrochen, bricht, *intr.* f., break forth, exclaim, *181; burst (out), *164.

ausbreiten, *tr.,* stretch out, extend, 3818; spread out, 452;

spread abroad (a rumor), 1059; ausgebreitet, *part. adj.,* outstretched, *114.

ausdeuten, *tr.,* expound, interpret.

Ausdruck, *m.,* –s, –ücke, expression.

ausdrücken, *tr.,* express.

ausdrücklich, *adj.,* express, explicit.

auseinander, *adv.,* asunder, apart.

ausfertigen, *tr.,* execute, 3030; draw up (*as a legal document*), 2650.

Ausflucht, *f.,* –üchte, evasion, subterfuge.

ausforschen, *tr.,* inquire after, search out, sound; ausforschend, *part. adv.,* inquiringly, *71.

ausführen, *tr.,* carry out, execute.

ausgehen, ging, gegangen, *intr.* f., go forth.

aushalten, hielt, gehalten, hält, *tr.,* hold out; stand, endure, *181.

Ausland, *n.,* –s, foreign country.

auslernen, *tr.,* learn thoroughly, master.

auslesen, las, gelesen, liest, *tr.,* choose, select.

auslöschen, *tr.,* extinguish, 2027; blot out, efface, 2181.

ausmachen, *tr.,* make, constitute.

ausnehmen, nahm, genommen, nimmt, *tr.,* except.

ausrufen, rief, gerufen, *tr.,* proclaim.

aussäen, *tr.,* sow (broadcast), disseminate.

aussagen, *tr.,* say, assert, state.

ausschließen, schloß, geschlossen, *tr.,* exclude.

aussehen, sah, gesehen, sieht, *intr.,* look, appear.

außen, *adv.*, out, without, out-side.

aussenden, sandte *and* sendete, gesandt *and* gesendet, *tr.*, send out *or* forth.

außer, *prep.* (*dat.*), without, out of, except, besides; — sich, beside oneself, 2105, 2443.

außerordentlich, *adj.*, extraordinary.

äußerst (*superl.* of äußer), *adj.*, utmost, extreme; *neut. as subst.*, the worst, 1839; extreme measure, 3026.

aussetzen, *tr.*, expose.

Aussicht, *f.*, –en, outlook, prospect.

aussinnen, sann, gesonnen, *tr.*, think out, devise.

ausspannen, *tr.*, spread out, extend.

aussprechen, sprach, gesprochen, spricht, *tr.*, speak out, express, 1736, 3299; pronounce, 322, 579, 994, *etc.*

ausstrecken, *tr.*, stretch out *or* forth.

austeilen, *tr.*, give out, issue.

austrinken, trank, getrunken, *tr.*, drink empty, drain.

ausüben, *tr.*, exercise; practise, 1575.

auswirken, *tr.*, procure, obtain.

Auswurf, *m.*, –s, –ürfe, outcast.

auszeichnen, *tr.*, distinguish.

Axt, *f.*, Äxte, axe.

B.

Babington. Anthony Babington, for a time page to Mary Stuart, subsequently an ardent champion of her cause and the author of a plot against Elizabeth. Born 1561, executed 1586.

Bahn, *f.*, –en, way, path; career, 1577.

bahnen, *tr.*, smooth *or* clear (a path *or* way); pave, 1884.

bald, *adv.*, soon.

Band, *n.*, –es, Bänder, ribbon, band, *55.

Band, *n.*, –es, –e, bond, fetter, 63, 334, 947 *etc.*; bond, tie, 1223, 1630.

bändigen, *tr.*, control.

Bannfluch, *m.*, –s, –üche, curse of excommunication, anathema.

Barmherzigkeit, *f.*, –en, mercy.

Barnabite (*Fr.*), *m. pl.*, –n, one of the Barnabites, an order of monks, 2623, *cf. N.*

Basilisk (*Gr.*), *m.*, –en, –en, basilisk, cockatrice, *cf. N.* 2440.

Bastard, *m.*, –s, –e, bastard.

Bastardkönigin, *f.*, –innen, bastard queen.

Bastardname, *m.*, –ns, –n, bastard's name.

Bastardtochter, *f.*, –töchter, bastard *or* illegitimate daughter.

bauen, *tr.*, build.

Baum, *m.*, –es, Bäume, tree.

be-, *insep. pref., never accented, Eng.,* be-.

beängstigen, *tr.*, make uneasy cause one anxiety *or* alarm.

Becher, *m.*, –s, —, goblet cup.

bedacht, *part. adj.*, discreet, careful, 1870.

bedecken, *tr.*, cover.

bedenken, bedachte, bedacht, *tr.*, consider, weigh, 2044, 2674, *etc.*; think of, plan, 2063; *refl.*, deliberate, consider, 166; hesitate, 3971.

bedenklich, *adj.*, hesitating, doubtful; scrupulous, 1618, 1857.

bedeuten, *tr.*, mean; signify, *158; bedeutend, *part. adj.*,

significant, important; *adv.*,
significantly, 1643, *44.

Bedeutung, *f.*, –en, significance,
importance.

bedeutungsvoll, *adj.*, significant,
full of meaning.

bedienen, *tr.*, serve.

Bediente, *m.*, (*decl. like adj.*),
servant, attendant.

bedrängen, *tr.*, press hard; vex,
harass, 820.

bedrohen, *tr.*, threaten.

bedürfen, bedurfte, bedurft, be=
darf, *intr.* (*with gen.*), be in
need of, need.

Befehl, *m.*, –s, –e, command;
order, 2648.

befehlen, befahl, befohlen, befiehlt,
tr. (*dat. of pers.*), command,
order.

befinden, befand, befunden, *refl.*,
find oneself, be.

beflecken, *tr.*, spot, stain; pollute,
954; beflect, *part. adj.*, polluted, defiled, 368.

befleißen, befliß, beflissen, *refl.*,
exert oneself, strive.

beflügelt, *part. adj.*, wingéd.

befolgen, *tr.*, follow, obey.

befördern, *tr.*, forward, transmit.

befragen, *tr.*, question, inquire of.

befreien, *tr.*, free, set free, deliver; exempt, 3041.

Befreier, *m.*, –s, –, liberator,
deliverer.

Befreiung, *f.*, –en, liberation, deliverance.

befreundet, *part. adj.*, friendly.

befürchten, *tr.*, fear, apprehend.

begeben, begab, begeben, begiebt,
refl., betake oneself, go, *111;
enter, set out (on, auf), 1665;
(*with gen.*),forego, waive, 3047.

begegnen, *intr.* (*dat.*) f., meet;
treat, 2215, *cf. N.*

Begegnung, *f.*, –en, meeting.

begehen, beging, begangen, *tr.*,
commit.

begehren, *tr.*, desire.

Begierde, *f.*, –n, desire.

beginnen, begann, begonnen, *intr.*
and tr., begin.

Beginnen, *n.*, –s, action, doings.

beglaubigen, *tr.*, accredit.

begleiten, *tr.*, accompany.

Begleiter, *m.*, –s, —, companion.

Begleitung, *f.*, –en, accompani-
ment, attendant, 3134.

beglücken, *tr.*, make happy, bless;
beglückt, *part. adj.*, favored,
2907, 3614; happy, 3832.

begnadigen, *tr.*, pardon.

begnügen, *refl.*, be content *or*
satisfied.

begraben, begrub, begraben, be-
gräbt, *tr.*, bury.

begreifen, begriff, begriffen, *tr.*,
comprehend.

begreiflich, *adj.*, comprehensible.

Begriff, *m.*, –s, –e, conception,
idea; im — sein, be on the
point of, be about to, *5, *181.

begrüßen, *tr.*, greet.

behalten, behielt, behalten, behält,
tr., keep.

behandeln, *tr.*, treat, deal with.

behaupten, *tr.*, maintain; assert,
2904.

Beherrscher, *m.*, –s, —, ruler.

Beherrscherin, *f.*, –innen (female)
ruler, sovereign.

Beherrschung, *f.*, –en, control;
1573, *cf. N.*

beherzt, *adj.*, courageous, bold.

bei, *prep.* (*dat.*), *adv. and sep.*
pref., by, near; with, 89, 675;
in, at, at the house of; among,
161; during, 2373.

Beichte, *f.*, –n, confession.

beichten, *tr.*, confess.

beide, *adj. pl.*, both; (the) two,
812, 1561.

Beifall, *m.,* –s, applause, approval.

Beil, *n.,* –es, –e, axe.

Beisein, *n.,* –s, presence.

Beispiel, *n.,* –s, –e, example.

Beistand, *m.,* –s, assistance, help; support, 3376; services, 3788.

beistimmen, *intr.* assent, agree.

beiwohnen, *intr.* (*with dat.*), attend, be present at.

bejahen, *tr.,* answer affirmatively.

bejammern, *tr.,* lament, mourn; *part. adj. as subst.,* 3126.

bekannt, *part. adj.,* known.

bekennen, bekannte, bekannt, *tr.,* confess, 879, 2932; acknowledge, own, 2403.

Bekenner, *m.,* –s, —, confessor; professor, 3501.

Bekenntnis, *n.,* –sses, –sse, confession.

beklagen, *tr.,* pity; regret, 2989.

Beklagte, *m. and f.* (*decl. like adj.*), accused (person), defendant.

bekleiden, *tr.,* clothe; invest, 1218; occupy, hold, 2945.

beklemmt, *part. adj.,* anxious.

bekränzen, *tr.,* garland, wreathe.

bekrönen, *tr.,* crown.

bekümmern, *tr.,* grieve, 3506; concern, 1599, 3908.

beladen, belud, beladen, beladet (*and* beläbt, *rare*) *tr.,* laden.

belasten, *tr.,* burden.

belegen, *tr.,* lay upon, impose.

belehren, *tr.,* instruct.

beleidigen, *tr.,* offend; insult, 3805; injure, 2205.

Beleidigung, *f.,* –en, offense, injury; outrage, 297.

belohnen, *tr.,* reward; *refl.,* be rewarded, 2576.

bemerken, *tr.,* remark, notice.

bemühen, *tr.,* trouble; *refl.,* take *or* give oneself trouble, 2665.

Bemühen (*verbal subst.*), *n.,* –s, effort, endeavor.

beneiden, *tr.* (*with* um), envy.

beobachten, *tr.,* observe.

berauben, *tr.,* rob, plunder; *part. adj. as subst.,* 3543.

Beredsamkeit, *f.,* eloquence.

beredt', *adj.,* eloquent.

bereichern, *tr.,* enrich.

bereisen, *tr.,* travel over, traverse.

bereit', *adj.,* ready.

bereiten, *tr.,* make ready, prepare; cause, 3019, 3790; *refl.,* prepare (*intr.*), 2178, 3763 *etc.*

bereits', *adv.,* already.

berennen, berannte, berannt, *tr.,* assault, attack, 1085, *cf. N.*

bereuen, *tr.,* repent; bereuend, *part. adj.,* repentant, 314.

Berg, *m.* –es, –e, mountain; the Mount, 490, *cf. N.*

bergen, barg, geborgen, birgt, *tr.,* hide, conceal.

Bergeslast, *f.,* –en, mountain's weight.

bergicht (*usually* bergig), *adj.,* mountainous, hilly.

Bericht', *m.,* –s, –e, report, account.

berichtigen, *tr.,* set right, settle.

Bertha, *f.,* Bertha, the name given by Schiller to one of Mary's Stuart's women; *cf. N.* 3550.

berücken, *tr.,* impose upon.

berufen, berief, berufen, *tr.,* call, summon; *refl.* (*with* auf *and* acc.), appeal to, 959, 2893.

beruhigen, *tr.,* quiet, calm; set at ease, 206; appease, 3063; *refl.,* calm *or* compose oneself, 154.

Beruhigung, *f.,* quieting; peace of mind, 3956.

berühmen, *refl.,* boast.

berühren, *tr.,* touch.

befänftigen, *tr.*, calm, appease; *refl.*, be calmed *or* appeased, 3259.

befchäftigen, *tr.*, busy, occupy.

Befchämung, *f.*, mortification.

befchauen, *tr.*, view, look at.

Befchauung, *f.*, -en, contemplation.

Befcheidenheit, *f.*, modesty.

befchlagen, befchlug, befchlagen, befchlägt, *tr.*, cover; drape, 3472.

befchleunigen, *tr.*, hasten, quicken.

befchließen, befchloß, befchloffen, *tr.*, determine, resolve.

befchuldigen, *tr.*, charge with (*gen.*).

befchützen, *tr.*, protect; defend, 654, 1356.

befchwatzen, *tr.*, talk over, persuade.

befchwören, befchwor, befchworen, *tr.*, swear to, 900, 3937; conjure, implore, 3922, 3951.

befeelen, *tr.*, inspire.

befeligen, *tr.*, bless.

befeßen (*for* befeffen), *part. adj.* possessed.

befeßen, *tr.*, occupy; befeßt, planted, *93.

befiegeln, *tr.*, seal, confirm.

befiegen, *tr.*, vanquish, overcome; conquer, 3134, 3760; befiegt, *part. adj.*, vanquished, 3831.

Befiß, *m.*, -es, possession.

befißen, befaß, befeffen, *tr.*, possess, 22, *cf. N.*

befonnen, *part. adj.*, resolved; plötzlich —, with a sudden resolve, *130.

beforgen, *tr.*, procure; bring, 3446.

Beforgniß, *f.*, -ffe, fear, apprehension.

beffer (*comp. of* gut), *adj.*, better; *neut., as subst.*, 1459.

beffern, *tr.*, better, improve.

Befferung, *f.*, -en, improvement.

beft (*superl. of* gut), *adj.*, best; *neut. as subst.*, 1610.

beftätigen, *tr.*, confirm.

beftechen, beftach, beftochen, befticht, *tr.*, bribe; corrupt, 759.

Beftechung, *f.*, -en, bribery, corruption.

beftehen, beftand, beftanden, *intr.* (*rarely* f.), exist, stand, 1452; — aus, consist of; — in (*dat.*), consist in; — auf (*dat.*), insist upon, 581, 1853, 2905; *tr.*, undergo, pass through, 3690, 3758.

befteigen, beftieg, beftiegen, *tr.*, mount, ascend.

beftellen, *tr.*, appoint.

beftimmen, *tr.*, determine, decide; destine *or* intend for (*dat.*), 3551, beftimmt, *part. adj.*, intended, 162; definite, 3981.

beftürmen, *tr.*, assail, besiege; importune, 3963.

beftürzt, *part. adj.*, amazed; perplexed, dismayed, 3912.

Beftürzung, *f.*, consternation.

befuchen, *tr.*, visit.

betäuben, *tr.*, stun, amaze; betäubt, *part. adj.*, stunned, dazed; *as subst.*, 223.

beten, *intr.*, pray; *inf. as subst.*, praying, 3419.

bethören, *tr.*, befool, infatuate, 1994; delude, 2336.

betrachten, *tr.*, look at, contemplate; regard (as, als), 2365.

Betrachtung, *f.*, -en, reflection.

betragen, betrug, betragen, beträgt, *refl.*, conduct oneself, behave.

betreten, *part. adj.,* confused, embarrassed.

betroffen, *part. adj.,* amazed, taken aback, perplexed, *140.

betrügen, betrog, betrogen, *tr.,* deceive; cheat, dupe, 2449.

Betrüger, *m.,* -ß, —, deceiver, impostor.

betrüglich, *adj.,* deceitful; illusory, 3578.

Bett, *n.,* -eß, -en, bed; (river) channel, 815.

Bette (*archaic*), *see* Bett.

betten, *refl.* (*with dat.*), make one's bed.

Bettler, *m.,* -ß, —, beggar.

beugen, *tr.,* bend, bow; *refl.,* bow (*intr.*), 3667; gebeugt, *part. adj.,* depressed, 268.

bewachen, *tr.,* guard.

bewaffnen, *tr.,* arm; *fut. perf.,* 2757, *cf. N.; refl.,* take up arms, 1454; *part. adj. as subst.,* armed men, *130.

bewahren, *tr.,* keep; — vor (*dat.*), keep *or* preserve from, 2328; guard, 550.

bewähren, *tr.,* verify, prove.

Bewahrung, *f.,* keeping, custody.

bewandert, *adj.,* versed (in), conversant (with).

bewegen, *tr.,* move; agitate, 949, 3088; *refl.,* move (*intr.*), 439.

Bewegung, *f.,* -en, movement, *166, *183; agitation, *145, *185; emotion, 1544.

bewehren, *tr.,* arm.

beweinen, *tr.,* weep for, bewail, lament.

Beweiß, *m.,* -eß, -e, proof.

beweisen, bewieß, bewiesen, *tr.,* prove.

bewilligen, *tr.,* consent to, grant.

bewußt (*with* sich [*dat.*] *and gen.*), conscious of, 2701.

bezahlen, *tr.,* pay.

bezeigen, *tr.,* show; Aufmerksamkeit —, pay attention, take notice, *16.

bezeugen, *tr.,* witness.

bezwingen, bezwang, bezwungen, *tr.,* conquer, overcome; *refl.,* control *or* constrain oneself, *192.

Bibel, *f.,* -n, Bible.

Biedermann, *m.,* -ß, -männer, upright man, man of honor.

bieten, bot, geboten, *tr.,* offer, 639; bid, 316, 1959.

Bild, *n.,* -eß, -er, image, 40, 1809; picture, portrait, 508, 550.

bilden, *tr.,* form.

Bildnergeist, *m.,* -eß, -er, creative *or* artistic spirit.

Bildniß, *n.,* -ffeß, -ffe, picture, portrait; image, 3539.

billig, *adj.,* just, proper; *neut. as subst.,* reasonable, 3768.

billigen, *tr.,* approve.

binden, band, gebunden, *tr.,* bind.

biß, *prep.* (*acc.*), *adv. and conj.,* till, until, as far as; — auf, except, *170.

Bischof, *m.,* -ß, -öfe, bishop.

Bischoffsitz, *m.,* -eß, -e, (bishop's) see.

Bitte, *f.,* -n, request.

bitten, bat, gebeten, *tr.,* ask, beg, request; *intr.,* pray *or* intercede for (für), 2819; ask *or* beg for (um), 180.

Bittende, *m. and f.* (*decl. like adj.*), suppliant.

bitter, *adj.,* bitter; *neut. as subst.,* 94, *cf. N.*

Bitterkeit, *f.,* -en, bitterness.

blankgeschliffen, *part. adj.* (*from* schleifen), brightly polished.

Blatt, *n.,* -eß, -ätter, leaf; sheet, 3267.

blau, *adj.,* blue.

bleiben, blieb, geblieben, *intr.* f., remain, stay; bei der Sache —, stick to the point, 928.

bleich, *adj.*, pale, pallid.

bleichen, *tr.*, pale, blanch.

blenden, *tr.*, blind; blendend, *part. adj.*, dazzling, 2556.

Blendwerk, *n.*, –s, delusion.

Blick, *m.*, –es, –e, look, glance.

blicken, *intr.*, look, glance.

blind, *adj.*, blind.

Blitz, *m.*, –es, –e, lightning, flash; bolt, 1272, 2462.

blitzen, *intr.*, lighten, flash; *tr.*, strike (*as with lightning*), 3240.

Block, *m.*, –es, –öcke, block.

Blödigkeit, *f.*, weakness of sight; bashfulness, timidity, 344.

bloß, *adj.*, bare, naked; mere, 11; *adv.*, merely, only, 1867.

Blöße, *f.*, bareness; weakness, 3222.

bloßstellen, *tr.*, lay open, expose (to, *dat.*).

blühen, *intr.*, bloom, flourish; blühend, *part. adj.*, blooming; lovely, 302; handsome, 1796; in loveliness, 1396.

Blumenstrauß, *m.*, –es, –äuße, nosegay, bouquet.

Blut, *n.*, –es, blood; letztes —, last drop of blood, 2518.

Blutbefehl, *m.*, –s, –e, fatal (bloody) order.

Blüte, *f.*, bloom, prime.

bluten, *intr.*, bleed.

Blutentwurf, *m.*, –s, –würfe, bloody *or* fell design.

Blutgerüst, *n.*, –es, –e, scaffold (of execution).

Blutgier, *f.*, bloodthirstiness.

blutig, *adj.*, bloody; brutal, 297; cruel, fierce, 669.

Blutschuld, *f.*, blood-guiltiness.

blutsverwandt, *adj.*, blood-related.

Blutsverwandte, *m. and f.* (*decl. like adj.*), blood-relation, kinsman.

Blutsverwandtschaft, *f.*, blood-relationship.

Blutthat, *f.*, –en, deed of blood, (capital) crime.

Boden, *m.*, –s, — *and* Böden, ground, 1711, 3930; soil 498, 1004; earth, 1932; floor, 34, 128, *155.

borgen, *tr.*, borrow.

böse, *adj.*, bad, evil, wicked, ill.

Bösewicht, *m.*, –s, –e *and* –er, wretch, villain.

Bosheit, *f.*, –en, wickedness.

Boswicht, *see* Bösewicht.

Bote, *m.*, –n, –n, messenger.

Bothwell, James Hepburn, Earl of Bothwell, the third husband of Mary Stuart. Born 1536, died 1578.

Botschaft, *f.*, –en, message, news, tidings.

Botschafter, *m.*, –s, —, envoy, ambassador.

Boulen, Anna von, Anne Boleyn *or* Bullen, the second wife of Henry VIII of England and mother of Queen Elizabeth. Born 1507, beheaded 1536; 2432, *cf. N.*

Brauch, *m.*, –es, –äuche, usage, custom.

brauchen, *tr.*, use, 858, 1024; need, 247, 748 *etc.; with gen.*, 3430.

Braut, *f.*, –äute, betrothed (woman), 2016; bride, 1877, 3576.

Brautgemach, *n.*, –s, –ächer, bridal chamber.

Brautgeschmeide, *n.*, –s, —, bridal jewels.

Bräutigam, *m.*, –s, –e, betrothed (man).

bräutlich, *adj.*, bridal.

Bräutlichkeit, *f.*, expectation of marriage, coming bridehood, 2034, *cf* N.

Brautwerbung, *f.*, -en, match-making, (bridal) suit.

brav, *adj.*, worthy, good, brave.

Brecheisen, *n.*, -ß, —, crowbar.

brechen, brach, gebrochen, bricht, *tr.*, break ; violate, 848.

brennen, brannte, gebrannt, *intr.* (*and tr.*), burn ; brennend, *part. adj.*, burning, 2183.

Brett, *n.* -eß, -er, plank.

Brief, *m.*, -eß, -e, letter.

bringen, brachte, gebracht, *tr.*, bring.

Britannien, *n.*, -ß, Britain.

britannisch, *adj.*, of Britain.

Britte, *m* , -n, -n, Briton.

Brücke, *f.*, -n, bridge ; = Zug-brücke, drawbridge, 2598.

Bruder, *m.*, -ß, -über, brother.

Bruderkuß, *m.*, -ffeß, -küsse, fraternal kiss.

brüderlich, *adj.*, brotherly, frater-nal ; *adv.*, in brotherhood, 825.

Brust, *f.*, -üste, breast.

Bube, *m* , -n, -n, knave, scoun-drel, villain.

Bübin, *f.*, -innen, jade.

Buch, *n.*, -eß, Bücher, book.

buchstäblich, *adj.*, literal ; *adv.*, literally, to the letter, 3286.

Buhle, *m.*, -n, -n, lover, para-mour.

buhlen, *intr.* (*with* um), court, 1987, 3195 ; leichtsinnig —b, by frivolous coquetry, by wanton amours, 2032.

Buhlerin, *f.*, -innen, lover, mis-tress.

Buhlernetz, *n.*, -eß, -e, amorous net.

Bühne, *f.*, -n, stage.

Bulle, *f.*, -n, bull, papal edict, 1490, *cf. N.*

Bund, *m.*, -eß, Bünde, alliance ; league, 639, 2790.

Bündnis, *n.*, -ffeß, -ffe, alliance ; league, 635, 1743.

Bürgerin, *f.*, -innen, (female) citizen.

Bürgerkrieg, *m.*, -ß, -e, civil war.

bürgerlich, *adj.*, civil.

Bürgerweib, *n.*, -ß, -er, woman of the citizen class, woman of the people.

Busen, *m.*, -ß, —, bosom.

Buße, *f.*, -n, penance.

büßen, *tr.*, atone for, expiate ; *refl.*, be expiated, 57.

C.

Calais, Calais (*pronounce* kä-lā'), a seaport city of France.

Canterbury, Canterbury, a city in England and the seat of an archbishopric ; *cf. N.* 750.

Charak'ter, *m.*, -ß, -te're, charac-ter ; title, 2668.

Christenheit, *f.*, christendom.

Christus, *m.*, Christ ; *gen.*, Christi, 3526 ; crucifix, 142, *cf. N.*

Committee' (*Eng.*), *f.* (*usually* Komitee', *n.*, -ß, -ß), committee ; Commission, 705, *cf. N.*

D.

da, *adv.*, there, here, then ; *conj.*, when, while, as, since.

dabei, *adv.*, thereby, thereat ; at that, 594 ; close by, 2467.

Dach, *n.*, -eß, Dächer, roof.

dadurch, *adv.*, thereby, through *or* by that.

dahin, *adv. and sep. pref.*, thither, there, along, away ; to this, 2433 ; hence, 3845 ; gone, de-parted, dead, 1163, 3541.

dahingeben, gab, gegeben, giebt, *tr.*, sacrifice.

dahinkommen, kam, gekommen, *intr.* ſ., come along *or* past.

damals, *adv.*, then, at that time.

Dame, *f.*, –n, lady.

damit, *adv.*, therewith, with it, with that; *conj.*, in order that.

daneben, *adv.*, beside it, beside that, by it; = neben welche, 2414.

Dank, *m.*, –es, thanks.

Dankbarkeit, *f.*, gratitude.

danken, *intr.* (*dat.*), thank; *tr.* (*dat. of pers.*), thank for, owe, 2123.

dann, *adv.*, then, thereupon.

daran, *adv.*, thereon, thereat, therein, on it, to it.

darauf, *adv.*, thereupon, thereon, upon it, on it; thereafter, afterward, 492; preparatory to, 636.

daraus, *adv.*, thereout, therefrom, thereof, out of that *or* it *or* them.

darbieten, bot, geboten, *tr.*, offer, proffer; dargeboten, *part. adj.*, *169.

darein, *adv.*, thereinto, therein, into that *or* it.

darin, *adv.*, therein, in that *or* it.

darnach, *adv.*, thereafter, after it *or* that, at it.

Darnley, Henry Stuart, Lord Darnley, Mary Stuart's second husband. Born 1541 (?), murdered 1567. *Cf.* Intr. §§ 7, 9.

darstellen, *tr.*, exhibit; *refl.*, appear, be displayed, 1133.

darthun, that, gethan, *tr.*, show, prove.

darüber, *adv.*, thereover, over it, about it *or* that, concerning it *or* that.

darum, *adv.*, thereabout, around it *or* that, therefore; for it *or* that; on that account, 2170; eben —, for that very reason, 796, 2210.

darunter, *adv.*, under it *or* that, among it *or* that *or* them; of them, 1704.

daß, *conj.*, that, so that.

dastehen, stand, gestanden, *intr.*, stand there, be present.

davon, *adv. and sep. pref.*, therefrom, thereof, from that *or* it, of that *or* it.

davontragen, trug, getragen, trägt, *tr.*, carry off.

davor, *adv.*, before that, from that *or* it.

dazu, *adv.*, thereto, to it *or* that *or* them, besides.

dazwischen, *adv. and sep. pref.*, between *or* among them; at intervals, *158.

dazwischenkommen, kam, gekommen, *intr.* ſ., come between; intervene, 2757.

Dechant', *m.*, –en, –en, dean, 187, *cf. N.*

Decke, *f.*, –n, ceiling.

decken, *tr.*, cover.

Degen, *m.*, –s, —, sword.

demütig, *adj.*, humble.

demütigen, *tr.*, humble.

denken, dachte, gedacht, *intr.* (*with* an *or* über *and acc.*), think; *with gen.*, think of, 471, 3705; imagine, conceive, 758; denkend, *part. adv.*, thoughtfully, 1386.

Denkmal, *n.*, –s, –äler *and* –e, monument.

denn, *adv.*, then, so, therefore; *conj.*, for, because.

dennoch, *conj.*, yet, nevertheless.

der (die, das), *def. art.*, demon. *and* rel. pron., the; this, that, that one, he, she, it; who, which, that.

bereinſt, *adv.*, once, one day, some (future) time.

berſelbe (bieſelbe, baſſelbe), *demon. adj. and pron.*, the same, he, she, it.

beſto, *adv.*, the, all the (*with comparatives*), 3950; so much the, 14.

beuten, *tr.*, interpret, 1042; explain, construe, 3983.

beutlich, *adj.*, plain.

Diabem', *n.*, –$\mathfrak{s}$, –e, diadem.

bicht, *adj.*, thick, dense.

Dibier, Didier Sifflard, a servant of Mary Stuart; *cf. N.* 3510.

bienen, *intr.* (*dat.*), serve.

Diener, *m.*, –$\mathfrak{s}$, —, servant.

Dienerin, *f.*, –innen, maid-servant.

Dienſt, *m.* –e$\mathfrak{s}$, –e, service.

Dienſtbarkeit, *f.*, servitude.

bienſtfertig, *adj.* obliging.

bieſer (–e, –e$\mathfrak{s}$), *demon. adj. and pron.*, this, this one, the latter.

biftieren, *tr.* dictate.

Ding, *n.*, –e$\mathfrak{s}$, –e, thing.

bingen, bang *and* bingte, gebungen *and* gebingt, *tr.*, hire.

boch, *conj.*, though, yet, still, but; (*for emphasis*), surely, really; (I) pray, 2074.

Dokument', *n.* –$\mathfrak{s}$, –e, document.

Dolch, *m.*, –e$\mathfrak{s}$, –e, dagger.

Donner, *m.*, –$\mathfrak{s}$, —, thunder.

Donnerſtreich, *m.*,–$\mathfrak{s}$,–e, thunderbolt.

Doppelſinn, *m.*, –$\mathfrak{s}$, ambiguity; equivocation, 3722.

boppelt, *adj.*, double, questionable, doubtful.

bornenvoll, *adj.*, thorny, difficult.

bort, *adv.*, there, yonder.

brängen, *tr.*, press, urge, 3094; *intr.*, press, crowd, 2227; *refl.*, crowd, 460, 1124 *etc.*; force one's way, 2856.

brauf, *see* barauf.

brau$\mathfrak{s}$, *see* barau$\mathfrak{s}$.

brauſzen, *adv.*, out there, without, outside; abroad, 2369.

brei, *num.*, three.

Dreifaltigkeit, *f.*, Trinity; *cf. N.* 440.

breimal, *adv.*, thrice, three times.

breiſt, *adj.*, bold, daring.

Dreiſtigkeit, *f.*, boldness, audacity.

bringen, brang, gebrungen, *intr. ſ.*, press, 574, penetrate, reach, 120, 3624; — in (*acc.*), press, urge, 1145; auf ben Grunb —, go to the bottom, 1613.

Dringen (*verbal subst.*), *n*, –$\mathfrak{s}$, insistence, importunity.

bringenb, *part. adj.*, pressing, urgent.

brinnen, *adv.*, in there, within, inside

britt–, *num. adj.*, third.

brohen, *intr.* (*dat. of pers.*) *and tr.*, threaten; brohenb, *part. adj.*, threatened, impending, 1953; *adv.*, threateningly, menacingly, 818.

Drohung, *f.*, –en, threat.

brücken, *tr.*, press; afflict, 3507.

brum, *see* barum.

bu, *pl.*, ihr, *pers. pron.*, thou, you.

Duc (*Fr.*), *m.*, Duke.

bulben, *tr.*, tolerate, 432; suffer, 511, 3778.

bumpf, *adj.*, close, stifling, 414; gloomy, 457; dull, *183.

Dunkelheit, *f.*, obscurity.

bünken, *intr.* (*dat.*), seem, appear.

burch, *prep.* (*acc.*) *adv., sep. and insep. pref.*, through, by, throughout.

burchboh'ren, *insep. tr.*, pierce, stab.

burchfei'len, *insep. tr.*, file through.

durch'gehen, ging, gegangen, *sep. intr.* f., pass (*as a law*), be enacted.

durchlau'fen, durchlief', durchlau'-fen, durchläuft', *insep. tr.*, run through, read hastily.

durchrei'ßen, durchriß', durchriſ'-fen, *insep. tr.*, tear asunder, break.

durchschau'en, *insep. tr.*, see through, fathom.

durchschnei'den, durchschnitt', durchschnit'ten, *insep. tr.*, sever.

durchstech'en, durchstach', durch-stoch'en, durchsticht', *insep. tr.*, run through, stab.

durchsu'chen, *insep. tr.*, search (thoroughly).

durchwach'en, *insep. tr.*, pass waking *or* awake.

durchzie'hen, durchzog', durch-zo'gen, *insep. tr.*, travel through, traverse, 416; pass through, 3128.

durchzo'gen, *part. adj.*, studded, set, 19.

dürfen, durfte, gedurft, darf, *intr. and modal aux.*, be permitted, may; 2586, *cf. N.;* dare, 743; *with neg. sometimes* = must not, 1027, 3292.

dürftig, *adj.*, needy.

dürr, *adj.*, dry, withered, leafless, 3626.

dürsten, *intr.*, thirst (for, nach).

durstig, *adj.*, thirsty.

E.

eben, *adj.*, even, level, smooth; *adv.*, even; just, exactly, 10, 1706; — die, the same, *16.

ebenso, *adv.*, likewise.

echt, *adj.*, genuine, 3937; pure, true; im —en Ehebett, in true wedlock, 3248.

edel, *adj.*, noble.

Edelfrau, *f.*, –en, lady, noble-woman.

Edelfräulein, *n.*, –s, —, noble maid, maid of honor.

edelherzig, *adj.*, noble-hearted.

Edelmut, *m.*, –s, magnanimity, generosity.

edelmütig, *adj.*, noble-minded, generous.

Edinburg, *n.*, –s, Edinburgh (*pronounce* ed'-n-bo-rō), the capital city of Scotland.

Edinburger, *indecl. adj.*, of Edinburgh.

eh(e), *conj.*, before, ere; = eher, sooner, 2202.

Ehe, *f.*, –n, marriage.

Ehebett, *n.*, –s, –en, marriage-bed, nuptial bed; wedlock, 3248.

ehebrecherisch, *adj.*, adulterous.

Ehebündnis, *n.*, –ſſes, –ſſe, mar-riage-alliance.

eh(e)lichen, *tr.*, marry.

eh(e)mals, *adv.*, formerly.

eher, *adv.* (*comp. of* ehe), sooner, rather.

ehern, *adj.*, brazen, of brass.

Ehrbarkeit, *f.*, modesty, purity, 2030; chastity, 2430.

Ehre, *f.*, –n, honor.

ehren, *tr.*, honor, revere, 2231; respect, 253, 3194, 3546.

Ehrenmantel, *m.*, –s, –mäntel, cloak *or* robe of honor.

ehrerbietig, *adj.*, respectful, def-erential.

ehrfurchtsvoll, *adj.*, respectful.

Ehrgeiz, *m.*, –es, ambition.

Ehrsucht, *f.*, ambition.

Eid, *m.*, –es, –e, oath.

Eifer, *m.*, –s, zeal.

Eiferer, *m.*, –s, —, zealot.

Eifersucht, *f.*, jealousy.

eigen, *adj.*, own; very, 351; peculiar, characteristic, 1188.

eigenmächtig, *adj.,* arbitrary.

Eigensinn, *m.,* -s, willfulness, caprice.

Eigentum, *n.,*-s,-ümer, property, possession.

Eiland, *n.,* -s, -e, island.

Eile, *f.,* haste.

eilen, *intr.* f. *and* h., hasten, make haste.

eilfertig, *adj.,* hasty.

ein, *indef. art. and num.,* a, an, one; *adj.,* one, the same, 554.

ein, *sep. pref.,* in, into.

einander, *indec. pron.,* one another, each other.

eindringen, drang, gedrungen, *intr.* f., press *or* close in (upon, auf *and* acc.), *131; — in, penetrate, 3925.

einfach, *adj.,* simple.

einfallen, fiel, gefallen, fällt, *intr.* f., fall in; break in, interrupt, *47, *91 *etc.; (with dat. of pers.),* come into one's mind, occur to, 1673.

einführen, *tr.,* bring *or* show into, 2662; appoint, 3329.

eingemauert, *part. adj.,* walled in, immured.

eingestehen, gestand, gestanden, *tr.,* confess, admit; avow, sanction, 1598.

einig, *adj.,* one, united; some; any, *16.

einlassen, ließ, gelassen, läßt, *tr.,* let in, admit.

ein'mal, *adv.,* one time, once; auf —, all at once, suddenly, 455.

einmal', *adv.,* once upon a time, some time, just; even, 1830.

einnehmen, nahm, genommen, nimmt, *tr.,* take in.

Einsamkeit, *f.,* solitude.

einschlagen, schlug, geschlagen, schlägt, *tr.,* follow, pursue, adopt (a way, course), 2950.

einschließen, schloß, geschlossen, *tr.,* shut in, enclose; confine, 2301.

einschreiben, schrieb, geschrieben, *tr.,* inscribe.

einsehen, sah, gesehen, sieht, *tr.,* perceive.

einst, *adv.,* once (upon a time), one time, formerly.

einstimmig, *adj.,* unanimous.

einstürmen, *intr.* f., rush in.

eintreten, trat, getreten, tritt, *intr.* f., enter; — in (acc.), enter upon, 1810.

Eintritt, *m.,* -s, -e, entrance, *146; admittance, 3914.

einverstanden, *part. adj.,* agreed; — sein, have an understanding *or* be in collusion with (mit), 868.

Einverständnis, *n.,* -ses, -sse, understanding; collusion, 924.

einweben, wob *and* webte, gewoben *and* gewebt, *tr.,* weave into.

einweihen, *tr.,* consecrate; ordain, 3637.

einwilligen, *intr.,* consent to (in *and* acc.).

einzeln, *adj.,* individual.

einzig, *adj.,* only, single, alone, sole.

Eisengitter, *n.,* -s, —, iron grating.

Eisenzange, *f.,* -n, iron tongs.

Eisesblick, *m.,* -s, -e, icy glance.

eitel, *adj.,* vain, 1395, 3686; needless, 618; empty, idle, 1385, 1508, 1646.

Eitelkeit, *f.,* -en, vanity.

Elend, *n.,* -s, misery, wretchedness.

elend, *adj.,* miserable, wretched: *as subst.,* wretch.

emp-, *see* ent-.

empfangen, empfing, empfangen, empfängt, *tr.,* receive.

empfinden, empfand, empfunden, *tr.*, feel.

empören, *tr.*, excite, agitate; shock, be revolting to, 3026; empörend, *part. adj.*, revolting, 357; empört, *part. adj.*, excited, agitated, 2188.

emporsteigen, stieg, gestiegen, *intr.* f., rise.

Empörung, *f.*, -en, insurrection, rebellion.

Ende, *n.*, -s, -n, end.

enden, *tr.*, end, put an end to, 1626; *intr.*, end, come to an end, 81, 138, *etc.*

endigen, *intr.* (*and tr.*), end.

endlich, *adv.*, finally, at last.

eng, *adj.*, narrow, 457; strait, 63; close, 91, 500, 1630; eng binden, contract, narrow, 1933.

Engel, *m.*, -s, —, angel.

Engelland (*poetic*), see England.

Engelsflügel, *m.*, -s, —, angel's wing.

England, *n.*, -s, England.

englisch, *adj.*, English.

Enkeltochter, *f.*, -töchter, grand-daughter.

ent– (*sometimes has the form* emp–), *insep. pref.*, *never accented.*

entbehren, *intr.* (*gen.*), be with-out, 182; be in want, 207; do without, 54.

entblößen, *tr.*, bare, uncover.

entdecken, *tr.*, discover, find out, 1481, 2741; disclose, reveal, 577, 1615, 1738.

entehren, *tr.*, dishonor.

enterben, *tr.*, disinherit.

entfernen, *tr.*, remove; avert, 3104; dismiss, *101; *refl.*, withdraw, retire, 380, 2898, *16, *33, *etc.*; depart, 2834.

Entfernung, *f.*, -en, distance.

entfesseln, *tr.*, unfetter, release.

entfliehen, entfloh, entflohen, *intr.* f., escape.

entführen, *tr.*, carry off, abduct.

entgegen, *prep.* (*dat., governed word preceding*) *and sep. pref.*, toward, against, to, to meet.

entgegeneilen, *intr.* f., hasten toward *or* to meet.

entgegenschreiten, schritt, geschrit-ten, *intr.* f., advance toward.

entgegensteigen, stieg, gestiegen, *intr.* f., rise before, loom up before.

entgegenstellen, *tr.*, set against, oppose.

entgegentreiben, trieb, getrieben, *tr.*, drive *or* impel toward.

entgehen, entging, entgangen, *intr.* f., escape.

enthalten, enthielt, enthalten, ent-hält, *tr.*, contain.

enthaupten, *tr.*, behead; *part. adj. as subst.*, 3117.

entkleiden, *tr.*, undress, disrobe.

entkräften, *tr.*, weaken; invali-date, 1420.

entladen, entlud, entladen, ent-ladet (*and* entlädt, *rare*), *tr.*, unload; unburden, 211; *refl.* (*with gen.*), relieve *or* rid one-self of, get rid of, 967, 1757, 1778, 2052.

entlarven, *tr.*, unmask.

entlassen, entließ, entlassen, ent-läßt, *tr.*, let go.

entledigen, *tr.*, free *or* relieve of (*gen.*).

entlehnen, *tr.*, borrow (from).

entraten, entriet, entraten, enträt, *intr.* (*with gen.*), do without, dispense with.

entreißen, entriß, entrissen, *tr.* (*dat. of person*), snatch *or* take (*forcibly*) from.

entsagen, *intr.* (*dat.*), renounce, give up.

entſcheiden, entſchied, entſchieden, *tr. and intr.,* decide.

Entſcheidung, *f.,* –en, decision; crisis, 573.

entſcheidungsvoll, *adj.* decisive.

entſchloſſen, *part. adj.* (*from* entſchließen), determined, resolute.

Entſchluß, *m* ,–ſſes,–üſſe, resolve.

entſchuldigen, *tr.,* excuse; ſich — laſſen, beg to be excused, 4033.

Entſchuldigung, *f.,* –en, excuse.

entſetzen, *tr.,* remove; depose (from, *gen.*), 99; discompose, upset, terrify, 3464; *refl.,* be shocked *or* terrified, 1931.

Entſetzen, *n.,* –s, horror.

entſetzlich, *adj.,* horrible, terrible.

entſteigen, entſtieg, entſtiegen, *intr.* ſ., rise (from).

entthronen, *tr.,* dethrone.

entwaffnen, *tr.,* disarm.

entweihen, *tr.,* profane, desecrate.

entwerfen, entwarf, entworfen, entwirft, *tr.,* design, plan, contrive.

Entwurf, *m.,* –s, –ürfe, design, plan.

entziehen, entzog, entzogen, *tr.,* remove, withdraw; *refl.,* exempt oneself, escape, 735.

entzücken, *tr.,* enchant, charm; entzückt, *part. adj.,* enchanted, enraptured, 439.

Entzücken (*verbal subst.*), *n.,* –s, rapture, ecstasy.

entzünden, *tr.,* set on fire, kindle.

entzweien, *tr.,* cut in twain, sever, divide; — mit, set at variance with, part from, 2874.

er, *pl.* ſie, *pers. pron.,* he, it; *gen.,* ſein, 2491.

er–, *insep. pref.,* never accented.

Erbarmen, *n.,* –s, pity, compassion.

erben, *tr.,* inherit.

Erbin, *f.,* –innen, heiress.

erbitten, erbat, erbeten, *tr.,* beg, entreat.

erblicken, *tr.,* behold, see; catch sight of, *163.

Erde, *f.,* –n, earth; *dat. sing.,* –n, 1190.

Erdengröße, *f.,* earthly greatness.

Erdenrund, *n.,* –s, earthly globe; auf dem —, on the face of the earth, 1960.

erdreiſten, *refl.,* make bold, dare, presume.

erdulden, *tr.,* bear, endure, suffer.

ereifern, *refl.,* get angry.

erfahren, erfuhr, erfahren, erfährt, *tr.,* learn, experience; suffer, 1076.

erfaſſen, *tr.,* seize, grasp.

erfechten, erfocht, erfochten, erficht, *tr.,* get *or* gain (by fighting).

erfinden, erfand, erfunden, *tr.,* invent, contrive, 1121; find (by experience), 912, 4014.

Erfinder, *m.,* –s, —, inventor; instigator, author, 2660.

erflehen, *tr.,* entreat, beseech.

Erfolg, *m.,* –s, –e, result, issue; outcome, end, 2468; glücklicher —, success, 1845.

erfolgen, *intr.* ſ., result from (aus).

erforſchen, *tr.,* search (out), examine; find out, detect, 2939.

erfreuen, *tr.,* delight, gladden; *refl.* (*with gen.*), rejoice in, enjoy, 1247, 3826.

erfüllen, *tr.,* fill; fulfill, 1243, 2282.

Erfüllung, *f.,* –en, fulfillment.

ergeben, ergab, ergeben, ergiebt, *tr.,* give up; *refl.,* surrender, 1100; ergeben, *part. adj.,* resigned, 3738.

Ergebung, *f.,* resignation, submission.

ergehen, erging, ergangen, *intr.* f., go forth; *refl.*, walk, stroll, 2061; wander, 2093; *impers.* (*with dat.*), f., fare, 3358, 3503.

ergießen, ergoß, ergossen, *refl.*, pour forth, flock, 3130.

ergreifen, ergriff, ergriffen, *tr.*, seize; take hold of, move, thrill, 505; lay hold on, 3408.

erhaben, *adj.*, elevated, noble, illustrious, 469, 1134, 1225; sublime, 490; — über (*with acc.*), raised *or* elevated above, 745.

erhalten, erhielt, erhalten, erhält, *tr.*, keep, preserve, save; receive, 124.

erharren, *tr.*, wait for.

erhärten, *tr.*, declare, affirm.

erheben, erhob *and* erhub, erhoben, *tr.*, lift, raise; *refl.*, raise oneself, *101; arise, 850, *cf. N.;* rise, 3473, 3585; erhoben, *part. adj.*, heightened, ennobled, 2033.

erheitern, *tr.*, brighten, gladden.

erhitzen, *tr.*, heat, inflame.

erhöhen, *tr.*, raise, elevate.

erholen, *refl.*, recover (one's health).

erhören, *tr.*, hear, hear of; grant, 2199; erhört, *part. adj.*, with *neg.*, unheard of, 221, *cf. N.*

erinnern, *tr.*, remind; *refl.* (*gen.* or an with *acc.*), remember, 3313.

Erinnerung, *f.*, -en, recollection, reminiscence.

erkaufen, *tr.*, purchase.

erkäuflich, *adj.*, purchasable, venal.

erkennen, erkannte, erkannt, *tr.*, perceive, 540, 2124; recognize, 271, 1418, 3919; acknowledge, 172, 2712, 2921; decide, 846.

erklären, *tr.*, make clear, explain,

679, 1730; declare, 892, 1334, 2366; erklärt, *part. adj.*, avowed, sworn, 1733.

erkühnen, *refl.*, venture, dare.

Erkühnen (*verbal subst.*), *n.*, -s, daring, audacity.

erlangen, *tr.*, attain, get.

Erlassung, *f.*, absolution.

erlauben, *tr.*, allow, permit.

Erlaubnis, *f.*, permission.

erleben, *tr.*, live to see, experience, witness.

erleichtern, *tr.*, lighten.

erleiden, erlitt, erlitten, *tr.*, suffer, endure.

erlesen, erlas, erlesen, erliest, *tr.*, select; erlesen, *part. adj.*, picked, select.

erleuchten, *tr.*, enlighten.

erlöschen, erlosch, erloschen, erlischt, *intr.* f., go out, be extinguished.

Erlöser, *m.*, -s, —, deliverer; der —, the Redeemer, the Saviour.

ermahnen, *tr.*, admonish, warn, 2212; exhort, 3870.

ermorden, *tr.*, murder.

ernennen, ernannte, ernannt, *tr.*, appoint.

erneuen, *tr.*, renew; *refl.*, be renewed *or* revived, 1952.

erneuern, *tr.*, renew; *refl.*, be renewed, begin again, *158.

erniedrigen, *tr.*, lower; humiliate, 2464, 2830; debase, 156.

Erniedrigung, *f.*, -en, humiliation.

Ernst, *m.*, -es, seriousness, earnestness; earnest, 1099.

ernst, *adj.*, earnest; serious, 1409; with *dat.*, in earnest, 1613, *cf. N.*

ernsthaft, *adj.*, earnest, serious; grave, *145.

ernstlich, *adj.*, earnest.

erobern, *tr.,* conquer.

eröffnen, *tr.,* open.

erproben, *tr.,* try, test; prove, 1333.

erquicken, *tr.,* refresh.

Erquickung, *f.,* -en, refreshment.

erregen, *tr.,* arouse, excite.

erreichen, *tr.,* reach, 734; attain, 2381; gain, 1908.

erretten, *tr.,* save.

Erretter, *m.,* -s, —, deliverer.

Errettung, *f.,* deliverance.

errichten, *tr.,* set up, erect.

erröten, *intr.* f., blush; errötend, *part. adj.,* blushing, 340.

erschaffen, erschuf, erschaffen, *tr.,* create.

erschallen, erscholl, erschollen, *intr.* f., sound, resound.

erscheinen, erschien, erschienen, *intr.* f., appear.

erschrecken, erschrak, erschrocken, erschrickt, *intr.* f., be frightened, start with fear; *part. adv.,* *87.

erschrecken, *tr.,* frighten, startle, alarm, 586, 1846.

erschrocken, *part. adj.,* frightened, startled; *adv.,* in alarm, *87.

erschüttern, *tr.,* convulse; move, affect, 2208.

ersehen, *tr.,* long *or* yearn for; *part. adj.,* 1137.

ersinnen, ersann, ersonnen, *tr.,* devise, 862, 1081; invent, 2787.

ersparen, *tr.,* spare, save.

erst, *num. adj.,* first; *adv.,* first, 1700; nun —, only *or* not until now, 1246.

erstatten, *tr.,* render, return; Bericht —, give account, inform, 2999.

erstaunen, *intr.* f., be astonished *or* amazed; erstaunt, *part. adj.,* astonished, amazed; in astonishment, *33.

Erstaunen (*verbal subst.*), *n.,* -s,

astonishment, amazement; in — setzen, astonish, surprise, 242.

erstehen, erstand, erstanden, *intr.* f., arise.

ersteigen, erstieg, erstiegen, *tr.,* climb, scale.

ersticken, *tr.,* stifle, smother.

erstorben, *part. adj.* (*from* ersterben), extinguished; benumbed, 3850.

erteilen, *tr.* (*dat. of pers.*), grant, give.

ertragen, ertrug, ertragen, erträgt, *tr.,* bear, endure.

erwägen, erwog, erwogen, *tr.,* consider.

erwählen, *tr.,* choose; Rat —, take counsel, 3787.

erwarten, *tr.,* wait for, await; expect, 1889.

Erwartung, *f.,* -en, expectation; suspense, 3879.

erwehren, *refl.* (*with gen.*), ward off, defend oneself against.

erweichen, *tr.,* soften; make weak, 3364.

erweisen, erwies, erwiesen, *tr.* (*dat. of pers.*), render, bestow; do for, 1507.

erweitern, *tr.,* widen, extend.

erwerben, erwarb, erworben, erwirbt, *tr.,* gain; erworben, *part. adj.;* teuer —, dearly bought, 1257.

Erwiderung, *f.,* -en, response.

erwürgen, *tr.,* strangle.

Erzbischof, *m.,* -s, -öfe, archbishop.

erzeigen, *tr.* (*dat. of pers.*), show, grant.

erzeugen, *tr.,* beget; *refl.,* be begotten, 1278.

erzittern, *intr.* f., tremble.

erzürnt, *part. adj.,* angered, wrathful, incensed.

es, *pl.,* **fie,** *pers. pron.,* it, *impers.,* there, 137; *as expletive sometimes not translatable,* 30; *cf. N.,* 30, 249.

Essenz, *f.,* –en, essence.

etwa, *adv.,* perhaps; perchance, 737.

etwas, *indec. pron. and adj.,* some, something; aught, 1057; *adv.,* somewhat, *160.

euer, *poss. adj. and pron. (corresponding to* ihr, *you),* your, yours.

Euro'pa, *n.,* –s *or* –pens, Europe.

ewig, *adj.,* eternal, 356, 491, 1942; everlasting, 659, 1605; perpetual, 569, 606, 1109, *etc.; neut. as subst.,* the eternal, eternity, 3405; *adv.,* ever, eternally; **auf** —, forever, 3307.

Ewigkeit, *f.,* eternity.

Exempel, *n.,* –s, —, example.

F.

Fach, *n.,* –es, Fächer, drawer, pigeon-hole.

fachen, *tr.,* fan.

Fackel, *f.,* –n, torch.

Fall, *m.,* –es, Fälle, fall; case, 1870.

fallen, fiel, gefallen, fällt, *intr.* f., fall; **in die Augen** —, strike the eye, 503.

fällen, *tr.,* let fall, fell; **ein Urteil** —, pronounce judgment, pass *or* impose sentence, 577, 3092.

Fallstrick, *m.,* –s, –e, snare, trap.

falsch, *adj.,* false.

fälschlich, *adv. (and adj.),* falsely.

falschverstanden, *part. adj.,* falsely understood.

fangen, fing, gefangen, fängt, *tr.,* catch, seize, capture.

Farbe, *f.,* –n, color.

fassen, *tr.,* seize, 1807, 3861; grasp, 3619; **comprehend,** 2825; express, state, 3297; prepare, draw up, 2649; *refl.,* compose *or* calm oneself, 147, 682, 2166, *etc.,* recover one's self-possession, *88, *130; gefaßt, *part. adj.,* prepared *or* ready (for, auf *and acc.*), 587.

Fassung, *f.,* composure, self-possession; frame *or* state of mind, 241; bearing, *178.

Fasten (*verbal subst.*), *n.,* –s, fasting, fast.

Faust, *f.,* Fäuste, fist.

Feder, *f.,* –n, feather; pen, *151; spring, 1938, *cf. N.*

Federstrich, *m.,* –s, –e, stroke of a pen, pen-stroke.

Federzug, *m.,* –s, –üge, stroke of a pen, pen-stroke.

Fehde, *f.,* –n, feud.

fehlen, *intr.* (*dat.*), fail, be wanting *or* lacking, 2740; be lack of (an *with dat.*), 42, 3900; err, 2936; sin, 2421, 3740.

fehlgehen, ging, gegangen, *sep. intr.* f., go wrong, miss.

feiern, *tr.,* celebrate, commemorate.

feig(e), *adj.,* cowardly; *as subst.,* coward, 2481.

feil, *adj.,* for sale, purchasable, 740; venal, 778; mercenary, hireling, 2806.

fein, *adj.,* fine, delicate.

Feind, *m.,* –es, –e, enemy, foe.

Feindin, *f.,* –innen, (female) enemy, foe.

feindlich, *adj.,* hostile.

Feld, *n.,* –es, –er, field.

Feldstück, *n.,* –s, –e, field-piece; mimic cannon, 1094.

Fels, *m.,* –en, –en, rock.

Felsenklippe, *f.,* –n, rocky cliff.

Fenster, *n.,* –s, —, window.

fern(e), *adj.,* far distant; *adv.*

far, far off; von ferne, from afar, at a distance, 1380, 2116.

Ferse, f., –n, heel.

Fertigkeit, f., readiness, unscrupulousness, 1636.

Fessel, f., –n, fetter.

fessellos, adj., unfettered.

fesseln, tr., fetter, bind; confine, 63.

fest, adj., fast, firm; secure, 129; das —e Land, mainland, continent, 413, 3215.

Feste, f., –n, stronghold.

festhalten, hielt, gehalten, hält, sep. tr., hold fast or firmly.

festlich, adj., festive; solemn, 999; adv., magnificently, *166, cf. N.

Festlichkeit, f., –en, festivity.

Festung, f., –en, fortress.

Feuer, n., –s, —, fire.

feurig, adj., fiery, 812; ardent, 1739, 3597; passionate, 1956.

Fieberwahn, m., –s, fevered fancy, hallucination.

finden, fand, gefunden, tr., find; pret. ind., 1830, cf. N.; refl., be found; be, 161; accommodate oneself, 53.

Finger, m., –s, —, finger.

finster, adj., dark, gloomy.

Fischer, m., –s, —, fisherman.

fixieren, tr., fix one's eyes upon; mit den Augen —, stare at, *101.

Flamme, f., –n, flame.

Flammenauge, n., –s, –n, flaming eye.

Flattersinn, m., –s, frivolity.

flechten, flocht, geflochten, flicht, tr., braid; involve, 2768, 2803.

Flecken, m., –s, blemish, stain.

flehen, intr., implore, beseech, supplicate.

Flehen (verbal subst.), n., –s, supplication, entreaty.

Flehenswort, n., –s, –e, word of entreaty or supplication.

fleißig, adj., diligent.

fliegen, flog, geflogen, intr. f. (rarely h.), fly.

fliehen, floh, geflohen, intr. f., flee, 2185; tr. (h.), flee from, 1029.

fließen, floß, geflossen, intr. f., flow.

Flitter, m., –s, —, tinsel; bauble, 51, 154.

Flor, m., –es, –e, crape; veil, 1628.

Flotte, f., –n, fleet.

Fluch, m., –es, –üche, curse.

fluchenswert, adj., accursed, execrable.

Fluchgeschick, n., –s, –e, accursed fate.

Flucht, f., flight.

fluchvoll, adj., curse-laden.

Flügel, m., –s, —, wing.

Flügelschnelligkeit, f., swiftness of wings.

flugs, adv., instantly; off-hand, 223.

Folge, f., –n, consequence.

folgen, intr. f. (dat.), follow.

Folter, f., –n, rack.

fordern, tr., demand; ask, 940, 2023, 3095; summon, 96, 3993.

fördern, tr., further; despatch, hurry, 882.

Form, f., –en, form.

Förmlichkeit, f., –en, formality.

forschen, intr., search, inquire; forschend, part. adv., searchingly, *66, *76.

fort, adv. and sep. pref., forward, forth, away; gone, 2849; adds to some verbs the meaning on, continue to, keep on.

fortan, adv., henceforth.

fortfahren, fuhr, gefahren, fährt, intr. f., continue, go on.

fortführen, *tr.,* carry on, bear onward.

forthallen, *intr.,* continue to sound.

Fotheringhay, Fotheringay, a village in Northamptonshire, England; *5, cf. N.;* 2060, *cf. N.*

Frage, *f.,* –n, question; eine — thun, ask *or* put a question, 1698.

fragen, *tr.,* ask, question; *intr.,* — nach, care about, heed, 3199; fragend, *part. adv.,* inquiringly, *22.

Franke, *m.,* –n, –n (*poetic, sometimes contemptuous, for* Franzose), Frenchman.

Frankreich, *n.,* –s, France.

Franzmann, *m.,* –s, Frenchman, *cf. N.,* 103.

Franzose, *m.,* –n, –n, Frenchman.

französisch, *adj.,* French.

Frau, *f.,* –en, woman, 176, 509, 3424; *gen. sing.,* –en, 1019 (*cf. N.* 49); lady, 613, 3995; wife.

Frauengunst, *f.,* woman's favor.

Frauenkrone, *f.,* crown of womanhood.

Frauenreich, *n.,* –s, –e, woman's realm; woman's rule, 1934.

Fräulein, *n.,* –s, —, unmarried woman, young lady.

frech, *adj.,* insolent, bold.

frei, *adj.,* free; voluntary, 900.

Freibrief, *m.,* –s, –e, license, 729, *cf. N.*

Freiheit, *f.,* –en, freedom, liberty.

freilich, *adv.,* to be sure, of course.

Freimut, *m.,* –s, frankness, candor.

fremd, *adj.,* strange, 874; foreign, 730, 1125; ignorant, 787;

another's, of another, 1064, 3417.

Fremde, *m. and f.* (*decl. like adj.*), stranger.

Fremdling, *m.,* –s, –e, stranger.

Fremdlingin, *f.,* –innen, (female) stranger.

Freude, *f.,* –n, joy, pleasure; *gen. sing.,* –n, 49, *cf. N.*

Freudenchor, *m.,* –s, –öre, chorus of joy, joyful chorus.

Freudenpost, *f.,* –en, joyful news.

Freudenreich, *n.,* –s, –e, realm of joy.

Freudenseite, *f.,* –n, joyous side.

freudig, *adj.,* joyful, joyous, glad.

freudlos, *adj.,* joyless.

freuen, *tr.,* delight; *refl.,* rejoice, 3480; (*with gen.*), delight in, enjoy, 1983.

Freund, *m.,* –es, –e, friend.

Freundesbrust, *f.,* breast *or* bosom of a friend.

Freundespflicht, *f.,* –en, duty of friendship.

Freundin, *f.,* –innen, (female) friend.

freundlich, *adj.,* friendly, kind, kindly.

Freundschaft, *f.,* –en, friendship; *collect.,* friends, kindred, 2370.

Frevel, *m.,* –s, —, crime, outrage.

freveln, *intr.,* commit crime, transgress; frevelnd, *part. adv.,* criminally, 4009.

Friede(n), *m.,* –ns, peace; *acc. sing.,* Friede, 274, *cf. N.*

Friedensinsel, *f.,* –n, isle of peace, peaceful isle.

Friedenssitz, *m.,* –es, –e, abode of peace.

friedlich, *adj.,* peaceful.

frisch, *adj.,* fresh; vivid, 452.

frischblutend, *part.,* bleeding afresh.

Frist, *f.*, –en, time, delay.
froh, *adj.*, glad, joyous, happy.
fröhlich, *adj.*, joyous, happy; *as subst.*, 459.
fromm (frömmer, frömmst–, *now usually without umlaut*), *adj.*, pious.
Frucht, *f.*, –üchte, fruit.
früh, *adj.*, early.
fügen, *tr.*, join, add.
Fügung, *f.*, –en, contingency, arrangement.
fühlen, *tr.*, feel; *refl.*, feel (oneself), 455, 3448.
fühllos, *adj.*, unfeeling.
führen, *tr.*, lead, 302, 491, 637, *etc.;* escort, *52; bring, 1118, 2025; take, 2166, 2721; deal (*a blow*), 1293, 2613; bear, wield (*weapons*), 2462, 3241; use (*language*), 1534; wage, carry on (*war*), 1270; carry away, 3098.
Führer, *m.*, –s, —, guide; guardian, 470.
Fülle, *f.*, fullness, abundance; wealth, 436.
füllen, *tr.*, fill; *refl.*, fill, be filled, 79.
für, *prep.* (*acc.*), for.
Furcht, *f.*, fear; timidity, 982.
furchtbar, *adj.*, fearful, terrible.
fürchten, *tr.*, fear, dread.
fürchterlich, *adj.*, frightful, terrible.
furchtlos, *adj.*, fearless.
Fu'rie, *f.*, –n, fury, curse.
Fürst, *m.*, –en, –en, prince.
Fürstenfurcht, *f.*, fear of princes.
Fürstentochter, *f.*, –töchter, princess.
Fürstin, *f.*, –innen, princess.
fürstlich, *adj.*, princely.
fürwahr, *adv.*, in truth, verily, forsooth.
Fürwort, *n.*, –s, intercession.

Fuß, *m.*, –es, Füße, foot; stehenden Fußes, *adv. gen.*, immediately, without delay, 3273; auf freien — setzen, set free, 3433; mit Füßen treten, tread under foot, trample upon, 144, 2693.

G.

galant', *adj.*, gallant'.
Gang, *m.*, –es, Gänge, walk, 3798; step, *183; course, 1562.
ganz, *adj.*, whole, entire; complete, perfect, 358, *cf. N.; adv.*, wholly, quite, utterly.
gar, *adv.*, quite, entirely, altogether; *with neg.*, at all, 2065.
Garn, *n.*, –es, –e, yarn; net, snare, 1753.
Garten, *m.*, –s, Gärten, garden.
Gärtner, *m.*, –s, —, gardener.
Gasse, *f.*, –n, street.
Gast, *m.*, –es, Gäste, guest.
gastfreundlich, *adj.*, hospitable.
Gastrecht, *n.*, –s, –e, right of hospitality.
Gatte, *m.*, –n, –n, husband.
Gaukelkunst, *f.*, juggling, trickery.
Gaukelspiel, *n.*, –es, jugglery, trickery, imposture.
Gaukler, *m.*, –s, —, juggler, trickster, impostor.
Gauklerin, *f.*, –innen (female) juggler; impostor, 2449.
ge–, *insep. pref., never accented.*
geängstigt, *part. adj.*, anxious.
Gebärde, *f.*, –n, gesture.
gebären, gebar, geboren, gebiert, *tr.*, bear (child), give birth to; geboren, *part. adj.*, born, 465.
geben, gab, gegeben, giebt, *tr.*, give; grant, 3444; *impers.* (*with acc.*), es giebt, es gab, *etc.*, there is, are, was, were,

etc., 363; *refl.*, fich (*dat.*) —, give oneself, assume, 1638.

Gebet, *n.*, -es, -e, prayer.

gebeugt, *part. adj.*, bowed; depressed, 268.

gebieten, gebot, geboten, *tr.* (*dat. of pers.*), command; impose upon, 3211; *intr.* (*with dat.*), control, subdue, 2188.

Gebieter, *m.*, -s, —, master.

Gebieterin, *f.*, -innen, mistress; sovereign, 1580.

gebieterisch, *adj.*, imperious.

Gebirge, *n.*, -s, —, (chain of) mountains.

geboren, *see* gebären.

Gebot, *n.*, -es, -e, command.

gebrauchen, *tr.*, use.

Gebrechen (*verbal subst.*), *n.*, -s, frailty, weakness.

gebrechlich, *adj.*, frail.

Gebühr, *f.*, -en, due, seemliness; nach —, fittingly, 1242.

gebühren, *intr.* (*dat.*), belong to, 521, 2367; beseem, 4005; gebührend, *part. adj.*, fitting, 1302.

Geburt, *f.*, -en, birth.

Gedächtnis, *n.*, -nisses, -nisse, memory.

Gedanke, *m.*, -ns, -n, thought.

gedankenlos, *adj.*, thoughtless.

gedenken, gedachte, gedacht, *intr.* (*gen.*), think of, 3793; mention, make mention of, 2783, 3306.

gediegen, *adj.*, sterling, solid.

Geduld, *f.*, patience.

Gefahr, *f.*, -en, danger, peril.

gefährlich, *adj.*, dangerous, perilous.

Gefährte, *m.*, -n, -n, companion.

gefallen, gefiel, gefallen, gefällt, *intr.* (*dat.*), please.

gefällig, *adj.*, pleasing; obliging, 2723.

gefangen, *part. adj.* (*from* fan-

gen), caught, captive; imprisoned, 91, 110, 453, *etc.*; — halten, keep a prisoner, 937; — nehmen, take prisoner, 2084, *131; — fitzen, be in prison, 3910.

Gefangene, *m. and f.* (*decl. like adj.*), prisoner.

Gefängnis, *n.*, -nisses, -nisse, prison; imprisonment, 1912.

Gefängnisnacht, *f.*, prison-night, prison-darkness.

Gefäß, *n.*, -es, -e, vessel.

gefaßt, *part. adj.*, prepared (for, auf *and acc.*), 587, 2151; composed, 3810.

geflügelt, *part. adj.*, wingéd, *adv.*, with wingéd speed, 3271.

Gefolge, *n.*, -s, —, train, retinue.

Gefühl, *n.*, -s, -e, feeling; feelings, 506.

gefühllos, *adj.*, unfeeling, destitute of feeling.

gegen, *prep.* (*acc.*), against; compared to, 2528; towards, 790, 804; to, 944.

Gegend, *f.*, -en. region, country; vicinity, parts, 2154; part (of), *93.

gegenüber, *prep.* (*dat.*, governed word usually preceding*), adv. and sep. pref.*, over against, opposite (to); face to face with, 2004.

gegenüberstehen, stand, gestanden, *intr.* (*dat.*), stand *or* be face to face with.

gegenüberstellen, *tr.*, confront.

Gegenwart, *f.*, presence.

gegenwärtig, *adj.*, present; in very presence, 438.

Gegner, *m.*, -s, —, adversary, enemy, 1761, 3225.

Gegnerin, *f.*, -innen, (female) adversary; enemy, 3670; rival, 1903, 4030.

gehaben, gehabte, gehabt, *refl.*, fare.

gehässig, *adj.*, malicious, odious.

geheim, *adj.*, secret; private, 1482; in —, in private, 1699, 2003.

Geheimnis, *n.*, —niffes, —niffe, secret, 9, 1851, 2937; mystery, 2706; secrecy, 342, 1631.

geheimnisreich, *adj.*, mysterious.

geheimnisvoll, *adj.*, mysterious.

gehen, ging, gegangen, *intr.* f., go; in fich —, examine oneself, 56, 1386.

Gehilfe, *m.*, —n, —n, assistant.

Gehör, *n.*, —s, hearing; — fchen= fen, give ear, listen (to, *dat.*), 2323.

gehorchen, *intr.* (*dat.*), obey.

gehören, *intr.* (*dat.*), belong.

Gehorsam, *m.*, —s, obedience.

Geist, *m.*, —es, —er, spirit, 134, 225, 281, 333, *etc.*; the (Holy) Spirit, 3669; soul, 456; mind, 13, 42, 465.

Geiz, *m.*, —es, avarice.

geizen, *intr.*, aspire to, be covetous of (nach).

gekrönt, *part. adj.*, crowned.

gelangen, *intr.* f., arrive at; — zu, reach, 214; come by (information), 2970.

Gelassenheit, *f.*, calmness.

gelegen, *part. adj.*, convenient, opportune; *adv.*, 3015.

gelehrt, *adj.*, learnéd.

geleiten, *tr.*, accompany, attend; Gott geleite, God speed, 2638.

Geliebte, *m.* and *f.* (*decl.* like *adj.*), beloved; lover, 3234; lady-love, 1924.

gelingen, gelang, gelungen, *intr.* (*usually impers. with dat.*), f., succeed.

geloben, *tr.*, vow, promise.

gelten, galt, gegolten, gilt, *intr.*, be worth *or* of value; be valid, count, 3596; be at stake, 3886; be the time to, be a question of, 3084.

Gelübde, *n.*, —s, —, vow.

Gemahl, *m.*, —s, —e, husband.

Gemälde, *n.*, —s, —, painting.

gemein, *adj.*, common; in common, 1562, 2773; die Gemeinen, the Commons, 580.

Gemüt, *n.*, —s, —er, mind, soul; feelings, 3099.

genießen, genoß, genoffen, *tr.*, enjoy; *with poetic gen.*, 2075.

genug, *adv. and indec. adj.*, enough.

Genüge, *f.*, sufficiency; — thun, satisfy, suffice, 1204.

Genügen (*verbal subst.*), *n.* —s, satisfaction.

genugthun, that, gethan, *intr.* (*dat.*), satisfy.

Genuß, *m.* —nuffes, —nüffe, enjoyment.

Gepräng (e), *n.* —s, pomp.

gepriesen, *part. adj.* (*from* prei= fen), praised, lauded, 416, *cf. N.*

gequält, *part. adj.*, tormented.

gerade, *adj.*, straight, erect, unbending, 4024; *adv.*, precisely, just, exactly.

geraten, geriet, geraten, gerät, *intr.* f., get into (a state or condition).

Geräusch, *n.*, —es, —e, noise, *177; stir, sensation, 1011.

gerecht, *adj.*, just, 1600, 2285, 3209; righteous, 732, 2654.

Gerechtigkeit, *f.*, justice.

gereichen, *intr.* h., tend; serve (for, zu), 863.

gereift, *part. adj.*, matured, ripe.

gereizt, *part. adj.*, irritated, exasperated, 2441; *as subst.*, provoked, 2444.

Gericht, n., -s, -e, judgment, 95, 4008; court (of justice), 171, 221, 688, etc.; tribunal, 2047, 2921.

gerichtlich, adj., judicial; adv., according to law, 853.

Gerichtshof, m., -s, -öse, court of justice.

gering, adj., little, trifling; comp. as subst., the less, 1708; adv., meanly, lightly, 3531.

Gertrud, f., Gertrude, the name given by Schiller to one of Mary Stuart's women, 3550, cf. N.

Gerücht, n., -s, -e, report, rumor.

gerührt, part. adj., moved, touched.

Gerüst, n., -es, -e, scaffold.

gerüstet, part. adj., equipped; comp., better equipped, 2038.

Gesandte, m. (decl. like adj.), messenger, 688, 2102; ambassador, *4.

Geschäft, n., -s, -e, business; matter, 1233; task, 198, *158.

geschäftig, adj., busy; fromm —, with pious activity or zeal, 494.

geschehen, geschah, geschehen, geschieht, intr. s. (used in 3rd pers. only), happen, occur; often = passive of machen or thun, 292, 2644, 3746, etc.

Geschenk, n., -s, -e, present, gift.

Geschichte, f., -n, history, story; pl., annals, 772.

Geschick, n., -s, -e, fate, destiny.

Geschlecht, n., -s, -er, race, 1183, 1287, 1325; sex, 175, 1132, 1187, 1375, 3802.

Geschmack, m., -s, (rare -äcke), taste.

Geschmeide, n., -s, jewelry, jewels.

geschmeidigt, part. adj., made pliant; bowed, softened, 2244.

Geschöpf, n., -s, -e, creature.

Geschrei, n., -s, -e, outcry, shriek(s).

Geschütz, n., -es, -e, cannon, artillery.

geschwind, adj., quick, speedy, ready, 2159.

Geschworene, m. (decl. like adj.), juror.

Gesellschaft, f., -en, society.

Gesetz, n., -es, -e, law; necessity, 2192.

gesetzt, part., granted, supposing that, 936.

Gesicht, n., -s, -er, face.

gesinnt, part. adj., minded; disposed, 1687.

gesittet, part. adj., orderly, good.

gespannt, part. adj., intense; fixed, *101.

Gespenst, n., -es, -er, spectre.

Gespräch, n., -s, -e, conversation, *122; interview, 2496.

Gestalt, f., -en, form, stature; image, 436, cf. N.; aspect, appearance, 1606, 1768.

Geständnis, n., -nisses, -nisse, confession.

gestehen, gestand, gestanden, tr., confess.

gestern, adv., yesterday.

Gesträuch, n., -s, -e, bushes; shrubbery, foliage, 2086.

gestürzt, part. adj., lit. hurled down; undone, ruined, 3972.

geteilt, part. adj., shared, common, 3614, cf. N.

Getöse, n., -s, —, noise.

getreu, adj., faithful; as subst., 207, 3510.

getrost, adj., confident.

Getümmel, n., -s, tumult.

gewagt, part. adj., hazardous, risky.

gewahr, adj., aware; — werden, catch sight of, perceive, *146.

Gewähr, *f.*, surety, guarantee.

gewähren, *tr.*, grant; afford, give, 828; *intr.* (*with dat. of pers.*), guarantee, give security, 2357.

Gewahrsam, *f.* (*now usually m.*), custody.

Gewalt, *f.*, -en, power, 711, 762, 992, 2572, 3743; force, 661, 942, 957, 962, 1863; violence, 21, 2597, 3942.

gewaltig, *adj.*, powerful.

gewaltsam, *adj.* violent; *adv.*, by force, 159, 1847, *etc.*

Gewaltthat, *f.*, -en, deed of violence.

Gewand, *n.*, -s, -änder, garment; garb, 968, 1276, 3367.

gewärtig, *adj.* (*predicate only, with gen.*), ready for, expectant (of).

Gewehr, *n.*, -s, -e, weapon.

geweiht, *part. adj.*, consecrated.

Gewicht, *n.*, -s, -e, weight.

gewinnen, gewann, gewonnen, *tr.*, win, 1985. 2589, 3835; gain, 1594, 1641, 1898, *etc.*

gewiß, *adj.*, sure, certain.

Gewissen, *n.*, -s, —, conscience.

gewissenhaft, *adj.*, conscientious.

Gewißheit, *f.*, certainty; certain knowledge, 684.

gewißlich, *adv.*, surely.

gewöhnen, *tr.*, accustom; accustom oneself, get used (to, an *and acc.*), 157.

gezeugt, *part. adj.*, begotten.

geziemen, *intr.* (*with dat.*), befit, beseem, become; geziemend, *part. adj.*, fitting, proper; *adv* , 1570.

Gezücht, *n.*, -s, breed, brood.

gezwungen, *part. adj.* (*from* zwingen), compelled, constrained; under compulsion, 3965.

giftig, *adj.*, poisonous, venomous.

gigantisch, *adj.*, gigantic.

Glanz, *m* , -es, brightness; splendor, glory, 264, 1126, 1764, *etc.*; glare, glitter, 1393.

glänzen, *intr.*, shine, 1799; beam, 1228; glänzend, *part. adj.*, radiant, 3662.

glanzvoll, *adj.*, brilliant.

glatt, *adj.*, smooth.

Glaube(n), *m.*, -es, belief; faith, 786, 1742, 3501, *etc.*

glauben, *tr. and intr.* (*dat. of pers.*), believe.

Glaubensänderung, *f.*, -en, change of faith.

Glaubenslehre, *f.*, -n, doctrine, dogma.

Glaubensverwandte, *m. and f.* (*decl. like adj.*), fellow-believer, brother or sister in faith.

glaubensvoll, *adj.*, devout; *cf. N.*, 424.

gläubig, *adj.*, believing; devout, 3622; credulous, 1407.

gleich, *adj.*, like, equal; same, 647; *as subst.*, 2895; *adv.*, alike, 1261; equally, 778, 1788; (= sogleich), directly, immediately, 2041, *118; *conj* (*for* obgleich *or* wenn . . . gleich)), though, although, 1304.

gleichfalls, *adv.*, likewise.

Gleichmut, *m.*, -s, equanimity, calmness, unconcern.

gleißen, gliß *and* gleißte, geglissen *and* gegleißt, *intr.*, shine, glisten; *fig.* (*properly a different word*, gleißen), to play the hypocrite, sham; *hence*

gleißend (*properly* gleisend), *part. adj.*, hypocritical; *adv.*, 2428.

gleißnerisch, *adi.*, hypocritical.

Glied, *n.*, -es, -er, limb.

Glocke, *f.,* –n, bell; trumpet, herald, 2953.

Glo'rie, *f.,* glory, halo.

glorwürdig, *adj.,* glorious.

Glück, *n.,* –es, happiness; fortune, 472, 1806.

glücklich, *adj.,* happy, fortunate; *as subst.,* 553 (*cf. N.*), 654; successful, 1845.

Glückwunsch, *m.,* –es, –wünsche, congratulations.

glühen, *intr.,* glow; **glühend,** *part. adj.,* glowing, 3322, 3574; red-hot, 2538; ardent, 2554, *111.

Glut, *f.,* –en, glow; ardor, 2429.

Gnade, *f.,* grace, 2258, 3709; pardon, 314, 1527; mercy, 1228, 1521, 1569, 3512; clemency, 1023.

gnadenvoll, *adj.,* gracious; *adv.,* 1687.

Gnadenweg, *m.,* –s, –e, avenue of mercy.

gnädig, *adj.,* gracious, 2859; merciful, 1382, 3478.

gnug, *see* genug.

Gold, *n.,* –es, gold.

golden, *adj.,* gold, golden.

gönnen, *tr.* (*dat. of pers.*), not grudge, 2006; grant, allow, 1351.

Gott, *m.,* –es, Götter, god, God; *pl.,* 1066, *cf. N.*

Götterfest, *n.,* –es, –e, festival *or* fête (fit) for gods, *i.e.* of divine splendor.

Götterhalle, *f.,* –n, hall of the gods.

Götterhand, *f.,* divine hand.

Gottesbild, *n.,* –s, –er, sacred image, shrine, 420, *cf. N.*

Gottesdienst, *m.,* –es, divine service, worship.

Gottheit, *f.,* –en, deity, divinity.

Göttin, *f.,* –innen, goddess.

göttlich, *adj.,* divine; *neut. sing as subst.,* 448, 3757; *acc. pl. as subst.,* those personages *or* forms divine, 440, *cf. N.*

Götze, *m.,* –n, –n, idol.

Götzendienst, *m.,* –es, idolatry.

Grab, *n.,* –es, Gräber, grave.

Gräbernacht, *f.,* sepulchral *or* grave-like darkness.

Grabesrand, *m.,* –s, –ränder, edge of the grave.

Grabstein, *m.,* –s, –e, gravestone, tombstone.

Graf, *m.,* –en, –en, count; (*English*) earl.

Grafschaft, *f.,* –en, county, shire.

Gram, *m.,* –es, sorrow, grief.

gräßlich, *adj.,* horrible, hideous.

grau, *adj.,* gray, 2094; ancient, remote, 806.

grauen, *intr. impers.* (*with dat.*), dread.

Grauen (*verbal subst.*), *n.,* –s, horror.

grausam, *adj.,* cruel; *neut. as subst.,* cruelty, 2306.

Grausen (*verbal subst.*), *n.,* –s, shudder.

Gray, Lady, Lady Jane Grey, a great-granddaughter of Henry VII of England. Born 1537, beheaded 1554, *cf. N.* 613.

greifen, griff, gegriffen, *tr.,* grasp, seize; *intr.* (*with zu*), have recourse *or* resort to, 3026.

greis, *adj.,* gray, hoary, aged.

Greis, *m.,* –es, –e, old man.

Grenze, *f.,* –n, boundary, border.

Greuelthat, *f.,* –en, deed of horror, atrocity.

Grille, *f.,* –n, whim.

grillenhaft, *adj.,* whimsical, capricious.

Grimm, *m.,* –es, fury, rage.

grimmig, *adj.,* furious, 3934; fierce, 1269, 2550.

grob (gröber, gröbst–), *adj.*, coarse, rude.

Groll, *m.*, –es, grudge; hatred, 2440.

groß (größer, größt–), *adj.*, great, large; *as subst.*, 2838.

Größe, *f.*, greatness.

Großmut, *f.*, magnanimity, generosity.

großmütig, *adj.*, magnanimous, generous.

großmutsvoll, *adj.*, magnanimous.

Großohm, *m.*, –es, –öhme, great-uncle, grand-uncle.

Großschatzmeister, *m.*, –s, —, grand treasurer, lord high treasurer.

grübeln, *intr.*, indulge in subtile inquiries, speculate; **grübelnd,** *part. adj.*, speculative, hypercritical, *cf. N.* 478.

Gruft, *f.*, Grüfte, vault, 2080; tomb, 290, 3144.

Gruftgewölbe, *n.*, –s, —, sepulchral vault, vaulted tomb.

grün, *adj.*, green.

Grund, *m.*, –es, Gründe, ground, 1664; bottom, 1613; cause, 1950; reason, argument, 711, 1458.

gründen, *tr.*, ground, found, establish.

Gruß, *m.*, –es, Grüße, greeting; — des Engels, the Annunciation, 441, *cf. N.*

grüßen, *tr.*, greet.

Guise, Guise, a former duchy of northeastern France, named from the town of Guise and very powerful in the 16th and 17th centuries.

Guise, Kardinal von, Charles de Guise, Cardinal of Lorraine, maternal uncle of Mary Stuart; *cf. N.* 387, 463, 1266.

Guisen, *pl.*, the Guise, members of the ducal family of Guise, a branch of the House of Lorraine; *specifically*, the cousins of Mary Stuart, *cf. N.* 387, 1266.

Gunst, *f.*, favor; privilege, 3749, *cf. N.*

günstig, *adj.*, favorable.

Günstling, *m.*, –s, –e, favorite.

Gürtel, *m.*, –s, —, girdle, belt.

gut (besser, best–), *adj.*, good; *neut. as subst.*, 2201; *adv.*, well, 791.

Gut, *n.*, –es, Güter, good, blessing, 2578, 2805; possession, 1167, 1395, 3578, *etc.*; tote Güter, earthly (perishable) goods, 1651; das höchste —, 3685, *cf. N.*

gütig, *adj.*, kind, gracious.

H.

ha, *interj.*, ha! ah!

Haar, *n.*, –es, –e, hair.

haben, hatte, gehabt, hat, *tr.*, have, possess; *past aux.*, have; *plup. subj.*, 85, *cf. N.;* was habt Ihr? what is the matter with you? 3465, *cf. N.*

Haft, *f.*, custody.

haften, *intr.*, cling to; attach to, 3959; — für, answer for, 2691, 3303.

Hain, *m.*, –es, –e, grove, wood.

halb, *adj.*, half.

Hälfte, *f.*, –n, half.

Halle, *f.*, –n, hall.

Hals, *m.*, –es, Hälse, neck: throat, *166.

halten, hielt, gehalten, hält, *t.*, hold; keep, 380, 725, 1080, 2781, *etc.;* deem, consider, 1771; es mit (einem) —, side with, 1015, *cf. N.*

Hammer, *m.,* -s, Hämmer, hammer.

Hand, *f.,* Hände, hand; die Hände bieten, offer aid, 639.

Handel, *m.,* -s, Händel, business, affair; deed, 2769.

handeln, *intr.,* act, 1237, 1768, 1923. *etc.;* operate, take (their) course, 1592; — an (*with dat.*), deal with, treat, 2295.

hangen, hing, gehangen, hängt, *intr.,* hang, 995.

hängen, *tr.,* hang; *refl.,* cling to, 2771, *180.

Harnisch, *m.,* -es, -e, armor.

harren, *intr.,* wait (for, auf *and* acc.).

hart (härter, härtest-), *adj.,* hard.

Härte, *f.,* harshness.

Haß, *m.,* -sses, hate, hatred; odium, 1597.

hassen, *tr.,* hate.

hastig, *adj.,* hasty.

Hatton, Sir Christopher Hatton (1540–1591), Lord Chancellor of England (from April, 1587), active in the prosecution of Mary Stuart; *cf. N.* 244.

häufen, *tr.,* heap.

Haupt, *n.,* -es, Häupter, head; person, 2681.

Haus, *n.,* -es, Häuser, house.

Hausbediente, *m.* (*decl. like adj.*), household servant.

Haushofmeister, *m.,* -s, —, house-steward, master of the household.

heben, hob *or* hub, gehoben, *tr.,* lift, raise; *refl.,* rise, 3599.

Heer, *n.,* -es, -e, army.

heftig, *adj.,* violent, 3005, 3336, *5 *etc.;* impetuous, passionate, 816, 1882, *147; *adv.,* violently, urgently, 581, 3054.

heftigdringend, *part. adj.,* importunate, 1370.

Heftigkeit, *f.,* violence, vehemence.

hegen, *tr.,* foster, cherish; *pres. subj.,* 117, *cf. N.*

Heide, *f.,* -n, heath.

Heil, *n.,* -(e)s, welfare; salvation, 491; absolution, 3642.

Heiland, *m.,* -s, Saviour, Redeemer.

heilen, *tr.,* cure; heilend, *part. adj.,* curative, healing, 3489.

heilig, *adj.,* holy; sacred, 1067, 2565, 2668.

Heilige, *m. and f.* (*decl. like adj.*), saint; Holy Spirit, 3590.

heiligen, *t ,* consecrate; sanction, justify, 2355.

Heimat, *f.,* -en, home, native country.

heimführen, *tr.,* lead *or* take home.

heimlich, *adj.,* secret, 631, 952, *etc.;* private, 2503; *adv.,* privately, apart, *67.

Heinrich, Henry VIII of England, father of Queen Elizabeth. Born 1491; reigned, 1509–1547, *cf. N.* 522.

heischen, *tr.,* demand, require.

heiß, *adj.,* hot, ardent, 417, 1246; eager, 1138, 3477.

Heißgeliebte, *f.* (*decl. like adj.*), dearly loved one, 2539.

heißen, hieß, geheißen, *tr.,* call; name; bid, 814, 2799, 3980; *intr.,* be called, 1008; mean, signify; be, 723 (*cf. N.*), 1288, 3106.

heiter, *adj.,* serene, 1408; bright, happy, 429, 1229.

Held, *m.,* -en, -en, hero.

Heldengeist, *m.,* -es, -er, heroic spirit.

Heldenmut, *m.,* -s, heroism.

Heldentugend, *f.,* –en, heroic virtue.

Heldin, *f.,* –innen, heroine.

Helena, Helen, the wife of Menelaus; a Grecian woman famed for her beauty, whose abduction by Paris, legend says, brought about the Trojan War. *Cf. N.* 84.

Helfer, *m.,* –s, —, helper; ally, 821.

hell, *adj.,* clear, bright; keen, 335.

hemmen, *tr.,* hinder, 718; bar, cut off, 677, 1835.

Henker, *m.,* –s, —, hangman, executioner, 625.

Henkerbeil, *n.,* –s, –e, executioner's *or* headsman's axe.

Henkerblock, *m.,* –s, –öcke, executioner's block.

her, *adv. and sep. pref.,* hither, here, along.

herab, *adv. and sep. pref.,* down from, down.

herabhängen (*properly* hangen), hing, gehangen), *intr.,* hang down.

herablassen, ließ, gelassen, läßt, *tr.,* let down; *refl.,* condescend, 474.

herabsteigen, stieg, gestiegen, *intr.* f., descend.

herabstürzen, *tr.,* hurl down; *intr.* f., plunge.

herabwerfen, warf, geworfen, wirft, *tr.,* throw down.

herauf, *adv. and sep. pref.,* up here, up, upwards.

heraufsteigen, stieg, gestiegen, *intr.* f., climb, ascend.

heraus, *adv. and sep. pref.,* out here, out of, out; out of it, 2787.

herbei, *adv. and sep. pref.,* hither. near by, here.

herbeibringen, brachte, gebracht, *tr.,* bring forward, produce.

herein, *adv. and sep. pref.,* in hither, in, into.

hereindringen, drang, gedrungen, *intr.* f., press in.

hereinkommen, kam, gekommen, *intr.* f., come (in), enter.

hereinstürzen, *intr.* f., rush in.

hereintreten, trat, getreten, tritt, *intr.* f., step in, enter.

herkömmlich, *adj.,* customary.

hernieder, *adv. and sep. pref.,* down hither, down.

herniederfahren, fuhr, gefahren, fährt, *intr.* f., descend.

Herold, *m.,* –s, –e, herald.

Herr, *m.,* –n, –en, master, 1926, lord, 1116 (*pl.,* –n), 2663, *4, *52; gentleman, 681; the Lord, 441, 3615.

herrlich, *adj.,* glorious, 2398, 2472; splendid, magnificent, noble, 3132; *neut. superl. as subst.,* 438.

Herrlichkeit, *f.,* glory, splendor, magnificence; *as title,* Excellency, 685, 2661.

Herrschaft, *f.,* –en, dominion, sovereignty.

herrschen *intr.,* rule, reign; prevail (over, über *and acc.*), 328; *inf. as subst.,* 3145.

Herrscher, *m.,* –s, —, ruler, sovereign.

Herrscherin, *f.,* –innen, (female) sovereign.

Herrscherwort, *n.,* –s, –e, word of command.

Herrscherzügel, *m.,* –s, —, *pl.,* reins of government, 1345.

herrschsüchtig, *adj.,* filled with a rage for ruling; mad with ambition (to rule), imperious, 2334.

hertragen, trug, getragen, trägt, *tr.*, bear (here *or* along)

heram, *adv. and sep. pref.*, round, about.

herumgehen, ging, gegangen, *int . f.*, go *or* walk about.

herumsehen, sah, gesehen, sieht, *intr.*, look around.

herumtreiben, trieb, getrieben, *tr.*, drive about; shift, 3261.

herunter, *adv. and sep. pref.*, down, downwards.

herunterlassen, ließ, gelassen, läßt, *tr.*, let down; *refl.*, condescend, 1719.

heruntersteigen, stieg, gestiegen, *intr. f.*, descend.

herunterstoßen, stieß, gestoßen, stößt, *tr.*, thrust down, precipitate.

hervor, *adv. and sep. pref.*, forth, forward, out.

hervorgehen, ging, gegangen, *intr. f.*, go forth; come forth, emerge, 565.

hervortreten, trat, getreten, tritt, *intr. f.*, step forth *or* forward; come forth, 2439.

hervorziehen, zog, gezogen, *tr.*, draw forth *or* out.

herwogen, *intr.*, surge onward.

Herz, *n.*, -ens, -en, heart; — fassen, take heart, feel confidence, 173.

herzerschütternd, *part.adj.*, heart-rending; moving, 515.

herziehen, zog, gezogen, *intr. f.*, go, proceed; — vor, go before, precede, 3135.

Heuchelschein, *m.*, -s, hypocrisy.

heut(e), *adv.*, to-day; — nacht, last night, 1624, *cf. N.*

heutig, *adj.*, of this day, to-day's.

hier, *adv.*, here.

hierauf, *adv.*, hereupon, hereafter, upon this, at this.

hie(r)her, *adv.*, hither, here.

Hifthorn, *n.*, -s, -hörner, hunting-horn, bugle.

Hilfe, *f.*, help, aid.

Hilfestehende, *f.* (*decl. like adj.*), suppliant (for help), 88.

Himmel, *m*, -s, —, heaven, sky; *gen pl.* (*with sing. meaning*), 435, 1650, 3844.

Himmeldecke, *f.*, -n, canopy, 32, *cf. N.*

Himmelreich, *n.*, -s, kingdom of heaven.

Himmelsbote, *m.*, -n, -n, messenger of heaven, heavenly messenger.

Himmelskraft, *f.*, -kräfte, heavenly power.

Himmelspeise, *f.*, heavenly *or* spiritual food, Holy Communion, 3592, *cf. N.*

Himmelsschoß, *m.*, -es, bosom *or* canopy of heaven.

Himmelssegen, *m.*, -s, —, blessing of heaven, heavenly blessing.

Himmelsthüre, *f.*, door of heaven.

himmlisch, *adj.*, heavenly; *neut.* as *subst.*, 3603.

hin, *adv. and sep. pref.*, hence, there, thither, along, away; gone, 3847.

hinab, *adv. and sep. pref.*, down (thither), downwards.

hinabschreien, schrie, geschrieen, *intr.*, call *or* shriek down.

hinabsteigen, stieg, gestiegen, *intr. f.*, descend.

hinabstürzen, *tr.*, hurl down, precipitate.

hinaus, *adv. and sep. pref.*, out, hence, away; wo . . . hinaus, to what point *or* end, 590, *cf. N.*

hinaustreiben, trieb, getrieben, *tr.*, drive out *or* hence.

hindern, *tr.*, hinder, prevent.

hinein, *adv. and sep. pref.*, in (there), into, into it.

hineingehen, ging, gegangen, *intr.* ſ., go in, enter.

hineinlegen, *tr.*, interpose, insert.

hineinreißen, riß, geriſſen, *tr.*, drag in *or* into.

hineinſehen, ſah, geſehen, ſieht, *intr.*, look in.

hinfahren, fuhr, geſahren, fährt, *intr.* ſ., go away *or* hence; *imper.*, farewell! 2246.

hinfliehen, floh, geſlohen, *intr.* ſ., flee thither; flee from here, 2638.

hinführen, *tr.*, lead *or* conduct (there *or* away).

hingeben, gab, gegeben, giebt, *tr.*, give up, surrender.

hingehen, ging, gegangen, *intr.* ſ., go (thither); go hence, depart, 3793.

hinnehmen, nahm, genommen, nimmt, *tr.*, take; take of, receive, 3747.

hinraffen, *tr.*, take away; cut off, kill, 1008.

hinreichen, *tr.*, reach *or* hold out, extend.

hinreißen, riß, geriſſen, *tr.*, carry away.

Hinrichtung, *f.*, –en, execution.

hinſchmelzen, ſchmolz, geſchmolzen, ſchmilzt, *intr.* ſ., melt away; languish, 3853.

hinſehen, ſah, geſehen, ſieht, *intr.*, look there, look towards.

hinſinken, ſank, geſunken, *intr.* ſ., sink down, fall.

hinſtellen, *tr.*, put, place; *refl.*, take one's stand *or* place, 378.

hinten, *adv.*, behind; in the background, *91.

hinter, *prep.* (*dat. and acc.*), *adv.*,

sep. and insep. pref., behind, back, after.

hintergehen, hinterging', hintergang'en, *insep. tr.*, deceive.

Hintergrund, *m.*, -ᵈ, –ünde, background.

hinterlaſſen, hinterließ', hinterlaſſen, hinterläßt', *insep. tr.*, leave behind.

hinterliſtig, *adj.*, perfidious, deceitful, cunning.

hintragen, trug, getragen, trägt, *tr.*, bear o carry (thither, off).

hintreten, trat, getreten, tritt, *intr.* ſ., step (there).

hinüber, *adv. and sep. pref.*, over, across.

hinüberlaufen, lief, gelaufen, läuft, *intr.* ſ. and h., run over; desert, 1427.

hinweg, *adv. and sep. pref.*, away, off.

hinwegführen, *tr.*, lead away, *109; remove, 537.

hinwerfen, warf, geworfen, wirft, *tr.*, throw away, fling away, 3843; throw out *or* utter carelessly; remark casually, *91.

hinzu, *adv. and sep pref.*, to, towards; besides, in addition.

hinzufügen, *tr.*, add.

Hirtin, *f.*, –innen, shepherdess.

hoch (höher, höchſt–), *adj.*, (*in declined forms*, hoh–), high, tall, lofty, great; noble, 475, 519; advanced, 3511; *neut. superl. as subst.*, 438, 1652.

Hochamt, *n.* -ᵈ, high-mass.

Hochland, *n.* –ᵈ, highland; the Highlands (of Scotland), 2141.

Hochmut, *m.* -ᵈ, haughtiness, haughty pride.

Hochverrat, *m.* -ᵈ, high treason.

Hochverräter, *m.* -ᵈ, —, one guilty of high treason, arch-traitor.

hochwürdig, *adj.*, most venerable; *neut. as subst.*, Hochwürdiges, host, consecrated wafer, 290, 3634.

Hochzeitsfackel, *f.*, –n, wedding torch, 1147, *cf. N.*

Hof, *m.*, –es, Höfe, yard, courtyard; court (*residence of royalty*), 48, 552, 681, *etc.*

Hofdiener, *m.*, –s, servant *or* officer of the court.

Hoffart, *f.*, pride, haughtiness, 142, *cf. N.*

hoffen, *tr.*, hope; *intr.* (*with auf and acc.*), hope for, 1772.

Hoffen (*verbal subst.*), *n.*, –s, hope.

Hoffnung, *f.*, –en, hope.

hoffnungslos, *adj.*, hopeless.

Höfling, *m.*, –s, –e, courtier.

Höhe, *f.*, –n, height, eminence.

Hoheit, *f.*, –en, highness, eminence; sovereignty, 1764; dignity, *166; nobility, 1192; (*as title*), Highness, 1212.

hohl, *adj.*, hollow.

Höhle, *f.*, –n, cavern, recess.

Hohn, *m.*, –es, scorn.

höhnend, *part. adj.*, mocking, scornful.

Hohngelächter, *n.* –s, scornful laughter.

höhnisch, *adj.*, scornful.

holen, *tr.*, fetch, bring, secure; get, 2695; Rat —, get counsel *or* advice, consult, 526.

Hölle, *f.*, hell.

Höllenangst, *f.*, anguish of hell; agonizing hell, 3337.

Höllengeist, *m.*, –es, –er, spirit of hell, infernal spirit; *pl.*, the Furies, 2187, *cf. N.*

Höllenkunst, *f.*, –künste, hellish *or* diabolical art.

Höllenpforte, *f.*, –n, gate of hell.

Höllenschlange, *f.*, –n, serpent of hell, infernal viper.

Höllenwaffe, *f.*, –n, weapon of hell, infernal weapon.

Honi soit qui mal y pense (*Fr.*), *lit.* "shamed (*or* dishonored) be he that thinks evil of it," the motto of the Order of the Garter, 1221, *cf. N.*

horchen, *intr.*, hearken, listen.

hören, *tr.*, hear.

Horn, *n.* –es, Hörner, horn.

Hostie, *f.*, –n, host, holy wafer, 2526, *cf. N.*

Hotel (*Fr.*), *n.*, –s, –s, palace, mansion.

Howard. Lord Howard of Effingham, Lord High Admiral of England, 752, *cf. N.*

Howard, Katharina. Catherine Howard, fifth wife of Henry VIII of England. Married 1540, beheaded 1542, *cf. N.* 613.

Huldigung, *f.*, –en, homage.

hundert, *num.*, hundred.

hurtig, *adj.*, quick, nimble; — machen, make haste, 3446.

Hut, *f.*, heed, guard; keeping, 1050.

hüten, *tr.*, watch, guard.

Hüter, *m.*, –s, —, keeper; guard, 2513.

J.

ich, *pl.*, wir, *pers. pron.*, I; *gen.*, mein, 451, 471, *cf. N.*

ihr (*pl. of* du, *formerly used in sing. and pl. of polite address*), ye, you.

ihr, *poss. adj. and pron.* (*corresponding to* sie), her, hers, its, their, theirs.

ihretwillen, um, *adv.*, for her (*also* their) sake, 78, *cf. N.*

ihrige (der, die, das), *poss. pron.* (*absolute*), hers, theirs; die Ihrigen, her friends, 3357.

Ihro, *poss. pron.* (*archaic, used only in titles*), Your, His, Her.

immer, *adv.,* always, ever.

immerdar, *adv.,* always, ever; auf —, forever, 2128.

immerhin, *adv.,* always, constantly; still; at any rate, 240.

in, *prep.* (*dat. and acc.*), in, into.

indem, *conj.,* while; as, *73.

indes, indessen, *adv.,* meantime, meanwhile; *conj.,* while, however.

Inhalt, *m.,* –s, contents, 167, 1727; purport, 3040.

innehalten, hielt, gehalten, hält, *sep. intr.,* stop, pause.

innen, *adv.,* within, inside.

inner, *adj.,* inner, interior; *neut. sing. as subst.,* interior, 434; heart, soul, 2191, 2677, 3726; *neut. sing. superl. as subst.,* inmost heart *or* soul, 2966, 3192.

Innere(s), see inner.

Innerstes, see inner.

Inquisitionsgericht, *n.,* –s, –e, court of inquisition.

Insel, *f.,* –n, island.

irdisch, *adj.,* earthly; *neut. sing. as subst.,* Irdisches, earthly things, 1540, *cf. N.*

irgend, *adv.* (*in composition with a pron. or other adv.*), some, any, ever.

irre, *adj.,* astray, wandering; restless, delirious, *114; *adv.,* irre führen, lead astray, mislead, 1552.

Irre, *f.,* wandering, maze, mistaken way; in der — leiten, lead in ways of error, 478.

irren, *intr.,* err, go astray; be wrong *or* mistaken, 1319, 2122; *refl.,* be mistaken, 1713, 1892.

Irrtum, *m.,* –s, –tümer, error.

Italien, *n.,* –s, Italy.

J.

ja, *aff. adv.,* yes, aye; surely, 359, *cf. N.;* indeed, you know.

Jagd, *f.,* –en, chase, hunt; die — machen auf (*with acc.*), hunt down, 2703.

Jagdgefolg(e), *n.,* –s, hunting train.

jagen, *tr.,* chase, hunt, drive; *intr.* h., hunt, 2154; *intr.* j., move swiftly, chase, fly, 2096.

Jagen (*verbal subst.*), *n.,* –s, hunting, hunt.

Jahr, *n.* –es, –e, year.

jahrelang, *adv.,* for years; *adj.,* lasting, 282.

Jahr(e)stag, *m.,* –s, –e, anniversary.

Jammer, *m.,* –s, lamentation, grief.

jammern, *intr.,* lament, wail.

Jammern (*verbal subst.*), *n.,* –s, lamentation, 3808.

jammernswürdig, *adj.,* lamentable, pitiable, miserable.

jammervoll, *adj.,* most lamentable; *as subst.,* my wretched lady, 25.

Jawort, *n.,* –s, yes, consent.

je, *adv.,* ever, always; von —, ever, of old, 763.

jeder (–e, –es), *adj. and pron.,* each, every, each one, every one.

jedermann, *pron.,* every one, everybody.

jedoch, *conj.,* however, yet, nevertheless.

jedweder (–e, –es), *adj. and pron.,* (*archaic for* jeder), each, every, each one, every one; each and every, 1185, 2379.

jeglicher (−e, −es), *adj. and pron.* = jeder; *neut. sing.*, everything, 1976.

jemand, *pron.*, some one, somebody.

jener (−e, −es), *demon. adj. and pron.*, that, that one, he, she, the former.

Jesus, *m. gen.*, Jesu, Jesus; die Gesellschaft Jesu, the Society of Jesus, the Jesuits, *cf. N.* 493.

jetzo, *adv.*, *archaic*, = jetzt, 913.

jetzt, *adv.*, now.

Joch, *n.*, −es, −e, yoke.

Jubel, *m.*, −s, jubilation, rejoicing.

jubeln, *intr.*, rejoice, exult; jubelnd, *part. adj.*, rejoicing, exultant.

Jugend, *f.*, youth.

Jugendkraft, *f.*, −kräfte, vigor of youth, prime.

Jugendland, *n.* −s, land of one's youth.

jugendlich, *adj.*, youthful.

Jugendlust, *f.*, −lüste, joy of youth, youthful joy.

jung (jünger, jüngst−), *adj.* young; *fem. comp. as subst.*, 2012.

jungfräulich, *adj.*, virgin, 1160; maiden, of maidenhood, 1166.

Jüngling, *m.*, −s, −e, youth.

jüngst (*superl. of* jung), *adv.*, lately, recently.

Juwel, *n.*, −s, −en, jewel.

K.

kahl, *adj.*, bald; bare, 30.

Kahn, *m.*, −es, Kähne, boat, skiff.

kalt (kälter, kältest−), *adj.*, cold; *adv.*, 1765.

Kammer, *f.*, −n, chamber, room.

Kämmerer, *m.*, −s, −, chamberlain.

Kammerfrau, *f.*, −en, woman-in-waiting, waiting-woman.

Kampf, *m.*, −es, Kämpfe, conflict, struggle.

kämpfen, *intr.*, fight, battle, struggle; kämpfend, *part.*, battling, in combat, 3220; *as subst.*, combatant, 817.

Kanzler, *m.*, −s, −, chancellor.

Kapelle, *f.*, −n, chapel.

Kardinal', *m.*, −s, −nä'le, cardinal.

Karte, *f.*, −n, card.

Katharina, *f.*, Catherine; *specifically*, Catherine de' Medici, 1128; *cf. N.* 48.

katho'lisch, *adj.* (Roman) Catholic; *as subst.*, 3058; as title of Philip II of Spain, 3527, *cf. N*

kaufen, *tr.*, buy.

kaum, *adv.*, scarcely, hardly; — . . . so, scarcely . . . when, no sooner . . . than.

Kavalier', *m.*, −s, −e, cavalier.

keck, *adj.*, bold, daring.

kehren, *tr.*, turn, 3933; *intr.* (s.), turn.

kein (keine, kein), *adj. and pron.*, no, none, not a, not any.

keineswegs, *adv.*, in no wise, by no means.

Kelch, *m.*, −es, −e, cup, 1977; chalice, communion-cup, *177.

kennen, kannte, gekannt, *tr.*, know, be acquainted with.

Kerker, *m.*, −s, −, prison.

Kerkerelend, *n.*, −s, misery of imprisonment.

Kerkerhaft, *f.*, imprisonment.

Kerkermauer, *f.*, −n, prison wall.

Kerkermeister, *m.*, −s, −, jailer.

Kerkerschmach, *f.*, ignominy of imprisonment; ignominious captivity, 2383.

Kerze, *f.*, −n, candle.

Kette, *f.*, −n, chain.

keuſch, *adj.,* chaste.

Kind, *n.,* –es, –er, child.

Kindheit, *f.,* childhood.

kindiſch, *adj.,* childish.

Kirche, *f.,* –n, church.

Kirchenfeſt, *n.,* –s, –e, church-festival.

Kirchenſtrafe, *f.,* –n, penance.

Kiſſen, *n.,* –s, —, cushion.

Klagarti'kel, *m.,* –s, —, indictment.

Klage, *f.,* –n, complaint, lament.

klagen, *intr.,* complain, lament.

Klagepunkt, *m.,* –s, –e, point of accusation, charge.

Kläger, *m.,* –s, —, accuser, complainant.

klar, *adj.,* clear.

Kleid, *n.,* –es, –er, garment, dress; *pl.,* clothes.

kleiden, *tr.,* dress; clothe, 968.

klein, *adj.,* little, small; petty, 1785; *neut. sing. as subst.,* 2126.

Klein'od, *n.,* –s, –e *or* –o'dien, jewel; treasure, 1202, 1813, 3560.

klingeln, *intr.,* ring (a bell).

klingen, klang, geklungen, *intr.,* sound.

Kloſter, *n.,* –s, Klöſter, cloister, monastery.

Kluft, *f.,* Klüfte, cleft, cavern, vault.

Klugheit, *f.,* prudence, discretion.

klüglich, *adv.,* prudently, cleverly.

Knabe, *m.,* –n, –n, boy.

Knecht, *m.,* –es, –e, servant.

Knechtſchaft, *f.,* bondage, servitude.

Knie, *n.,* –s, –e, knee.

knie(e)n, *intr.,* kneel.

knüpfen, *tr.,* tie, join.

Koloſſeum, *n.,* –s, Colosseum, a great amphitheater of ancient Rome.

kommen, kam, gekommen, *intr.* ſ., come.

Kommiſſa'rius, *m.,* —, –ien, commissioner, 217, *cf. N.*

König, *m.,* –s, –e, king.

Königin, *f.,* –innen, queen.

königlich, *adj.,* royal, regal; *neut. as subst.,* 153.

Königreich, *n.,* –s, –e, kingdom.

Königsblut, *n.,* –s, royal blood.

Königsmord, *m.,* –s, –e, regicide, murder of a king.

Königspflicht, *f.,* –en, duty of royalty.

Königsſohn, *m.,* –s, –ſöhne, prince.

Königstitel, *m.,* –s, royal title.

Königswille(n), *m.,* –ns, royal will.

Königswürde, *f.,* royal privilege.

können, konnte, gekonnt, kann, *tr. and modal aux.,* can, be able.

konſekrie'ren, *tr.,* consecrate.

Konzept', *n.,* –s, –e, rough draft, outline.

Kopie', *f.,* –(e)n, copy.

körperlos, *adj.,* incorporeal, 433, *cf. N.*

koſtbar, *adj.,* costly; precious, 1259.

Koſtbarkeit, *f.,* –en, costliness; *pl.,* valuables, *181,158, jewels, 7.

koſten, *tr.,* cost.

köſtlich, *adj.,* costly, precious.

Kraft, *f.,* Kräfte, strength, 529; power, 2273.

kraft, *prep.* (*gen.*), by *or* in virtue of.

kraftvoll, *adj.,* powerful.

krank (kränker, krank[e]ſt–), *adj.,* sick, ill.

Krankheit, *f.,* –en, sickness, illness.

Kränkung, *f.,* –en, mortification, vexation.

Kranz, *m.,* –es, Kränze, wreath, garland.

kredenzen, *tr.,* serve *or* present food and drink; *originally, of such as had been tasted by the person presenting it, to attest its harmlessness, and of the act of so foretasting;* 630, "*attested,*" *i. e.* poisoned.

Kreis, *m.,* –es, –e, circle.

Kreuz, *n.,* –es, –e, cross.

kreuzigen, *tr.,* crucify; *part. as subst.,* der Gekreuzigte, the Crucified Lord, 3539.

Krieg, *m.,* –es, –e, war.

Krone, *f.,* –n, crown.

krönen, *tr.,* crown.

krümmen, *tr.,* curve, bend; ge-krümmt, *part.,* writhing, 3922.

Kruzifix, *n.,* –es, –e, crucifix.

Kugel, *f.,* –n, ball; bead, *166.

kühn, *adj.,* bold.

Kühnheit *f.,* boldness, daring.

Kummer, *m.,* –s, sorrow, grief.

kümmern, *tr.,* grieve, trouble; concern, 2765.

kund, *indecl. adj.* (*predicate only*), known, public; — thun, make known, 3284; sich — geben, manifest itself (*or* oneself), 2071.

Kunde, *f.,* information.

kundig, *adj.,* learned, expert, versed; *as subst.,* 528.

Kundschaft, *f.,* –en, information.

künftig, *adj.,* future.

Kunst, *f.,* Künste, art.

kunstfertig, *adj.,* practised, skillful.

Kurl. Curl *or* Curle, a Scotchman, one of Mary Stuart's secretaries.

kurz (kürzer, kürzest–), *adj.,* short, brief; seit –em, a short time since, 123; *superl. as subst.,* 2628.

Kuß, *m.,* –sses, Küsse, kiss.

küssen, *tr.,* kiss.

Küste, *f.,* –n, coast, shore.

L.

Lächeln (*verbal subst.*), *n.,* –s, smile.

laden, lud, geladen, ladet (*and* lädt, *rare*) *tr.,* load; bring upon, 295; auf sich —, incur, 1555.

Lady (*Eng.*), *f.,* –ies, lady.

Lager, *n.,* –s, —, couch.

lähmen, *tr.,* lame; cripple, 2380.

Lamm, *n.,* –es, Lämmer, lamb.

lammherzig, *adj.,* lamb-hearted, lamb-like.

Land, *n.,* –es, Länder *or* Lande, land, country.

landen, *intr.* s., land, disembark.

länderlos, *adj.,* without lands *or* possessions; pauper, 1411.

Landesrecht, *n.,* –s, law of the land.

Landsitz, *m.,* –es, –e, estate.

Landsmannschaft, *f.,* –en, company (of people from the same country), 461, *cf. N.*

lang (länger, längst–), *adj. and adv.,* long.

lange, *adv.,* long, for a long time.

langentbehrt, *part. adj.,* long missed.

langsam, *adj.,* slow; *adv.,* *93.

längst (*superl. of* lang), *adv.,* long ago, long since.

langverhalten, *part. adj.,* long suppressed.

Larve, *f.,* –n, mask, 395, 2420; face, 1996.

lassen, ließ, gelassen, läßt, *tr.,* let, let alone, give up; leave, 413; *with dat. of pers.,* 43; let, permit, allow, 230, 292, *cf. N.,* 323, *cf. N.; with dependent inf.,* let (be done), have (done), cause (to be done), 318, 346, 626, 1364.

laſten, intr., weigh or rest (upon, auf and dat.).

Laſter, n., -s, —, vice, crime.

laſterhaft, adj., vicious, wicked.

Läſt(e)rung, f., -en, calumny, blasphemy.

laſtervoll, adj., vicious, profligate, abandoned.

lauern, intr., lurk, lie in wait; lauernd, part. adv., secretly, covertly, 1751.

Lauf, m., -es, Läufe, course; speed, 415; pace, *93.

laufen, lief, gelaufen, läuft, intr. ſ. and h., run.

laut, adj., loud; adv., aloud.

Laute, f., -n, lute.

leben, intr., live; survive, remain, 2182; lebend, part. adj., living; alive, 880; fem. sing. as subst., 3116; leb(e) wohl, lebt wohl, farewell, 3569, 3832, etc.

Leben, n., -s, —, life.

lebendig, adj., living; alive, 118, 3600.

Lebensgott, m., -es, -götter, god of life.

Lebensteppich, m., -s, -e, tapestry. 452, cf. N.

Lebewohl, n., -s, -s, farewell.

lebhaft, adj., lively; quick, animated, *13, *185; eager, *91.

ledig, adj., free (from, gen.).

leer, adj., empty.

Legat', m., -en, -en, legate (of the Pope), 3175, cf. N.

legen, tr., lay, put, place; refl., lie down, 1625; abate, be allayed, 2691.

lehnen, tr., intr. and refl., lean; past part. = Eng. pres. part., leaning, *100.

lehren, tr., teach; instruct, 3188.

Leib, m., -es, -er, body, person; auf — und Leben, on penalty of death, 97, cf. N.

Leibarzt, m., -es, -ärzte, house physician.

Leibeserbe, m., -n, -n, offspring, issue.

Leibwache, f., -n, body-guard.

Leichnam, m., -s, -e, dead body, corpse.

leicht, adj., light, nimble, 2078; easy, 1980.

leichtbedeckt, part. adj., lightly covered; 287, cf. N.

Leichtſinn, m., -s, indiscretion, frivolity.

leichtſinnig, adj., frivolous, wanton.

leid, indecl. adj. (used only in predicate, usually impers. with dat)., troublesome, sorrowful; es thut mir —, I am sorry for it; laßt es Euch nicht — thun, be not grieved, do not feel hurt, 1627.

leiden, litt, gelitten, tr. and intr., suffer; leidend, part. adj., suffering, 2438; adv., passively, 1837.

Leiden, n., -s, —, suffering, sorrow.

Leidende, m. and f. (decl. like adj.), sufferer.

Leidenſchaft, f., -en, passion.

leidenſchaftlich, adj., passionate.

Leidensprobe, f., -n, crucial suffering.

leihen, lieh, geliehen, tr., lend.

leiſe, adj., soft, low.

leiſten, tr., render, give, 1464, 2322; do, perform, 3803.

leiten, tr., lead, conduct; direct, 2700; start, 1883.

Leiter, f., -n, ladder.

Leitung, f., -en, lead, guidance.

lenken, tr., guide, direct, sway.

lernen, *tr.,* learn.

lesen, las, gelesen, liest, *tr. and intr.,* read.

Lesen (*verbal subst.*), *n.,* -s, reading.

Leßley. John Lesley (*or* Leslie), a Scottish Roman Catholic prelate; a partisan and adviser of Mary Stuart. Born 1527, died 1596, *cf. N.* 498.

letzt, *adj.,* last, final; recent, 612.

leuchten, *intr.,* light, shine; leuchtend, *part. adj.,* shining, bright, radiant.

leugnen, *tr.,* deny.

Leutnant (*Fr.*), *m.,* -s, -s (*and* -e), lieutenant.

Licht, *n.,* -es, -er, light.

Lichterscheinung, *f.,* -en, vision of light, heavenly vision.

lieb, *adj.,* dear, beloved.

Liebe, *f.,* love.

lieben, *tr.,* love.

liebenswert, *adj.,* lovable.

liebenswürdig, *adj.,* lovely.

lieber, *adv.,* (*comp. of* lieb, *used as comp. of* gern), rather.

Liebesband, *n.,* -s, -e, bond of love, amorous bond.

Liebesbitte, *f.,* -n, love's request.

Liebesbote, *m.,* -n, -n, messenger of love; lover's messenger, 1944.

Liebesfackel, *f.,* -n, torch of love.

Liebesglut, *f.,* flame of love; passion, 325.

liebkosen, *tr.,* caress, fondle.

Liebling, *m.,* -s, -e, favorite, darling; 318, *cf. N.*

Lied, *n.,* -es, -er, song.

liegen, lag, gelegen, *intr.* h. (*and* f.), lie, be situated.

Lilie, *f.,* -n, lily; fleur-de-lys, 19, *cf. N.*

Lippe, *f.,* -n, lip.

List, *f.,* -en, cunning, craft.

listig, *adj.,* cunning, crafty, artful; *fem. sing. as subst.,* 132, 1994.

Lob, *n.,* -es, praise.

loben, *tr.,* praise.

lobenswürdig, *adj.,* praiseworthy.

Locke, *f.,* -n, lock (of hair); curl, ringlet, 2561.

locken, *tr.,* lure, 293, 2718; entice, 1927; tempt, allure, 1646, 2381; lockend, *part. adj.,* tempting, alluring, 1665.

Lohn, *m.,* -es, Löhne, reward.

lohnen, *tr.,* reward; *intr. impers.* (*with gen.*), pay for, be worth, 2734.

Lond(o)ner, *adj.* (*invariable*), London, 2604, *cf. N.*

Lord (*Eng.*), *m.,* -s, -s, lord.

Lordmarschall, *m.,* -s, Lord Marshal, 2661, *cf. N.*

Los, *n.,* -es, -e, lot; destiny, fortune, 304.

lösen, *tr.,* loose, 2128, 2358; unloose, release, 2274; solve, 679; sich — von, let go, relinquish, 3402; *refl.,* be loosed, 2530, 2810.

Löseschlüssel, *m.,* -s, —, key of absolution.

lossprechen, sprach, gesprochen, spricht, *sep. tr.,* acquit (of, *gen.*), 353.

Losung, *f.,* -en, watchword, rallying-cry.

Loth'ringen, *n.,* -s, Lorraine.

Loth'ringer, *m.,* -s, —, Lothringian.

loth'ringisch, *adj.,* of Lorraine, Lothringian, die -en Brüder, 1266, *cf. N.*

Luft, *f.,* Lüfte, air; *pl.,* breezes, 2098.

Lüge, *f.* -n, lie, falsehood; (einen) Lügen strafen, give (one) the lie, 3979.

lügen, *intr.*, lie, tell a falsehood.

Luft, *f.*, Lüfte, joy, delight, 572; lust, 2429.

lüften, *intr. impers. (with acc.)*, desire, long.

Lüftling, *m.*, -s, -e, voluptuary.

M.

machen, *tr.*, make; — zu, make, make into, 864; *refl.*, fich — über (*with acc.*), go at, busy oneself with, *5.

Macht, *f.*, Mächte, might; power, 2422; *pl.*, powers, 3214.

mächtig, *adj.*, mighty, powerful, strong; *masc. and fem. sing. as subst.*, 781, 961; *with gen.*, having control of, able to control, 506, 2512.

Madrigal, *n.*, -s, -e, madrigal, 1090, *cf. N.*

Majestät', *f.*, -en, majesty; sovereignty, 3150.

majestätisch, *adj.*, majestic.

Mal, *n.*, -es, -e, time; mit einem —, suddenly; zum letzten-mal, for the last time, 3462.

man, *indef. pron. (oblique cases supplied by forms of* ein*)*, one, they, people, we, you; man, *with active, often best rendered by passive.*

Mangel, *m.*, -s, Mängel, want, lack; distress, hardship, 2303, 3507.

mangelhaft, *adj.*, deficient, incomplete.

mangeln, *intr.*, be wanting *or* lacking; *impers. (with dat.)*, want for, be in want of, 568.

Mann, *m.*, -es, Männer, man; husband, 2409, 3432, 3573.

Männerkraft, *f.*, -kräfte, manly *or* virile power.

Männerschönheit, *f.*, manly beauty.

Männerwille(n), *m.*, -ns, masculine will.

männlich, *adj.*, manly, manful.

Mantel, *m.*, -s, Mäntel, mantle, cloak.

Märchen, *n.*, -s, —, tale.

Mari'a, *f.*, -s *or* -riens, Mary; die spanische —, Mary Tudor, *or* "Bloody Mary" (born 1516, reigned 1553-1558), daughter of Catherine of Aragon and wife of Philip II of Spain, 102, *cf. N.;* die himmlische —, the Virgin Mary, 2814.

Marschall, *m.*, -s, -s *or* -älle, marshal.

Märtyrkrone, *f.*, -n, crown of martyrdom.

Märtyrtum, *n.*, -s, martyrdom.

Maß, *n.*, -es, -e, measure.

mäßigen, *tr.*, control, restrain.

Mäßigung, *f.*, self-control.

Mauer, *f.*, -n, wall.

Medicä'erin, *f.*, (the) Medicean Queen; Catherine de Medici (*pronounce* mä'-dē-chē), Queen of France, as wife of Henry II, mother of Francis II (Mary Stuart's first husband), Charles IX and Henry III. Born 1519, died 1589. *cf. N.* 48.

Meer, *n.*, -es, -e, sea.

mehr (*comp. of* viel), *adj.*, more; kein ... mehr ... als, no other ... than, 121; = mehrere, more than one, several, 613; nicht ... mehr, no longer.

mein, *poss. adj. and pron.*, my, mine; die Meinen, my people *or* family, 3779.

meinen, *tr. and intr.*, mean; think, 1039, 1170.

meinesgleichen, *indecl. adj.*, my equal(s).

Meinung, *f.* -en, opinion; public opinion, 1015, 3194; meaning, 3297; intention, 1051, 2947.

Meister, *m.*, -$, —, master; = Hofmeister, 3430.

Mendoza. Mendoza, ambassador of Philip II to England, 929, *cf. N.*

Menge, *f.*, -n, multitude, crowd.

Mensch, *m.*, -en, -en, man, human being; *collect.*, mankind, humanity, 478; *pl.*, people, 1428.

Menschenangesicht, *n.*, -$, -er, human face, [ity.

Menschheit, *f.*, mankind, human-

menschlich, *adj.*, human, 1325, 2421; humane, 1551.

Menschlichkeit, *f.*, humanity, humaneness.

Merkmal, *n.*, -$, -e, mark, sign.

Meßdiener, *m.*, -$, —, assistant at mass; acolyte, 289, *cf. N.*

messen, maß, gemessen, mißt, *tr.*, measure; mit den Augen —, scrutinize, *69, *139; *refl.*, compete, cope (with, mit), 765.

Messer, *n.*, -$, —, knife.

Meßgewand, *n.*, -$, -änder, vestment(s), chasuble.

Meuchelmörder, *m.*, -$, —, assassin.

Meuchelrotte, *f.*, -n, band of assassins.

Miene, *f.*, -n, mien, air; sich die — geben, affect, 1498.

mild, *adj.*, mild, gentle; lenient, merciful, 1300; *neut. superl. as subst.*, 1911.

Milde, *f.*, clemency.

mildern, *tr.*, mitigate.

minder, *adj.*, *and adv.*, less.

Minutenzeiger, *m.*, -$, —, minute-hand.

mischen, *tr.*, mix, mingle.

Mission, *f.*, -en, mission; *pl.*, missionaries, 1275.

miß'brauchen, *insep. tr.*, misuse, abuse.

mißgön'nen, *insep. tr.*, (*dat. of pers.*), begrudge.

mißhan'deln, *insep. tr.*, maltreat, ill-treat.

Mißhand'lung, *f.* -en, ill-treatment, cruelty.

mißtrau'en, *insep. intr.* (*with dat.*), distrust, mistrust.

Miß'trauen, *n.*, -$, distrust.

Mistreß (*Eng.*), *f.*, mistress.

mit, *prep.* (*dat.*), with, together with; *adv. and sep. pref.*, along, along with.

miteinander, *adv.*, with each other, together.

Mitgefangene, *m.*, (*decl. like adj.*), fellow-prisoner.

Mitleid, *n.*, -$, sympathy, compassion. [passionate.

mitleidig, *adj.*, sympathetic, com-

mitleidsvoll, *adj.*, full of pity *or* compassion, sympathetic.

Mittag, *m.*, -$, mid-day, noon; the south, 2096.

Mitte, *f.*, middle, *183; midst, 652, 1408, 2643.

Mittel, *n.*, -$ —, means, way.

mitten, *adv.*, in the middle, midway.

Mitwisser, *m.*, -$, —, accessory.

mögen, mochte, gemocht, mag, *tr. and modal aux.*, may, can, be able, like

möglich, *adj.*, possible.

Moment', *m.*, -$, -e, moment.

Monarch', *m.*, -en, -en, monarch.

Monarchie', *f.*, -(e)n, monarchy.

Monar'chin, *f.*, -innen, (female) monarch.

Monat, *m.*, -$, -e, month.

Mönch, *m.*, -es, -e, monk.

Mond, *m.*, -es, -e, moon; = Monat, month, 3314.

Monsieur (*Fr.*), *m.*, –s, Monsieur, 1104, *cf. N.*

Mord, *m.*, –es, –e, murder.

Mordanstifterin, *f.*, –innen, instigator *or* author of murder.

Mordblick, *m.*, –s, –e, murderous glance.

morden, *tr.*, murder.

Mörder, *m.*, –s, —, murderer.

Mörderhand, *f.*, –hände, murderer's *or* assassin's hand, murderous hand.

Mörderhilfe, *f.*, murderer's *or* murderous help.

Mörderin, *f.*, –innen, murderess.

Mörderstreich, *m.*, –s, –e, murderous *or* deadly thrust.

Mordgerüst, *n.*, –es, –e, murderous *or* fatal scaffold.

Mordgesell, *m.*, –en, –en, accomplice in murder, fellow-murderer.

Mordstreich, *m.*, –s, –e, murderous stroke *or* blow, murder.

Morgan. Sir Thomas Morgan, a Welshman, sometime Shrewsbury's secretary, a devoted partisan of Mary Stuart. *cf. N.*, 496.

Morgen, *m.*, –s, —, morning.

morgen, *adv.*, to-morrow.

müde, *adj.*, tired, weary of, (*gen.*).

Mühe, *f.*, –n, trouble, pains; mit —, with difficulty, 150.

Mund, *m.*, –es, –e, mouth, lips; tongue, 690, 762; mouthpiece, spokesman, 3637, 3666.

mündig, *adj.*, of age, a man, 1575, *cf. N.*

munter, *adj.*, lively, merry.

Musik', *f.*, music.

müssen, mußte, gemußt, muß, *intr. and modal aux.*, must, be obliged to, have to.

müßig, *adj.*, idle.

Muster, *n.*, –s, —, pattern, model, paragon, 466; example, 3204.

Mut, *m.*, –es, mood, humor; mir ist zu —, I feel, 2171; mind, 2175; courage, 1571; — fassen, take courage, 372.

mutig, *adj.*, courageous, bold; (*of a horse*), spirited, mettlesome, 2136.

mutlos, *adj.*, spiritless, discouraged.

mutvoll, *adj.*, courageous.

mutvollstark, *adj.*, strong in courage; *masc. sing. superl. as subst.*, the bravest and strongest, 1371.

Mutter, *f.*, Mütter, mother.

Mylady (*pronounce* mela'dy), *in address*, my lady.

Mylord (*pronounce* melord'), *in address*, my lord.

N.

nach, *prep.* (*dat.*), after, towards, to; according to, 1022; *adv. and sep. pref.*, after, behind, to, along.

nachahmen, *tr.*, imitate.

nachdem, *conj.*, after.

nachdenken, dachte, gedacht, *intr.*, reflect, meditate; nachdenkend, *part. adj.*, thoughtful, pensive; *adv.*, *55.

Nachdenken, *n.*, –s, reflection, meditation.

nacheilen, *intr.* f., hasten after.

Nachen, *m.*, –s, —, (small) boat, skiff.

nachfolgen, *intr.* f., follow after, pursue.

nachgeben, gab, gegeben, giebt, *intr.*, give way, yield (to, *dat.*).

nachlässig, *adj.*, careless.

nachreißen, riß, gerissen, *tr.*, drag after *or* along.

Nachruhm, *m.,* –8, posthumous fame; good name, 3499.

nachschallen, *intr.* (*with dat.*), resound after, ring behind, 348.

nachschlagen, schlug, geschlagen, schlägt, *tr.,* refer to, consult (a book), 527.

nachsehen, sah, gesehen, sieht, *intr.,* look after.

Nachsicht, *f.,* forbearance, indulgence.

nächst (*superl. of* nahe), adj., next, nearest, closest, 2839; readiest, 1861, 2628 (*neut. sing. as subst.*).

Nacht, *f.,* Nächte, night; heute —, last night, 1624, *cf. N.*

nächtlich, *adj.,* of night; sable, sombre, 3367.

nachts, *adv.,* at night, by night, o' nights.

Nacken, *m.,* –8, —, neck.

nagen, *tr. and intr.,* gnaw (at, an *with dat.*).

nahe (näher, nächst–), *adj.,* near, nigh, close, close by.

Nähe, *f.,* nearness, 3704; presence, 1527, 2467; in der —, near by, at hand, 3189.

nahen, *intr.* f., *and refl.,* draw near, approach.

nähern, *tr.,* bring near; *refl.,* draw near, approach.

nähren, *tr.,* feed, nourish; foster, 1588; cherish; 829, 1264; support, 2110.

Name, *m.,* –n8, –n, name; reputation, 1621.

namenlos, *adj.,* nameless; unspeakable, 1953.

nämlich, *adj.,* (the) same, identical.

Nation′, *f.,* –en, nation.

Natter, *f.,* –n, adder.

Natur′, *f.,* –en, nature.

Naturzweck, *m.,* –8, –e, intent *or* purpose of nature.

Nau. Nau, a Frenchman, one of Mary Stuart's secretaries, 884, *cf. N.*

Nebelberg, *m.,* –8, –e, *pl.,* misty mountains, 2094.

neben, *prep.* (*dat. and acc.*), by, beside, near, close.

nebst, *prep.* (*dat.*), together with.

Neffe, *m.,* –n, –n, nephew.

nehmen, nahm, genommen, nimmt, *tr.,* take, receive; take from (*dat.*), 50, 2291.

Neid, *m.,* –es, envy.

neidisch, *adj.,* envious.

neigen, *tr.,* bend, incline; *refl.,* bow, *56.

Neigung, *f.,* –en, inclination, 1975; disposition, 1328; affection, 2071, 2921, 3829.

nein, *neg. adv.,* no.

nennen, nannte, genannt, *tr.,* name, 2671, 3359, *etc.;* call, 1537, 2307, *etc.;* mention, 748, 1856.

Netz, *n.,* –es, –e, net; snare, 1751.

neu, *adj,* new; was —, 148, *cf. N.,* late, recent, 1485; *adv.,* anew, again, 1810; von neuem, anew, 3952.

neulich, *adv.,* lately, recently.

Neumond, *m.,* –8, –e, new moon.

nicht, *adv.,* not; gar —, not at all; noch —, not yet; — mehr, no longer.

nichts, *indecl. indef. pron.,* naught, nothing, not anything.

nichtswürdig, *adj.,* worthless, contemptible; *masc. sing. as subst.,* 2737.

nie, *adv.,* never; noch —, never yet.

nieder, *adv. and sep. pref.,* down, downwards.

niederfallen, fiel, gefallen, *intr.*

niebergeben, ging, gegangen, *intr.*
f., go down; auf= und —, walk
up and down, *185.

niederfnieen, *intr.*, kneel (down).

niederlaffen, ließ, gelaffen, läßt,
tr., let down; *refl.*, fall, *65.

niederlegen, *tr.*, lay down.

niederfchlagen, fchlug, gefchlagen,
fchlägt, *tr.*, strike down, smite,
fell, 2466; refute, disprove,
2947; befall, 3236.

niederfchreiben, fchrieb, gefchrie-
ben, *tr.*, write down.

niederfehen, fah, gefehen, fieht,
intr., look down.

niederftürzen, *tr.*, hurl down;
prostrate, 2264; *intr.* f., fall
down, fall prostrate (before,
dat.), 3621.

niederwerfen, warf, geworfen,
wirft, *tr.*, throw down; *refl.*,
cast oneself down, prostrate
oneself, 2248.

niedlich, *adj.*, neat, pretty.

niedrig, *adj.*, low; base, 307,
744; *adv.*, basely, 155.

niemals, *adv.*, never.

niemand, *pron.*, no one, nobody.

nimmer, *adv.*, never.

nimmermehr, *adv.*, never, never
more, never at all; *often =
emphatic* nimmer, *as* 1512,
2194; by no means, 1027,
1101.

nirgends, *adv.*, nowhere.

noch, *adv.*, yet, as yet, still, besides, in addition, more; —
nicht, not yet; — nie, never
yet; — ein, one more, 251.

noch, *conj.*, nor, 3186.

Norden, *m.*, –s, north.

Norfolk. Thomas Howard,
Duke of Norfolk, an English
nobleman of high rank who

sought to release Mary Stuart
and marry her. Born 1536,
beheaded 1572; *cf. N.* 73.

Not, *f.*, Nöte, need; necessity,
809; not thun, be necessary *or*
needful (for, *dat.*), 481.

Nota'rius, *m.*, —, -ta'rien,
notary, 190, *cf. N.*

Notdurft, *f.*, necessaries, necessity; kleine —, needed trifle,
39.

nötigen, *tr.*, necessitate; urge,
compel, 583.

notwendig, *adj.*, necessary, needful. *neut. sing. as subst.*, 1553;
adv., necessarily, 1705.

Notwendigkeit, *f.*, necessity.

nun, *adv.*, now; *as interj.*,
well!

nunmehr, *adv.*, now, by this
time.

nur, *adv.*, only, merely; even,
979.

Nutzen, *m.*, –s, use; profit, advantage, 794; benefit, 851.

O.

O, *interj.*, O! oh!

ob, *prep.* (*dat. archaic*) *and adv.*
(*as sep. pref. in compounds*),
over, above.

ob, *conj.*, whether, if; to see
whether, 1480.

ober-, *adj.*, upper.

Oberhaus, *n*, –es, Upper House,
(*in England*) House of Lords.

Oberrichter, *m.*, –s, Chief Justice.

obgleich, *conj.*, although; *sometimes written* ob ... gleich, 1920.

obliegen, lag, gelegen, *intr.* (*with
dat., usually impers.*), be in-
cumbent upon, be one's duty.

obfiegend, *part. adj.*, victorious.

oder, *conj.*, or.

offen, *adj.*, open; open to (*dat.*), 361.

offenbar, *adj.*, manifest, evident, public; *adv.*, openly, 631.

offenba'ren, *tr.*, reveal.

öffentlich, *adj.*, open; public, 2049; *adv.*, openly, 1923; publicly, in public, 1106, 1123.

Offizier', *m.*, –s, –e, officer.

offiziös', *adj.*, official; *adv.*, formally, *123.

öffnen, *tr.*, open; *refl.*, open (*intr.*), 2810, 3397; unbosom oneself, 176, 672.

oft, *adv.*, often, oft.

Oheim, *m.*, –s, —, uncle.

Ohm (*contraction of* Oheim), *m.*, –s, –e, uncle.

Öhm (= Oheim), *m.*, –s, –e, uncle.

ohne, *prep.* (*acc.*), without.

ohngefähr (*now* ungefähr), *adj.*, casual, accidental; von —, by chance, 2062.

ohnlängst (*now* unlängst), *adv.*, lately, not long since.

Ohnmacht, *f.*, weakness, impotency, 3165; powerlessness, 3508.

ohnmächtig, *adj.*, impotent, vain, 2246; weak, powerless; *fem. sing. as subst.*, 3241; fainting, *101; swooning, unconscious, *183; — werden, faint, swoon.

Ohr, *n.*, –es, –en, ear.

Ölbaum, *m.*, –s, –bäume, olive tree, 831, *cf. N.*

Opfer, *n.*, –s, —, offering; sacrifice, 1251, 3028, 3738, *etc.*; victim, 832, 859, 1021, 1557, *etc.*; ein — bringen, make a sacrifice, 963.

opfern, *tr.*, sacrifice; offer, 3747.

Ora'kel, *n.*, –s, —, oracle.

Orden, *m.*, –s, —, order (of nobility).

Ordnung, *f.*, –en, order, arrangement.

Organ', *n.*, –s, organ; instrument, 740.

Ort, *m.*, –es, –e *and* Örter, place.

O'zean, *m.*, –s, –e, ocean; sea, 2097, *cf. N.*

P.

Page (*Fr.*), *m.*, –n, –n, page, attendant.

Paket', *n.*, –s, –e, package, parcel.

Palast', *m.*, –es, –äste, palace.

Papier', *n.*, –s, –e, paper.

Papist', *m.*, –en, –en, papist.

Papis'tin, *f.*, –innen (female) papist.

Papst, *m.*, –es, Päpste, pope.

Papsttum, *n.*, –s, papacy.

Paris' (*pronounce* pa-rees'), *n.*, Paris.

Park, *m.*, –es, –e *and* –s, park.

Parlament', *n.*, –s, –e, parliament.

Parry. Dr. William Parry, a Welshman, instigator of a plot to murder Elizabeth and put Mary on the throne, 70, *cf. N.*

Partei', *f.*, –en, party.

Partei'enhaß, *m.*, –sses, partisan hate.

Paß, *m.*, –sses, Pässe, pass, passport.

Pause, *f.*, –n, pause.

Peer (*Eng.*), –s, –s, peer.

peinigen, *tr.*, torment, harass, 1788, 2023; torture, 2026.

peinlich, *adj.*, painful.

Percy. Thomas Percy, Earl of Northumberland, executed 1572 for conspiring against Elizabeth.

Perle, *f.*, –n, pearl.

Person', *f.*, –en, person; character, part, 2725.

Peter, Sankt, Saint Peter, 2360, *cf. N.*

Pfand, *n.,* –es, Pfänder, pledge, 2357; symbol, token, 3602; trust, 4010.

Pfeil, *m.,* –es, –e, arrow, shaft.

pflanzen, *tr.,* plant.

pflegen, pflog, gepflogen, *tr.,* carry on, conduct, 2979; *intr.* (*with gen.*), take, enjoy, 3422.

pflegen, *intr.,* be accustomed *or* wont, 269, 2952.

Pflegerin, *f.,* –innen, foster-mother, nurse.

Pflicht, *f.,* –en, duty, 492, 1181, 1383, *etc.;* obligation, 945, 1209, 2354; *pl.,* discipline, 410.

Pforte, *f.,* –n, gate.

Pilgerschar, *f.,* –en, throng of pilgrims.

Plagegeist, *m.,* –es, –er, tormenting spirit.

Plan, *m.,* –es, Pläne (*rarely* –e), plan.

planvoll, *adj.,* carefully planned; *adv.,* systematically, artfully, 870.

Platz, *m.,* –es, Plätze, place.

Plauderer, *m.,* –s, —, prattler.

plötzlich, *adj.,* sudden; *adv.,* suddenly, on a sudden.

Pöbel, *m.,* –s, mob, rabble; populace, 738, 3061.

pochen, *intr.,* knock; auf etwas —, boast of, presume on, 2022.

Pochen (*verbal subst.*), *n.,* –s, rapping, pounding.

Possenspiel, *n.,* –s, –e, farce.

Post, *f.,* –en, post; relay, 1141.

Posten, *m.,* –s, —, post, place.

Pracht, *f.,* splendor.

Prachtgerät, *n.,* –s, splendid (silver) plate.

prächtig, *adj.,* magnificent, splendid.

prägen, *tr.,* stamp; enact, 779.

Prahler, *m.,* –s, —, boaster, braggart.

prangen, *intr.,* be splendid, shine; prangend, *part. adj.,* splendid, 304.

Prediger, *m.,* –s, —, preacher.

Predigtstube, *f.,* –n, preaching-room, meeting-place, conventicle, 414, *cf. N.*

Preis, *m.,* –es, –e, prize.

preisen, pries, gepriesen, *tr.,* praise; gepriesen, *part. adj.,* lauded, 416; preisend, *part. adv.,* with praise, 769; glücklich —, call happy, 1779.

preisgeben, gab, gegeben, giebt, *sep. tr.,* expose (to, *dat.*), 312, *cf. N.*

pressen, *tr.,* press.

Priester, *m.,* –s, —, priest.

priesterlich, *adj.,* priestly.

Primas, *m.,* —, —, primate, archbishop.

Probe, *f.,* –n, proof.

prophezei'en, *tr.,* prophesy.

Protestant', *m.,* –en, –en, Protestant.

Prozeß', *m.,* –sses, –sse, process, lawsuit; case, 236; procedure, trial, 999.

prüfen, *tr.,* prove; examine, 1458; try, 2078.

Prüfung, *f.,* –en, trial, ordeal.

Prüfungsjahr, *n.,* –s, –e, year of probation.

Prunk, *m.,* –es, pomp, show.

Pult, *n.* (*and m.*), –es, –e, desk.

Punkt, *m.,* –es, –e, point.

Purita'ner, *m.,* –s, —, Puritan, 414, *cf. N.*

Putz, *m.,* –es, finery, adornment.

Q.

Qual, *f.*, -en, torture, torment.
quälen, *tr.*, torment, torture; ge=
quält, *part. adj.*, tormented,
134; *as subst.*, 3917; harass,
worry, 1429, 3310.
Quelle, *f.*, -n, source, 535;
spring, 3628.
quellen, quoll, gequollen, quillt,
intr., f., spring, well; stream,
437.

R.

Rache, *f*, revenge, vengeance.
rachefordernd, *part. adj.*, de-
manding vengeance.
Rachegeist, *m.*, -es, -er, avenging spirit.
rächen, *tr.*, avenge; *refl.*, revenge
oneself *or* itself, 321.
Rächer, *m.*, -s, —, avenger.
Rachgedanke, *m.*, -ns, -n, re-
vengeful thought, thought of
vengeance.
ragen, *intr.*, tower, rise.
Rand, *m.*, -es, Ränder, edge;
verge, brink, 3588; brim, 628.
Rang, *m.*, -es, Ränge, rank,
station; standing, 1712; position, 2910.
Rank, *m.*, -es, Ränke (*now used
in plural only*), intrigue, mach-
ination.
ränkespinnend, *part. adj.*, intriguing, machinating.
ränkevoll, *adj.*, intriguing, artful.
rasch, *adj.*, quick, swift; rash, 1868.
rasen, *intr.*, rave, be mad, 2590;
rasend, *part. adj.*, mad; *fem.
sing. as subst.*, frenzied woman,
2444; *neut. sing. as subst.*,
mad *or* desperate deed, 2623.
Rasende, *m. and f.* (*decl. like
adj*), madman, maniac.

Raserei, *f.*, -en, frenzy, madness.
Rat, *m.*, -es, Räte, counsel, advice, 229, 544, 1350, 1450, *etc.*;
expedient, 1300; plan, 2058;
council, 1399; counsellor, 4014;
— holen, get counsel, 526.
raten, riet, geraten, rät, *tr.* (*dat.
of pers.*), counsel, advise.
ratlos, *adj.*, helpless, perplexed.
Rätsel, *n.*, -s, —, riddle, mystery.
Raub, *m.*, -es, robbery; abduction, 2575; mit Eurem -e,
by robbing you, 202, *cf. N.*
rauben, *tr.* (*dat. of pers.*), rob.
Räuberin, *f.*, -innen, robber,
usurper, 1289.
rauh, *adj.*, rough, rude.
Raum, *m.*, -es, Räume, space,
2093; room, 3896; opportunity, 1896.
räumen, *tr.*, vacate, leave.
Rechenschaft, *f.*, account; ac-
counting, 2695, 3695; responsibility, 735, 3331.
Rechnung, *f.*, -en, account.
recht, *adj.*, right, true, real; die
Rechte, the right hand, 2255;
— machen, account to, satisfy,
3196.
Recht, *n.*, -es, -e, right, 530, 905,
1023, *etc.*; claim, 530, 852;
justice, 234, 739, 1603; law,
917, 957; Rechtens, according
to law, 915, *cf. N.*; mit —,
rightly, 507; recht haben, be
right, 555, 1905.
rechtfertigen, *insep. tr.*, justify.
Rechtsanspruch, *m.*, -s, -üche,
legal claim, title.
Rechtsform, *f.* -en, process of
law.
Rechtsgelehrte, *m.* (*decl. like
adj.*), one learned in the law,
jurist.
Rechtsspruch, *m.*, -s, -üche, verdict, sentence.

Rechtsstreit, *m.,* –s, litigation; action, trial, 986.

Rede, *f.,* –n, speech, 489; words, *87, 3440; matter, question, 958, 1441; — stehen, answer to (auf *with acc.*), 224; (*dat. of pers.*), 2738.

reden, *tr. and intr.,* speak.

redlich, *adj.,* upright; honest, 164, 2938; *masc. sing. as subst.,* the worthy man, 513.

Redlichkeit, *f.,* integrity, honesty.

Redner, *m.,* –s, —, speaker, orator.

Rednerkunst, *f.,* oratory.

regen, *tr. and refl.,* stir, move.

Regentenstamm, *m.,* –s, –stämme, royal line.

regieren, *tr. and intr.,* rule; reign, 2378; govern, 795.

Regierung, *f.,* –en, government; reign, 908, 3786.

Regung, *f.,* –en, emotion.

reich, *adj.,* rich.

Reich, *n.,* –es, –e, realm, kingdom.

reichen, *tr.,* extend (to, *dat.*), 1547, 2255; give, 355, *177; *intr.,* reach, extend, 1141.

Reichsgesetz, *n.,* –es, –e, law of the land *or* realm.

Reichsreligion, *f.,* –en, state religion.

Reichsschluß, *m.,* –sses, –üsse, royal decree, Act of Parliament.

Reichsverräter, *m.,* –s, —, traitor to the realm.

Reichtum, *m.,* –s, –tümer, riches; treasure, *158.

Reif, *m.,* –es, –e, ring; band, 1214.

reihen, *tr.,* put in a row; *refl.,* range oneself, take one's place, 2137.

reimen, *tr.,* lit. rhyme; explain, reconcile, 2129.

Reims. Rheims *or* Reims (*pronounce* rēmz), a city in France, *cf. N.* 493.

rein, *adj.,* clean; 1053, 1677; pure, 1291; spotless, 1058, 3618.

reinigen, *tr.,* clean, clear, 927, 2992.

Reise, *f.,* –n, journey.

reisen, *intr.* s. *and* h., journey, travel.

reißen, riß, gerissen, *tr.,* tear, snatch; drag, 3929; carry, 424, 1932.

Reiz, *m.,* –es, –e, charm.

reizen, *tr.,* excite, irritate; provoke, 298, 3089; gereizt, *part. adj.,* exasperated, 2441; rei-zend, *part. adj.,* charming, 1132, 1948.

Reizung, *f.,* –en, charm.

Religion, *f.,* –en, religion.

rennen, rannte, gerannt, *intr.* s. *and* h., run.

Ressort (*Fr.,* t *silent*), *m.,* –s, –s, spring; spring drawer, *6.

Rest, *m.,* –es, –e, rest, remainder.

retten, *tr.,* rescue, save; rettend, *part. adj.,* rescuing, 2114.

Retter, *m.,* –s, —, deliverer.

Rettung, *f.,* –en, rescue, 1641; deliverance, 660, 1735; salvation, 2758.

Rettungsbrücke, *f.,* –n, bridge of deliverance.

Rettungshand, *f.,* –hände, rescuing hand.

Reu(e), *f.,* repentance, penitence; mit jahrelanger —, with years of penitence, 282.

reuen, *tr.* (*usually impers. with acc.*), repent, regret.

reuvoll, *adj.,* repentant.

Richmond. Earl of Richmond, the title of Henry VII before his accession. Great-grandfather of Mary Stuart and grandfather of Elizabeth; founder of the Tudor line. Born 1457, reigned 1485—1509. *cf. N.*, 837.

richten, *tr.*, direct, 1488, *101 ; turn, cast (upon, auf *and acc.*), 2240; judge, 62, 704, 971, 1069, *etc.;* ins Werk —, effect, accomplish, 2958.

Richter, *m.*, -s, —, judge.

Richterhof, *m.*, -s, -höfe, court, tribunal.

Richterschwert, *n.*, -s, -er, sword of judgment.

Richterspruch, *m.*, -s, -üche, judgment, 697 ; sentence (of a judge), 3033.

Richterstuhl, *m.*, -s, -ühle, judgment-seat, tribunal.

Riegel, *m.*, -s, —, bolt.

Riesenkraft, *f.*, giant strength.

Ring, *m.*, -es, -e, ring.

ringen, rang, gerungen, *intr.*, struggle.

rings, *adv.*, round about, all round.

Ritter, *m.*, -s, —, knight.

ritterlich, *adj.*, knightly; chivalrous, 951.

Ritterschaft, *f.*, gallantry.

Ritterspiel, *n.* -s, -e, tournament.

Rizzio. David Rizzio (*or* Riccio), an Italian in the service of Mary Stuart, first as court musician and subsequently as private secretary and adviser. Murdered at the instigation of Darnley, 1566. *cf. N.*, 320.

roh, *adj.*, rude, coarse; brutal, 969; *masc. sing. as subst.*, brute, 262.

Rohr, *n.*, -es, -e, reed.

Rolle, *f.*, -n, rôle, part.

Rom, *n.*, -s, Rome.

römisch, *adj.*, Romish.

Rosamund, *f.* Rosamond, the name given by Schiller to one of Mary Stuart's women, 3550, *cf. N.*

Rose, *f.*, -n, rose.

Rosenkranz, *m.*, -es, -kränze, rosary.

Roß, *n.*, -sses, -sse, horse, steed.

Roße, Bischof von. Bishop of Ross (a county in northern Scotland) *see* Leßley, *and cf. N.*, 498.

ruchlos, *adj.*, reckless, unscrupulous.

rücken, *tr.*, move; *intr.*, s., move.

Rücken, *m.*, -s, —, back.

Rückfall, *m.*, -s, -fälle, relapse.

rückwärts, *adv.*, backwards.

Rückweg, *m.*, -s, -e, way back, return.

Ruf, *m.*, -es, -e, call, summons, 541; fame, 1047; reputation, 1058, 2426; mächtigen -es, *adv., gen.*, with mighty blast, 2135.

rufen, rief, gerufen, *tr.*, call, 1449, 1577; summon, 334, 3335.

Ruhe, *f.*, rest, quiet; — schaffen, get relief, 624.

ruhen, *intr.*, rest.

ruhig, *adj.*, quiet.

Ruhm, *m.*, -es, fame, 1311, 2416. 3907; glory, 1157, 1187, 1468, *etc.*

ruhmbegierig, *adj.*, ambitious.

rühmen, *tr.*, praise, 1996; *refl.*, boast, 3451.

ruhmvoll, *adj.*, glorious, illustrious.

rühren, *tr.*, move, 2274, 2584; touch, 1543, 1827, 2180; rührend, *part. adj.*, moving, 2571; touching, 504.

rüsten, *tr.*, equip.

Rüsthaus, *n.*, -es, -häuser, arsenal.

S.

Saal, *m.*, –es, Säle, room.

Sache, *f.*, –n, thing; affair, 2766; business, 693; matter, 844, 1869, 3186, *etc.;* cause, 768, 1600; bei der — bleiben, stick to the point, 928.

Säge, *f.*, –n, saw.

sagen, *tr.*, say, tell.

Sakrament', *n.*, –s, –e, sacrament.

sammeln, *tr.*, gather, 2791; collect, compose, 3099; gain, 1670; *refl.*, compose oneself, 1386.

sanft, *adj.*, gentle.

Sänfte, *f.*, –n, sedan-chair.

Sanftmut, *f.*, meekness.

Sänger, *m.*, –s, —, singer; musician, 319.

Sankt, *adj.* (*only before proper names, uninflected*), Saint, St.

Sankt Barthel'emi, die, Saint Bartholomew; a massacre of French Huguenots beginning on the night of St. Bartholomew's Day (Aug. 24), 1572; 2352, *cf. N.*

Sankt Peter, St. Peter, 2360 *cf. N.*

Sarg, *m.*, –es, Särge, coffin.

Säule, *f.*, –n, column, pillar.

säumen, *intr.*, delay.

Säumen (*verbal subst.*), *n.*, –s, delay.

Sauvage (*Fr.*). Savage, the name given by Schiller to the fictitious assailant of Elizabeth, 2613, *cf. N.*

Schade(n), *m.*, –ns, Schäden, damage, mischief; schade! pity!

schaden, *intr.* (*dat. of pers.*), injure, harm, 899; do harm, 22.

schaffen, schuf, geschaffen, *tr.*, create, make.

schaffen, *tr.*, get, obtain, 624; *intr.*, be busy, be at work, 13.

Schafott', *n.*, –s, –e, scaffold.

Schale, *f.*, –n, bowl, dish; vessel, *172.

Schall, *m.*, –es, –e, sound.

schalten, *intr.*, dispose, direct (über *and acc.*), 3544.

Scham, *f.*, shame, sense of shame, 3850.

Schamerröten, *n.*, –s, blushing.

schamhaft, *adj.*, bashful.

schamlos, *adj.*, shameless.

Schande, *f.*, shame, disgrace; zu schanden machen, bring to grief, confound, 2658.

schänden, *tr.*, disgrace.

schändlich, *adj.*, disgraceful, infamous, shameful, 2660, 3411; *as subst.*, 311, 2895.

Schandthat, *f.*, –en, infamy.

Schar, *f.*, –en, band, 663, host, 139.

scharf (schärfer, schärfst–), *adj.*, sharp, keen.

Scharfblick, *m.*, –s, keen glance, acuteness.

schärfen, *tr.*, sharpen.

Schatten, *m.*, –s, —, shade, 272; shadow, 830, 2382, 3959.

Schatz, *m.*, –es, Schätze, treasure.

schätzen, *tr.*, value.

Schatzmeister, *m.*, –s, —, treasurer.

Schau, *f.*, show, view; zur — stellen, expose to view, exhibit, 345.

Schauder, *m.*, –s, shudder, horror, dread.

schauderhaft, *adj.*, horrible, dreadful.

schaudern, *intr.*, shudder; schaudernd, *part. adv.*, with dread, 3135.

schauen, *tr.*, see, behold; *intr.*, look, 1249.

Schauspiel, *n.*, -s, -e, spectacle.

Scheide, *f.*, -n, sheath, scabbard.

scheiden, schied, geschieden, *tr.*, separate, cut off, 213; es muß geschieden sein, we must part, 3796; *intr.*, f., depart, 2399, 3583, 3681, *etc.*

Schein, *m.*, -es, -e, brightness, splendor, 446; appearance, semblance, 973, 1901, 2423; appearances, 1598, 2925.

scheinen, schien, geschienen, *intr.*, shine; seem, 1601, 1775; appear, 974.

schelten, schalt, gescholten, schilt, *tr.*, scold, 1792; chide, blame, 271, 1968.

Schemel, *m.*, -s, —, foot-stool.

schenken, *tr.*, give.

Schergenamt, *n.*, -s, bailiff's office.

Scherz, *m.*, -es, -e, jest.

scheu, *adj.*, shy, fearful; *adv.*, timidly, *21.

Scheu, *f.*, shyness, timidity; respect, 338, *cf. N.*

scheuchen, *tr.*, frighten away.

scheuen, *tr.*, fear; shun, avoid, 2719.

schicken, *tr.*, send.

Schicksal, *n.*, -s, fate, destiny.

Schickung, *f.*, -en, dispensation, providence.

schießen, schoß, geschossen, *tr.*, shoot; dart, *109.

Schiff, *n.*, -es, -e, ship; ist zu —, has taken ship, 4033.

Schiffbruch, *m.*, -s, -brüche, shipwreck.

schiffen, *intr.* f. *and* h., sail.

schildern, *tr.*, depict, portray.

Schilderung, *f.*, -en, description.

Schimmer, *m.*, -s, —, gleam, 1229; splendor, 1963.

schimmerlos, *adj.*, without splendor, unpretentious.

schimmern, *intr.*, shimmer, glitter.

schimpflich, *adj.*, shameful, 96; scandalous, outrageous, 21, 2304.

Schlachtopfer, *n.*, -s, —, victim.

Schlaf, *m.*, -es, sleep.

Schläfe, *f.*, -n, temple.

schlafen, schlief, geschlafen, schläft, *intr.*, sleep.

Schlag, *m.*, -es, Schläge, blow.

schlagen, schlug, geschlagen, schlägt, *tr.*, strike, smite, 1711, 3628; *intr.*, strike, 2035; beat, throb, 1305.

Schlange, *f.*, -n, serpent, snake.

Schlangenhaar, *n.*, -s, -e, snaky hair *or* locks.

schlau, *adj.*, cunning, crafty.

schlaugefaßt, *part. adj.*, cunningly worded *or* drawn.

schlecht, *adj.*, bad, low, base; mean, humble, 35, *cf. N.*; *masc. as subst.*, villain, 2805.

schleichen, schlich, geschlichen, *intr.*, f., slink, steal (away).

Schleier, *m.*, -s, —, veil; im —, veiled, *11.

schleifen, *tr.*, drag.

schleudern, *tr.*, hurl.

schleunig, *adj.*, quick, speedy; auf das -ste, as quickly as possible, 2667.

schlicht, *adj.*, plain, simple, homely.

schließen, schloß, geschlossen, *tr.*, close, 1313; conclude, 606, 1488; *part. adj.*, concluded, 2682; enclose, embrace, 429; sich — an (*with acc.*), unite with, join, 459, 500.

schlimm, *adj.*, bad; *comp. as subst.*, 2701; *superl.*, 1599.

Schloß, *n.*, -sses, Schlösser, castle; lock, 2359.

schluchzen, *intr.*, sob.

Schlummer, *m.*, -s, slumber.

Schlund, *m.*, -es, Schlünde, gulf, abyss.

schlüpfrig, *adj.*, slippery.

Schluß, *m.*, -sses, Schlüsse, end, conclusion; decree, act (of Parliament), 1420.

Schlüssel, *m.*, -s, —, key; — eines Weibes, petticoat dominion, 1937.

Schmach, *f.*, ignominy, 567, 2054, 2249; dishonor, 3491; disgrace, 345.

schmachvoll, *adj.*, ignominious; in ignominy, 2254.

schmachten, *intr.*, languish.

schmählich, *adj.*, ignominious, disgraceful.

schmal, *adj.*, narrow.

schmeicheln, *intr.* (*with dat.*), flatter, 1998; pander to, 776, 3192; schmeichelnd, *part. adj. and adv.*, by my enticements, 293; coaxing, *104.

Schmeicheln (*verbal subst.*), *n.*, -s, flattery, 1804, 1994.

Schmeichelrede, *f.*, flattering words.

Schmeichler, *m.*, -s, —, flatterer.

schmeichlerisch, *adj.*, flattering, fawning, cajoling.

schmeidigen, *tr.*, make pliable; geschmeidigt, *part. adj.*, softened, subdued, 2244.

schmelzen, schmolz, geschmolzen, schmilzt, *intr.*, s., melt, dissolve.

schmelzen, *tr.*, melt, dissolve, 258.

Schmerz, *m.*, -es, -en, pain, 1952; grief, *150, *158.

schmerzenvoll, *adj.*, painful.

schmerzlich, *adj.*, painful.

schmerzvoll, *adj.*, painful.

schmieden, *tr.*, forge (*as metal*), 1272; devise, concoct, 1479.

Schmuck, *m.* -es, -e, adornment, 24; decoration, 1219; jewels, 2.

schmücken, *tr.*, adorn.

Schmuckkästchen, *n.*, -s, —, jewel-casket.

schneiden, schnitt, geschnitten, *tr.*, cut.

schnell, *adj.*, fast, swift; eine -e Hand, 197, *cf. N.; adv.*, quickly, 108, 219.

schon, *adv.*, already.

schön, *adj.*, beautiful; fair, 92.

schonen, *tr. and intr.* (*with gen.*), spare, 451, 1880.

Schönheit, *f.*, -en, beauty.

Schönheitsgarten, *m.* -s,-gärten, garden of beauty.

Schönheitsglanz, *m.*, -es, splendor of beauty.

Schonung, *f.*, -en, mercy.

schonungslos, *adj.*, pitiless, relentless.

Schöpfung, *f.*, creation.

Schoß, *m.*, -es, Schöße, lap; bosom, 486.

Schotte, *m.*, -n, -n, Scotchman.

schottisch, *adj.*, Scotch.

Schottland, *n.*, -s, Scotland.

Schrank, *m.*, -es, Schränke, cabinet, chest of drawers.

Schranke, *f.*, -n, barrier; bar, 95, 218, 3441; *pl.*, bounds, 1558.

schrecken, *tr.*, frighten, terrify; alarm, 3393.

Schrecken, *m.*, -s, —, terror; alarm, 2642, 3055.

Schreckensauftrag, *m.*, -s, -aufträge, dread errand.

Schreckenskraft, *f.*, power of terror.

schreckenvoll, *adj.*, terrified.

schrecklich, *adj.*, fearful, horrible; *masc. sing. as subst.*, 329; *neut.*, 366.

Schrecknis, *n.* -nisses, -nisse, terror.

ſchreiben, ſchrieb, geſchrieben, *tr. and intr.,* write.

Schreiben, *n.,* -ſ, —, letter.

Schreiber, *m.,* -ſ, —, secretary.

ſchreien, ſchrie, geſchrieen, *intr.,* scream, cry.

ſchreiten, ſchritt, geſchritten, *intr.* ſ., stride.

Schrift, *f.,* -en, paper, document, 3269, 3309, 3966, *145; *pl.,* papers, 14, 149, 161, *6.

ſchriftlich, *adj.,* written; *adv.,* in writing, 3420.

Schritt, *m.,* -eſ, -e, steps, 3905; *pl.,* doings, 2775.

ſchroff, *adj.,* rough, harsh.

Schuld, *f.,* -en, debt, fault; = Sünde, sin, 285, 2505; guilt, 294, 1363; ſchuld geben (*dat.*), charge with, 1496.

ſchuldig, *adj.,* indebted; — ſein, owe, 1058; guilty, 579; *masc. sing. as subst.,* 353; *fem. sing. superl. as subst.,* 82; ſchuldigſt, *superl. of adv.,* most dutifully, 2664.

ſchuldlos, *adj.,* guiltless, innocent.

Schuldnerin, *f.,* -innen (female) debtor.

Schule, *f.,* -n, school.

Schulter, *f.,* -n, shoulder.

ſchütteln, *tr.,* shake.

Schutz, *m.,* -eſ, protection (from, vor *with dat.*), 89, 719, 943, 1443; defense, 949, 1607.

Schütze, *m.,* -n, -n, shooter, marksman.

ſchützen, *tr.,* protect.

ſchwach (ſchwächer, ſchwächſt-), *adj.,* weak; *fem. sing. as subst.,* 961, 1369.

Schwäche, *f.,* -n, weakness.

Schwachheit, *f.,* -en, weakness, frailty.

Schwager, *m.,* -ſ, Schwäger, brother-in-law.

ſchwank, *adj.,* wavering, tottering.

ſchwärmen, *intr.,* be carried away (by fancy *or* enthusiasm), dream, 2106.

Schwärmer, *m.,* -ſ, —, fanatic.

Schwärmereifer, *m.,* -ſ, fanaticism.

ſchwarz (ſchwärzer, ſchwärzeſt-), *adj.,* black.

ſchwärzen, *tr.,* blacken.

ſchwatzen, *intr.,* talk, prate.

ſchweben, *intr.,* hover, float.

ſchweigen, ſchwieg, geſchwiegen, *intr.,* be silent, keep silence.

Schweigen, *n.,* -ſ, silence.

Schwelle, *f.,* -n, threshold.

ſchwer, *adj.,* heavy, 296, 648; hard, 283, 1052, 1181, 3450; difficult, 545; grave, 222; grievous, 1545; heinous, 100; *adv.,* sorely, grievously, 2254, 2281.

Schwermut, *f.,* melancholy.

Schwert, *n.,* -eſ, -er, sword.

Schweſter, *f.,* -n, sister, 162, *cf. N.*

ſchweſterlich, *adj.,* sisterly.

ſchwierig, *adj.,* difficult, troublesome.

ſchwimmen, ſchwamm, geſchwommen, *intr.* h. *and* ſ., swim.

Schwindel, *m.,* -ſ, dizziness, dizzy madness, 1932.

ſchwinden, ſchwand, geſchwunden, *intr.* ſ., vanish, 1221, 2453; fail (in health), be in a decline, 1059.

Schwinge, *f.,* -n, wing.

ſchwingen, ſchwang, geſchwungen, *tr.,* swing; *refl.,* swing oneself, vault, 2136; soar, 3484.

ſchwören, ſchwor *and* ſchwur, geſchworen, *tr.* (*and intr.*), swear.

Schwur, *m.,* -eſ, Schwüre, oath; vow, 1942, 2835.

Seele, *f.,* –n, soul.

Segen, *m.,* –8, —, blessing, 544; prosperity, 1164; sign of the cross, *176.

segenbringend, *part. adj.,* bringing blessing, beneficent.

segenvoll, *adj.,* blessed, blissful.

Segler, *m.,* –8, —, ship.

segnen, *tr.,* bless.

Segnung, *f.,* –en, blessing.

sehen, sah, gesehen, sieht, *tr. and intr.,* see; sieh! look! see! 17.

sehr, *adv.,* very, much; so —, so greatly; very well, 788.

seiden, *adj.,* silken.

sein, war, gewesen, bin, *intr.* s., be, exist; *past aux.,* have, be.

sein, *poss. adj. and pron.,* his, its.

seinesgleichen, *indecl. adj.,* his equal(s).

seit, *prep.* (*dat.*), since, for (time).

seitdem, *conj.,* since.

Seite, *f.,* –n, side.

Seitenthüre, *f.,* –n, side-door.

selber, *indecl. pron.,* self; myself, himself, *etc.;* mein Leben —, my life itself, my very life, 185.

selbst, *indecl. pron.,* self; myself, himself, *etc.; adv.,* even.

Selbst, *n.,* —, self.

selbständig, *adj.,* independent.

selbsteigen, *adj.,* own, 1503, *cf. N.*

Selbstsucht, *f.* selfishness.

Selbstvergessen, *n.,* –8, self-forgetfulness, oblivion.

selig, *adj.,* blessed, happy.

seltsam, *adj.,* strange, curious; *adv.,* 2000.

Senat', *m.,* –8, –e, senate.

senden, sandte *or* sendete, gesandt *or* gesendet, *tr.,* send.

Seneschall, *m.,* –8, –e, seneschal, Lord Steward.

Sentenz', *f.,* –en, sentence.

Serail' (*Fr.*), *n.,* –8, –8, seraglio.

setzen, *tr.,* set, put, place; *refl.,* sit down, *57; gesetzt, *part. adj.,* granted, assuming that, 936.

seufzen, *intr.,* sigh.

Sheriff (*Eng.*), *m.,* –8, –8, sheriff.

sich, *indecl. refl. pron., 3d pers. sing. or pl., dat. or acc.,* himself, herself, itself, themselves; *as recip.,* each other, 818, 220:.

sicher, *adj.,* sure, secure; safe, 2686; true, 464.

Sicherheit, *f.,* safety, 2361; security, 963.

sichtbar, *adj.,* visible.

sie, *pl.* sie, *pers. pron.,* she, it, they; Sie (*with plural verb*), you.

sieben, *num.,* seven.

Sieg, *m.,* –es, –e, victory.

Siegel, *n.,* –8, —, seal.

siegen, *intr.,* conquer, be victorious; triumph, 229, 2238, 2469; siegend, *part. adj.,* victorious, triumphant, 484, 711.

Siegesbogen, *m.,* –8, —, triumphal arch, 426, *cf. N.*

silbern, *adj.,* silver.

sinken, sank, gesunken, *intr.* s., sink, fall.

Sinn, *m.,* –es, –e, sense, 335, 432, 1241, 3041; mind, 1532, 2608; meaning, 810, 3983; von Sinnen, out of one's senses, 3347, 3947.

sinnen, sann, gesonnen, *intr.,* think (of, auf *with acc.*), 1315.

Sitte, *f.,* –n, habit, custom; ways, 3317; *pl.,* manners, 255, 308.

Sitz, *m.,* –es, –e, seat.

sitzen, saß, gesessen, *intr.,* sit.

Sitzung, *f.,* –en, session; council, 482, *cf. N.*

Sixtus, Papst. Pope Sixtus V (1585-1590), 1490, *cf. N.*

Sklave, *m.,* -n, -n, slave.

Sklavendemut, *f.,* slavish humility.

Sklaverei', *f.,* slavery.

so, *adv. and conj.,* so, as, thus, then; 1736, *cf. N.*

sobald, *adv.,* so soon; *conj.,* as soon as.

sogar, *conj.,* even.

sogleich, *adv.,* immediately.

Sohn, *m.,* -es, Söhne, son.

solang(e), *conj.,* as long as.

solch (-er, -e, -es), *pron. and adj.,* such.

sollen, sollte, gesollt, soll, *intr. and modal aux.,* shall, should, ought; be to, 4, *cf. N.;* be said to, be intended to; was soll, what business has, 2902; what means, 3456.

sondergleichen, *adv.,* without equal *or* parallel.

Sonne, *f.,* -n, sun; sunlight, 1466,

sonst, *adv.,* otherwise, else, 1830, 3781; formerly, 269, 339.

Sorge, *f.,* -n, care, 1235, 2408; anxiety, 619, 1250; sorrow, 3587; — tragen, take care, 1604.

sorgen, *intr.,* fear, worry, 1852; see to, 385; provide (for, für), 208, 3533.

sorgenvoll, *adj.,* anxious.

Souverän', *m.,* -s, -e, sovereign.

Späher, *m.,* -s, —, spy.

Spähertritt, *m.,* -s, -e, spy's footstep.

Spanien, *n.,* -s, Spain.

spanisch, *adj.,* Spanish.

Spannung, *f.,* suspense.

sparen, *tr.,* spare, save.

spärlich, *adj.,* scanty; *adv.,* scantily, scarcely, 2110.

spät, *adj.,* late.

Speise, *f.,* -n, food.

speisen, *intr.,* eat; *tr.,* give to eat, feed, 37.

sperren, *tr.,* close, bar.

Spiegel, *m.,* -s, —, mirror, looking-glass.

Spiel, *n.,* -es, -e, game, play.

spielen, *tr. and intr.,* play.

Spielzeug, *n.,* -s, -e, plaything, toy.

spinnen, spann, gesponnen, *tr.,* spin; plan, plot, 1472.

Spitze, *f.,* -n, point, 2736; head, 750.

Spott, *m.,* -es, scorn; — treiben (mit), ridicule, make sport of, 2821.

spotten, *intr.* (*with gen.*), scorn, 2807; ridicule, 2829.

Sprache, *f.,* -n, speech, language.

sprachlos, *adj.,* speechless.

sprechen, sprach, gesprochen, spricht, *tr. and intr.,* speak; pronounce (sentence *or* judgment), 249, 768, 802, *etc.*

sprengen, *tr.,* burst.

spröde, *adj.,* brittle; reserved; mit —em Stolz, with proud reserve, 1787.

Spruch, *m.,* -es, Sprüche, saying, utterance; judgment, 760.

Spur, *f.,* -en, track.

Spurkunst, *f.,* sagacity.

St. Germain. St. Germain, a suburb of Paris, formerly a fashionable quarter and the favorite residence of royalty and the nobility; 1119, *cf. N.*

Staat, *m.,* -es, -en, state.

Staatsamt, *n.,* -es, -ämter, (public) office.

Staatskunst, *f.,* statecraft.

Staatsmann, *m.,* -s, statesman.

Staatsrat, *m.,* -s, -räte, council (of state).

Staatsverbrechen, *n.,* -s, —, political crime.

Staatsvorteil, *m.*, –s, –e, political advantage.

Stab, *m.*, –es, Stäbe, staff, *180; rod, 3626; bar, 125; prop, support, 3374; den — brechen, pronounce sentence, condemn, 1069, *cf. N.*

Stachel, *m.*, –s, –n, sting.

Stadt, *f.*, Städte, city.

Stamm, *m.*, –es, Stämme, race, family.

Stammbaum, *m.*, –s, –bäume, genealogical tree, pedigree.

stampfen, *intr.*, stamp.

Stand, *m.*, –es, Stände, station, 1966; condition, 1155.

standhaft, *adj.*, steadfast, 1550; firm, 3369.

stark (stärker, stärk[e]st–), *adj.*, strong.

Stärke, *f.*, strength.

stärken, *tr.*, strengthen.

starr, *adj.*, fixed, rigid; unbending, 4024; obstinate, 1682; transfixed, *130.

Statthalter, *m.*, –s, —, vicar, lieutenant.

Staub, *m.*, –es, dust.

staunen, *intr.*, be amazed, wonder; staunend, *part. adj.*, wondering, amazed, 428, 762.

stecken, steckte *or* stak, gesteckt, *intr.*, stick; be hidden, 8.

stehen, stand, gestanden, *intr.* h. (*and* f.), stand; *impers.*, — um, be *or* fare with, 731; (stünd', *pret. subj.*), 2641; steht nicht zu ändern, cannot be, is not to be changed; stehen nach, be set on, turn towards, 1265.

stehlen, stahl, gestohlen, stiehlt, *tr.*, steal; *refl.*, steal one's way, 1480.

steigen, stieg, gestiegen, *intr.* f., mount, ascend, 841, 2616; rise, 1408, 1328; — von, descend,

3155; steigend, *part. adj.*, increasing, *183.

Stein, *m.*, –es, –e, stone, 3859; gem, 18, 3559.

stellen, *tr.*, place, put; lay, spread, 1751; frame, 2289; *refl.*, affect, pretend to be, *101.

Stellung, *f.*, –en, position, attitude.

sterben, starb, gestorben, stirbt, *intr.* f., die; *pres. part. as subst.*, 195.

Sterben (*verbal subst.*), *n.*, –s, dying, death, 3811.

sterblich, *adj.*, mortal.

Sterbliche, *m. and f.* (*decl. like adj.*), mortal.

Sterblichkeit, *f.*, mortality.

Sterlyn, Stirling Castle, a stronghold near the Forth, in Scotland; 37, *cf. N.*

Stern, *m.*, –es, –e, star.

stets, *adv.*, always.

sticken, *intr.*, embroider.

stiften, *tr.*, found; make, 1631.

Stifter, *m.*, –s, —, founder, 1344; author, instigator.

Stifterin, *f.*, –innen, (female) author, instigator, 1002.

still, *adj.*, still, 595; quiet, 622, *114.

stillen, *tr.*, still; quiet, allay, 2479.

stillschweigen, schwieg, geschwiegen, *sep. intr.*, keep silence, be silent; stillschweigend, *part. adv.*, silently, 1423.

Stillschweigen, *n.*, –s, silence.

Stimme, *f.*, –n, voice, 3068; vote, assent, 1825.

stimmen, *intr.*, vote.

Stimmenmehrheit, *f.*, –en, majority of votes; majority, 1323.

Stimmung, *f.*, –en, temper, mood.

Stirn(e), *f.*, –en, brow, 122, 733, 1468, 1636; face, 2719; front,

345, 2793; — gegen —, face to face, 883.

Stirnband, n., -s, -bänder, head-band, frontlet.

Stock, m., -es, Stöcke, stick, cane; floor, story (of a house), 3.

stocken, intr., stop, falter; be choked, 2277.

stolz, adj., proud.

Stolz, m., -es, pride.

Stoß, m., -es, Stöße, thrust.

stoßen, stieß, gestoßen, stößt, tr., thrust; refl., stab oneself, 3007.

Strafe, f., -n, punishment.

strafen, tr., punish.

straflos, adj., unpunished; adv., with impunity, 730.

Strahl, m., -es, -en, beam, flash; bolt, 3270.

stranden, intr. f., strand, be wrecked; der Strandende, the stranded, shipwrecked [sailor], 2270.

Straße, f., -n, street; dat. sing., -n, road (to London), 2604.

streben, intr., strive.

strecken, tr., stretch.

Streich, m., -es, -e, stroke; blow, thrust, 2614.

Streit, m., -es, -e, contention, conflict; dispute, *5; contro-versy, 757; strife, 837, 3142.

streiten, stritt, gestritten, intr., contend, dispute; inf. as subst., 844.

streng, adj., strict, 234, 676, 917, etc.; severe, 1025, 1377, 1984, etc.; stern, 410, *103.

Strenge, f., severity; austerity, 2583.

streuen, tr., strew; scatter, 3617; sow, 2877.

Strom, m., -es, Ströme, stream.

strömen, intr. f. and h., stream; flow, 1304.

Stufe, f., -n, step.

Stuhl, m., -es, Stühle, chair.

stumm, adj., dumb, 749; mute, 1032, *164; speechless, *77.

Stunde, f., -n, hour; time, 895, 2042; moment, 2176.

Sturm, m., -es, Stürme, storm; assault, 1095.

stürmen, tr., storm; attack, 2688.

sturmvoll, adj., storm-laden, stormy.

Sturz, m., -es, Stürze, fall.

stürzen, tr., hurl down, precipi-tate, 3840; plunge, 1815, 2878, 3348; overthrow, 933; ruin, 1717; gestürzt, part. adj., un-done, ruined, 3972; refl., cast oneself, plunge, 78; intr. f., fall, 1805, 1920, 3008, etc.; plunge, rush, 866.

Stütze, f., -n, prop, support.

Suada, f., persuasiveness, 485, cf. N.

suchen, tr., seek, look for; intr., seek, try, *109.

Suchen (verbal subst.), n., -s, seeking, search.

Sultanslaune, f., -n, sultanic whim, despotic caprice.

Sünde, f., -n, sin.

Sünderin, f., -innen, (female) sinner.

sündig, adj., sinful.

süß, adj., sweet.

Szene, f., -n, scene, scenery; scenes, *117.

T.

Tadel, m., -s, blame, censure.

tadeln, tr., blame, censure.

Tafel, f., -n, table.

Tag, m., -es, -e, day; adv. gen, eines Tages, one day, 501.

tagen, intr., dawn.

Tagesanbruch, m., -s, -brüche, daybreak, dawn.

Tand, *m.,* –es, trifles.

tapfer, *adj.,* brave, valiant; *mcsc. sing. as subst.,* hero, 2577.

Tapferkeit, *f.,* bravery, valor.

Tasche, *f.,* –n, pocket.

Tausch, *m.,* –es, –e, exchange.

täuschen, *tr.,* deceive, 310, 390, 1633, *etc.;* cheat, 1794; disappoint, 3664.

Täuschung, *f.,* –en, deception.

tausend, *num.,* thousand, a thousand.

Tausend, *n.* –s, –e, thousand.

Teil, *m.* (*and n.*), –es, –e, part, share, lot; *neut.,* 3575; zu teil werden, fall to the lot of (*dat. of pers.*), be given to, 1395, 3498.

teilen, *tr.,* share.

Tempel, *m.,* –s, —, temple.

Teppich, *m.* –s, –e, carpet.

Testament, *n.,* –s, –e, testament, will.

teuer, *adj.,* dear, precious; *adv.,* dearly, 1256, 1671.

teuflisch, *adj.,* devilish, fiendish.

That, *f.,* –en, deed; in der —, indeed, in fact, 1760.

Thäter, *m.,* –s, —, perpetrator.

thätig, *adj.,* active.

Themis, *f.,* Themis, a Greek goddess, the personification of law, order and justice.

Thor, *m.,* –en, –en, fool, 257.

Thor, *n.,* –es, –e, gate, 664.

Thorheit, *f.,* –en, folly, act of folly.

thöricht, *adj.,* foolish; *fem. sing. as subst.,* 1290.

Thräne, *f.,* –n, tear.

Thron, *m.,* –es, –e, throne.

thun, that, gethan, *tr. and intr.,* do; make, 1720, 2112; *intr.;* stolz — (mit), boast of, plume oneself on, 2021.

Thun (*verbal subst.*), *n.,* –s, doings, acts, 3198.

Thüre, *f.,* –n, door.

Tichburn. Chidive Tichbourne, an accomplice of Babington, and executed with him, 1586.

tief, *adj.,* deep, low.

tiefgebeugt, *part. adj.,* bowed low, humbled; *fem. sing. as subst.,* 2242.

tiefgefallen, *part. adj.,* fallen low, 1547, *cf. N.*

tiefsinnig, *adj.,* deep in thought, pensive.

tiefstgesunken, *part. adj.,* fallen lowest, most degraded, 3492, *cf. N.*

Tiger, *m.,* –s, —, tiger.

tilgen, *tr.,* blot out, efface.

Tisch, *m.,* –es, –e, table.

Titel, *m.,* –s, —, title.

toben, *intr.,* rage, struggle; tobend, *part. adj.,* raging; boisterous, 2142.

Toben (*verbal subst.*), *n.,* –s, frenzy, storm, 3251.

Tod, *m.,* –es, –e, death; des –es sein, be a dead man, 2618.

Todesmacht, *f.,* –mächte, power of death.

Todesnetz, *n.,* –es, –e, net of death, fatal net.

Todesopfer, *n.,* –s, —, deathoffering, victim.

Todespost, *f.,* –en, fatal news.

Todesstunde, *f.,* –n, hour of death.

Todesurteil, *n.,* –s, –e, deathsentence, death-warrant.

Todesweg, *m.,* –s, –e, way of *or* to death.

tödlich, *adj.,* deadly, fatal.

Tollkühnheit, *f.,* foolhardiness, recklessness.

Ton, *m.,* –es, Töne, tone, sound.

tönen, *intr.,* sound.

tot, *adj.*, dead ; lifeless, 1657.

töten, *tr.*, kill.

Toulon. Toulon, a city in France on the Mediterranean Sea.

Tower. Tower of London: the ancient palace-citadel of London, comprising a group of buildings and towers erected chiefly during the 12th and 13th centuries ; some time a royal residence, subsequently a state prison, and now a national arsenal. Many persons of note were executed and buried here.

Trabant, *m.*, –en, –en, guard, 2794, *cf. N.*

tragen, trug, getragen, trägt, *tr.*, bear, 823, 2454; carry, 675; wear, 396, 3547, *166; bear, endure, 254, 686, 3839.

trauen, *intr.* (*with dat.*), trust, 525; (*with* auf *and acc.*), 1637.

Trauer, *f.*, mourning.

Trauerflor, *m.*, –s, mourning-crape.

Trauerkleid, *n.*, –s, –er, mourning-dress.

trauern, *intr.*, mourn, grieve; *inf. as subst.*, grief, *158.

Traum, *m.*, –es, Träume, dream.

träumen, *tr.* (*and intr.*), dream, 2089; *impers.* (*with dat.*), 2607.

traurig, *adj.*, sad, sorrowful, mournful, 1295, 2326, 2406; dismal, dreary, 12, 2080.

treffen, traf, getroffen, trifft, *tr.*, hit, 3886; strike, 1152, 1486, 3242; fall, on, 1597; meet, 2739; Anstalt —, make preparations, 1844.

trefflich, *adj.*, excellent; *masc. sing. as subst.*, 474.

treiben, trieb, getrieben, *tr.*, drive, 3908; urge, impel, 3075, 3643; bear, put forth, 3627.

trennen, *tr.*, separate, 204; divide, 815; sever, 2354.

Trennung, *f.*, –en, separation.

Treppe, *f.*, –n, stairway.

treten, trat, getreten, tritt, *intr. f.*, step, go; — in, enter, 435; *tr.*, tread, trample, 2469; mit Füßen —, trample underfoot, 144, 2693.

treu, *adj.*, faithful; true, honest, 260, 468; loyal, 1303.

Treubruch, *m.*, –s, –brüche, breach of faith, disloyalty.

Treu(e), *f.*, faith, 888, 2359; faithfulness, fidelity, 135; good faith, 1714.

treulos, *adj.*, faithless, perfidious.

Trieb, *m.*, –es, –e, impulse, 1566, 2284; instinct, 3395; motive, 1296.

trinken, trank, getrunken, *tr.*, drink.

Triumph, *m.*, –s, –e, triumph.

trocknen, *tr.*, dry.

Trost, *m.*, –es, consolation; comfort, 3186, 3644.

trösten, *tr.*, console, comfort.

trostlos, *adj.*, inconsolable, disconsolate.

Trotz, *m.*, –es, defiance; — bieten, bid defiance (to, *dat.*), 316, 1959.

trotz, *prep.* (*dat.* [*and gen.*]), in spite of.

trotzen, *intr.* (*with dat.*), defy; — auf, insist (defiantly) upon, 2196.

Trübsal, *f.*, –e, *and n.*, –s, –e, affliction.

trunken, *part. adj.*, intoxicated (with joy), enchanted, 1144.

Trunkenheit, *f.*, intoxication.

Tuch, *n.*, –es, Tücher, cloth; handkerchief, 3564.

Tudor. Tudor, an English dynasty, descended on the male

side from Owen Tudor, comprising the sovereigns Henry VII, Henry VIII, Edward VI, Mary, and Elizabeth, and covering the period 1485–1603.

Tugend, *f.,* –en, virtue.

Tugendruf, *m.,* –s, reputation for virtue, virtuous fame.

Tumult, *m.,* –s, –e, tumult, disturbance, 850.

Turm, *m.,* –es, Türme, tower.

Turnierplatz, *m.,* –es, –plätze, tourney-place, lists.

Tweede, *f.,* Tweed, a river in Scotland that forms part of the boundary between Scotland and England.

Tyburn, Tyburn, to the north of Hyde Park in London, formerly (till 1783) the place of public execution.

Tyrann', *m.,* –en, –en, tyrant.

Tyrannei', *f.,* tyranny.

Tyrannenmacht, *f.,* tyrannical power, tyranny, despotism.

tyrannisch, *adj.,* tyrannical.

U.

üben, *tr.,* exercise, 3751; practise, 2356, 3200.

über, *prep.* (*dat. and acc.*), *adv., sep. and insep. pref.,* over, above, across, beyond, about, concerning.

überbleiben, blieb, geblieben, *sep. intr. f.,* be left, survive.

überbringen, überbrachte, überbracht, *insep. tr.,* deliver, 1820; bring to, 3653.

übereilen, *insep. tr.,* over-hasten, hasten unduly, 3077; *with impers. obj.,* use undue haste, 3346, 3951; übereilt, *part. adj.,* overhasty ; *adv.,* precipitately, 3955.

überfallen, überfiel', überfallen, überfällt', *insep. tr.,* fall upon (suddenly); surprise, 218, 239, 385.

Überfluß, *m.,* –sses, plenty, abundance.

überführen, *insep. tr.,* convict.

übergeben, übergab', übergeben, übergiebt', *tr.,* give *or* hand over, 2993; deliver, 160, 1504, 1658; give in charge. 538; commit to (*dat.*), 1053.

übergehen, ging, gegangen, *intr. f.,* go over, pass.

überheben, überhob', überhoben, *insep. refl.,* presume upon.

überlassen, überließ', überlassen, überläßt, *insep. tr.,* abandon, 3172; leave to, 3185; *refl.,* give oneself up to, give way to, 3372.

überlästig, *adj.,* troublesome ; *masc. sing. as subst.,* 2897.

überlegen, *insep. tr.,* consider.

überliefern, *insep. tr.,* deliver.

Übermut, *m.,* –s, insolence.

übermütig, *adj.,* arrogant, insolent.

übernehmen, übernahm', übernommen, übernimmt', *insep. tr.,* take upon oneself, 1055, 2685, 3048; accept, 3330.

überraschen, *insep. tr.,* surprise, take unawares ; *past. part. as subst.,* 223.

überreden, *insep. tr.,* persuade.

überreichen, *insep. tr.,* hand to, present.

überschreiten, überschritt', überschritten, *insep. tr.,* overstep, exceed.

überstrahlen, *insp. tr.,* outshine, eclipse.

übertragen, übertrug', übertragen, überträgt', *insep. tr.,* commit *or* assign (to, *dat.*).

überwäl'tigen, *insep. tr.,* overpower.

überwun'den, *part. adj.* (*from* überwin'den), beaten, conquered.

überzeu'gen, *insep. tr.,* convince; überzeugt', *part. adj.,* confident, assured, 3733.

Überzeugung, *f.,* –en, conviction.

überzie'hen, überzog', überzo'gen, *insep. tr.,* cover; drape, 3471.

ü'brig, *adj.,* over; left, 1186; remaining, other, *56; — bleiben, be left, remain, 3292; das übrige, the rest, 20.

Übung, *f.,* –en, exercise.

Ufer, *n.,* –s, —, shore.

um, *prep.* (*acc.*), *adv., sep. and insep. pref.,* around, about, near, for, concerning; *of time,* at; um ... zu (*inf.*), in order to, to; um ... (*gen.*) willen, for the sake of (somebody *or* something), 78, 511, 2265.

umar'men, *insep. tr.,* embrace.

Umar'mung, *f.,* –en, embrace.

umfang'en, umfing, umfang'en, umfängt', *insep. tr.,* embrace, 2539; encircle, surround, 428, 2091.

umfas'sen, *insep. tr.,* encircle, 2401; embrace, 3516.

umflech'ten, umflocht', umfloch'ten, umflicht', *insep. tr.,* enmesh, entwine.

umflie'ßen, umfloß', umflos'sen, *insep. tr.,* surround, encompass.

umge'ben, umgab', umge'ben, umgiebt', *insep. tr.,* surround, 448, 1871, *etc.;* environ, 2055.

um'gehen, ging, gegangen, *sep. intr.* f., go around *or* about.

umge'hen, umging', umgang'en, *insep. tr.,* avoid, evade.

umgit'tern, *insep. tr.,* surround with a grating.

umglän'zen, *insep. tr.,* surround with radiance *or* splendor.

um'hängen, hängte *or* hing, gehängt *or* gehangen, *sep. tr.,* hang about; put on, *55.

umher', *adv. and sep. pref.,* around, about.

umher'blicken, *sep. intr.,* look around.

umher'gehen, ging, gegangen, *sep. intr.* f., go about.

umhül'len, *insep. tr.,* envelop, enwrap.

umklam'mern, *insep. tr.,* clasp.

um'kommen, kam, gekommen, *sep. intr.* f., perish, die.

umlach'en, *insep. tr.,* smile about.

umla'gern, *insep. tr.,* surround, beset.

umring'en, umring'te, umringt' *and* umrung'en, *insep. tr.,* surround, 349, 1369.

umschling'en, umschlang', umschlung'en, *insep. tr.,* embrace; entwine, 1223.

um'sehen, sah, gesehen, sieht, *sep. refl.,* look around *or* about.

umsonst', *adv.,* vainly, in vain; without reason *or* purpose, 2119.

umste'hen, umstand, umstan'den, *insep. tr.,* surround.

umstrah'len, *insep. tr.,* shine round, dazzle, 2039.

umstrick'en, *insep. tr.,* ensnare.

um'wenden, wandte *or* wendete, gewandt *or* gewendet, *sep. tr.,* turn about; *refl.,* *87, turn round.

umzing'eln, *insep. tr.,* encircle, surround.

unabseh'bar, *adj.,* immeasurable, incalculable.

un'anständig, *adj.,* unseemly, indecent.

unauflös'lich, *adj.,* indissoluble, inextricable, 2544.

unbedacht'sam, *adj.,* indiscreet; *adv,* rashly, 1939.

un'bedeutend, *part. adj.,* insignificant, unimportant.

un'befleckt, *part. adj.,* unspotted.

un'bereitet, *part. adj.,* unprepared.

un'berufen, *part. adj.,* unbidden, 2315; *adv.,* officiously, presumptuously, 2697.

un'bescholten, *part. adj.,* unblemished.

unbestech'lich, *adj.,* incorruptible.

un'bewegt, *part. adj.,* unmoved.

unbezwing'lich, *adj.,* unconquerable.

und, *conj.,* and.

unein'geschränkt, *part. adj.,* unlimited; *adv.,* unreservedly, 1689.

unend'lich, *adj.,* endless; *adv.,* infinitely, 2010.

un'entschlossen, *part. adj.,* irresolute.

unerhört', *part. adj.,* unheard of, unprecedented; *adv.,* beyond example *or* parallel, 2986.

unermü'det, *part. adj.,* unwearied; unremitting, indefatigable, 793, 1180.

unerschöpf'lich, *adj.,* inexhaustible.

unerträg'lich, *adj.,* intolerable.

unerwar'tet, *part. adj.,* unexpected.

Un'geduld, *f.,* impatience.

un'geduldig, *adj.,* impatient.

un'gefähr, *adj.,* casual, accidental; von —, by chance; *adv.,* about, nearly.

ungeheu'er, *adj.,* monstrous.

un'gekränkt, *part. adj.,* unmolested.

un'gelehrt, *part. adj.,* unlearnéd.

un'gemessen, *part. adj.,* unmeasured.

un'genützt, *part. adj.,* unemployed.

un'gerecht, *adj.,* unjust.

un'gesäumt, *part. adj.,* immediate; *adv.,* without delay, promptly.

ungesche'hen, *part. adj.,* undone; as if it had not happened, 2395.

un'gestraft, *adj.,* unpunished; *adv.,* with impunity, 2414.

un'gestüm, *adj.,* impetuous, turbulent; clamorous, 1428.

Un'gestüm, *n.,* –s, impetuosity, violence.

un'geteilt, *part. adj.,* undivided.

un'getreu, *adj.,* faithless.

un'geweiht, *part. adj.,* unconsecrated.

Un'gewißheit, *f,* uncertainty.

un'gleich, *adj.,* unequal.

Un'glück *n.,* –s, misfortune; unhappiness, 275.

un'glücklich, *adj.,* unfortunate; *masc. sing. as subst.,* 1016; unhappy, 649.

Un'glücksbrief, *m.,* –s, –e, fatal letter.

un'glückselig, *adj.,* unfortunate, 3080; unhappy, wretched, 278; *fem. sing. as subst.,* 86, 1238; *also of the one who causes unhappiness,* wretched, 327, 834, 2742.

Un'glücksthat, *f.,* –en, unhappy *or* unfortunate deed.

un'glücksvoll, *adj.,* most unhappy.

Un'grund, *m.,*–s, groundlessness.

Un'heil, *n.,* –s, mischief, calamity.

un'heilbringend, *part. adj.,* fraught with harm, calamitous.

un'heilbrütend, *part. adj.,* mischief-hatching, 132, *cf. N.*

un'heilspinnend, *part. adj.*, mischief-plotting, 114, *cf. N.*

un'hold, *adj.*, ungracious, unkind.

un'föniglich, *adj.*, unkingly, unroyal.

un'kundig, *adj.*, ignorant (of, *gen.*).

unlängst', *adv.*, lately, not long since.

un'mäßig, *adj.*, immoderate.

Unmensch'lichkeit, *f.*, inhumanity.

Un'mut, *m.*, –s, indignation.

Un'recht, *n*, –s, –e, wrong.

Un'ruhe, *f.*, uneasiness, disquiet; agitation, *109, *128.

Un'schuld, *f.*, innocence.

unser, *poss. adj. and pron.*, our, ours.

un'sichtbar, *adj.*, invisible.

un'sinnig, *adj.*, mad; *masc. as subst*, madman, 2540.

un'stät, *adj.*, unsteady.

unsterb'lich, *adj.*, immortal.

unten, *adv.*, below.

unter–, *adj.*, lower.

unter, *prep.* (*dat. and acc.*), *adv.*, *sep. and insep. pref.*, under, below, beneath, between; among, 3636; amid, 3005.

unterbrech'en, unterbrach', unterbroch'en, unterbricht', *insep. tr.*, interrupt.

unterdrück'en, *insep. tr.*, oppress.

Unterdrück'ung, *f.*, –en, oppression.

unterfang'en, unterfing', unterfang'en, unterfängt', *insep. refl.*, dare, presume.

Un'tergang, *m.*, –s, destruction.

un'tergehen, ging, gegangen, *sep. intr.* s., perish.

unterhal'ten, unterhielt', unterhal'ten, unterhält', *insep. tr.*, entertain, 42; *refl.*, converse, commune, 3463.

unterhan'deln, *insep. intr.*, negotiate.

Unterhand'lung, *f.*, –en, communication.

unterjoch'en, *insep. tr.*, subjugate.

unterlie'gen, unterlag', unterle'gen, *insep. intr.*, succumb (to, *dat.*).

unterneh'men, unternahm', unternom'men, unternimmt', *insep. tr.*, undertake.

Unterre'dung, *f.*, –en, interview.

unterschrei'ben, unterschrieb', unterschrie'ben, *insep. tr.*, sign.

Un'terschrift, *f.*, –en, signature.

untersu'chen, *insep. tr.*, investigate.

Untersu'chung, *f.*, –en, investigation.

un'terthan, *adj.* (*with dat.*), subject to.

Un'terthan, *m.*, –s *and* –en, –en, subject.

un'terthänig, *adj.* (*with dat.*), subject to.

unterweg'(e)s, *adv.*, on the way.

unterwer'fen, unterwarf', unterwor'fen, unterwirft', *insep. tr.*, subject, 956, 1037; subdue, 1936; *refl.* (*with dat.*), submit to, 694, 1784, 1981, 2245.

Unterwer'fung, *f.*, submission.

unterwor'fen, *part. adj.*, subject (to, *dat.*), 845.

unterwür'fig, *adj.*, subject (to, *dat.*), 1184; *adv.*, submissively, 2217.

unterzeich'nen, *insep. tr.*, sign.

un'verdient, *part. adj.*, undeserved.

un'verdrossen, *adj.*, indefatigable.

unverein'bar, *adj.*, incompatible.

un'verhofft, *part. adj.*, unhoped for, unexpected.

un′verhohlen, *part. adj.*, unconcealed; *adv.*, plainly, unreservedly, 1197.

un′vermählt, *part. adj.*, unmarried, unwedded.

unvermeid′lich, *adj.*, unavoidable, inevitable.

un′verschämt, *adj.*, impertinent, insolent; *masc. sing. as subst.*, 2879.

unversöhn′lich, *adj.*, irreconcilable; implacable, *fem. sing. as subst.*, 2461.

un′versöhnt, *part. adj.*, unreconciled; implacable, 1267.

un′verwahrt, *part. adj.*, unguarded.

un′verwandt, *part. adj.*, unmoved; *adv.*, fixedly, *55.

un′vollstreckt, *part. adj.*, unexecuted.

Un′wille, *m.*, −ns, indignation.

unwillkür′lich, *adj.*, involuntary.

un′würdig, *adj.*, unworthy, base, 1236; *masc. sing. as subst.*, 306; *neut. sing. as subst.*, indignity, 564, 3486; beneath the dignity of (*gen.*), 1523.

unzäh′lig, *adj.*, countless, innumerable; *pl. as subst.*, 646.

Un′ziemlichkeit, *f.*, −en, impropriety.

un′zugänglich, *adj.*, inaccessible.

üppig, *adj.*, luxurious.

uralt, *adj.*, very old, ancient.

Urlaub, *m.*, −s, leave.

Urteil, *n.*, −s, −e, judgment, 860, 1318, 3087; opinion, 1329, 1979; verdict, 691; doom, 322; sentence, 576, 1525, 1905, 4004, *etc.*; death-warrant, 2845, 3065, 3334, 3960.

urteilen, *intr.*, judge; have *or* express an opinion, 1437; pass *or* give judgment, 245.

urteln, see urteilen, 245, *cf. N.*

Urteilspruch (*usually* Urteils=), *m.*, −s, −sprüche, verdict, sentence.

V.

Vasall′, *m.*, −en, −en, vassal.

Vater, *m.*, −s, Väter, father.

Vaterland, *n.*, −s, native country, fatherland.

Vatikan′, *m.*, −s, Vatican.

ver=, *insep. pref.*, *never accented*.

verabscheuen, *tr.*, abhor, abominate.

verachten, *tr.*, despise.

verächtlich, *adj.*, contemptible, despicable.

Verachtung, *f.*, contempt.

verachtungswert, *adj.*, contemptible.

verändern, *tr.*, change, 979; *refl.*, 1769; *part. adj.*, altered, 1819.

Veränderung, *f.*, −en, change.

verbannen, *tr.*, banish.

Verbannte, *m. and f.* (*decl. like adj.*), exile.

Verbannung, *f.*, banishment, exile.

verbergen, verbarg, verborgen, verbirgt, *tr.*, hide, conceal.

verbieten, verbot, verboten, *tr.* (*dat. of pers.*), forbid.

verbinden, verband, verbunden, *tr.*, bind; *refl.*, unite, 3753; bandage, blindfold, 3564.

verblassen, *intr.*, pale, turn pale.

verborgen, *part. adj.*, hidden, concealed, *6; secret, 279, 1918.

Verbot, *n.*, −s, −e, prohibition.

verbrechen, verbrach, verbrochen, verbricht, *tr.*, commit, perpetrate (a crime); *with impers. obj.*, sin, transgress, 3739.

Verbrechen, *n.*, −s, —, crime.

Verbrecher, *m.,* –8, —, criminal; culprit, 2470.

verbreiten, *tr.,* spread; *refl.,* be spread, spread, 1108.

verbringen, verbrachte, verbracht, *tr.,* pass, spend, waste (time), 1180.

verbuhlt, *adj.,* amorous, wanton.

verbünden, *refl.,* unite, ally.

verbürgen, *refl.,* vouch *or* answer for (für).

Verdacht, *m.,* –8, suspicion.

verdammen, *tr.,* damn, 2658; condemn, 888, 956, 2923; verdammt, *part. adj.,* damned; *pl.* as subst., 139, 3846.

Verdammniß, *f.,* damnation, 2783; perdition, 333.

verdanken, *tr.* (*dat. of pers.*), owe, be indebted for.

verderben, verdarb, verdorben, verdirbt, *intr.* f., perish, 1879; *tr.,* destroy, 857.

Verderben, *n.,* –8, destruction.

verdienen, *tr.,* merit, deserve; deserve from (um), 2698.

Verdienst, *n.,* –es, –e, merit; service, 1188.

verehren, *tr.,* reverence, revere, 433, 2263; respect, 1990, 2392; worship, do reverence, 3611.

Verehrer, *m.,* –8, —, worshiper.

Verein, *m.,* –8, –e, union; totality, 1325.

vereinen, *tr.,* unite, combine.

vereinigen, *tr.,* unite, combine.

vereiteln, *tr.,* frustrate.

verfahren, verfuhr, verfahren, verfährt, *intr.* f. *and* h., proceed.

verfallen, verfiel, verfallen, verfällt, *intr.* f., fall under, incur the penalty of, 848; be forfeited to, 2562.

verfassen, *tr.,* compose (in writing); draw up, frame, 857.

verfluchen, *tr.,* curse: verflucht,

part. adj., cursed, accursed, 71 2602.

verfolgen, *tr.* (*acc.*), pursue; persecute, 1836.

Verfolger, *m.,* –8, —, pursuer; persecutor, 669.

verfügen, *refl.,* betake oneself; proceed *or* repair to (nach), 3274, 3902.

Verfügung, *f.,* disposal, disposition; — treffen über (*acc.*), make disposition of, 200.

verführen, *tr.,* lead astray, 1667, 2422; seduce, 2374, 2407; mislead, 1291, 1355; verführt, *part. adj.,* misled, misguided, 649.

Verführer *m.,* –8, —, seducer.

vergangen, *part. adj.,* past; last, 847; of the past, 1327.

vergeben, vergab, vergeben, vergiebt, *tr.,* give away, 1651; *with dat. of pers.,* forgive, 285, 1993, 2523, *etc.*; compromise, forfeit, 701.

vergeben, *part. adj.,* vain; needless, idle, 620.

vergeblich, *adj.,* vain, useless.

Vergebung, *f.,* forgiveness.

vergehen, verging, vergangen, *intr.* f., pass away; wither, be annihilated, 2241; *refl.,* go wrong, transgress, 59.

vergessen, vergaß, vergessen, vergißt, *tr.,* forget.

Vergessen (*verbal subst.*), *n.,* –8, oblivion.

vergießen, vergoß, vergossen, *tr.,* shed, 3748.

vergleichen, verglich, verglichen, *tr.,* compare.

vergönnen, *tr.* (*dat. of pers.*), permit; vergönnt sein, be granted *or* given, 554.

vergrößern, *tr.,* enlarge; aggravate, 2896.

Vergünstigung, *f.,* –en, privilege.

verhaften, *tr.,* take into custody, arrest.

verhandeln, *tr.,* discuss.

verhaßt, *part. adj.,* hated, 404, 967, *etc.;* hateful, 395, 1034, 1658; odious, 1555, 3048.

verhehlen, *tr.,* conceal.

verheimlichen, *tr.,* keep secret.

verheißen, verhieß, verheißen, *tr.,* promise.

verherrlichen, *tr.,* glorify.

verhindern, *tr.,* hinder, prevent.

verhöhnen, *tr.,* scorn, mock; deride, 2463.

Verhör, *n.,* –s, –e, examination; ins — nehmen, cross-examine, take to task, 1790.

verhüllen, *tr.,* veil, cover.

verhüten, *tr.,* prevent, avert; Gott verhüte, God forbid! 1314, 3290; beware, 1448.

verjagen, *tr.,* expel.

verjüngen, *tr.,* rejuvenate, make young; *refl.,* grow young again, 1991.

verkaufen, *tr.,* sell.

verklagen, *tr.,* accuse (*of gen.*); indict, 4012.

verklären, *tr.,* transfigure, glorify; verklärt, *part. adj.,* glorified, 3845.

Verklärung, *f.,* Transfiguration, *cf. N.* 440; glory, 3742.

verkünden, *tr.,* announce, inform of.

Verkünderin, *f.,* –innen, herald, harbinger, 2122.

verkündigen, *tr.,* announce, make known.

verkürzen, *tr.,* shorten.

verlangen, *tr.,* desire, 1234; demand, 1241; request, 190; — nach, ask for, 3426.

Verlangen, *n.,* –s, desire.

verlängern, *tr.,* prolong.

verlassen, verließ, verlassen, verläßt, *tr.,* leave, 1492, 2692; abandon, 1173; desert, forsake, 338, 392, 1443; *refl.,* depend *or* rely upon (auf *with acc.*), 1689, 1857, 3772.

verlegen, *part. adj.,* embarrassed.

Verlegenheit, *f.,* –en, embarrassment, perplexity.

verleihen, verlieh, verliehen, *tr.,* give, grant, confer upon (*dat.*).

verleiten, *tr.,* mislead.

verletzen, *tr.,* wound, 2204; harm, 1013; offend, 1672, 2290; outrage, 2681.

verleugnen, *tr.,* deny, repudiate, 1676.

verlieren, verlor, verloren, *tr.,* lose.

verloren, *part. adj.,* lost; wasted, 261, 1776, 2115.

Verlorene, *m. and f.* (*decl. like adj.*), outcast, 358, *cf. N.;* reprobate, wretch, 738.

Verlust, *m.,* –es, –e, loss.

Vermächtnis, *n.,* –nisses, –nisse, legacy, bequest.

vermählen, *tr.,* marry, have married, 1430; wed, ally by marriage, 838; *refl.,* ally oneself (*or* itself) in marriage, 2684.

Vermählung, *f.,* –en, marriage.

vermeiden, vermied, vermieden, *tr.,* avoid, evade.

vermengen, *tr.,* mingle.

vermessen, vermaß, vermessen, vermißt, *refl.* (*with gen.*), venture, presume upon, 3990; vermessen, *part. adj.,* presumptuous; insolent, 2587.

vermischen, *tr.,* mix, mingle; *refl.,* be mingled, mingle, 816.

vermissen, *tr.,* miss.

vermögen, vermochte, vermocht, vermag, *tr.,* able to do *or* ac-

complish, 1581, 2573, *cf. N.;*
avail, 1711.

vermummen, *tr.,* mask, disguise.

vernehmen, vernahm, vernom=
men, vernimmt, *tr.,* perceive;
hear, 1392; learn of, 3412;
sich — lassen, let oneself be
heard, express oneself, make
answer, 708.

vernichten, *tr.,* annihilate.

Vernichtung, *f.,* annihilation.

Vernunft, *f.,* reason.

veröden, *tr.,* desolate; make desolate *or* deserted, 3136.

verordnen, *tr.,* decree, enact.

verpflanzen, *tr.,* transplant.

Verrat, *m.,* -s, treason, 130,
3168; treachery, 3411.

verraten, verriet, verraten, ver=
rät, *tr.,* betray.

Verräter, *m.,* -s, —, traitor.

Verräterei, *f.,* treason.

verräterisch, *adj.,* treacherous.

verrichten, *tr.,* perform, execute.

verrinnen, verrann, verronnen,
intr. f., pass (of time).

Verrückte, *m.* (-r) *and f.* (*decl.
like adj.*), maniac.

verrufen, verrief, verrufen, *tr.,*
revoke.

versagen, *tr.* (*dat. of pers.*), refuse, deny, 906, 2067, 3591,
etc.; fail (*dat. of pers.*), *181.

versammeln, *tr.,* assemble, call
together, 2502, 3615; *refl.,* assemble, meet, 640; versammelt,
part. adj., gathered together,
3635; united, 1133.

Versammlung, *f.,* -en, meeting.

verschaffen, *tr.,* procure, 3914;
afford, gain, 1896.

verscharren, *tr.,* bury.

verscheiden, verschied, verschieden,
intr., f., depart, die, pass away.

verschenken, *tr.,* give away, bestow.

verscheuchen, *tr.,* scare *or* frighten
away.

verschieden, *adj.,* different, opposite, *120.

verschleudern, *tr.,* fling away.

verschließen, verschloß, verschlossen,
tr., shut, close, lock; enclose,
3604.

verschlingen, verschlang, verschlun=
gen, *tr.,* swallow up, engulf.

verschlossen, *part. adj.,* closed,
1104, 2802; locked, 3661,*183.

verschmähen, *tr.,* disdain, scorn.

verschmerzen, *tr.,* get over (pain *or*
vexation), recover from, 158.

verschonen, *tr.,* spare, exempt
(from, mit), 1510.

Verschulden, *n.* -s, fault.

verschweigen, verschwieg, ver=
schwiegen, *tr.,* keep secret.

verschwenderisch, *adj.,* lavish,
prodigal.

verschwinden, verschwand, ver=
schwunden, *intr.* f., vanish, dis-
appear.

verschwören, verschwor, verschwo=
ren, *tr.,* forswear, abjure; *refl.,*
conspire, 2553; verschworen,
*part. adj.,*conspired, 3058; conspiring, as a conspirator, 101.

Verschwörung, *f.,* -en, conspiracy.

versehen, versah, versehen, versieht,
tr., provide with (mit), 2650.

Versehen, *n.,* -s, —, error, blun-
der.

versichern, *tr.,* make sure *or* secure, 599; *with dat. of pers.,*
assure (to), 1257, 1700, 1821.

Versicherung, *f.,* -en, assurance.

versiegeln, *tr.,* seal (up), *158;
set the seal to, 4025.

versinken, versank, versunken,
intr. f., sink, fall.

versöhnen, *tr.,* reconcile, 3789;
propitiate, make one's peace

with, 3590, 3675; expiate, 3739; verſöhnt, *part. adj.*, reconciled, 3681.

Verſöhnung, *f.*, -en, reconciliation.

verſpotten, *tr.*, mock.

verſprechen, *n.*, verſprach, verſprochen, verſpricht, *tr.* (*dat. of pers.*), promise.

Verſprechen, *n.*, -s, promise.

verſpritzen, *tr.*, shed.

Verſtand, *m.*, -s, understanding.

verſtändigen, *refl.*, come to an understanding with (mit), 2914.

Verſtändnis, *n.*, -niſſes, -niſſe, understanding.

verſtatten, *tr.*, (*dat. of pers.*), permit.

verſtecken, *tr.*, hide, conceal.

verſtehen, verſtand, verſtanden, *tr.*, understand.

Verſtellung, *f.*, dissimulation.

verſtohlen, *adj.*, clandestine, secret.

verſtoßen, verſtieß, verſtoßen, verſtößt, *tr.*, repel; expel, 2848.

verſtricken, *tr.*, ensnare, entangle.

verſtummen, *intr.* ſ., be dumb, 2924, *or* silent, 3859, *or* speechless, 767.

verſuchen, *tr.*, try, attempt, 1334, 1907; tempt, 3106, 3829.

vertauſchen, *tr.*, exchange; vertauſcht, *part. adj.*, changing, altered, 785.

verteidigen, *tr.*, defend.

verteilen, *tr.*, distribute, divide (among, unter *with acc.*), 3545.

vertilgen, *tr.*, exterminate.

Vertilgungskrieg, *m.*, -s, -e, war of extermination.

Vertrag, *m.*, -s, Verträge, agreement; treaty, 106, 2694.

vertragen, vertrug, vertragen, verträgt, *refl.*, agree, be consistent.

vertrauen, *intr.* (*with dat.* [or auf *and acc.*]), trust, 1697, 3625; trust to, 113; confide in, 680; vertrauend, *part. adj.*, trusting, confiding, 2727; vertraut, *part. adj.*, trusty, faithful, 1756; *tr.*, entrust, 1050, 1074, 1482, 1689 *etc.*; confide (to *dat.*), 1729, 2631, 3587.

Vertrauen, *n.*, -s, confidence.

vertrauern, *tr.*, pass (time) in mourning *or* sorrow.

vertraulich, *adj.*, intimate, confidential.

Vertraute, *m.* (-r) *and f.* (*decl. like adj.*), confidant.

vertreiben, vertrieb, vertrieben, *tr.*, drive away, expel, banish.

Vertriebene, *m.* (-r) *and f.* (*decl. like adj.*), exile.

verun'treuen, *tr.*, prove false to, abuse (a trust).

verurteilen, *tr.*, condemn.

verwahren, *tr.*, keep (safe), 20, 3977; guard, 1930; secure, 2359.

Verwahrung, *f.*, keeping, 3962; custody, 2795.

verwalten, *tr.*, administer; discharge, 1295.

verwandeln, *tr.*, transform, 3631; *refl.*, change, 1339.

Verwandlung, *f.*, -en, transformation, change; transubstantiation, 3620, *cf. N.*

Verwandte, *m.* (-r) *and f.* (*decl. like adj.*), relative, kindred.

verwegen, *adj.*, bold, 2576; audacious, insolent, *as subst.*, 8, 2767, 2881.

verwehren, *tr.* (*dat.*), prevent.

verweigern, *tr.* (*dat. of pers.*), refuse, deny.

verweilen, *refl.*, tarry, stay.

verweint, *part. adj.*, red with weeping.

verweisen, verwies, verwiesen, *tr.* (*dat. of pers.*), reprove, rebuke.

verwerfen, verwarf, verworfen, verwirft, *tr.*, cast away, reject; disown, 524, 1685; deny, 715, 2931; refuse to acknowledge, 736.

verwildert, *part. adj.*, wildly torn, dishevelled.

verwirken, *tr.*, forfeit.

verwirren, verwirrte, verwirrt *and* verworren, *tr.*, confuse, confound.

Verworfene, *m.* (-r) *and f.* (*decl. like adj.*), outcast, wretch.

verwunden, *tr.*, wound.

verwundern, *tr.*, astonish, amaze.

Verwunderung, *f.*, wonder, amazement.

Verwünschung, *f.*, -en, curse, imprecation.

Verzeichnis, *n.* -nisses, -nisse, list.

verzeihen, verzieh, verziehen, *tr.* (*dat. of pers.*), pardon, 695, 1502; forgive, 1748, 1821, 2444.

Verzeihung, *f.*, pardon.

Verzweiflung, *f.*, despair.

verzweiflungsvoll, *adj.*, despairing, desperate.

Vetter, *m.* -s *and* -n, -n, cousin.

viel (mehr, meist-), *adj.*, much, many.

vielbedeutend, *adj.*, influential, 1710; *adv.*, most significantly, 1032.

vielgeliebt, *part. adj.*, much *or* dearly beloved.

vielleicht, *adv.*, perhaps, perchance.

viermal, *adv.*, four times.

vierzig, *num.*, forty.

Volk, *n.*, -es, Völker, people, 610; nation, 2300; men, 2592.

Völkerhaß, *m.*, -hasses, international hate.

Völkerhirt, *m.*,-en,-en, shepherd of the people.

Völkerrecht, *n.*, -s, -e, law of nations.

Völkerschaft, *f.*, -en, people, nationality.

Volksdienst, *m.*, -es, service of the people.

Volksgunst, *f.*, popular favor, popularity.

voll, *adj.*, full, complete; *adv.*, *sep. and insep. pref.*, fully, wholly, entirely.

vollbring'en, vollbrach'te, vollbracht', *insep. tr.*, perform, accomplish, 3044; carry out, execute, 2632; *inf. as subst.*, accomplishment, 3598.

vollen'den, *insep. tr.*, finish.

vollfüh'ren, *insep. tr.*, accomplish, 3103; carry out, 3858.

völlig, *adj.*, full complete.

vollkom'men, *adj.*, complete, perfect.

Voll'macht, *f.*, -en, authority, 3800; power, 4009.

vollstreck'en, *insep. tr.*, carry out, execute.

Vollstreck'ung, *f.*, carrying out, execution.

vollzie'hen, vollzog', vollzo'gen, *insep. tr.*, fulfil, 3577; put into effect, 1579, carry out, execute, 250, 1525, 1906, 3092 *etc.*

Vollzie'hung, *f.*, execution.

von, *prep.* (*dat.*), of, from, by.

vor, *prep.* (*dat. and acc.*), *adv. and sep. pref.*, before, in front of, from, for, with, because of; (*of time*), ago.

voran', *adv. and sep. pref.*, before, at the head of, in front.

voran'gehen, ging, gegangen, *sep. intr.* f. (*dat.*), go before, precede.

voraus', *adv. and sep. pref.*, be-

fore, ahead; nichts — vor (*dat.*),
no advantage over, 1208; im
— (*now usually pronounced*
im vor'aus), in advance, beforehand, 2506.

voraus'eilen, *sep. intr.* f., hasten
on before.

Vorbedeutung, *f.*, foreboding,
omen.

vorbei', *adv. and sep. pref.*, by,
past.

vorbei'führen, *sep. tr.*, lead past.

vorbei'kommen, kam, gekommen,
intr. f., come past.

vorbereiten, *tr.*, prepare.

Vorbereitung, *f.*, -en, preparation.

Vorfahr, *m.*, -s, *and* -en, -en, pre-
decessor.

vorfordern, *tr.*, summon, cite.

vorführen, *tr.*, bring before, produce (a witness).

vorgeben, gab, gegeben, giebt, *tr.*,
put forward, advance, allege.

vorgehen, ging, gegangen, *intr.*
f., occur.

vorgreifen, griff, gegriffen, *intr.*
(*with dat.*), forestall.

Vorhang, *m.*, -s, -hänge, curtain.

vorher, *adv. and sep. pref.*, before, beforehand.

vorher'bedenken, bedachte, bedacht, *sep. tr.*, premeditate;
vorherbedacht, *part. adj.*, pre-
meditated, prearranged, 2752.

vorhin, *adv.*, a little while ago,
just now.

vorig, *adj.*, former, foregoing.

vorleuchten, *intr.* (*with dat.*),
shine before; als Muster —,
set a brilliant example, 1189.

vorn, *adv.*, before, in front; in
the foreground, *93.

Vorrecht, *n.*, -s, -e, privilege.

Vorsaal, *m.*, -s, -säle, hall, anteroom.

Vorsatz, *m.*, -es, -sätze, purpose,
resolution.

Vorsicht, *f.*, foresight, care.

vorstellen, *tr.*, place before, 2304;
confront with, 910; represent,
1083.

Vorteil, *m.*, -s, -e, advantage,
795; expediency, 1441; zu —
(*gen.*), in behalf of, 1352.

vortragen, trug, getragen, trägt,
tr., carry before, submit to,
3187.

vortreten, trat, getreten, tritt, *intr.*
f., step forward.

vorü'ber, *adv. and sep. pref.*, by,
past.

vorü'berziehen, zog, gezogen, *intr.*
f., move past; pass, 1542.

Vorwand, *m.*, -s, -wände, pretext.

vorweisen, wies, gewiesen, *tr.*,
produce, exhibit.

vorwerfen, warf, geworfen, wirft,
tr. (*dat. of pers.*), reproach;
vorwerfend, *part. adj.*, reproachful, 2056.

Vorwurf, *m.*, -s, -würfe, reproach.

vorziehen, zog, gezogen, *tr.*, pre-
fer.

Vorzimmer, *n.*, -s, —, anteroom.

Vorzug, *m.*, -s, -züge, preference,
preferment.

W.

wach, *adj.*, awake; — werden,
awake, 1816.

Wache, *f.*, -n, watch; guard,
*131; — stehen, stand guard.

wachsam, *adj.*, watchful.

Wachsamkeit, *f.*, watchfulness,
vigilance.

wachsen, wuchs, gewachsen, wächst,
intr. f., grow.

wachstehend, = Wache stehend,
140, *cf. N.*

Wächter, *m.,* –s, —, watchman; guard, 135, 663; keeper, 123, 1993.

Waffe, *f.,* –n, weapon, 1494 2341; arms, 350, 609.

waffnen, *tr.,* arm; *refl.,* arm oneself, 608.

wagen, *tr.,* venture, risk, 990, 1700, 1865, *etc.;* dare 41, 246, 600, *etc.;* gewagt, *part. adj.,* risky, dangerous, 2941.

Wag(e)stück, *n.,* –s, –e, hazardous deed; risk, 1863.

Wagnis, *n.,* –nisses, –nisse, hazard, jeopardy.

Wahl, *f.,* –en, choice, 3208; alternative, 3247.

wählen, *tr.,* choose.

Wahn, *m.,* –es, illusion, fancy, 2090; delusion, error, 3088.

wähnen, *intr.,* fancy, think.

Wahnbegriff, *m.,* –s, –e, false conception.

Wahnsinn, *m.,* –s, insanity, 3916, 3930; madness, 2460, *114; frenzy, 2341.

wahnsinnig, *adj.,* insane; mad, 2314.

Wahnwitz, *m.,* –es, madness; delirium, 2605.

wahr, *adj.,* true, real; *adv.,* truly; — machen, verify, 137.

wahren, *tr.,* keep, guard; *poetic gen.,* 752.

während, *prep. (gen.),* during; *conj.,* while, *67.

wahrhaft, *adj.,* truthful, upright.

Wahrheit, *f.,* –en, truth; reality, 1337.

Wald, *m.,* –es, Wälder, forest, wood.

Wall, *m.,* –es, Wälle, wall, rampart.

wallfahren, wallfahrte, gewallfahrt, *intr.* s., go on a pilgrimage.

Walsingham. Sir Francis Walsingham (b. 1536, d. 1590), sometime English ambassador to France; *cf. N.,* 1489.

walten, *intr.,* manage, rule, govern.

wälzen, *tr. and refl.,* ro'l.

Wand, *f.,* Wände, wall.

Wandel, *m.,* –s, conduct, (course of) life, 3638.

wandelbar, *adj.,* changing, variable, fickle, 1329.

wandeln, *intr.* s. *and* h., walk, wander.

wandern, *intr.* s. *and* h., wander, travel; *pret. subj.,* roam, 2099.

Wanderung, *f.,* –en, migration.

Wange, *f.,* –n, cheek.

wankelmütig, *adj.,* fickle.

wanken, *intr.* h. *and* s., totter, waver.

wann, *adv. (interrog.),* when.

Wappen, *n.,* –s, —, coat of arms.

Wappenbuch, *n.,* –s, –bücher, book of heraldry, 527. *cf. N.*

warm (wärmer, wärmst–) *adj.,* warm.

warnen, *tr.,* warn; warnend, *part. adv.,* as a warning, 645.

Warnung, *f.,* –en, warning.

Warnungsstimme, *f.,* –n, voice of warning, warning voice.

warten, *intr. (gen., or usually* auf *with acc.,)* wait, wait for; await. 2133, 2395.

warum, *adv. (interrog.),* why, wherefore.

was, *interrog. pron.,* what; *indef. rel. pron.,* whatever, that which, that, which; = warum, why, 3480, 3807; = etwas, something, anything, 252; — auch, whatever, 373.

waschen, wusch, gewaschen, wäscht, *tr.,* wash.

Wasser, *n.,* –s, —, water.

Wafferflut, *f.*, -en, flood, deluge.

weben, webte *and* wob, gewebt *and* gewoben, *tr.*, weave.

Wechfel, *m.*, -s, —, change.

wecken, *tr.*, wake, waken; rouse, 1747.

Weg, *m.*, -es, -e, way, 107, 677; road, 419, 616; track, 1883, *cf. N.;* den großen — machen, make the grand tour, 1470; Londner —, road to London, 2632.

weg, *adv and sep. pref.,* away.

wegen, *prep. (gen.),* on account of.

wegführen, *tr.*, carry off, abduct, 3387; remove, 1833.

wegnehmen, nahm, genommen, nimmt, *tr.*, take away.

wegschleudern, *tr.*, hurl away.

Weh, *n.*, -es, woe sorrow.

weh, wehe, *interj.*, woe! 858, 1849; *adj.*, sore, painful; *adv.*, — thun, hurt, pain, 53, 2069.

Wehmut, *f.*, melancholy.

wehren, *tr. (dat. of pers.),* prevent, hinder, 1064; ward off, avert, 2656.

wehrlos, *adj.*, defenseless.

Weib, *n.*, -es, -er, woman.

Weiberlift, *f.*, woman's cunning.

Weiberthräne, *f.*, -n, woman's tear, feminine tear.

weibisch, *adj.*, womanish, effeminate.

weiblich, *adj.*, female, womanly; feminine, 992; woman's, 503, 3740.

Weiblichkeit, *f.*, womanhood.

weich, *adj.*, soft, 257, 3161; tender, 360, 1343.

Weichbild, *n.*, -es, -er, precincts, 424, *cf. N.*

weichen, wich, gewichen, *intr.* f., give way, 3149; retire, 3764, *100; yield, be inferior (to, *dat.*), 2011.

Weicherzogene, *f. (decl. like adj.),* one tenderly reared, 47, *cf. N.*

weichgewöhnt, *part. adj.*, soft, accustomed, used to softness, 33, *cf. N.*

weichlich, *adj.*, effeminate, mawkish.

weiden, *tr.*, feed; feast, 3537; *refl.*, feast on, gloat over (an *with dat.*), 1557.

weigern, *tr.*, refuse, deny.

Weihe, *f.*, -n, order (ecclesiastical), 3652, *cf. N.*

weihen, *tr.*, consecrate, 2557, 3654; devote, 1284; doom, 1524.

Weihrauch, *m.*, -s, incense.

weil, *conj.*, because, since.

Weile, *f.*, while, space of time; leisure, 13.

weilen, *intr.*, tarry, linger.

Wein, *m.*, -es, -e, wine.

weinen, *intr.*, weep; *inf. as subst.,* weeping, 3755, *169.

weife, *adj.*, wise.

Weife, *f.*, -n, manner, way; habit, 2954.

weifen, wies, gewiesen, *tr.*, show; *intr.* (*with* auf *and acc.*), point to, signify, 1209.

Weisheit, *f.*, wisdom.

weiß, *adj.*, white.

weit, *adj.*, wide, broad, 2091; distant, 1462, *93; *adv.*, far, 745, 2285; *comp.*, 354.

weiten, *tr.*, widen, extend.

weiter (*comp. of* weit), *adv.*, further.

welcher (-e, -es), *interrog. adj. and pron.*, which, what, what a; *rel. pron.*, who, which, that.

welken, *intr.* f., fade, wither.

Welle, *f.*, -n, wave.

Welt, *f.*, -en, world; alle —, everybody, 213.

Weltgeräusch, *n.,* –es, bustle *or* tumult of the world.

Weltlust, *f.,* worldly desire, worldliness.

Weltteil, *m.,* –s, –e, part *or* quarter of the world.

wenden, wandte *and* wendete, gewandt *and* gewendet, *tr.,* turn, 1473, 3120; avert, 3014, 3141; *refl.,* 2496, 2596, 2814; sich anders —, change (direction), 1328.

Wendung, *f.,* –en, turn.

wenig, *adj.,* little, few; klein –es, little bit, 2084; mit –em, in few words, 1741.

wenigstens, *adv.,* at least.

wenn, *conj.,* if, when.

wer, *interrog. pron.,* who; *indef. rel. pron.,* whoever, who, he who.

werben, warb, geworben, wirbt, *intr.* (with um), sue for, woo, 3833; *inf. as subst.,* wooing, 1776, 1795.

werden, ward *and* wurde, geworden, wird, *intr.* f., become; get, grow, 1060; *in various idioms with a personal pron. in dat.,* fall to one, 131; have, 235, 2131; feel, 425, *cf. N.;* wie wird Euch, what is the matter with you, 2156; *fut. aux.,* shall, will; *pass. aux.,* be.

werfen, warf, geworfen, wirft, *tr.,* throw; cast, 2032, 2036.

Werk, *n.,* –es, –e, work; ins — richten, effect, accomplish, 2958; zu — gehen, proceed, deal, 238.

Werkzeug, *n.,* –s, –e, instrument, 1943, 2108, 3296; tool, 1752, 2974.

wert, *adj.,* worth; worthy, esteemed, 1685, 3413; worthy of

(*gen.*), 358; dear, 256, 3535, 3797.

Wert, *m.,* –es, worth, value.

Wesen, *n.,* –s, —, being, creature, 1373, 3842; conduct, demeanor, *111; bearing, *135.

Westminster. Westminster, a former city, now a part of London.

Westminsterhall. Westminster Hall, a structure adjoining the houses of Parliament, forming part of the ancient palace of Westminster; *cf. N.,* 244.

Westminsterhof. Westminster Court. Westminster Palace was sometime a royal residence, but was partially destroyed by fire, and consequently abandoned, in 1512.

weswegen, *adv.,* for what reason, wherefore.

wetteifern, *intr.,* contend, emulate. vie with.

wichtig, *adj.,* weighty, important.

wider, *prep.* (*acc.*), *adv. and insep. pref.,* against; contrary to, 90, 937; = ohne, without, 2884.

widerlegen, *insep. tr.,* refute.

widerrufen, widerruf', widerrufen, *insep. tr.,* revoke, retract.

Widerspruch, *m.,* –s, contradiction, 2129; opposition, 1419.

widerstreben, *intr.* (with *dat.*), strive *or* struggle against, resist.

widerwärtig, *adj.,* offensive, repugnant.

Widerwille, *m.,* –ns, aversion, reluctance.

widmen. *tr.,* dedicate.

widrig, *adj.,* obnoxious.

wie, *adv.,* how, in what way; *conj.,* how, as, like; when, 2690; — auch, however, 1674.

wieder, *adv., sep. and insep. pref.,* again.

wiederho'len, *insep. tr.,* repeat.

wie'derkehren, *sep. intr. ſ.,* return.

Wie'derſehen, *n.,* –s, meeting, reunion.

Wiege, *f.,* –n, cradle.

Wieſe, *f.,* –n, mead, meadow.

wild, *adj.,* wild; savage, 2429.

Wille(n), *m.,* –ns, will, wish; letzter —, last will, testament, 191, 1422; willens ſein, have a mind, intend, 160; um ... willen, for the sake of, 78, 511, 2265.

willenlos, *adj.,* without will.

willfährig, *adj.,* ready, compliant.

willig, *adj.,* willing.

willkommen, *adj.,* welcome.

Willkür, *f.,* arbitrary caprice, despotism.

wimmeln, *intr.,* swarm.

Wind, *m.,* –es, –e, wind.

winken, *intr.,* beckon.

wir, *pres. pron.,* we.

wirklich, *adj.,* real, genuine; *adv.,* really, indeed, 1995, 2148.

wiſſen, wußte, gewußt, weiß, *tr.,* know; *with dep. inf.,* know how, 1042, 2718; be able, 64, 1413, 3891; ſich (*dat.*) viel — mit, pride oneself on, set much store by, 2020; wiſſend, *part. adv.,* knowingly, 3710.

Wiſſenſchaft, *f.,* knowledge.

Witwe, *f.,* –n, widow.

wo, *adv. and conj.,* where, when; — nicht if not.

wodurch, *adv.,* through what *or* which, by what *or* which, whereby.

Woge, *f.,* –n, wave.

wohin, *adv.,* whither, where.

wohl, *adv.,* well, 137, 195; indeed, 257, 507; perhaps, 10·9; probably, doubtless, I suppose, 980, 1009, 3511; truly, forsooth, 1997; wie mir — iſt, how happy I feel, 2455·

Wohl, *n.,* –es, welfare, well-being.

wohlanſtändig, *adj.,* becoming, proper.

Wohlfahrt, *f.,* welfare.

wohlfeil, *adj.,* cheap.

wohlriechend, *part. adj.,* sweet-smelling, fragrant.

Wohlthat, *f.,* –en, good deed, kindness; benefit, 720, 9·0; boon, 183 3792.

wohlthätig, *adj.,* beneficent.

wohnen, *intr.,* dwell, live.

Wohnplatz, *m.,* –es, –plätze, dwelling-place.

Wohnung, *f.,* –en, dwelling, residence.

Wolke, *f.,* –n, cloud.

wollen, wollte, gewollt, will, *tr. and modal aux.,* will, be willing, wish; want, 188, *cf. N.;* require, 2048; be about to, *14, *16; ich will hoffen, I should hope, 1051; ich will nicht hoffen, let me not suppose, 3973.

Wollen (*verbal subst.*), *n.,* –s, volition, will.

womit, *adv.,* wherewith, with what *or* which.

Woodſtock. Woodstock, a town in Oxfordshire, England; *cf. N.* 1382.

worin, *adv.,* wherein, in what *or* which.

Wort, *n.,* –es, Wörter (*single, unconnected words, as such*) and Worte (*connected, coherent words*), word, 163, 433, 944; saying, 805; ins — fallen (*dat. of pers.*), interrupt, 696; (einem) das — reden, defend, excuse, 1363.

Wortgefecht, *n.*, -s, -e, disputation, argument,

worüber, *adv.*, over which, about *or* concerning which *or* what.

wovon, *adv.*, whereof, wherefrom; of, from, *or* by which *or* what.

wovor, *adv.*, before which *or* what.

wozu, *adv.*, whereto, wherefore, for what purpose.

Wunder, *n.*, -s, —, miracle.

wundergroß, *adj.*, prodigious.

Wunderhand, *f.*, wondrous *or* miraculous hand.

wundersam, *adj.*, wondrous.

wundervoll, *adj.*, wonderful.

Wunderwelt, *f.*, wonder-world.

Wunsch, *m.*, -es, Wünsche, wish.

wünschen, *tr.*, wish, desire; *pret. subj.*, 1669, *cf. N.*

Würde, *f.*, -n, dignity, 687, *108; honor, 700; position, office, 3047.

würdig, *adj.*, worthy (of, *gen.*); *pl. as subst.*, 500.

würdigen, *tr.*, hold *or* deem worthy.

Wurm, *m.*, -es, Würmer, worm.

Wut, *f.*, rage, fury; madness, 2575.

wüten, *intr.*, rage; be furious, 3061; wütend, *part. adj.*, furious, 2445, 2633, 3218, *etc.*; rabid, 1268, 2974; *as adv.*, frantically, 3928; *masc. as subst.*, madman, 3109.

3.

zaghaft, *adj.*, faint-hearted, timid.

zählen, *tr.*, number, 409, 1262; *intr.* (with auf *and acc.*), count *or* rely on, 1624, 1899.

zart (zärter, zärtest–, *now without umlaut*), *adj.*, tender; delicate, 1714.

zärtlich, *adj.*, tender fond.

Zärtlichkeit, *f.*, tenderness, fondness, 1786; delicacy, 308.

Zauber, *m.*, -s, charm.

Zauberkunst, *f.*, -künste, magic art, magic.

Zaubertrank, *m.*, -s, -tränke, magic potion, philter, 329, *cf. N.*

zaudern, *intr.*, delay, hesitate.

zehen, *see* zehn, *cf. N.*, 548.

zehn, *num.*, ten.

Zeichen, *n.*, -s, —, sign.

zeigen, *tr.*, show; *refl.*, appear, 1123, 1840, *21, *etc.*; present itself, 3915.

zeihen, zieh, geziehen, *tr.*, accuse (of, *gen.*), 3674.

Zeit, *f.*, -en, time; zu seiner —, in due time, 29, *cf. N.*

Zeitlang, eine, *adv.*, for a time.

zeitlich, *adj.*, temporal; *neut. as subst.*, 3404; alles Zeitliche, all my temporal affairs, 3581.

Zeitung, *f.*, -en, tidings, news.

Zepter (*better* Scepter), *n.*, -s, —, sceptre.

zer-, *insep. pref.*, *never accented.*

zermalmen, *tr.*, crush.

zerreißen, zerriß, zerrissen, *tr.*, tear, 571; rend, 2317; tear *or* rend to pieces, 2689; sever, 2682, 3691.

zerschlagen, zerschlug, zerschlagen, zerschlägt, *tr.*, beat, smite, 3933.

zerstören, *tr.*, destroy.

zerstreuen, *tr.*, scatter, 2789; divert, distract, 1385; dispel, 476.

Zeuge, *m.*, -n, -n, witness.

zeugen, *tr.*, beget, 522; *intr.*, testify, bear witness, 808, 891, 3439, *etc.*

Zeugnis, *n.*, -nisses, -nisse, evidence, testimony.

ziehen, zog, gezogen, *tr.*, draw;

intr. ſ., go, march; gezogen kommen, come in state, 3176.

Ziel, *n.*, –eš, –e, goal, 1794; limit, 145; end, 1590, 3481; target, 2831.

ziemen, *intr.* (*with dat.*), become, befit, 687, 1149, 2907; be suited to, 3042.

Zierde, *f.*, –ır, ornament, grace.

zieren, *tr.*, adorn.

Ziffer, *f.*, –ır, cipher.

Zimmer, *n.*, –š, —, room.

Zimmerer, *m.*, –š, —, carpenter.

Zinn, *n.*, –eš, tin.

zittern, *intr.*, tremble.

zögern, *intr.*, delay, hesitate.

Zorn, *m.*, –eš, anger, wrath.

zu, *prep.* (*dat.*), *adv. and sep. pref.*, to, at, towards, with, for, besides, in addition, to.

zubereiten, *tr.*, prepare.

zucken, *intr.*, quiver, wince; zuckend, *part adj.*, convulsive, spasmodic, *183.

zudenken, dachte, gedacht, *tr.*, destine *or* intend for (*dat.*), 1762.

zueignen, *tr*, appropriate; ſich (*dat.*) —, appropriate (to oneself), 3603; assume, 2337; seize, 159.

zueilen, *intr.* ſ., hasten to *or* towards.

zuerkennen, erkannte, erkannt, *tr.*, award, concede.

zuerſt, *adv.*, at first, first.

zufachen, *tr.*, fan to.

Zufall, *m.*, –š, –fälle, chance, 2058; accident, 1007.

Zufluchtsort, *m.*, –š, –e *and* –örter, place of refuge.

Zug, *m.*, –eš, Züge, line; feature, 2232; train, 2137; draught, 2081; haul, 2112.

zugegen, *adv.*, present.

zugehen, ging, gegangen, *intr.* ſ., go towards *or* up to (auf *with*

acc.), *101, *114; happen, 2643.

zugeſellen, *refl.*, join, ally oneself, 821.

zugeſtehen, geſtand, geſtanden, *tr.*, concede.

zugleich, *adv.*, at the same time, simultaneously.

zukehren, *tr.*, turn towards.

zukommen, kam, gekommen, *intr.* ſ., come to, reach, 536.

Zukunft, *f.*, future.

Zunder, *m.*, –š, tinder; fuel, 823.

Zunge, *f.*, –ır, tongue.

Zungendreſcher, *m.*, –š, —, idle babbler, pettifogger.

zürnen, *intr.*, be angry *or* wrathful.

zurück, *adv. and sep pref.*, back, backwards, behind.

zurückbleiben, blieb, geblieben, *intr.* ſ., remain behind.

zurückbringen, brachte, gebracht, *tr.*, bring back.

zurückfahren, fuhr, gefahren, fährt, *intr.* ſ., come back; return, *183; start, be startled, *21, *96.

zurückgeben, gab, gegeben, giebt, *tr.*, give back, return.

zurückhalten, hielt, gehalten, hält, *tr.*, hold back, restrain.

zurückkehren, *intr.* ſ., return.

zurücklaſſen, ließ, gelaſſen, läßt, *tr.*, leave behind.

zurücknehmen, nahm, genommen, nimmt, *tr.*, take back.

zurückrufen, rief, gerufen, *tr.*, recall; call back, *69; recover, 313.

zurückſchlagen, ſchlug, geſchlagen, ſchlägt, *tr*, throw back, *166.

zurückſchrecken, *tr.*, frighten back; deter, 76.

zurückſtoßen, ſtieß, geſtoßen, ſtößt,

tr., repel; repulse, 1787; spurn, 3407.

zurücktreten, trat, getreten, tritt, *intr.* [. , step back.

zurückweichen, wich), gewichen, *intr.* [. , fall back, retire.

zurückweisen, wies, gewiesen, *tr.*, reject; refuse admittance, 2863; motion away, *177.

zurückziehen, zog, gezogen, *tr.*, draw back, withdraw; *intr.* [. , back out, retract, 996; *refl.*, retire, retreat, 1096.

zusagen, *tr.* (*dat. of pers.*), promise; *intr.*, consent, 1893.

zusammen, *adv.* and *sep. pref.*, together.

zusammenbinden, band, gebunden, *tr.*, bind together.

zusammenbringen, brachte, gebracht, *tr.*, bring together; collect, rally, 1915.

zusammenfahren, fuhr, gefahren, fährt, *intr.* [. , start, shudder.

zusammenfassen, *tr.*, collect, compose, 2175.

Zusammenkunft, *f.*, –künfte, meeting.

zusammenlaufen, lief, gelaufen, läuft, *intr.* [. , run or flock together, congregate, 3943.

zusammenraffen, *refl.*, collect oneself.

zusammenschaudern, *intr.* [. , shiver, shudder. [der.

zusammenschauern, *intr.*, shud-
zusammenschrecken, schrak, geschrocken, schrickt, *intr.* [. , start (with terror or alarm).

zuschließen, schloß, geschlossen, *tr. and refl.*, shut up, close tightly.

zusehen, sah, gesehen, sieht, *intr.*, see to, take care, 2739.

zusenden, sandte and sendete, gesandt and gesendet, *tr.*, send to.

zuspitzen, *tr.*, point, sharpen.

Zutrauen, *n.*, –s, confidence.

zutraulich, *adj.*, trusting, confiding.

zuvor', *adv. and sep. pref.*, before.

zuvor'kommen, kam, gekommen, *intr.* (*with dat.*) [. , get ahead of, forestall, 2785.

zuwenden, wandte and wendete, gewandt and gewendet, *tr. and refl.*, turn to or towards.

zuwider, *prep.* (*dat., governed word preceding*) and *adv.*, against, contrary to; repugnant, distasteful, 2064.

Zwang, *m.*, –es, compulsion, constraint, 1760, 3063; restraint, 1757, 1777; — anthun, constrain, 3087.

Zwangsrecht, *n.*, –s, compulsory right, 946, *cf. N.*

zwanzig, *num.*, twenty.

zwar, *adv.*, in fact, indeed.

Zweck, *m.*, –es, -e, purpose.

zwei, *num.*, two; *decl. gen. pl.*, 2913.

zweierlei, *indecl. adj.*, of two sorts, two different, 1703.

Zweifel, *m.*, –s, —, doubt.

zweifelhaft, *adj.*, doubtful.

Zweifelmut, *m.*, –s, indecision, irresolution.

zweifeln, *intr.* (*with an and dat.*), doubt.

Zweig, *m.*, –es, -e, branch.

zweit –, *num. adj.*, second.

zweiundvierzig, *num.*, forty two, 578, *cf. N.* [sion.

Zwietracht, *f.*, discord, dissen-
Zwietrachtsgöttin, *f.*, –innen, goddess of discord.

zwingen, zwang, gezwungen, *tr.*, force, compel, 352; constrain, 3082, 3211.

zwischen, *prep.* (*dat. and acc.*), between, among.

zwölf, *num.*, twelve.